EVERYTHING TO LOSE

EVERYTHING TO LOSE

Diaries 1945–1960

by

FRANCES PARTRIDGE

LITTLE, BROWN AND COMPANY

Boston   Toronto

LIBRARY OF CONGRESS CATALOG CARD NO. 85-81444

FIRST AMERICAN EDITION

To Janetta and Jaime Parladé
with love

RRD–VA
PRINTED IN THE UNITED STATES OF AMERICA

Contents

Illustrations

James Strachey
Alix Strachey
V.S. Pritchett and Freddie Ayer
Eddy Sackville-West with Ralph at Cooleville House, Ireland
Pansy Lamb
Robin Campbell, Cyril Connolly and Ralph at Buena Vista,
 Churriana
Burgo, Joanna Carrington and Gamel Brenan in a Spanish café
Cyril Connolly in the 'music position'
Rose Jackson
Janetta and children at Ham Spray
Desmond Shawe-Taylor and Raymond Mortimer at Crichel
Robert and Georgie at Ham Spray
Nicko Henderson and Boris Anrep playing chess at Ham Spray
Janetta with Paddy Leigh Fermor being reminded of Piero della
 Francesca
Simon Raven
Ralph with the Brenans in Spain

Prologue

On May 8th 1945 the tiny Wiltshire village of Ham, like every other town and hamlet in the British Isles, celebrated by its V.E. Day the end of the second Great World War in Europe. An almost audible sigh of relief rose from the whole country. If some of our reactions were strange or inappropriate, we had no need to pinch ourselves mentally, so to speak, to be aware that PEACE was really *here*, even though several months were to pass before V.J. Day would strike the gong of finality.

I was living at this time with my husband Ralph and our ten-year-old son Burgo at Ham Spray House, where we had spent the entire war except for a few breaks taken in London, staying with friends or escaping to farmhouse rooms in Wales or Devonshire.

Ham is the first village to be reached as one crosses the Berkshire border going westwards. It lies among fine chalk downs, a thousand feet high, like Walbury Camp, or the Gibbet Hill, where a replica of the old gallows still marks the scene of the execution (and the dramatic murder story behind it) described by W. H. Hudson in *Afoot in England*.

Forty years ago the village consisted merely of a pub, a village shop and post office combined (selling pyjamas and Wellington boots as well as groceries), the small school whose few inmates could be heard monotonously chanting, three middle-sized houses and a handful of thatched cottages, some of which had been prettified and sold to the gentry. One had been the home of a witch, we were seriously told; when she was forced to move to make way for newcomers no one saw her leave, 'but a rabbit ran across the road, and when the door was opened the cottage was empty'. Another belonged to a Mrs Abercrombie, whose name the school-children believed in all good faith to be 'Mrs Apple Crumpet': perhaps this was due to the lively imagination of 'Little Phyllis', who used to come 'up to Spray' to play with Burgo, and who once told me they learned 'Sharpspike' at school.

It was indeed three-quarters of a mile and uphill most of the way before one turned off down an avenue of immensely tall wych-elms leading to Ham Spray itself, huddled among farm buildings. Its charming pink-washed Jane Austen front was on the further side facing the long ridge of the downs and gathering all the sun from the south in its glass-roofed verandah. From here the lawn sloped gently down to a ha-ha, and to reach the world beyond our garden we had to cross a footbridge, elegantly overhung by a drooping ilex tree. Our favourite walk took us across the 'Park' with its formal circles and semi-circles of beech trees planted by a previous owner of the land, to climb the downs diagonally by a grass track of great antiquity. Here grew a number of orchids among other chalk plants — Bee, Fly, Butterfly, Burnt Stick, and even the rare Musk, whose tiny green spikes I used to search for and count each year for the Wiltshire Botanical Society.

We believed there was no view more beautiful, more inexhaustible in England, and no house more lovable than Ham Spray. Lytton Strachey and Ralph had together bought it in 1924 for the sum of £2,000, which they could then ill afford, and Lytton and Carrington had spent their last seven years and died there. This fact did not fill the house with an atmosphere of gloom, but of course with many memories of them both, and Carrington's pictures and inspired and gay decorations — tiles, painted furniture and papers — continued to beautify the interior for many years to come. We had colour-washed the walls of most of the rooms ourselves. Lytton's old library was completely surrounded with bookshelves made by the village carpenter and both Ralph and I worked there at our separate tables; the dining-room dresser was covered in Spanish plates and English lustre ware; and a large, otherwise featureless room known as the Music Room contained a piano, gramophone and sometimes a ping-pong table. Everywhere were paintings by Duncan Grant, Vanessa Bell and Carrington; drawings by Henry Lamb and Augustus John, mosaics by Boris Anrep. Two four-poster beds and a good deal of Regency and Provençal furniture were not in the best possible condition and often menaced by woodworm. (James Strachey's chair once collapsed in a cloud of dust in the middle of dinner). Upstairs a long corridor that rocked beneath the feet led past visitors' rooms to the old granary that had been converted first into a studio for Carrington, then Burgo's nursery.

During the war we had had all too many practical tasks to do, though Ralph was an expert pruner and I know enjoyed providing us with pears and peaches, figs, nectarines and grapes. As more official 'work' he wrote reviews, mainly for the *New Statesman*, whereas for my part ever since May 1944 I had been under contract to Allen Lane to write a book on English wild flowers in a number of volumes — a sort of modern Sowerby — in co-operation with a young artist called Richard Chopping, who was making delicate and faithful illustrations of each plant. (I mention this project as its fortunes will figure in what follows).

I first started keeping a diary early in 1940, some of which has been published as *A Pacifist's War*. In it I described many of the friends and refugees who came to Ham Spray; but one of them had by the end of the war qualified as an inmate. This was Janetta, whom we had first met in Spain with her mother, Jan Woolley, at the beginning of the Civil War in 1936. We were staying in the house of our old friend Gerald Brenan in Churriana, and he it was who introduced us to Jan and 'her little daughter, who made everyone's heart beat faster'. The Woolleys had some terrifying experiences in Malaga, which was at that time almost in the front line, and when they returned to England we invited them to stay. At fourteen Janetta was young enough to be our daughter, but she also quickly became one of our dearest friends, and there was always room for her at Ham Spray. Jan died soon after the death of her son in the R.A.F.

Diary-keeping is a difficult habit to break, and I must confess that I have failed to do so. I take up the thread, therefore, where I left off.

Note

Passages in square brackets do not come from my diary. I have included in this way short portraits of friends now dead and other later comments.

F.P.

1945

May 19th — Ham Spray. Have we already got used to Peace, and drained the cup to the bottom, of all its savour? I believe it is rather that we have been unconsciously holding back from the pleasure of full realization, just as children often hold back from looking forward to a treat, for fear of the agony of disappointment. Only very gradually are we recovering our old peace-time outlook, and the process is like the pins and needles with which blood rushes back into a crushed limb. It may one day seem absurd to remember what childish delight it gave us today for instance, to take our car out *simply for fun*, with a picnic basket in full view on the seat, and drive up to the top of Walbury Camp, bent on nothing but enjoyment. Even so I was conscious of a faint twinge of guilt, and a feeling that we ought to have been on bicycles. After lunching under the great clump of trees on the highest summit we walked down to Combe village and looked at the little church.

A lot of images have been left in my mind by our outing: Burgo screeching with excitement among the crazy old tombs all scrawled over with ivy and pink and yellow lichens; then peppering me with questions about burials, and with obstetric ones aroused by the graffiti in the air-raid shelters. 'Why I'm interested in dying,' he said, 'is that I simply can't imagine it and long to know what it can be like.' Then, taking a botanical excursion by myself, and finding leopard's bane gleaming under the trees in Combe wood, the starry faces of stitchwort balanced in the long grass and valerian sprouting even from the chimneys of Combe Manor. Coming back to see the two people I love most in the world sitting blown about on the top of the downs — Ralph's bent corduroy knee level with Burgo's rough brown head.

'What a lovely day we've had!' said Ralph.

May 21st. Shopping this morning. The grocer was anxious to dispel any hope of increasing supplies. 'You're in for a shock, I'm afraid,' he said ominously — from a general desire to take us down a peg, I thought at the time; but on the wireless tonight, far from an increase in the rations, *cuts* were announced: less bacon, less fat, less butcher's meat, and 'no possible improvement this year'.

Raining all day. Inspired by his history lesson at school, Burgo spent hours making what he called 'a Bayeux tapestry' of his own, representing Louis XVI at the Guillotine. As a needleman he isn't at all expert, but he contrived a dramatic scene, with a small, pathetic king and a bloodthirsty executioner.

May 24th. A lot of letters. Bunny [David Garnett] writes about his new daughter,[1] and says he 'met at a party an amazingly, an almost embarrassingly beautiful girl, who turned out to be Janetta'. Angelica, recovering from childbed, writes in a serious mood about the Wandering Scholars and the importance of learning Latin and Greek, while Julia [Strachey] ends a wonderful description of V.E. Day in London: 'Personally I no longer feel human any more; I mean the dynamic principle has given way and one feels like a sheet of old newspaper or pressed dried grass.'

[1] Henrietta, who was to become our daughter-in-law by marrying Burgo.

[I wrote back to her: 'We rustic mice feel very much out of the world now that civilization has begun again in London — it is apparent in every line of your letter, and also from others "up there". I suddenly feel there are so many things I want to do, exhibitions of pictures to see, Britten's new opera to hear, and so forth. Your description of the effect on yourself of the war being over interested me greatly. Personally I am suffering from a conviction that each moment of my day has to be carefully packed in a last-minute hurried way, as one packs a week-end suitcase. There's no doubt that though it seems nothing much the advent of Peace has been a severe shock to all our nervous systems.'

Julia Strachey, elder daughter of Lytton's brother Oliver, was my best friend from childhood, and remained so until she died in 1979. I have described the tragi-comic vicissitudes of her life in considerable detail in my book *Julia, a Portrait*, therefore I do not propose to do more here than say that she was the most original, amusing and eccentric of my friends, and possessed a natural gift for writing which caused her both intense pleasure and agony. All too little of her work was finished, but what little was published won recognition from the critics and many devoted readers. She was married first to Stephen Tomlin, sculptor, in 1926; secondly in 1952 to Lawrence Gowing.]

May 27th. The effects of the Peace are certainly very strange. My feeling is that my 'dynamic', whatever that may be, has run amok somehow and got disassociated from its proper functions. This last week I have often felt as though I were racing to catch a train, and am possessed with a demon of relentless energy which (if I don't stuff its eager maw with housework or botany) will spend itself in futile restlessness. My engine is turning round too fast without properly engaging its gears. The sensation is not altogether unpleasant, in a way rather exciting, but I wish I had not forgotten how to do nothing for an hour or so.

This morning Mrs Chant[1] told me that her brother-in-law, home from Germany, had 'brought back ever such a lovely bedspread and a coat and a suit — and he only just missed a gold watch worth £50 off a German prisoner. It's rather awful, isn't it?' she added, with a naughty pussycat smile, 'they just go into shops and houses and take the things.' I couldn't help feeling shocked, though I don't think she noticed.

After dinner I began on Koestler's Russian revelations;[2] what an appalling indictment it is, even allowing for his fanatical personality. I sat brooding over the horrors of the world — feeling too hot with the electric fire burning my outer crust, yet a chill numbness within; physical discomfort symbolizing the mental. Without actually believing in progress, I used unconsciously to assume that there was some degree of stability in the stream of human existence which would prevent any great loss of civilization already won. Now it seems as though that very thing had happened, and an almost prehistoric barbarity had spread over the earth. And the *violence* of the present world! Oh how one longs for tolerance, humanity, kindness, and for thought and discussion to come into their own again and drive out black, blind feelings. I wonder if these reflections were the cause of a full-dress argument defending Socialism that I embarked on later with Ralph, and which continued with emotion but not much heat, until after we were in bed. Ralph felt for some reason that my views were an attack upon his liberal ones, but actually I wanted to see if he could put up arguments which I couldn't logically meet. I don't think he did, but I'm not convinced there are none.

[1] Daily help from the village.
[2] *Darkness at Noon.*

May 29th. Weather gusty and impetuous. My mood likewise, full of vague apprehensions; my body all day as tense as a fiddle-string.

New war-clouds are gathering in Syria and the Lebanon. As I now believe that every man-jack alive is at present keyed-up to the verge of insanity, and that Europe is spread over indiscriminately with gunpowder and matches side by side just waiting to go off, this hardly surprises me.

Burgo staggered into our bedroom this morning carrying a huge parcel addressed to himself. Numberless wrappings revealed — a bust of Julius Caesar made by Kitty West[1] out of dental plaster! This was her response to my telling her that I had found him about to order such an object C.O.D. But I can't think of anyone else in the world who would have actually made him one. He remained profoundly Roman-minded all day: as we walked down the avenue he said, 'I think cows ought always to wear togas, they have such Roman faces.'

[1] First wife of Anthony West; painter.

June 13th. Before Burgo developed measles we took tickets for Britten's opera *Peter Grimes*. He is now nearly but not quite well, and Ralph has nobly volunteered to take my place as sick-nurse while I go and enjoy myself. So I am taking Janetta, and off I go, with a bag stuffed with eggs and gooseberries for her, and presents for Nicky.[1]

To lunch alone with Clive [Bell] at the Ivy: conversation fast and furious; delicious wine, pâté, chicken and rice. About what did we talk? I hardly remember. Politics, Flaubert, Anthony and Kitty West. There is a noticeable lack of tension in peace-time London. When it was under attack, Londoners were united into a species of whole by their common anxiety, the common threat. Now the unifying plasm has melted away and they are an incoherent mass, moved by different urges, no longer pawns in a game.

[1] Her two-year-old daughter.

[In the Twenties when I was working at Birrell and Garnett's bookshop, Clive Bell was one of the first members of Old Bloomsbury to invite me out. He liked girls, and I knew that it was partly because I was one that I was asked: but he was much too sensitive to press unwanted attentions, and we quickly became very great friends, as we remained for the rest of his life.

Clive led two separate but interlinked lives. In London he owned a comfortable bachelor flat in Gordon Square, and here he liked to entertain his friends to dinner, often dressed in a suit of purple sponge-cloth with black frogs, and surrounded by well-filled bookshelves set between panels painted by Duncan Grant, with pictures by Vlaminck, Picasso and Juan Gris on the walls. He was an excellent host, who had the rare gift of preferring others to shine rather than doing so himself; yet he never seemed to conduct the conversation in an obvious way — it ranged far and wide and usually went on late over brandy and cigars. Among those I met at these dinners were Desmond MacCarthy, Roger Fry, Bertrand Russell, Vita Sackville-West, Lionel Penrose and Rebecca West. Lunch-time guests were invited to the Ivy Restaurant.

In Clive's second life at Charleston there was no central focus, nor even a particular host or hostess, it was more like a collection of people with various absorbing occupations and interests, into which one felt lucky to be admitted. He was more relaxed there: he would get into old tweeds and bedroom slippers, go walking on the downs or sit out in the sun with a book. He was a great enjoyer, whose enjoyment was as infectious as his laughter, and who appreciated the details of country life almost as much as the hours he spent reading and writing every day. He saw the public world through liberal and rational spectacles, and (besides his better-known books on art) defended his views in *On British Freedom* and two pacifist pamphlets: *Peace at Once* (1915), burned by order of the Lord Mayor of London, and *Warmongers* (1938).

Clive often visited us at Ham Spray. He and Ralph were devoted to each other, and Burgo too enjoyed his high spirits and vitality. (I remember overhearing a conversation between Clive and Burgo — aged about 5 — in which they were describing meals one would *not* like to eat. It ended by Clive saying: 'No, Burgo, ink and spearpoints wouldn't be *at all* nice.') Fond of gossip, in which there was sometimes a strain of mischief or even malice, he endeared even by his comic characteristics, such as larding his talk with French phrases and words, or anxiously rearranging the thick carroty hair which grew on only part of his cranium and had a way of getting out of place. He travelled a lot in Europe, particularly in France, where he had many friends and spoke the language fluently. He had been known to make an after-dinner speech in it full of jokes that brought blushes to the cheeks of the ladies present.]

June 14th. Last night Janetta and I went to Sadlers Wells, where a large, excited and mainly youthful audience was collected. Then the opera began and we were all attention, immediately caught by the beauty and startling originality of what we were seeing and above all hearing. I often longed to have some interesting, thrilling passage back to hear it again. In the first act the most arresting scene was the trial and acquittal of Grimes for the murder of his apprentice, when he sings a marvellous aria, expressing the agony of the outcast. The second act included a passage of intense and mounting dramatic excitement which moved both Janetta and me profoundly, where Grimes is pursued and hounded by all the inhabitants of the little town, indignant at his ill-treatment of the boys, and suspicious that he had murdered the last. 'Grimes is at his exercise!' they had chanted earlier — haunting words from Crabbe's poem set to haunting music; and now the ever louder and more terrifying cries of 'Gri–imes! Grimes!' deepen the horror of his plight.

In the interval I went to talk to Henry Lamb, whose pale tonsure I had observed in the front row of the stalls. He is painting Britten's portrait and is, as always, obsessed by his sitter's personality.

'But you know I'm getting old and I like more sweetness in music,' he said, 'and I find this rather too arid.' Then, of the dramatic theme: 'I suppose these buggers have to get their pariah-feelings off their chests.'

Later that evening, when I pondered Henry's comments, something that had confused me became clearer. One feels a difficulty in sympathizing with a man whose isolation is caused by his brutality — his ill-treatment, possibly even murder of young boys in his power. Yet that this is what both composer and librettist mean us to do seems clear from the angelic music sung by a beautiful tenor voice. But if for 'ill-treatment' 'love' is substituted, the knot in the emotional thread is untied, and we can feel wholeheartedly for the outcast's position. So what I believe Britten was consciously or unconsciously expressing in *Peter Grimes* was a plea for the freedom from persecution of homosexuals.[1]

In any case I left feeling I had had a major experience.

[1]In Britten's later works there is often a strong moral streak — for instance pacifism in the *War Requiem* and *Owen Wingrave*.

June 15th. Pleasant messy breakfast in bed with Nicky and Janetta and lots of talk. She still sees no solution of her relation with Kenneth[1] — he never refers to returning from Belgrade and she feels the position is hopeless. I went with her to see the new house she is to share with Cyril Connolly in Regent's Park, and was stunned by its grandeur and beauty.

[1]Father of Nicky.

June 20th — Ham Spray. Now that Burgo's measles are over I resolve to get out of the waiting-room and into the train, and start living my life again. (One of his *bons mots* during convalescence: 'I offer you a penny, Burgo,' said I, 'if you won't mention your sufferings today.' But he lost it in two minutes. 'I'd much rather lose *ten* pennies than not say.')

In summery weather we drove to see the Pritchetts. This was my suggestion, made with some qualms at my audacity, for we scarcely know them but would like to know them more. We settled in the dark shade of a Wellingtonia, to talk to V.S.P. and Dorothy, while the three children went off happily together. Such intelligence and friendliness radiates from V.S.P.'s animated face and gestures that it is a pleasure to watch them. He keeps his eye on reality with a blend of scientific detachment and artistic sensibility, qualities discreetly revealed by his talk, just as letters reveal the writer's originality, whatever they may seem to say. We took our picnic down by the river, fringed with yellow cress and the china blue faces of water forget-me-nots, everything spangled with freshness. I felt suddenly starved of conversation and fell upon it as a hungry man a meal. Pritchett told us about his experiences with the Army in Germany as a newspaper correspondent.

'I was amazed by how much hanging about there was,' he said. 'I thought the Army would either be *advancing*,' — and here he made a sweeping, forward gesture — 'or *retreating*' — pointing behind himself. 'I didn't picture them just *standing perfectly still ironing their trousers!*' Then he told us about his time among the dockers, and how earnest and serious they were, reading their *New Statesman* each week and even trying their best to understand the Arts pages. They had a passion for solid reading. One said: 'I've been reading nothing but Kant these last three years.'

June 23rd. Ralph is not quit of his war-time melancholy and says
he wakes each morning to a profound feeling of sadness. I wish I
knew how to comfort him. Is it physical, as he sometimes thinks?
One thing is certain, the crushing effects of this hideous war on
the human spirit will go on for a long time.

I returned from an afternoon at our old bathing-place in the
Kennet with Catharine [Carrington][1] and our two boys in time to
cook supper for Nicko [Henderson][2] and 'a friend'. I don't know
why but I expected a girl. Instead it was a handsome, intelligent
and altogether delightful young man, just back from three years
in a German prison camp. After dinner he started talking about
his life there: it was of fascinating interest. I was struck by the
calm and sanity with which he spoke of it, but Ralph noticed that
his hand was trembling, especially as he said that in spite of the
positive relief it was that there were no small decisions to make in
prison, the reverse was also true, and it was torment to feel that
you weren't free to take important ones affecting your whole life.
He had been released by Russians, who were friendly, full of
gaiety and vitality, but barbarians. They raped and looted
unchecked by their officers, and the Germans turned with relief
to the English and Americans. 'You are *good* soldiers,' they said to
him. No complaint about the Germans, who were unfailingly
correct. It was typical of them that when they found hacksaws
being smuggled into the camp inside gramophone records they
didn't destroy the lot as we should have done, but X-rayed each
one and passed the innocent ones.

His stories of escape made Ralph laugh until he nearly cried. It
was an R.A.F. camp, full of very enterprising young men, who
never stopped tunnelling and planning to escape, and many got
away, though most were later caught. They undertook the
tunnelling chiefly for something to occupy their minds, and
reaching daylight was a terrifying moment. The tunnels were
inconceivably elaborate. One had a shaft twenty feet deep, with
buckets going up and down carrying earth; there was a railway
track, with electric lighting and a switchboard worked by a man
wearing a green eye-shade. Above them the Germans were
constantly probing and listening, but they never found the
tunnel. When the outer air was reached the excitement was so
tremendous that the first man generally made the hole too small
and everyone who followed stuck. Some men made gliders and
balloons. Another planned to turn his flying-coat inside out and

disguise himself as the Airedale dog of one of the German officers. Some passed out as members of the Swiss Red Cross. Generally the punishment for attempted escape was fourteen days' imprisonment. Suddenly a large number of men were shot as an example — and there were no escapes after that.

Most of the prisoners started some sort of serious study in the camp. Those who didn't went to pieces.

Both Ralph and I took enormously to Nicko's friend, whose name is Robert Kee, and wondered whether he and Janetta would like each other. 'That's the man for her,' Ralph said.

[1] Sister-in-law of (Dora) 'Carrington'.
[2] Afterwards British Ambassador in Warsaw, Paris and Washington.

June 26th. This afternoon we went to tea with Nicko and his sister Toby in their cottage. Talked mostly of politics and the forthcoming Election. Everyone assumes Winston will get in. Nicko told us he had been lunching with someone who had been in Buchenwald, who remarked that he didn't know if he was mad or not. 'And did *you?*' I asked Nicko. After some thought he said: 'No.'

July 5th. Election day. Janetta and Nicky arrived last night and we had a lovely evening of talk. Burgo was reasonable and good on the whole, but rather over-excited by the plump squeezableness of Nicky. Soon after ten we posted big red labels on the car's windows saying: Vote for JOSEPHY,[1] and set off to the poll, but felt sheepish when we could find no one to be taken from their cottages, all having gone to Newbury to shop. 'I shall *die* if Miss Josephy doesn't get in,' Burgo intoned. A few female voters were at the polling-station, wearing their best clothes and with their false teeth in. Ralph then drove off further afield, but came back at lunch-time, full of stories about the fantastic old people he had been driving to vote. A mad old lady had tried to tip him with a saving-stamp when he left her; another, of vast proportions, floated out of her house and had a heart-attack at the polling station, a third declared she was going to vote for Lloyd George. All were voting on the emotional grounds that they had always been Liberals and this might be their last chance.

As we sat in deck-chairs during the afternoon there came the sound of a stupendous but far-off explosion, the blast of which hit us like a blow from a giant's hand, slowly lifting the hair at the back of my head and letting it fall again. It was the biggest bang we had heard at Ham since the *beginning* of the war. 'Ammunition dump blowing up,' said Ralph.

So it proved to be — the great heap of ammunition in Savernake Forest, camouflaged green and brown to protect it from 'the enemy', had somehow been set off, carrying with it only one American soldier, a pretty little cottage and a monkey-puzzle tree.

[1] The Liberal Candidate.

July 18th. Burgo came home from school yesterday evening and told us in agitated tones that the headmaster, Mr Starr, is leaving the Grammar School. Then, with a look of absolute consternation, he burst into tears. Several times he came back and tried to eat his tea only to collapse in tears again. He was obviously surprised at his own reaction.

'I didn't realize I loved him as well as liked him,' he said sadly, gazing out of the window. All the evening he behaved like a man in love, playing Mozart on the gramophone, unable to get to sleep 'because I was so miserable about Mr Starr'.

Today began to the tune of 'Oh, Mr Starr.' The irony of it is that there is probably no other boy in the whole school who has manifested such grief at his headmaster's going, not that Burgo is in any way a favourite. This evening we went to see Mr Starr before taking Burgo home. What a pity he is going — he is an intelligent, sensitive and rather charming man. Burgo is to stay on at the Prep. another year; Starr isn't confident in his ability to pass exams, though he has the highest IQ in the school and 'will go far'.

Janetta and Nicky came back from London. We were delighted to see them. They both look rather dirty: there's still no hot water in their new house. Kenneth is suggesting that they go out to Belgrade, but she doesn't want to, resists thinking about it. She has been seeing Nicko's friend Robert Kee, but I don't know how much.

July 26th. In to Hungerford to meet Janie [Bussy],[1] who has been back in England from France only three weeks. Will it be the same Janie? Yes, it is. Her bright little brown eyes retain their concentrated birdlike intelligence, but her face has mellowed and become less farouche, and her manner more confident and happier. We talked all evening of course about life in France, the food shortages, the landings, the arrival of the Americans. The worst thing she described was the agony of waiting for the Gestapo to pounce on some villages, as they did from time to time, and carry all the men and perhaps some of the girls off to work in Germany. A lorry full of men would go by, and small white notes would flutter out of it: on these they had written their names and addresses so that their relations could be told.

I noticed two things: one must be careful not to complain of any shortages we have had here, and one must assume that all collaborators were monsters. Janie becomes speechless at the name of Pétain, and wants him executed without fail. It is hard to understand such lust for revenge against a gaga old man of ninety whose crime is that he made peace.

Election results today. Janetta pinned up the list of candidates and prepared graph paper on the ping-pong table to show the progress of parties. It soon became evident to all our surprise and excitement, that the Labour Party was having a sweeping victory. None of our friends who stood as Liberals got in. True we supported the Liberals ourselves, but they seemed the only party who had a chance against the Tories.

During the long proceedings Janetta asked for 'a little encouraging music on the gramophone'. I put on some Bach and waited expectantly for it to add its colour and triumph to the electoral victory which filled our minds, just as music or the beauty of the garden seen through the window, so often overflow into one's thoughts. But it didn't work — the scene we were contemplating looked squalid and tawdry. Perhaps it was.

[1] Only child of Lytton Strachey's sister Dorothy. The Bussy family had spent the whole War at Roquebrune on the Riviera.

[In August we took three weeks' holiday in the Scilly Isles, partly to look for some botanical rarities there. Richard (Chopping)[1] and his friend Denis (Wirth-Miller) came with us. All of us were taking the first flight of our lives.]

[1] My artist collaborator in our botany book.

August 1st. Penzance airport was a grey tin hut. Here we were weighed and signed forms declaring that we didn't hold the Company responsible for our lives. Beside our party of five were two young women going over for the day; they too had never flown before. The tiny aeroplane appeared and we seven souls climbed in, each into our little pocket. It was like fitting oneself into a sponge-bag and seemed hardly more solid. I looked back at Burgo's pale but calm face behind. The engine roared and we were off, gently, then swiftly, bumping a little, making straight for the cliff, over it, and up over the sea as easy as anything. During our preliminary turns, as we curtsied and stooped over the valleys, a most satisfying fatalism possessed me, and I thought, 'I am a part of this machine, if we crash, then we crash.' Now we were travelling smoothly over the sea lying calm and touched with silver light below; it was lovely and exciting. All too soon the islands appeared — fields, bays, lakes, hedges. We're there; it's over — the realization was half-pleasant, half-sad. We were driven to our lodgings — a grey house near the port kept by two mountainous ladies.

August 2nd. Ralph has hired a boat, with a boatman, Mr Nance by name, a statuesque figure with a red carved face. Where to go? Tresco lies ahead and the dromedary humps of Samson to the left. Other distant shapes surround this inland sea. We ask Nance to put us on Tresco. We walk past the orange trumpets of thorn-apples and other brilliant tropical flowers, across the waist of the island to a great sweeping bay, whose snow-white beach is made up of glittering silver spangles, such that rolling one's hands in it they are dressed in sequin gloves. Unspeakably pure and ice-cold turquoise blue water, quantities of pretty shells (purple, white and yellow), strange fleshy plants coiled over the shingle, and no one but ourselves to enjoy these beauties. We bathed naked and ate our picnic on the beach.

August 5th. To St Helen's. The sun is blazing still; all our faces are becoming like riding-boots and beginning to peel.

It has just been announced on the News that a new and terrific bomb has been dropped on Japan, with effects incomparably more horrible than anything yet.

August 7th. No one talks of anything but the Atom bomb, and most voices are raised in horror. But the mother of a serving soldier said: 'Surely you'd rather have the atomic bomb and war over than the war going on for ever? Total extinction has much to recommend it and anyway I don't care what happens after I'm dead in the very least.' Her daughter hotly: 'That's one of the things you shouldn't say before the young.'

August 13th. Nance brought a rumour that Japan had asked for peace, and we are all waiting expectantly for V.J. Day to be announced.

Ralph and I were in bed and nearly asleep when a strange cacophony penetrated our consciousness: the church bells began tolling, and a cracked trumpet hooted out military refrains. Next began the sound of young voices singing, feet marching, cheering and beating on tins.

We woke up completely. Ralph said: 'It can only mean one thing. Peace.'

The contrast between the long tedious frightfulness just ended and the pitiful desire of puny human beings to make *some* sort of noise at all costs was more than I could manage to swallow, and I lay saying bitter things about them, while Ralph rightly laughed at me for not appreciating the greatness of the occasion. The procession clanked off along the pier; then the momentary quiet was shattered by the hooter of the *Scillonian* lying in the harbour, which gave tongue again and again like the last trump. Shouts; more trumpets, rockets and then maroons going off with a deafening whoosh followed by an echo like a whole town collapsing. Silence once more. The sound of a solitary tin being kicked along the street woke Burgo, who came and snuggled into bed with us. 'The whole world is now at PEACE!' we said to each other.

August 15th. V.J. Day number 2. We had promised to take Burgo to see the torchlight procession and bonfire, so about ten o'clock, dressed in warm jerseys, we took the road to Penninis. It was very still and no one was about in the velvet darkness. Far off we saw a red blaze tearing along the skyline of St Agnes, where a bonfire must have caught the heather, and the quiet flashing of distant lighthouses, as well as the semi-circular path thrown on near rocks and far horizon alike from Penninis itself, an un-manned lighthouse whose impartiality impressed me as if it belonged to the Solar System. Now human shapes began to gather in the darkness, and soon we heard far-off singing and beating of drums as the torchlight procession came winding down the hill under the inky sky like a pagan festival — beating, singing, flaring. In front were children carrying candles in jam jars, and we saw Richard and Denis arm in arm with two girls, all their heads wagging like dervishes. The bonfire was lit, the flames crackled up, and when all was over we three walked back to the beat of drums. I shall always remember this evening with great pleasure; it was a beautiful and moving scene of abandonment to rejoicing.

August 23rd — Ham Spray. Here we are back at Ham Spray for the first time in Total Peace for the last six years. Everyone is disgruntled by the unwelcome news that both food and clothes rations are to be immediately *reduced*. And goodness how it rains! The earth sucks it up like a sponge.

September 5th. The Times this morning had a correspondent's account of the effects of the atomic bomb. They are beyond words horrible and sickening to the heart. Now, days and weeks after the explosion, people unhurt at the time are falling ill and dying; even the doctors who came to take care of the wounded are succumbing. The symptoms are terrible — the skin becomes patched with blue, there is bleeding from nose and mouth, and when inoculations are given the flesh rots away from the needle. Death always follows. I thought with despair of poor Burgo, now so full of zest for life and unaware of its horrors. My own instincts lead me to love life, but as I read on, a desire welled up inside me to be dead and out of this hateful, revolting, mad world. Ralph and I talk and talk about it, and the conviction is growing in my mind that this is the *end* of the world and civilization we have known and enjoyed. Either by accident or design, how can it possibly be that someone will not destroy the earth? Any power wishing for world domination can get it in a single night by blotting out all its rivals, without any declaration of war, and Fear, that most potent force, will reign supreme. I see the earth reduced to a few meteorites and moons circling round in empty space. Nobody can deny all this if you put it to them, but human beings are too emotionally drained to react as violently as one might expect. It's as if exhausted humanity had sunk back into inarticulacy.

September 13th. Phil and Phyllis[1] came for the night, arriving to a very late supper. We prepared our warmest welcome for them, Ralph getting out a magnum of delicious wine, whose influence was stimulating rather than soporific, so that an impassioned argument began, mainly between Phil and me, about the Public Schools and the Empire, concerning both of which he takes an ever more ambassadorial view. Thence to the more interesting subject of what was the principal purpose of life. 'Happiness,' said I, 'of course.' Phyllis was looking very fine, and I loved seeing her again, even though it reminded me of the anxious first months of the war, when the whole family were lodged with us here. I grew very fond of her then. I admire her enormous honesty, her perseverance in learning Czech, and in all other ways being unlike one's idea of an ambassadress. They had a lot to tell us about life in Prague. They say the Russians are childlike barbarians, who kill all the milking cows, strip the Czechs of everything (I fleetingly remembered Mrs Chant's brother-in-law), particularly cars and bicycles, and rape all the women. An improbable story they told us was about a Russian who was riding along on a magnificent stolen chromium-plated bicycle, when he met a Czech errand-boy riding a fearful old crock with his arms folded and whistling. 'Give me your bicycle,' said the Russian, 'you can have this one in exchange.' The boy was delighted. The Russian leapt on his old bike, folded his arms and immediately crashed to the ground.

I taxed Ralph with not coming to my aid in my argument with Phil. He says this was because he thought I was getting the best of it.

[1]Sir Philip Nichols, then British Ambassador at Prague, and his wife.

September 16th. It seems to me that this post-war universe is more fraught with horrifying and combustible dangers even than that of 1938–9. This then, this grey joyless prospect seeded with ghastly explosives, is what the world has torn itself in pieces to produce. But though such reflections haunt my mind I'm also aware of a very strong inclination to turn away from them and merely survey the inner scene — chimney corner, husband and child, friends, plants, cats and crockery. Janetta and Nicky came on the morning train. Sat over the fire all afternoon talking to Janetta, Nicky asleep upstairs. Kenneth has managed to get a permit for them both to join him in Belgrade, and it is now only a matter of waiting for their passage to be arranged. She has written to him very little, while his letters grow anxious and show that he is beginning to realize that 'something is the matter'. Indeed, something — or somebody rather — *is* the matter and that is Robert Kee. Ralph and I are amazed that having decided two young people were made for each other, they too should seem to think so. Yet Janetta feels in duty bound to go out to Belgrade, though gritting her teeth and dreading it; nor does she want to leave her new London house. She described a week's holiday she had taken in the Welsh mountains, never mentioning her companion, nor even if she had one, but we suppose it was Robert. As a returned prisoner of war he may well suffer from indecision and uncertainty; but holding the view I do of Janetta's special attractions I can't help feeling sorry for Kenneth, whose stock I believe to be lower than he knows. We begged her to try and persuade him to come over here rather than plunge herself and Nicky into possible emotional anguish in a background of utter strangeness and the horrors of a Belgrade winter. And then not to be able to get away should she want to! But she sticks to her plan — perhaps from a sort of pride. Or fatalism.

September 26th. All caught the early train to London. Then to Sussex Place to see what Janetta has made of the house. Without signs of tremendous planning, she has made her part of it charmingly alive, fresh, with touches of inspiration in the way she has painted cupboards and windows, and chosen her colours. There is also some of the chaos and higgledy-piggledy of youth. She has the lower floors, opening on to the garden, Cyril Connolly the *piano nobile*. We stole upstairs to look. Oh my lord, what a contrast! I had seen these rooms empty and fallen in love with them. But instead of treating them in any way visually, as a painter his canvas, he has stuffed them with symbols of success and good living — massive dark furniture, sideboards groaning with decanters and silver coffee-pots, Sèvres porcelain, heavy brocade curtains, safe but dim pictures. I think the worse of him after seeing it.

Janetta found a pathetically anxious letter from Kenneth, realizing something was happening and begging to be told what. She sank down into a chair with a lost tragic expression, and said: 'Oh *dear* — I feel I shall really have to go on with him. I can't face it all.'

Off to the Ivy for lunch with Clive, his brother the Colonel, Dora [Romilly] and Yvonne Hamilton.[1] What with shouting at the deaf Colonel, little was heard above the din.

[1] Wife of the publisher, Hamish Hamilton.

September 27th — Ham Spray. Sebastian [Sprott] is paying us his yearly visit. One always forgets how incorruptibly he remains the same as the years go by, and is slow to fill in the picture of his immense virtues and his few limitations. His angelic good temper, serenity, sympathy for and detached interest in his fellow mortals, also of course his intelligence, are all in the first class. In the second is a curious lack of soaring power in his mental processes. He surprises by the things he has *not* thought or wondered about.

Talk turned naturally to the war — a tube tunnel, seen from the lighted platform. One was at no time aware of actually coming out; it is just that now *out* we certainly are and there is a curious silence embracing us — not an altogether pleasant silence either.

[When, at Cambridge, I attended the same lectures as Sebastian Sprott — McTaggart's on Hegel for instance — I was much too frightened of him to address a word to this assured prize-pupil who actually dared to question our lecturer, and little dreamed that he would one day become a dear friend with whom I should feel totally at ease and to whom I would confide my troubles. He had a neat appearance and stiffly erect bearing that reminded me of an old-fashioned wooden soldier. All his movements were precise; he even looked a little demure. If asked a direct question during a discussion of general ideas he would probably answer 'yes *and* no,' but go on to elaborate what was more an attitude than a belief. If this suggests dullness, that was most certainly not his failing. He had been a close friend of several older Bloomsbury characters — particularly Maynard Keynes, Lytton and E. M. Forster. Quite without personal ambition, he spent most of his working life lecturing at Nottingham University, refusing better offers from Cambridge, living in a modest terraced house and making many friends among the miners and their families. Could he be called an egalitarian? In the Class sense, yes. He hadn't an ounce of snobbishness in his disposition. Lytton liked going abroad with him — his equableness and wide interests made him a good travelling companion.

After the tragic deaths of Lytton and Carrington I remember him taking me for a walk up the downs and gently and sympathetically eliciting the whole story. It was from this time that my intimacy with him began; I realized his gift for understanding, but he also liked to confide. He was a devoted son and brother, and when his mother died he surprised me by confessing how lost and unprotected he felt without her.

With Ralph he had been on close terms for some time. Thereafter he occupied a special place among our friends and visited us at least once a year, usually in the autumn. He enjoyed picking mushrooms and blackberries, and while we filled our baskets he would unroll for our benefit some drama of Nottingham life, in as much detail as a Trollope novel. Later when I was living alone in London he came regularly to lunch with me.]

September 29th. Waking early, I saw from my window a sea of white mist spread over the fields, with the cows appearing to swim in it. An exquisite morning, the sky pure and cloudless, the air still, the grass netted with shimmering cobwebs.

Sebastian left after breakfast, and I spent the rest of the morning roasting myself on the verandah and writing. I know I ought to start work on my Botany book again, but I put it off till Monday. It is going to be lovely weather for Burgo's weekend, and he even admits he likes school better, and is alert, interested and gay. We took him for a picnic to Netherton, where there was a church marked in Gothic type on the map. Perhaps there would be more tombs for him, perhaps it was a ruin? We found the gate all right; inside it we entered what looked like a ballet scene, with shafts of sunlight glancing through huge trees onto yellowish Victorian tombs. One with two broken columns bore an inscription to a young woman drowned from a sailing ship in the nineteenth century; oddest of all, and rather like a Hans Andersen fairy story, the church was not made of brick and mortar, but cut out of yew trees in the *shape* of a church, with nave and spire. This bosky little churchyard had a magic character of its own and I never saw anything like it elsewhere.

October 1st. Existence has suddenly become exciting and interesting though nothing happens in particular. I eagerly anticipate each morning's post; it gives me a thrill to hear Burgo's treble voice say to Ralph: 'Darling! Look, there are the German prisoners going out to work in the field.' It is with rapture that I take my last cup of coffee to the fire. It's as if the beauty of the pattern in an old carpet I had been walking on for years all at once caught my eye and delighted me. I went up to the library resolved to do some work, and the morning flew by studying violets.

A letter from Janetta telling us she had written Kenneth a 'useless, awful letter, saying she wouldn't go to Belgrade and he must come back to London'. Meanwhile Cyril Connolly has been acting the bad angel trying to persuade her she should go. Why? As Janetta has the sense to see, he would like her to be always unattached. She has heard there is a girl living with Kenneth in his flat in Belgrade, which, she says, 'wouldn't help the situation I'm in for'. I rather fear she may be jockeyed into it by material things like the arrival of permits and passports.

To Aldbourne to lunch with the Brenans. It was only our second meeting since the end of the war[1] and Gerald was much more his old self with us today. He amused us very much with his characteristic talk and gestures. I have come to value Gamel's 'goodness' more and more: it is a combination of humanity, kindness and complete lack of aggression. Yet her mind mercifully has a sharp bite. Talking of her great friend Ronald Duncan[2] she said: 'Nearly everyone is mad on the subject of money — sex simply isn't in it.' I said I heard Beryl de Zoëte[3] had become nicer lately. 'Oh?' said Gerald. 'Well, I met her in London the other day and I wanted to hit her on the head with a hammer. It seems she has been converted to Communism, only she will call it "Democracy".'

We were expecting Alix and James [Strachey] to tea, but it wasn't till much later that they arrived in their little beetle car, with pale and exhausted faces looming through the darkness. We had a delightful evening and I thought how wonderfully elegant James was with his distinguished air and long legs and shining silver hair that leaves no print on his pillow at nights. We talked, needless to say, of the atomic bomb. James claimed to know through scientific friends that the Germans were experimenting wildly with it during those last frenzied months before defeat, and those in command were really afraid that in their desperation they might blow up the whole earth.

James and Alix gave us a mocking account of their own life at Gordon Square. They are looked after by a daily woman who was blown up by a bomb and 'is rather queer in the head'. Alix can't cook and refuses to try, so they take their meat ration in corned beef and eat it at a table so close to the sink that they can reach out and hold each dirty plate under the tap while they go on eating bread and marge. And yet James, at least, loves luxury, good food and wine!

[1]Ralph and Gerald Brenan had quarrelled during the war and Gerald refused to see us for a while because we were Pacifists.
[2]Poet.
[3]Consort of Arthur Waley.

[Talking about Alix and James Strachey, of whom he was deeply fond, Ralph told me that Alix had been the active one in the courtship which ended in their marriage, and that the sight of her determined pursuit and ultimate success in face of all obstacles had convinced him that in love all things are possible. I tended for a while to envisage her as *Vénus toute entière, à sa proie attachée.* Certain it was that everyone spoke of 'Alix and James' rather than 'James and Alix' (as is more usual), and yet in a subtle and unobtrusive way James was the dominant member of that extraordinarily devoted couple by the time I got to know them in the Twenties. Ralph and I started our joint life under their wing at 41 Gordon Square; it was they who made our elopement possible, and ever since — until their dying days — I felt for them both warm love and the strongest admiration and respect, based on the lucky chance of getting to know them at such close quarters. With their detachment, their integrity, truthfulness, perfect manners and saving streak of eccentricity and hilarious comedy, they seemed to exude a concentrated aroma of Bloomsbury, without occupying a central position in it.

Physically James had something of Lytton's spidery elegance as well as long thin arms and legs. His hair, however, unlike Lytton's, turned early to a beautiful shining silver and his face was small and round. His speaking voice revealed his intense musicality, though at moments of emotion he would turn a vivid pink and be overcome with total inarticulacy. This I saw happen to my dismay when in a reckless moment I made some criticism of Freud's theory of the Id, Ego and Superego; and in very different circumstances — when Lytton was dying — this speechlessness in emotion became a painful straitjacket, and in a stifled voice he told Ralph how greatly he envied him his ease in expressing what he felt.

Alix, very handsome, lean, big-boned, with level grey eyes and a thick thatch of dark brown hair, appeared often to be trying to solve the problems set her by life as if they were sums in arithmetic. She was the first to see how ludicrous were some of the answers but she stuck to her guns nonetheless. For instance, when the hall porter of the Savoy tried to refuse her admittance on the grounds that the severe black silk Chinese coat she was wearing 'was not evening dress', she set herself to prove to him logically that it was; and won.]

October 13th. Busy preparing Helen Anrep's[1] room, shopping and picking flowers. She arrived wearing a hat full of waving bright blue plumes, and carrying a pink sock she had been knitting in the train. Ralph couldn't get over the hat, though he isn't very clothes-conscious. He said: 'I can't *think* what she's up to with it. She must realize no one else wears anything like it. It's really funny — like a hat out of a cracker.'

She amused us with stories about Roger [Fry]'s Quaker sister, with whom she had been staying. With Helen in the house it's very difficult to think of anything else. I wonder if she would have been different if she had never left Boris [Anrep], and not developed the literary and artistic pretensions got from living with Roger. Yet there is something very warm, mellow and alive in her; also an amazing freshness, taking physical form in her pink cheeks and lips, upright and graceful carriage and springy walk. She makes me feel restless by flattering me too much, and also rather indignant that she appears to think I will take it seriously. Whence does the impulse spring? To want to please others, for instance, by repeating the nice things said about them, is an endearing quality, but the flatterer must take care not to overestimate one's credulity.

I have finished planting my rockery with bulbs — miniature irises and tulips, squills — it is now almost all bare earth between the stones, perhaps the most delightful stage of a garden. Nothing but hope!

[1] Estranged wife of Boris Anrep.

[Helen Maitland came as a girl from California to study music in Paris, where she became involved with the world of Augustus John, Henry Lamb and Boris Anrep, whom she married. In the mid-Twenties, when over forty, she left him to live as his wife with Roger Fry until he died — thus making a striking move from one aesthetic sphere to another as different from it as possible. Anrep and Fry disliked each other heartily, and the transfer of Helen caused a considerable disruption (if not as great as the Trojan War). At one time it was rumoured that Boris was threatening to tar and feather Roger — an alarming idea to his friends, since he was neither young nor strong. With Roger she led an evidently very happy, domestic life both in Bloomsbury and Suffolk — where Ralph and I often visited them. He was a kind, understanding man, less dominating than Boris; what was more, he adored Helen and credited her with great intelligence and appreciation of art and aesthetics. Some thought he over-encouraged her confidence in the latter sphere. She looked upon herself as the chief patroness of the Euston Road Group of painters, many of whom were her great friends, but I have heard her say that she insisted on respect — they were not allowed to call her 'Helen'.

Her most delightful gifts concerned the art of living — of decorating her house, throwing a shawl over an old chair, arranging flowers, creating a warm atmosphere for guests, cooking them delicious meals with what looked like the minimum of trouble. All these things she appeared to do instinctively, producing a Vuillard-like interior, richly coloured and satisfying to the eye. As a hostess she was charming and outgoing, her manner remained flirtatious and her appearance pretty till she was well on in middle life. I have said she was a flatterer, but this at least showed one of her prime motives — a desire to please. And her sympathetic nature brought her close to people — for instance Vanessa after Roger's death in 1934, and Julian Bell's in the Spanish Civil War. She had quantities of friends and confidants, among whom were Dorelia John, Gerald [Brenan] and Ralph.]

October 17th. Drove with Helen and Burgo (who had a half holiday) to the first of a series of concerts at Marlborough School. I wondered if he would stand the length of it, and the enforced stillness and silence. He did, very well, and I think enjoyed it. The gestures of the conductor, Fistoulari, were somewhat fantastic, and I saw Burgo unconsciously imitating them as he watched. The auditorium was a steep amphitheatre of pale, unhealthy boys' faces, and there on the stage behind Fistoulari's antics Adila Fachiri wielded her bow superbly and swept her fiddle round the circle of the hall. We sat above the double basses, so that we were more than usually aware of their restrained but important contribution to the whole, as well as of the comic dignity of the shapes made by player and instrument combined.

October 18th. Helen leaves us this evening. I was doing housework when she came into Burgo's room and talked to me, while the cold misty air streamed in from the garden. It was mostly about Isobel Fry, in whom she attacks (under very slight cover) all Quakers — even Roger, dearly as I'm sure she loved him. At times I was surprised by the violence with which she trounced the Frys for meanness and puritanism. Of Margery Fry she said: 'If only her connection with Roger didn't make her feel that she must have views about literature and the arts. And she won't let one disagree with her, though she is mostly approving what she thinks she ought to like, rather than having real feelings for painting or music.' And all of it fitted Helen herself to a tee. Then she talked of the pleasure of living and sleeping alone — 'the worst of Men is that they have this curious passion for sharing a bed'. With the introduction of Men with a capital M, I had the distinct impression she was inviting me to complain of Ralph, so that she could sympathize from her feminine heart. But I have nothing to complain of, and share his passion for double beds. Next she turned to cowardice, accusing the Frys of being nervous of the bombing and not trying to conceal it. And yet when she came here in the war I *saw* her fear of raids with my own eyes. Was this an attempt to 'draw' me for my pacifism? When I went off to play quartets this afternoon, Ralph told me she opened direct fire on his views and tried to get him to admit that the war had done good. I think it is because she won't let people 'be themselves' that she is such restless company.

October 19th. A disquieting letter from Richard [Chopping], who has worked out the time it takes him to draw each flower (a modest estimate, I must say), and affirms that on a basis of 200 working days and 165 non-working ones (not so modest) in each year, our book will take twelve years to complete. Allen Lane has accepted this, so there is nothing to be said, although I am filled with gloom, for when interested in a project it comes naturally to me to go at it full tilt. But from now on I shall make

no attempt to hurry Richard, which would be patently absurd,
and try and concentrate on the relief of no longer having to
nanny him.

A telephone call from Janetta. Cables have been flying between
her and Kenneth, and he is coming to England on the 27th. 'Can I
come down and discuss the appalling muddle I'm in?'

October 22nd. Janetta and Nicky arrived at tea-time. She looks
pale and tired and it was difficult to keep off the subject burning
to be discussed until Nicky and Burgo were in bed. Then, each
with a glass of gin and vermouth, 'Now,' we said, 'if you can
bear it, will you begin to tell us everything that has happened
since we saw you last.' Turning rather pink she did so, and we
talked of nothing else till bedtime. In reply to her letter to
Kenneth saying she wouldn't come to Belgrade but would like
to see him here, he had bombarded her with letters and cables.
He doesn't appear to take in the serious threat presented by
Robert. Yet she hasn't abandoned all thought of Belgrade, and
has even got her passport as asked. *Why* does she still entertain
the idea? For it is plain that all trace of love for Kenneth is gone,
and that what is left is liking, pity, some respect and a sense of
responsibility. Yet she must somehow or other summon up the
energy to face him on Saturday and spend a fortnight with him
which may well be agonizing. She says she will not marry him,
but his energy and powers of persuasion may well get her out to
Belgrade. She asks why shouldn't one be happy making a life
with a person one likes but doesn't love? And she is twenty-
three!

With someone so young and vulnerable we are naturally afraid
of being too interfering or dominant. (I more so than Ralph, I
think.) Or should I for once say what I really believe, that love is
far the most important thing in life, a stronger, potentially more
permanent and all-pervading force than the wildest of girlhood
dreams suggest. People talk, out of a sort of prudery, as if it
vanished entirely after five or six years of marriage, and only an
affable, humdrum relation was left, enabling couples to jog along
pretty well if they allowed each other plenty of freedom. But it
needn't be like that at all. It's a hopeless failure if it is. After
twenty years together one can be in a sense just as deeply in love
as ever one was. Love doesn't simply fade away like 'old soldiers';
it changes its character, naturally, and matures, but its depth and

richness can be as great as ever. And I feel Janetta to be capable, if anyone I know is, of such a relation.

But what of Robert? He is the mystery. Ralph understands his standing back and apparently refusing to try and take her from Kenneth. I'm not sure that I do. The Bloomsbury philosophy of sex, surrounded by which Ralph and I have lived for twenty years, disregards conventions but certainly not human feelings, nor does it sanction causing unnecessary pain. G. E. Moore's *Principia Ethica* set personal relations on a pinnacle for Bloomsbury, yet I think they are less promiscuous than their image in the eyes of the more conventional, whose sexual deviations may be under cover, or — in the case of the very rich — who buy as many mates as they can afford.

The telephone rang: Robert for Janetta. She came back beaming. 'Everything seems to have changed,' she said.

October 25th. Now that Kenneth is coming back, most of Janetta's friends are chary of giving her advice, perhaps because they don't want to be thought of as enemies if she stays with him. Robert has had to dash up to Yorkshire to his R.A.F. Station. This afternoon I drove a pale, sad-faced Janetta to the station.

October 30th. Ralph had to go to London to do a broadcast about *romans policiers* in French. He appeared strangely un-nervous and didn't even practise his French accent.

I went to the Padels[1] for music. They had a violin-playing school-mistress staying — one of those schoolgirls withered into middle-age without ever blooming or ripening. We were just settling down to play a Mozart quintet when another voice was heard in the hall. It was Mr Collier the cellist.

'We must have sextets!' cried Mr Padel, and got out the child's cello which I am hoping to buy for Burgo's Christmas present. Mr Collier, a largish man, wrapped himself round this instrument and drew magnificent sounds from it. We played both Brahms sextets — fine fun. I have got much better at reading, but my technique isn't up to the difficult passages.

Burgo and I drove in to meet Ralph. 'It was terrible!' he cried. 'The broadcasting room was hot and silent, and I got twisted up in my French!'

[1] A grammar-school headmaster and his wife living at Inkpen, who had persuaded me to buy a violin and try to play quartets on it with them, to relieve the dreary wartime days.

October 31st. Just before lunch Ralph was summoned to a second session at the B.B.C., to re-do his broadcast. Now that he knew what he was in for, he was as nervous as a cat and read his script all through lunch.

He left saying he would ring up if he missed the earlier train, but no message came and nor did he. Anxiety and pictures of imagined disasters swamped my mind, and I stood staring into the darkness, sherry glass in hand. Fighting against fuss, I at last gave in and rang up the station. The train had docked three-quarters of an hour ago and Ralph's car was still uncollected. When the time for his arrival by the late train came and went my agitation returned in full force. What *could* have happened? and what *should* I do if he didn't come at all? I remembered Dorothy Pritchett describing her anxiety when V.S.P. was late. 'Oh *yes*! I go through the whole thing — funeral and widow's weeds. . . . ' Then the car lights swept the drive.

It was a repeated pleasure throughout the night to turn and find Ralph's solid presence beside me.

I forgot to say that Burgo and I listened to his French broadcast which came through perfectly, as though he were in the room. I was amazed how good he was, how interesting he made it, and that his French sounded convincing and not at all worried.

Since Janetta went to London the thought of the agonizing position she is in has lain like a sediment at the bottom of my mind. This morning she broke her silence with a letter written 'in a frame of mind as near lunacy' as she had ever been in.

November 2nd. We both wrote to Janetta, trying in different ways to give her support, and telling her that of course she could come here whenever she liked, especially if things became too awful.

Meanwhile Burgo's half-term holiday began, and plans were made for his enjoyment, including a week-end visit from Esme, Pippa and Vicky [Strachey],[1] also fireworks, a bonfire and the burning of a guy. As I whisked round the house making beds I little thought what other events were due to happen that day. For while Ralph and Burgo were meeting the Stracheys the telephone rang, and Janetta's quiet voice told me in tones of absolute exhaustion that everything *was* too awful and she had finally decided against Kenneth and Belgrade, and having done so felt she must leave him at once. Between us we arranged that she and Nicky and Robert should come here this evening, a plan immediately endorsed by Ralph when he arrived back with the Stracheys, who gaped with adolescent amazement at finding themselves in the middle of an elopement.

Ham Spray has been filled all day with a feverish disquiet, punctuated by the ringing of the telephone. Once it was Kenneth for me, merely to say 'Take care of Janetta and Nicky. Robert is a weak immature character and not to be trusted with their happiness.' He went on to say that his relationship with 'the girl in Belgrade' was not important.[2] Ralph and I drove in the dusk to meet the refugees, and there they were looking worn-out and pale, a pathetic group on the dark station platform. Poor Robert, it must have been awful for him arriving among people who were practically strangers, but he put a very good face on it, and possibly it made things easier that he was at once whirled into a scene of eerie festivity, when the old guy was set crazily on a broken chair and burnt in a blazing bonfire under the Portuguese laurel. Unrecognizable figures stood round huddled in coats, and the blaze and the nostalgic smell of burning branches acted as a good solvent to our strange mixed party, blending them together. But Janetta looks quite exhausted, and after two endless telephone calls from Kenneth was almost in tears. All to bed — what a day!

[1] Mother and her daughters, who had spent part of the War with us as refugees. Burgo adored Vicky, who was about four years his senior.
[2] He afterwards married her.

November 4th. Burgo is happily closeted with Vicky making home-made fireworks. Pippa and I spent some time playing the Bach Double Concerto for two violins, and reversing the roles in violin-piano sonatas. Amongst these activities I had a long talk with Janetta in the nursery, and Ralph another in the library with Robert, who said afterwards how delighted he was 'that at last he had an ally'. The old house is bursting with all this drama and tension, and as well as everything else there is of course a mountain of work looking after so large a party. But I wouldn't have preferred to be without the Stracheys, who add quite a lot to our curious plum-pudding. Pippa and I drove after lunch to the Padels, and played some Mozart and the Mendelssohn Octet. Pippa loved the whole thing and the frenzied musical atmosphere, and I love it more and more and gain a little in confidence.

November 5th. Janetta was resolved to go to London to see Kenneth. Ralph tried to dissuade her, or alternatively offered to go with her, and I could hear their voices going on and on in the library; meanwhile beds had to be made and housework done. Robert also offered to go up with Janetta, but she said she felt she must 'do it herself' — which was completely understandable — but would come back on the 4.45 train. Nicky was left in my care, in spite of which Pippa and I managed to squeeze in some more music, while in the afternoon the rest of the party walked up the downs. Towards teatime a subterranean crescendo of anxiety could be felt, but as no message came through, the tension relaxed. After tea we had our firework display, Burgo wild with excitement and Nicky sitting on my lap watching them through the sitting-room window, saying 'Oh pretty! Isn't it naïs?' and chuckling softly to herself.

When Ralph and I are alone together we chorus Robert's praises. He's not only unusually attractive, but an intelligent, thoughtful and realistic character. I don't remember Ralph ever before taking such a liking to a younger man. When Ralph and Robert had driven off in the darkness and brought Janetta safely back again, Robert's expansive pleasure was delightful to witness. Janetta herself looked greatly relieved; she said Kenneth had been quiet and matter-of-fact and accepted everything.

November 6th. All the Stracheys left after breakfast. Burgo has been as good as gold with his beloved Vicky; I found a poem he had written to her in his bedroom. It is still his holiday, and the elopers were in the most light-hearted mood they have been in yet, seeming at last to believe there is happiness in store for them. Janetta said Kenneth had been perfectly reasonable yesterday, and had a good deal to say about his girl Angela who is coming to London. He had been 'talking himself blue' to all Janetta's friends, especially Cyril. She and Robert discuss their plans, and at the moment are considering taking refuge in Devon or Cornwall, but it will of course be a honeymoon handicapped by a ready-made child, something full of problems. It has been very moving and disquieting to have these two enacting their drama of All for Love under our roof — as if electricity had been let loose in the house.

Very tired tonight, but just as I was off to bed Robert started talking about his prison life, so enthrallingly that I sat up for many hours more.

November 9th. A letter from a friend saying how distressed she was by Janetta's lack of love for Kenneth. 'She expects too much of husbands, if only for Nicky's sake they should stay together. No one else could be expected to take such an interest in her.' How *can* one expect too much? Or rather, what is the use of husbands if one doesn't expect the highest and the best? And I don't think I'm being romantic, but severely rational. Moreover is there not great cruelty in condemning a girl of twenty-three to spend the rest of her life with a man she doesn't love and who has for some time been living with someone else? Even from Nicky's point of view, would the inevitable disagreements not be disturbing for her too?

The wind blows from the bitter East; we all retract a little into our shells, whether from the chill in the air or sense of anti-climax, and there is a noticeable undercurrent of irritability. Nicky reacts in her own way to the situation, and at breakfast she entered the room at a red-faced tearful gallop, one arm out-stretched towards Janetta, her hair flying, a tiny Tintoretto bacchante. Only Robert remains apparently imperturbable, writing and writing away in an exercise book in the midst of every disturbance.[1]

[1]He was at work on his first book *A Crowd is Not Company.*

November 12th. Robert left in the school car, intending to look in London for a letter from the R.A.F. and possibly go north that night. Nicky calmer. We all subside into normality.

In the evening a call from Robert. Janetta returned from it smiling. She said he was full of plans, had spent the afternoon with Cyril, did not have to go to his Air Force camp, but would like to come down here tomorrow and then go to Devon.

November 13th. Robert arrived in good spirits, looking very elegant in a grey suit and brown velvet tie. He described his visit to Cyril, who was sympathetic though also worried and concerned. He seemed full of plans, with no sign of 'immaturity'. After lunch I retired to my room and fell deeply asleep. Just before I dropped off, 'How do people live through these things,' I

thought, 'when even witnessing them is so exhausting?' I can't
think of any three people (for Nicky must be counted) to whom I
feel and wish more warmly. Tomorrow they will go, and
wearing and distracting though it has been, we shall miss them
terribly.

At dinner Robert talked for the first time about his experiences as a bomber pilot before he was shot down. I asked if he
would like to fly again in peace-time, and he described the
pleasure of 'whisking round up in the air' as being rather like
learning to swim. He had always liked flying in England for the
pleasure of what he saw. He talked with some cynicism about
'operations' and said that quite a proportion of bombers never
went near the target, but dropped their load at the first flak. The
crew tended to have a blind belief in their pilot — why? —
probably just because he *was* the pilot and they depended on
him. But as they came within range of flak there were times
when they would lose their nerve and shout at him: 'Oh God!
More to the left! They'll get us! Turn back!' Easy enough to
believe, but how much can weak imagination really grasp what
they all went through?

November 14th. Off they all went in the school car, Burgo mad
with excitement because his morning was to be spent at the film
of *Henry V*. Ralph and I were left alone to take up the threads of
our life again.

After a delicious lunch off a brace of pheasants shot by Clive
and beautifully roasted (I must say) by me, we drove to
Marlborough for the concert at the school — a French string
quartet playing Mozart, César Franck and Debussy. I realized I
hadn't watched a string quartet since I tried to play in one myself,
and I found it mesmerically fascinating — the sudden concentration of four individuals into a single unit; the first violin's raised
bow, and they are off! The weaving of four threads of different
sounds to ravish the ear was expressed in very different movements: the first violin, a mild little fellow, raised his bottom on
short pin-striped legs in moments of crisis and sank again into his
chair. The grey-haired second, looking like a distinguished
surgeon, bent and becked as if the music were some invisible
royalty, the viola rode it like a conscientious jockey; but best of all
to watch was the sultry-eyed cellist, who rolled and swayed in
orgiastic ecstasy, while his dark eyes in his pale face swam from

one to another of his fellow-players and shudders of unutterable feeling floated across his features.

November 30th. Drove over to the Brenans for lunch. Gerald's talk was full of comic surprises. The effect of coughing on family life, for instance, he described as 'the artillery of the home'.

Raymond [Mortimer] for the weekend and an evening of much more talk, of which all I can remember is Raymond saying: 'I'm not against the atom bomb,' and Ralph: 'Come, Raymond, that's a mere sound without any possible meaning.' To which Raymond replied: 'I believe it will make war impossible.'

['Can you remember your first meeting with So-and-so?' one is sometimes asked. Yes, for once I can. It was as early as 1924 that Raymond Mortimer and I were both invited to stay the weekend at the Mill House, Tidmarsh, with Lytton, Carrington and Ralph. Our nervousness of a new and strange experience and an alarming host brought us together, and I was grateful to Raymond for taking me off for a walk beside the river, to comment at our ease on the world we found ourselves in. Many years later I remembered this occasion, when he expressed his intolerance of shyness, was even inclined to deny that such a state existed: those who claimed to suffer from it, he said, were merely self-absorbed and shockingly uninterested in others. Certainly the young Raymond of the Twenties (or ever since for that matter) could not have been so described. Lively, quick-witted, interested in every subject, amusing, affectionate and companionable, he became a cherished friend, someone with whom Ralph and I took several happy holidays motoring through France, who visited us often at Ham Spray, and with whom we felt perfectly at ease and able to voice those differences in our views which may have become a little more marked as we grew older. Of course we held others that united us — we were all three Hedonists, we adored travel, were roughly Liberal in outlook, nourished curiosity and were passionate readers, though Raymond was the most dedicated. (If he ran out of books on a journey he would look round with an expression of anxious hunger impossible to ignore.) Where we differed was in our attitudes to War and Wealth. We were pacifists, he was not. We had something of an allergy to the rich and privileged; Raymond once told us that he found wealth and what it bought sexually attractive. He had a much higher standard of comfort than we did, and sometimes lectured us about the lack of ashtrays or the wrong placing of shaving-mirrors and reading-lights at Ham Spray, yet in the pursuit of some thrilling and exotic 'sight' he would put up with real discomfort — he had been known to sleep on bare boards. I cannot forgive Evelyn Waugh for his stupidity in describing him as a 'wild beast'.

Raymond was not good-looking, but he made up for that by the brightness of his eyes, his animated expression, and his readiness to smile and laugh. His thick hair never fell out but turned into handsome grey sculptured curls; his figure was lithe, he loved clothes and his ties were justly famous. He had many pleasures — looking at pictures, games like croquet, activities like skating. He claimed to be unable to sing *God Save the King*, but enjoyed listening to music in moderation particularly if it was French. Long, shuttlecock conversations about such subjects as aesthetics, prehistory or psycho-analysis could be enthralling with Raymond. I think it saddened him to be in disagreement with the young, yet he found it hard to adapt to new tastes and ways and he was not displeased to hear that his juniors thought him alarming, nor did he put people at their ease, angelically kind as he was at heart. I have heard him say that he would have liked to have had a child, and I can see him as a loving father, but woe betide the child if it didn't turn out 'bookish' (a favourite word of his) and pass its examinations.]

December 1st. No Mrs Chant. I've had rather too much of this lately and begin to feel that boring duties are endless. Raymond is very sympathetic — too much so. 'Oh dear! the philosopher in the kitchen! I don't like to see that at all,' he exclaimed today.

The alternative horrors of servantlessness and new faces loom before me, and I don't feel in a mood to face either. I was beginning to hope that perhaps now the war is over better times might be coming. But the whole subject is for me fraught with guilt, for I feel deeply ashamed to think that 'our class' should depend on those less fortunate to hoist us bodily through our physical lives as well as managing this feat for themselves. On Saturday our pig was killed. On Sunday it was cut up and great blood-stained chunks of meat invaded the larder. I attempt, fairly successfully, to think about them as little as possible.

December 11th. Called at the Hungerford labour exchange in search of 'daily help' and found myself all at once in the mangle of the bureaucratic machine. 'Is your husband disabled? Or is there any special hardship?'

'I have a contract to write a book,' I said on the spur of the moment, 'but if I'm doing all the work of the house it's impossible to get on with it.' This went down rather well.

'Well I'll have to send up a report on your case.'

A case! So that's what I have become.

1946

January 1st. For Christmas we had Janetta and Nicky, Saxon [Sydney-Turner] and no help; but we did have a mass of good things to eat and drink, turkey and plum pudding, extra butter and sugar on the ration, whisky, chocolates and cigars, and a pretty little Christmas tree. Saxon was I think glad to be here again, though he couldn't go further than murmuring that 'he thought it a good thing that his old habit of spending Christmas at Ham Spray was renewed'. He fascinated Nicky by dint of almost invisible nods and gestures in her direction; she and Burgo enjoyed themselves wildly, and it was certainly the happiest Christmas for years.

I gave Burgo his cello, which he was more pleased with than I would have guessed. On Boxing Day he insisted on going to the Padels to have a lesson, but tried to follow everything he was told with such intensity and anxiety that he was quite worn out by the effort. For a day or two he kept running to put records by Casals on the gramophone before breakfast, but already (alas and of course) the spell is loosening its hold, and practising is just another thing I want him to do. He is in rebellion against my desires at present, and though I respect him for it I can't quite think how to deal with it.

[Saxon was the mystery man of Old Bloomsbury and an early intimate of the circle of Vanessa, Virginia and Adrian Stephen. From Cambridge he brought a reputation for brilliant classical scholarship, for having written at least one opera, and even for skill at drawing. However, he spent his whole working career at the Treasury, refusing promotion because it would mean changing to a room with a less sympathetic view, and he was reputed to be the only man beside the Chancellor who could be trusted with knowledge of the contents of the Budget. He certainly had a gift for silence — perverse at times, for he might well remain dumb when talk was required of him and hold forth at length when there was some other urgent call on one's attention, just as he would go pink in the face with the effort of *not* laughing at a joke that amused him. A life-long unreciprocated passion for Barbara Bagenal had turned him into that now nearly extinct species 'a bachelor'. He never forgot one of her or her children's birthdays, and she told me that he wrote her a letter every day, written in his elegant hand with its overtones of Greek script — beginning just 'Barbara'!

He came often to Ham Spray, particularly during the war, a distinguished-looking figure with his finely modelled ivory-white features and hands, and his well-cut suits of great antiquity — white silk in summer, and at other seasons black, with a shirt of royal blue or plum colour maybe and button boots.

In the morning he might be seen advancing down the passage to the bathroom in a silk dressing-gown as shredded by wear and tear as a Hawaiian dancer's skirt, holding a tumbler of water containing his false teeth defiantly in front of him. There was always a volume of Horace or Thucydides in the original by his bedside.

His ability — indeed sometimes his desire — to aggravate could not disguise the fact that beneath this bottled-up eccentric there was a deeply affectionate man, and Ralph and I both loved him and enjoyed his company. Other friends were not exactly expected to do likewise, but received high marks if they did.]

January 23rd. Burgo has had flu, but his convalescence moves steadily along, he is sweet and reasonable and anxious to get well. In fact we are both delighted with his frame of mind. He is becoming very much an individual. The chess craze persists, but is being supplanted by a mania for acting Shakespeare on his Pollock model theatre. He and I divide all the parts between us and keep at it so that we are quite hoarse by evening. I enjoy it as much as he does, I believe; it is exactly like one I had as a child, with cardboard scenes of snowy woods and baronial halls, 'wings', and a boxful of characters who slide in and out on metal stands. Burgo thinks and talks of nothing but Shakespeare, takes the greatest trouble over the details of scenery — enhancing it by castle walls built of minibrix, or doll's-house furniture, and reads increasingly well. All this afternoon has been given over to *Macbeth*. This seems so healthy a sign of life that we don't feel anything else matters. The sap is certainly rising.

January 28th. Burgo's new vein of silent stoicism is most unexpected. He never mentioned school last night, so that I feared he might not have realized that term began today. Yet realize it he evidently did, and this morning we witnessed that heroic and pathetic ceremony — the sad pale figure clapping on its head and round its neck the insignia of slavery and suffering. Or so it seems to him at the moment, even though later on fun and excitement will be involved. We both found this spectacle harrowing in the extreme, and many times a term I ask myself whether it is really right and necessary to put children through such torments in order to get them used to the horrors of life.

Burgo's return from school in the evening is a moment when we prick up our ears, or send out feelers to sound the atmosphere. He came back today jovial and full of talk, and after prep. returned eagerly to Shakespeare. But at bed-time it was: 'I *hate* school. I know I shan't get a wink of sleep tonight thinking about it.'

January 30th. A letter from Janetta. Everything had been going frightfully well, 'Wonderfully lovely well' until three days ago when Robert was suddenly summoned north by the R.A.F. and threatened with Court Martial for writing some articles in a Sunday paper on life in prison camp in Germany, which the paper had omitted to get censored. So poor Robert is up there plunged in gloom, hanging about the camp with nothing to do, waiting for he knows not what. And Janetta fears for him all sorts of things, the worst of all being a possible prison term, and is trying to get help from various M.P.s. It's difficult not to get the feeling that 'the Forces' can't really take in the fact that the war is now over — or perhaps don't really want to.

February 2nd. Yesterday at last I was able to dig in at my Botany table, and did a good morning's work there, nor did it seem so formidable as I had feared. Burgo has returned each day cheerful from school, and sometimes with good news of top marks or other successes. We act *Hamlet* on the toy theatre, and then Ralph reads *Ivanhoe* aloud.

This morning Burgo came into our bedroom talking about Shakespeare as usual. He had been brooding over the 'fellow almost damned in a fair wife' in *Othello* and had some quite good ideas about what it meant.

Drove through streaming rain to Marlborough for a concert by Peter Pears and Benjamin Britten. I had only seen Pears as Peter Grimes, when wig and fancy clothes effectively concealed the fact that he is a large, broad-shouldered man with the profile of a Roman Emperor. He sang most beautifully. Britten, slim, nervous, and with the bright face of a little animal, began each piece looking shyly away as if he couldn't quite face eyeing the music or even the piano keys. But as the music ended he brought his rather pointed nose round sharply towards the audience as if to say 'What do you think of *that*?' The Marlborough boys punctuated the music with gruff and heart-racking coughs, all so alike that they seemed to come from a single ghostly monstrous throat.

February 6th. It has rained and rained from leaden skies. Sudden gusts blot out the downs in a sheet of whiteness; and to get out of our soaked garden we must wade through moulded ridges of rich coffee-coloured mud. A suitable background for the dismal news dished out to us last night by the Minister of Food that fats and animal fodder are to be cut, and that there is a serious world shortage of wheat, so that it is entirely possible we may have to have bread rationing to save millions from starvation. Well-off and well-fed as we are here I couldn't help a twinge of resentment at being suddenly faced with these facts, when so short a while ago we were being encouraged to think we would soon be enjoying peace-time conditions. But no: the thought of famine in Europe hangs overhead like the dark roof of Paddington Station.

At tea Burgo remarked: 'You and Ralph are unkind to me, you know, by being *too* kind. You let me have my own way too much. Now don't go and be brutally unkind because I say that.'

February 9th. We've come out at long last from the endless blanket of rain, into a pale clear blue sky, rosy towards the horizon. The beech tree in the park must have been blown down in last night's blast, and lies with its roots in the air, a melancholy spectacle. All through the winter months the forces of destruction have been beating on us — wind and weather, cold and disease. By now we are quite tired of huddling on the defensive; our muscles of withdrawal and staving off are exhausted, and we long to give way to the impulses of spring and growth which now faintly make themselves felt in the swelling buds and tentative twittering

of birds. So, wanting to go out and merge ourselves Pantheistic-
ally with the natural kingdom, we drove to Vernham Dean and
walked up the long grass track to the deserted farm of Hippenscombe, seated so surely among the high walls of the surrounding downs, with its few effectively placed dark trees, and
tumbledown walls sat on by a row of cats. This long-since
deserted farmhouse in its beautiful valley never fails to exert its
magic.

February 28th. A day in London. First to Sussex Place; Janetta let
us in. Robert and Nicky descended like a cascade. Beside the
horrible business of Robert's Court Martial, they had had a
burglary, and dry rot had been discovered under the Connollys'
bathroom door. Robert described two days of an Enquiry to see
whether a Court Martial is necessary; he thinks he is safe, but had
obviously had his nerves rasped by the futility of it all.

Lunch at the Ivy with Clive. There were Mary Hutchinson,
Lys (Connolly's girl) and later Cyril himself arrived and sat down
beside me. Lys is very pretty and she prattled of housewifely
things, like linoleum and dry rot. Cyril was amusing; his
conversational technique is to send out volleys of words,
surprising in content, in a quiet, level voice. I felt he thought
Ralph and I were enemies, which we are not in the least.

[I could never claim to have been more than an acquaintance of
Cyril Connolly's — one reason being that my pleasure in
friendship is as a two-way concern. Of course he had many close,
warm friends, but he had even more admirers and people who
were proud to know him. Indeed there was a great deal to admire
— he was exceptionally intelligent, clever (not quite the same
thing), witty and brilliantly funny, all qualities I greatly enjoy
and respect. I still laugh aloud when I remember some of his
characteristic witticisms, delivered in his famous 'flat' unmodu-
lated voice preceded by an intensified gleam in his eyes; for
instance the description of the traveller returning from abroad to
be greeted by an invisible loudspeaker saying: 'Wipe that smile
off your face — this is London!' He had great charm when he
chose to switch it on, and could look as if he was pleased to see
one again. But no one could venture a remark that transgressed
his system of values without bringing a hint of the schoolmaster
into his manner. What were those values? Obviously literature

came in lengths ahead with the other arts following. I doubt if politics interested him much except insofar as they involved the arts. It's rather difficult to relate moral concepts to Cyril. He had a bad reputation about money when he was young and poor; but even when his victims were equally young and poor they bore him little resentment. They enjoyed his company too much for that. Also when he grew more prosperous he was an extremely generous host, and could show supporting and affectionate kindness, as he did to his neighbour Duncan Grant, during the lonely years of his old age at Charleston.

I am sure the same current of warmth flowed towards his children, his loves and his chosen friends; what matter if those outside his inner circle reacted to his company rather as an audience does to a play or concert? On the whole he was unresponsive to other people's sallies, even by the quiver of an eyelid. When he was a guest, Cyril certainly expected best feet to be put forward: we tried to please him and were happy if we succeeded, even if there was a grain of resentment in our happiness.

He probably knew his own failings better than others did — far the most disastrous seems to have been sloth, which so strangely curtailed the output of an original and stimulating talent.]

March 23rd. The intervening time has not been very cheerfully spent. Awful cold: even snow and searing east winds. Five weeks of whooping-cough for Burgo, intractable political world, riots, famine, threats of a new war and the Atom bomb.

June 20th — Ham Spray. Richard and I sit waiting in considerable feverishness for the arrival of the 'Tycoons' — in other words Allen Lane of Penguin Books, publisher of our Botany book, and the printer Geoffrey Smith. We have a feeling that its whole future is threatened in some way incomprehensible to me by the financial by-products of Peace. This meeting has been arranged by the book's midwife Noel [Carrington] for the whole thing to be discussed. I have some important queries about scope and size, and Richard some others mainly concerned with time and money. As for money, none at all has been offered to me until the first volume comes out, and when oh when will that be? All yesterday I was tidying up the library and my Botany table. All this morning I have been trying to straighten out my thoughts and at the same time keep my confidence afloat. I am very much aware of it as a bobbing entity like a ping-pong ball on a jet of water at a fair, perilously kept up by an effort more of auto-suggestion than intelligence. But I must go and make tea ready for them.

June 21st. The Tycoons have come and gone. After an anxious time of trying to prevent all I had to say draining away and leaving complete blankness, I saw the smooth, long-nosed Bentley draw up in the drive. Allen Lane, a stocky figure squeezed into a smart suit of palest grey, was purely and simply the millionaire in an American film. He appeared to be acting a part, an important element of which was manifesting the 'common touch' by revealing a passion for choc-ices. Yet I'm sure he never ceased thinking of himself as the personification of power through money, benevolent but not to be 'had'. This for some reason made him rather pathetic. Geoffrey Smith the printer was a nice solid man, understanding his job and inspiring confidence, while Richard looked very wrought-up and defended his life-work with burning eyes in a pale face. We drank a glass of Madeira and then repaired to the library. I found my wits and my tongue once we started talking, but very little comfort or advice was to be got from any of them because they knew absolutely nothing about the subject. Lane is determined to exclude trees from the book, and when I tried to point out that there is no natural line of demarcation between plants, shrubs and trees, he waved me aside with a winning gesture saying, 'Oh, I think of a tree as something whose trunk I can put my arms round.'

So the afternoon spun by, while two incompetent electricians who had come to put in a single plug tore up the floorboards in the corridor with a loud rending noise, or shouted boomingly in the cellarage like Hamlet's father's ghost.

As our visitors were driving off I couldn't resist saying to Allen Lane: 'We've met before, you know — more than twenty years ago when I worked in Birrell and Garnett's bookshop.' His millionaire pomposity crumpled just a fraction at this reminder of his boyish diffident self, travelling the books of his firm and making up to me in the process.

But I slept lightly, full of forebodings about the book's fate. And Burgo too had trouble getting to sleep, disturbed by a story read to him at school 'about skeletons in blackened sun-bonnets'.

July 12th. Janetta, Robert and Nicky have come for the weekend. We love to have them here, and love all three of them. Also it is going to be gloriously fine and hot. Heat produces a sense of calm and expansiveness, and just as the flowers are bursting out of their buds all over the garden, everything that had become knotted and constricted within oneself loosens and expands and brings delicious relaxation. All day the warm air poured in at open windows, the garden is a bath full of faintly buzzing stillness. All day we lay on rugs spread on the lawn, talked, bathed and picked fruit. The presence of Robert and Janetta, both so beautiful and charming, enhances everything for both Ralph and me, and in exactly the same way.

July 13th. Everyone seems happy, particularly Burgo who is celebrating his eleventh birthday and undoes his presents with frantic delight. A kite, a camera, a tent, books — all are a success, and in each case he rushes round the breakfast table and hugs the giver nearly to death. Drove to the top of the downs where the kite was flown, while Janetta and I wandered about picking flowers and making miniature gardens and houses of pebbles to amuse Nicky.

A bathe before lunch: the water in the swimming-pool is getting much warmer and our bathes last longer and are pandemonic. Ralph bounces in with a roar and a splash, Janetta knots her hair on top of her head and swims about very fast, breast-stroke but crab-wise, with her head and neck well out of the water, her nose wrinkled with laughter; Robert dives in with a wild gleam in his eye and a wolfish smile and comes up with his black hair all over his face; Burgo squeals and hops without stopping; he carries on like billy-o with Robert, and there is a lot of horseplay and shouts of 'you dirty rotter!' Nicky sits demurely on the edge, naked but refusing to be coaxed into the water. Burgo's birthday tea followed.

It's extraordinary how even in what may seem the smoothest and most felicitous circumstances tiny signs may show that all is not perfectly well between two people, and irritate the inattentive ear like the faint buzzing of a mosquito or the drip of water from a tap. So it was that when Janetta and Robert decided to spend the golden evening walking to the top of the downs, and indeed set off in that direction only to come to a halt in the field and stand there talking for almost an hour, something in the attitude of their drooping heads struck a chill into my heart. I felt it again when at dinner what sounded like a random remark of Robert's produced a sudden movement in Janetta, making her upset her glass of gin and vermouth and murmur: 'It's the last straw.' 'The last straw to what?' 'Just life.'

July 9th. All left us this morning, by car and bicycle, but how they linger in our minds, attach themselves to tunes and remain with us as the echo of voices or images of beautiful bodies in the pool. It would be strange if several years in prison camp left no tension, and Janetta told Ralph when they were picking fruit and vegetables to take to London that Robert was 'terrifically up and down'. Sometimes everything she did would be wrong. Then he would turn and blame himself. But why, oh why do human beings have to spoil the sweetness of companionship by tossing the burden of guilt and blame between them like some macabre form of football? No lovers can escape quarrels, but these two are too exceptional for one to be aware of them without pain.

[Some combination of circumstances — now partly forgotten — led to my stopping writing my diary for over a year, the only real break there has been in it until today. I had never thought of it as a thing to be kept religiously, and perhaps it would be more relevant to ask why I ever started it again (in January 1948). After all, it had begun life as an uneasy tail tied to the kite of the war, or in other words the war had focused my desire to write, as very likely the Peace could not.

One reason certainly was that in the late summer of 1946 Burgo left Newbury Grammar School and went as a weekly boarder to a conventional boys' prep school at Kintbury about ten miles from Ham Spray. Surprisingly happy and successful there at first, he wasn't a conventional little boy, and to our dismay he suddenly began quietly taking to the road and walking in the direction of home. 'What was wrong?' we asked, scenting bullying and other horrors. But he had no complaints. There had been a bad thunderstorm, and at length he confessed that he had got it into his head that Ralph and I might have been struck by lightning and be dead. The pattern repeated itself, and there followed many uneasy months for us all, for there is nothing that wrings the entrails more savagely than one's child's inarticulate misery. There were more escapes, and all Burgo could say was that the moment he left the school gates and started 'running away' a feeling of intense happiness invaded him. The trouble was there was no day school within reach and we obviously couldn't leave Ham Spray. We consulted the charming old Scottish psycho-analyst Dr Edward Glover, who talked of 'fugues' and 'fantasies about the death of parents' as common currency, and spoke of the Junior School at Eton (which Burgo had been put down for) as a 'jungle', but the problem remained. Our worry and fear that we were bungling a difficult situation, as well as the fact that it was one about which Ralph and I didn't always see eye to eye, I'm sure made up one reason I stopped writing. Angst is not something one enjoys recording.

Quite a different cause was that the difficulties I had unconsciously foreseen between Robert and Janetta became serious. There was a temporary separation that grieved us deeply, followed by reunion.

But this was by no means an entirely gloomy year. There was a very happy interlude in the summer of 1946 when we all three enjoyed the thrill of going abroad for the first time for six years. We chose Switzerland as a country mercifully untouched by war, and arranged to join James, Alix and Marjorie Strachey at Lugano. What joy it was to feel the prison doors swing open and find ourselves speeding across France again, even though it meant sitting up all night in a full railway carriage. I remember that Burgo had a bad attack of hiccups and that a genial Swiss couple told him of an infallible cure, which I have several times passed on to perfect strangers. And I remember too the amazed delight of arriving at Basle station early in the morning, to find a huge banner of Welcome to us poor sufferers from the austerities of war — a welcome tangibly expressed in bananas (without coupons!), hot coffee and croissants with lashings of butter and black cherry jam. How clean everything was! and how kind the admirable Swiss, who treated us with almost embarrassing sympathy — undeserved we felt. Even the Lugano trams were spotless, and conductors in impeccable grey uniforms picked up the used tickets from the floor with a long pair of tongs. We began to identify the Swiss nation with the Red Cross, and admire without qualification all we heard about their impartially humane activities during the war. We swam in the lake, rowed on it and took steamers to picnic on its further shores. Burgo took lessons in diving and the crawl, and the society of our Strachey

friends was punctuated by bursts of laughter. Three weeks' bliss
in fact. As we left I was struck with pleasurable surprise to realize
that a small, non-belligerent nation such as Switzerland, completely surrounded by a terrible war, could yet have survived so
well.

It was now time to return to our working lives — Ralph to
writing for the *New Statesman*, Burgo to school and I to my
Botany. A new character had appeared in the latter sphere: an
expert from Kew had been found to advise Richard and myself
and see that we made no howlers in our book. The choice could
not have been more fortunate. Noel Sandwith was a distinguished botanist, specializing in the plants of South America; he
came often to Ham Spray and we all soon became much attached
to him. Of young middle age and medium build, he walked with
a long springing tread, his eyes flashing with expectation behind
his gold-rimmed spectacles. He led us to the sites of several rare
species — the last known patch of the Monkey Orchid (*Orchis
Simia*), for instance, saying as we approached it: 'I really ought to
blindfold you here'. When I took him to see our local Bath
Asparagus (*Ornithogalum Pyrenaicum*) he was more interested in
an unpleasant reddish dust on its stems and leaves than in the
plant itself, exclaiming excitedly: 'A rust, a *marvellous* thing!',
pounced on it and sent it off to Kew. It was somehow tempting to
tease him and even shock him a little. Richard once asked him
why he had never married. 'Because of my great love for the
flowers,' he replied without hesitation. He fitted in well with all
our friends. As Julia wrote to me with her usual acumen:
'Sandwith is a very soothing element, is he not?']

1948

January 6th. All three to London for a few days' holiday treat. In Hungerford Station waiting-room a number of prosperous, well-dressed families were collected, who talked loudly about their personal affairs, ignoring the rest of the world and making me ponder the phenomenon of Class, and ask myself how the war had affected it. When the pressure was on us all, it had seemed as though the relation between master and man, for instance, was suffering a sea-change, and it was a common sight to see a Colonel in a good but worn suit almost cringing to a waitress as he pleadingly enquired 'Do you think I might have a little water?' Today I felt we were in the presence of 'conspicuous padding' — that is to say I was aware that the gentry had re-assumed their right to the privileges and support that money gives. Two elderly ladies got into our carriage in the train and drew back their lips from their yellowing teeth with identical snarls of concentration as they pecked about in their handbags. 'Thought for a moment I'd forgotten my handkerchief,' said one. '*Very* nosy day, isn't it?'

Left our things at the Great Western Hotel and went to meet Boris [Anrep] and Maroussa [Volkova] at a Chinese restaurant where we ate from numerous delicately flavoured dishes. Both looked smoothly plump and seal-like and were wonderfully hospitable and friendly, yet there was a waft of sadness hanging about them.

Our evening was spent having supper with Julia and Lawrence [Gowing] before going to the Aldwych Farce. A delicious repast of lobster Newburg and a rich cake. Ralph, Julia and I laughed uproariously at Ralph Lynn and Robertson Hare. Burgo often looked serious, but I think he was enjoying it. After the theatre I went on to the second meeting I have ever attended of the Memoir Club. Bunny [Garnett], Oliver [Strachey], Clive and Quentin [Bell], Dermod and Desmond [MacCarthy], Duncan and Vanessa, Morgan Forster were the company. I was wearing a

new suit of black watered silk trimmed with gold braid; I had
designed it myself and was rather pleased with my appearance.
'Fanny has a new dress,' said Clive. 'Oh no,' said Desmond, 'I
remember seeing her in it *years* ago at Birrell and Garnett. It's a
pity that braid doesn't make words.' 'Such as what?' I asked. 'Oh,
I don't know. Something like "Darling".' Dermod read a good
paper about his father; Morgan a very long and slightly boring
one about his aunts. He at least appeared to be amused by it, and
often laughed at his own jokes, tipping up his curiously-shaped
head and exposing a mouthful of neat false teeth to the electric
light. My doom is sealed — I am to read a Memoir next time we
meet.

[The Memoir Club began as a Novel Club, created by Molly
MacCarthy in 1918 with the object of inciting Desmond to write
one. This it failed to do and was therefore transformed into a
Memoir Club a year later. The idea was that papers should be
both confidential and completely frank, and that no one should
take offence at anything read. Invitations were sent out by 'Mary
MacCarthy, Secretary and drudge of the Club', to the Keyneses,
the Woolves, Roger Fry, Duncan, Vanessa, Clive and E. M.
Forster. New members were elected by secret ballot, but as one
blackball sufficed to exclude a nominee the Club naturally failed
to grow very fast. By the time I was elected it had been
augmented by Bunny Garnett, Adrian Stephen, Oliver Strachey,
Janie Bussy and Quentin Bell; but it had lost — by death —
Roger, Virginia, Lytton and Maynard. Later on, in the teeth of
fierce blackballing we co-opted Dermod MacCarthy, Julia
Strachey, Olivier Bell, Angelica Garnett, Sebastian Sprott and
Denis Proctor.
Dinner was arranged by the Secretary, usually in a Soho
restaurant, and after it we repaired to the rooms of one of the
members, sank into armchairs and sofas and listened while two
papers were read aloud. I never knew a more attentive or
appreciative audience, and there was usually plenty of laughter.
After the papers came questions and general conversation. It was
a delightful way to spend the evening, and notes made after
several meetings will be found in what follows. The trouble was
that it was difficult for the various secretaries (I was the last) to
find dates suiting everyone, and also enough new blood to get
through the barrage of blackballs. Molly had intended the papers

to be kept by the secretary, but as more and more members became writers they all carried them home to act as material for their published works.]

January 7th. Lunched at the Ivy with Clive and Desmond Shawe-Taylor whom we had long wanted to meet. We found him very sympathetic, and full of eager vitality which makes him bounce up and down as he talks.

To tea with Isobel [Strachey][1] in her elegant feminine flat, full of the fragance of mimosa, and then on to the Ballet at Covent Garden — Burgo completely absorbed but unable to describe what he felt. Each evening we come back to the red corridors of the Great Western Hotel and feel that it is home. Often we go down into the station to buy an evening paper and look at the night expresses, well-stuffed with passengers and hear their bird-like shrieks as they chug off on their long journeys to Plymouth or Penzance.

[1]Writer and artist, first wife of Lytton's nephew John.

January 9th. A fine crisp morning. Burgo and I went to the H.M.V. Gramophone shop where he wanted to spend some record tokens; among other things he chose the music of the Tschaikovsky ballet, which has hooked him. Home on the afternoon train with Robert, Janetta and Nicky, back to beloved Ham Spray, cold, but sweet-smelling, with flowers in pots in every room, black Minnie[1] and a supper of home-made brawn. We meant to go to bed early, but Janetta and I got into a long rambling conversation about Capital Punishment which kept us up for hours.

Robert works hard at a German translation. It wasn't till this evening after a bottle of wine and sitting over a roaring fire that he suddenly said what must have been for hours on the tip of his tongue: 'I hope you are free on the twentieth.' We didn't pretend not to understand that it was an announcement of their marriage, and Ralph said in a very melancholy voice which failed to conceal his emotion: 'I suppose we mustn't say how glad we are.' For however little one may believe in ceremonies, this one will be surely both a symbol and solid evidence of something that has every claim to make one glad. And happy planning for their party filled the rest of the evening.

[1]Cat.

January 15th. Re-reading Proust is rather like having a fever. So stimulating is the effect of drawing in his subtle, intoxicating complexities that one is left restless, breathing fast and shallow, so that those moments come as a relief when one is carried away by the flood — drowned in it. I cannot decide whether I get more from the translation or the original, and so move from one to the other, at times getting so much interested in the problems of translation itself that I have to have both versions in front of me.

Burgo goes back to school on Monday, and seems only to have realized the fact today, passing as a result into a sort of Laputa, neither in our world nor that of school. We drove in to Newbury for some school shopping and I tried to give my mind to thick grey socks (which must be marked) and speckled sand-shoes. In the afternoon the arrival of Boris and Maroussa made a happy diversion. It takes one all one's time to attend to Boris; he is such a potent force quite apart from his huge size, increased I think since we last saw him. At tea his bulk alarmingly overlapped our fragile Regency chairs. He spreads his legs wide to make room for the giant stomach; and beneath his mouth with its turned down rather bitter expression the double chins hang like those of a monitor lizard. Yet there isn't the least contradiction in saying that he is a pleasure to look at, is full of charm and captivates the eye by his delicate movements with his large hands or the subtle drift of expression over his face, and the ear by the musical play of his voice — even by the long drawn-out '*Eu — eu — eu*' with which he fills in a gap in a sentence. He said one was wrong to put a child's happiness at school first; he must learn, and that involved a certain amount of being unhappy. He described how, when he got a specially bad mark at school, his mother said to him: 'If you get that again, *I'll skin you alive.*'

[Boris von Anrep, as he should properly be called, was a Baltic Baron. He was also a descendant of Catherine the Great and one of her lovers, though he told us that his father grew angry when his children asked about their forbears, believing it to be a purely snobbish interest. Once when we were staying with his great friend Maud Russell at Mottisfont, Ralph and I walked with him into the garden where huge trees stooped to embrace white-painted seats and streams glided under bridges festooned with roses, and stood leaning on the parapet of one of them. The shallow water flowing swiftly beneath must have reminded Boris of the Volga, for he began to tell us about his childhood home on its banks — the large house built of granite below and wood above, the low cliffs and little beaches bordering the river and the paddle-steamers chugging past; he described them all most vividly.

After the 1917 Revolution Boris was in Paris for a while, studying painting and meeting Augustus John, Henry Lamb, Man Ray and Helen Maitland whom he married. When he turned to mosaics I do not know, but before the Second World War he had become a master, perhaps the only master, making floors for the Tate, the National Gallery and the Bank of England, murals in the Russian Church and the Roman Catholic Cathedral, as well as many mosaics for private commissions. He made two fireplaces for Ham Spray, the first commissioned by Lytton, the second as a wedding-present for Ralph and myself. It was characteristic of him that he entered into the tastes and interests of those he worked for. Along the top of Lytton's fireplace was the prostrate naked torso of a young man, looking provocatively over his shoulder. In our dining-room he took his cue for the border 'from the crookedness of the books in our shelves'. For my present London flat he made me a cat warming itself before a blazing fire. I was astonished to find a large wall decorated by him in a church in the middle of Ireland, but not surprised that its prevalent colour was green and its theme St Patrick driving out the snakes.

He occupied in every sense a very large place in our lives and came often to Ham Spray with his delightful 'consort' Maroussa Volkova. Their visits usually began dramatically on the station platform, when Boris used to salute Ralph with a bear's hug and kisses on both cheeks. He was as good a guest as host, and entered with equal originality and energy into cooking or conversation. As good a listener as talker, he would greet other people's remarks with a broad Slavonic smile and a long drawn-out 'No-o-o-O! Ree-ee-ally!'

When, after Ralph's death, I decided to sell Ham Spray in 1961, Boris wrote me a letter which would have made me change my mind if anything could:

I read your letter with the greatest sorrow in my heart. To abandon the house where you lived so long and where happy memories supersede the sad ones is a terrible uprooting.

Whatever unhappiness you feel now it will mellow with time, and happy days of many years will come back in watching your old friends gathering round under the roof which for all of us is a centre of loving hospitality and enlightment and the greatest civilized taste in all things.

Soon afterwards I went to see him putting up the mosaics in the Roman Catholic Cathedral. Boris looked (and was) ill, a splendid crumbling ruin in the midst of what he believed to be his last works.

The last time I saw him was at Mottisfont again, only ten days before his death. At dinner one night he leant across the table and to my astonishment urged me to write about the past and old friends. So strong was my impulse to please him that I said: 'All right, Boris, I will.' Very uncharacteristically, he then repeated twice in a gentle, unemotional voice: 'I love you.'

I never saw him after this weekend, and shall never forget him.]

January 18th. Maroussa came down to breakfast in an elegant yellow wool housecoat. She smokes without stopping, using a long holder, otherwise she seems in a less nervous state than she was, though she startled me by saying: 'Of course I cannot go to the cinema, for fear of thieves at the flat.'

Burgo is becoming as much under Boris' spell as we are — a great blessing as it has distracted him from his uneasy, pre-school state. Today he took Boris up to his room to show him all his treasures, including those in his secret cache under the floor-boards — a signal mark of favour. Boris told us a story about his brother Glyep who is a doctor in Cairo and an ardent stamp-collector. He happened to find a freak sheet without perforations in a small post-office. Soon afterwards King Farouk's Secretary wrote to say that he had heard of Glyep's purchase and would like to buy the stamps from him. 'They have been sent to a friend, a professor in Germany,' was Glyep's reply. Another letter from the King's Secretary asked for the friend's address, but was told the stamps had not arrived. 'Unfortunately lost in the post.' Even this was not the end. When Glyep was out his flat was completely ransacked by the King's agents, but the stamps, hidden in a special poison cupboard, were not found.

January 19th. The fascination that Boris exercises over Burgo has reached such a point that last night at supper he couldn't take his eyes off him, and from time to time put out a hand and — as if magnetized — touched his enormous cheek. We all drove to Hungerford to see our Russian friends off, and then returned to our packing and preparations. If Burgo minded going back (and he said a few days ago that he did) he was wonderfully philosophical and seemed to be trying to make his departure go off as smoothly as possible. At last Ralph drove him away into the darkness with his trunks and his cello, while I sank extenuated on to the sofa. How I hate the whole business! How unnatural it seems! I do believe he was partly excited to be rejoining the world of boys, but for my part I hated seeing the door of his bedroom yawning vacantly, and finding his blue jersey and his sandals lying on the bathroom floor.

[Most parents of my generation had been brought up impersonally by nurses and in the belief that father and mother knew best, so that when the war handed us responsibilities for our own beloved children for which we were ill-prepared, many of us worried too much whether we were doing right — a worry not diminished by knowing something of the theories of Freud.

I hope I have conveyed in the few references to him that Burgo was a happy, funny, original if sensitive little boy before the guillotine fell that took him away from home. I have noticed the same change in many other children. Before the prep. school age they are unselfconscious, amusing, and so full of energy and high spirits that they cannot walk along a pavement, but need to let off steam by going hoppity-skip. Then what happens? They are forced into the company of their contemporaries, undiluted except for a few adults of a special species among whom are to be found love of power, paedophilia, and — with luck — one or two born teachers gifted to stimulate budding intelligences. Under the influence of transplantation from the flower-pot of home to an environment fraught with fear and bewilderment, what a sad change takes place! They become fidgety, competitive, suspicious, wanting to be exactly like everyone else, and ready to bang or punch the other boys before they have it done to them. I am of course exaggerating and over-generalizing, but there is some truth in my picture.

I suggest that our English system of packing children off to boarding-school at the age of eight or even six is brutally cruel, as can be seen from watching the departure of any school train at the start of the year. Of course children should learn to mix with their contemporaries, and can have glorious fun and laughter with them — if only they are allowed back to base in the evenings until they are old enough and firm enough not to be battered out of their original shape. I find something very unnatural in herding those of the same age together, and would prefer something approaching the microcosm envisioned in the households described by Tolstoy and Turgenev, where children, adolescents and lovers mix together and the old babushka makes her comments from a corner by the samovar.]

January 20th. We had to catch the early train to be in time for Janetta and Robert's wedding. Fine and frosty weather; a brilliant flame from a hedger's fire, caster sugar covering the fields, and puffs of smoke coming from the mouths of men bicycling to work.

At Sussex Place there were flowers everywhere, champagne bottles on the white-covered table, and the old charwoman's face cracked by a permanent smile. We walked with Janetta and Robert, and Janetta's half-brother Mark [Culme-Seymour] to the Registry office nearby. Back at the house again, wonderful food was appearing — oysters, smoked salmon, chicken mayonnaise. Then the guests swarmed in, about sixteen of us in all; someone was filling my plate with food and my glass with champagne, while the heat of the fire brought out and spread abroad the scent of mimosa, so that the whole experience merged into one, and I was borne on the wings of semi-intoxication combined with the sympathetic feelings I had been simmering in all day, through conversations with the other friends — Cyril Connolly, Angela [Culme-Seymour], Julia, Diana Witherby, all of whom seemed as mellow as I felt.

January 27th — Ham Spray. Ralph and I are working in the library — the first real day's work this term. Only during the quiet days between weekends can I seriously plunge into reading or work, and even so it often takes me a day to get into my stride, and I think I read unusually slowly: it seems to me I hear every word resounding through the corridors of my brain, but if one does not, how to appreciate the style — if there is one? Tonight I was reading Virginia's book of essays, some are quite dull, and then comes a brilliant sentence, like this about Proust: 'Suddenly in flash after flash, metaphor after metaphor, the eye lights up that cave of darkness and we are shown the hard tangible material shapes of bodiless thoughts hanging like bats in the primeval darkness where light has never visited before.'

How tired I get of being imprisoned in my own vocabulary — the words I choose to fit my thoughts into when talking or writing. If it had no other purpose, reading would be enjoyable for the change alone.

January 28th. How delicious our winter breakfasts at Ham Spray are, I thought this morning as I looked at all the dear delightful familiar objects on the breakfast table, and the pale clean winter sunlight slanting in at the windows to light up a cyclamen flower just coming out in its pot, and black Minnie sitting in Burgo's chair with her furry chin resting on the table-cloth; and Ralph beaming because the bacon was so good this morning; and a snug warm night in bed behind us, not to mention years and years of happiness together. How very fortunate I am!

January 30th. Feeling over-sedentary after a hard morning's work in the library I decided to go for a walk, but couldn't persuade Ralph to come too. 'Why do you like going for walks so much?' he asked me. Well, why do I? Because I like the look of the world around me seen from a different position (from that in the car, say); because I like the feel of the wind on my face, the sun also, and the mere pleasure of physical movement.

It wasn't a particularly attractive day. I turned up the grass track that follows Wan's Dyke. At the top, two old chaps, one with a pretty rosy face like a Morland, were digging holes in the bank, and as I passed one shouted to the other. I looked back and saw him hauling up the limp yellowish body of a ferret. Coming up back the lane I suddenly caught several whiffs of purest Spanish village — damp wood smouldering on a bonfire — which brought back a cobbled street odoriferous with hot dust, mules, white walls, everything most different from my surroundings, like a stab from a hatpin.

January 31st. In lovely sunny moments this morning I went out without a coat and picked snowdrops, aconites and wild sweet violets.

The Brenans to lunch. We hardly mentioned politics, not even the assassination of Gandhi heard about last night. Everyone seems to be sick and tired of them. Instead we talked about people, books and writing. Gerald said to Ralph: 'Your review on Nelson was very good. You always seem to write what you want to say: now I can never do that — I write what my pen wants me to do or something. The man at the points is at fault, it appears to me, and gets onto the wrong line and I can't get off it.' Talked about Bertie Russell and his broadcast discussion the other night with a Jesuit about the existence of God. Bertie put up a bad showing for the agnostics, and the clever Father ran rings round him.

February 2nd. We had planned to spend two days in London, mainly for me to consult the botanical journals in the Lindley Library. The Librarian is the most damping man imaginable. 'How's the book going?' he asked briskly. 'Now Clapham, Tutin and Warburg's Flora — *that* really *is* going to be good. I've been looking at some of it: it's first rate and the keys *work*, which you can't say of some.'

February 4th — Ham Spray. Breakfast conversation with Ralph about Londoners and country people. How Londoners are all the time under observation and therefore to some extent acting. For instance in a restaurant people are often so busy *looking* as if they were having a good time, and being careful to laugh and talk in an animated style for the benefit of the perfect strangers round them, that they can hardly attend properly to the conversation going on at their own table. We had dined with Phyllis [Nichols] at the Caprice Restaurant last night, and since Phil was having wisdom-teeth out, Roger Senhouse was asked instead, who while keeping his end up with perfect aplomb in every topic of conversation was all the time eyeing the other diners as they came in and out. 'There's Lady Seafield. You know she had an heir when she was over forty and everyone thought it was hopeless. Ah, there's Viva King — now I wonder who she is with — looks like a Museum boy. What are the initials on his case? C.S.R.C.? I'm just waving to Ken Ritchie.'

[I first met Roger Senhouse when I was an undergraduate at Cambridge, and he came over from Oxford with a party of friends, nearly all men. All seemed alarmingly brilliant, witty and confident, but Roger was far the handsomest of them all, or indeed of any young men I had met. Tall, brown-haired with regular aquiline features and a charming smile; his looks were not striking, they were merely perfect.

His best friend was the clever, amusing but far less good-looking Philip Ritchie, and as is well known to readers of Lytton Strachey's biography, he fell deeply in love with Philip (who died young in 1927), and afterwards and until the end of his life with Roger, to whom he left the most valuable part of his library. Philip and Roger both loved music, and I quite often met them together at a Prom. or Chamber Music concert, to which I had most likely gone alone. They were invariably forthcoming and friendly to me, for which I was grateful because I felt I didn't really belong in their charmed circle. However, I shared with Philip a passion for string quartets and trying to understand Philosophy, and with Roger for Brahms. It was sad that Roger began to lose his marvellous looks very young: he put on weight and lost some hair; but his charm remained and I never saw him without it. He had one failing — he couldn't be counted on to tell the truth. I think this came from a streak of pure fantasy in his character, and his lies usually concerned trivial, social matters. He would obstinately maintain that he had met the Duchess of X on such-and-such a day, repeating their conversation, and only when it was conclusively proved to him that she was in Egypt at the time would he say airily: 'Oh well, have it your own way.'

Roger became a partner in Secker and Warburg's, the publishers, and also translated some of Colette for them. I visited him there when Julia was their reader — his room was a shambles of books, manuscripts and unopened letters in toppling towers of confusion, mixed with dirty tea-cups and plates of fossilized sandwiches. As usual he gave me a debonair, friendly welcome, and seemed quite unaware of the strangeness of his surroundings.

The last years of his life were spent at Rye in Sussex. He had inherited a great many books and pictures, as well as those Lytton had left him. The confusion was beyond words, Miss Havisham could not have competed. If two kind local ladies had not looked in now and then, I dread to think what would have happened. The disease from which he was dying was wasting him away, with the moving result of bringing out the fine bone structure of his face and restoring his youthful beauty.]

February 19th — Ham Spray. Yes, we are to be frozen now, just when we thought we had squeaked through the winter intact. Piled up a roaring wood fire and sat in front of it reading the text of my Volume III out loud, for smoothness and lack of repetitions. There seems to be no limit to possible re-furbishings.

Went to lunch with Juanita [Turton][1] and there met her mother-in-law Euphemia.[2] She must be over sixty; she is tall and really beautiful still. Her short bobbed hair is dyed yellow with a fringe; she has a pair of splendid blue eyes, a classical nose and a skin that still keeps its look of bloom and softness. Her car, which stood outside, had at least eight yapping poodles and pekes inside it. She said: 'I've got about eighteen altogether. I can't resist them.' She brought one of the pekes indoors, where it sat trembling and bubbling on her knee with its tongue permanently hanging out, as if it had never in its life owned any teeth. What a ménage! With the wide smile of an amiable alligator Euphemia promised us 'black' butter and chickens, I wonder if we shall ever see them.

[1]Daughter of Darsie and Lucila Japp.
[2]Married first to Henry Lamb, then Ned Grove. The father of her only son (Christopher Turton) was killed in the First War.

March 1st. Robert rang up yesterday, sounding cheerful and eager to come down. He was writing his first review for *The Spectator*, and hoped to get it done before the six o'clock train. What a pleasure to see them both again! Also they seem to be completely in control of their life, no longer buffeted by it, and Robert's book[1] has been having a lot of favourable, some enthusiastic reviews. He is working away industriously at his translation.

Clive arrived at tea-time with a tiny suitcase and a large briefcase containing three bottles of sherry. What would our guests make of each other? we wondered. We warned Robert and Janetta of Clive's comic side. We needn't have worried — they all got on perfectly and conversation never stopped.

[1]*A Crowd is Not Company*.

March 3rd. We decide to institute the Charleston regime of spending the morning quietly at our various occupations. Otherwise the constant talk would finish us off. But there is great goodwill afloat in the house to make this visit a success. Clive remarks often on Janetta's beauty and sweetness, and obviously likes Robert, saying he is 'very attractive'. Meanwhile Janetta sparkles in the light of Clive's admiration, and has been very funny. Clive was delighted when she produced gestures turning herself into the caryatids which support Cyril's sideboard.

On Cyril's recommendation we had invited two new neighbours, Robin and Mary Campbell, to have drinks with us. They were a pleasant surprise — informal and easy, fairly tough, realistic. In no time we were discussing the reason for the failure of the Ruskin marriage, described in a book we had all been reading.[1] Was it Ruskin's surprise and horror at the first sight of Effie's bush (his experience of the naked female having hitherto come from Art alone)? Mary Campbell is self-confident, rather small, with neat pink and white features. In the evening Clive was captivated by Janetta's description of having her bottom pinched black and blue by Italians. He got rather drunk, and though no one else was more than merry, kept saying: '*Some* of us have had too much brandy.' All of us notice and are amused by his compulsive gestures when talking — the sweeping movements of his hands as though sowing seed, pulling up his trouser legs to reveal a pink leg and then buttoning his coat tightly round him with defiant looks in both directions, as if at imaginary enemies.

[1] *The Order of Release*, by Admiral Sir William James.

March 5th. The last few hours before Clive's departure were spent like most of the rest, talking our heads off. After he had gone I felt I had talked all the breath out of my body and was quite hoarse and deflated. His vitality is tremendous, almost exceeding Robert's. He and Janetta made as if to go, but we asked them to stay on and were delighted when they said they would. Robert was curious to hear more about Clive and Charleston and old Bloomsbury, and both he and Janetta seemed impressed by Clive — as indeed they might — he is so rosy and lively at sixty-six and keeps the conversation at such an interesting level. An unfortunate misprint in Robert's review for *The Spectator* has made him feel persecuted and as if nothing he did could come right. One glimpsed his potentiality for unhappiness in the fiercest of his repertory of smiles. Janetta took him off for a walk across the fields and he came back marvellously cured but still inclined to panther-like prowling.

March 9th. A summer day in March. The sky was already blue when Ralph pulled the curtains, and immediately after breakfast it was like June on the verandah. Birds sing loudly. Purple crocuses, following on the yellow, are bursting up and bursting out into wide cups in which the bees revel. Minnie appears to be on heat, and wanders round letting out unearthly yells, with an agonized expression and half-shut eyes. Her lover, the farm cat, follows her half-heartedly, while she makes all the running, rolling herself on the ground before him and stretching out her furry arms.

One cannot bear to go indoors, so we take out books, papers and writing-cases, and let them curl up in the heat or float away on a waft of air. I can only give half my mind to anything. I think vaguely about sex (because of Minnie, I suppose) — or *wonder* rather. Is a one-man woman or one-woman man born or made? What is the best technique for a permanent couple to adopt when one of them is attracted elsewhere? And is jazz the music of promiscuous sex only? Spring thoughts! Later I returned to writing my Memoir for the next meeting of the Memoir Club, something which has been causing me a good deal of worry and self-disgust, and then back to Proust and the superb M. de Charlus.

March 10th. A letter from Clive says of Robert: 'It's a long time since I met any male creature to whom I took a more immediate fancy.' This miraculous warmth soon dissolves one into a pat of butter, and it is overpowering to have the heat of July coupled with the growth and freshness of early spring. The fields turn greener under our eyes, plants start up out of their beds, the cows in the park lie down exhausted by the sun. In such weather one puts off and puts off, without any sense of guilt, feeling that when Nature is staging such a fine performance it would be foolish to do anything but watch it. I did write to Julia, and that was all.

March 11th. Most of today we spent with the Brenans, driving to Aldbourne and lunching in their garden. Gerald was very amusing, and ceaselessly fished odd creations out of his mind, like a conjurer producing rabbits. He complained of exhaustion however, caused by seeing a lot of Dylan Thomas who threatens to come and live in their village. At a certain hour of the day, Gerald told us, and a certain degree of drunkenness, his conversation is brilliant, amusing, imaginative and poetical. Then he refuses to go, and gets drunker and drunker, and has to be propped out of the house and away, with his large baby's head wobbling on its stalk. As he left the last time, he started dramatically at the sight of Gerald's row of dustbins, and exclaimed: '*FORty* thieves!'

Talked also of politics — the Communist coup in Czechoslovakia and Jan Masaryk's suicide — and almost agreed.

March 18th. Off to London, poor Ralph in considerable gloom, as he was dreading his visit to the dentist. How to convey to the sufferer in any valuable way how deeply one feels for them, but the truth is that (however much that may be) they feel even more keenly for themselves. In our crowded train I saw the eyes of the business man next to me popping out in the direction of *Sodome et Gomorrhe* which I was reading.

Leaving Ralph to his fate I drove to 41 Gordon Square, with a heavy suitcase of letters to Lytton which James wants to have microfilmed. James looked pale and ill, Alix's clothes are unbelievably patched and darned; I think she takes a masochistic pleasure in what is a task for most of us — making very old clothes do.

Lunch with Clive at the Ivy, with Desmond [MacCarthy] and Mary Hutchinson. It was rather an elaborately conversational affair, wherein Clive (as Stage Manager or Conductor) wound each person's strand carefully into the whole. He does it very well, but makes a too conscious business of it — for me at any rate. Desmond was the only person whose talk reached the necessary standard and his was, I must say, very good. He would begin to roll a little in his chair, growling in a low tone, and then would come some remarkable phrase, such as his comment on Professor Joad: 'He's a fungus sprouting in the tub of Bertrand Russell.'

March 20th — Ham Spray. Saxon and Pippa[1] are here for the week-end. I took Pippa off to the piano and we played Haydn sonatas for the best part of the morning, in fact until our callers James and Jean Macgibbon arrived. Saxon was completely silent

during their visit, except when they said that Adrian Stephen was
believed to be dying. (He and Saxon were great friends and
shared a flat long ago.) It was rather a success having him with
Pippa, for each takes a certain interest in the other, and tonight
after a bottle of wine Saxon burst into one of his unexpectedly
fiery monologues, about opera-singers and operas of long ago.
Burgo came back, frightfully dirty but in good spirits, and
pleased because he had gone up in his form.

¹Sister of Vicky Strachey.

March 22nd. The news — I can't write about it. Ever since the
Communist coup in Czechoslovakia, open war-talk is rising in a
steady booming drone. One can't allow the total import to
penetrate because of being too horrified and also at the same time
au fond too apathetic, too weary of the long dismal story, to think
about suicide, or any other means of escape. And so, like
cornered rabbits we hope for some lucky chance to save us all.
But not *one* voice is raised against this horrible war-talk. Not *one*.

March 25th. Celestial weather, day after day. After breakfast we
step out into the sun on the verandah, where Minnie often spends
the night in a box of straw and can be seen doing her maidenly
morning stretches in the sunlight. The fields look incredibly neat:
all the hedges have been trimmed and plaited back, and the earth
rolled out into smooth flat ribs. Yesterday we had tea on the lawn
and sat out till nearly six. After dark it was still and warm, like a
summer night, with bright stars twinkling.

Burgo is back for the holidays and we have the Gowings here
for a week. Lawrence is very genial and beaming, and keeps
saying: 'This is the nicest Easter I have ever had.'

Burgo's comment on a boy at his school: 'He has a distasteful
face.'

April 5th. Richard is here, not this time mainly on botanical
business, but because the interest we have shown in his stories
about the Criminal Lunatic Asylum at Broadmoor (of which his
cousin is at present the Superintendent) has led to his arranging
for Ralph and me to visit it this week. Dr Hopwood has been told
that we are not like some of his wild artist friends, but a 'sensible
middle-aged couple'.

April 7th. Our visit to Broadmoor fully came up to our
expectations. Ralph, Richard and I booked in to a hotel at
Reading, and took the bus to Crowthorne. From the bus-stop we
walked through pines, past rows of modern warders' houses to
the precincts themselves, which looked just as I had expected —
rather like Euston Station, red-brick Romanesque, Victorian
model. Richard took us to the house of his cousin Dr Hopwood,
a short benign figure, with a comfortable drawling doctor's
voice, and teeth like old piano keys, a spaniel dog, a Siamese cat,
and an invisible old mother bedridden up aloft.

Almost at once we started on a round of the prison — no,
'institution' it must be called, and we soon realized we must not
speak of 'warders' but 'nurses' '. We were escorted by several male
nurses looking much like stalwart sergeant-majors; they produced in us a spice of danger by closing in round us whenever we
entered a building, and ever behind and in front of us sounded the
clanking of keys, which hung on enormously broad belts round
Dr Hopwood's and the 'nurses' ' waists. Apart from this the whole
place looked like a well-run hospital. Standing on a height with a
vast view over several counties, it gave no sense of confinement.
Gardens stretched below us in which the inmates were working.
Others were rolling the bowling-green. All were dressed normally except for their trousers, of a somewhat faded orange
corduroy. Some very old men were sitting with their mouths
open, one who was blind was feeling his way round a plot of
grass and scattering crumbs to non-existent sparrows. Some of
their faces were as vacant as most old men's, others had a curious
mask-like beauty as if all expression had been washed away from
them. Most of them had some distortion or imperfection in their
appearance. Often they were awkward in shape or movement,
their mouths a little twisted, their foreheads sloping back too far.

In the great bakery the male murderers were making bread; in
the laundry murderesses washed the clothes and sheets. But they
gave no impression of being engaged in drudgery: the scene was
dramatic rather than dull, as if their madness itself was a form of
originality which must make them far from boring for the
admirable people who looked after them, who seemed intelligent, humane and careful, moved by kindness and interest. The
rooms were spacious, spotlessly clean and painted in pleasing
colours. There were armchairs, a piano, wireless, a library,
tennis, croquet, ping-pong. Some of the more afflicted slept in

small rooms of their own, with a glass window through which the nurse could peep. Most had photos, flowers and personal belongings — except for a few who couldn't be trusted with anything but a bed. A splendid operating theatre; a dentist's surgery.

Glimpses: — a crazy old woman with two plaits, smiling to herself as she hurried to the lavatory, which was open at the bottom so that patients' legs could be seen. Another woman, wrapped in a rug, sitting in a passage rocking her head to and fro between her hands with every appearance of tragic desperation; a completely ·sane-looking man doing wood-carving in the carpenter's shop; a strong handsome girl with a bell of thick hair, working a machine with vigorous, violent gestures; an old woman making a rug. 'How many have you made, Laura?' asked Dr Hopwood. 'Oh, I don't like to think of things like that. How many beans in a bushel?'

Quite exhausted by so much food for emotion and thought, we were now summoned to the theatre, to see the patients perform *The Earl and The Girl*. We were in the very centre of the front row, just above the small orchestra of fiddles and double-basses. Then the curtain rose and we were confronted by an amazing, an overwhelming scene: a row of mostly young, tall and strong murderers dressed in hunting pink were singing the opening chorus at the top of their voices! Richard whispered, 'I'm going to cry in a minute.' The performance was absorbingly strange, it could never have been mistaken for a show put on by normal amateurs. Perhaps the most surprising thing, and in its way touching, was the immense enthusiasm and care that was going into it. Was it stranger that they were mad or that they were murderers? Those hands, what had they done? The women were mostly ugly and far from young, except for one healthy, blooming beauty, whose perfection was marred by a permanent smile. Afterwards I asked Dr Hopwood if she would be released soon? 'Oh no, I wouldn't like to see *her* go out yet. Oh dear, no, *she's* not well yet.' (He had told us before this that the majority of the women had been cases of puerperal mania, who had killed their own babies, and often stayed a few years only, but it was arranged that they should have no more children.)

The hero of the play was a small neat young man with a rosebud mouth from which emerged a light tenor voice, and the typical sloping forehead. He was evidently delighted with himself, and I found him terrifying. One could easily imagine him suddenly changing a caress into strangulation. The 'Super', as he is called, is immensely popular for the humane attitude to the patients, and all these amenities are his creation.

When the performance was over we went back to his house. Of course we had dozens of questions for him, and his stories were fascinating. Some like to talk of their crimes, he told us, and some do not. One was telling the Super how he had murdered his wife and three children, when he suddenly looked at him suspiciously and said: 'But I don't really see what business it is of yours. Nor could I see it was any of the Judge's for that matter. It was purely a family affair.' Back to our Reading Hotel, feeling surprised that this most encouragingly progressive institution should be a Criminal Lunatic Asylum.

April 16th — Ham Spray. Roger Senhouse arrived at supper-time last night. Allowing for an increase in age he is almost as handsome and quite as charming as ever. The fact that he is fully confident of this charm, and plays one with it like a trout on a line doesn't detract from it in the least. He is in fact a perfect visitor, never at a loss for something of his own to do, and always ready to enter into anything that's going, such as a walk or croquet — though I have never in my life known anyone cheat so blatantly as he does at games. Next day came Marjorie Strachey, looking pretty eccentric in a capacious fur coat, with a helmet of black felt decorated with pink flowers crushed down over her bespectacled eyes.

Our stories about Broadmoor meet with very different reactions — Marjorie's for instance was '*Nothing* would have induced me to go and I don't want to hear ANYTHING about it!'

We had all been invited for drinks with the Campbells; Mary had known Marjorie twenty years ago and I think her changed appearance was something of a shock, though bravely taken. The Connollys were there. Cyril kept the conversation relentlessly on literary subjects, particularly his own writings, while Lys was untiring in her wifely deference — 'Clever people like Cyril', or 'Good talkers like Cyril' — but got little attention from him in return. The large beakers of yellow intoxicant soon did their work and all were very jolly. We like the Campbells very much, and think they will be a great asset to our lives. Burgo also liked Mary's girls, Serena and Nell, went boating with them on their pond and all managed to fall in.

[Marjorie Strachey was Lytton's youngest and plainest sister. She had trained as a teacher, and during the war taught a class of little Bloomsburies at Charleston, among others Angelica Bell and Nicko Henderson. Children were either doubled up with laughter at her brilliant comic gift or paralysed with fear and shame by her imitations of them. She was especially good at clarifying the mysteries of mathematics to those allergic to them. Ralph and I once asked her to explain why logarithms worked and I remember she did so with great lucidity, though I have alas forgotten it all. Marjorie had many other gifts — she understood and loved music, was extremely warm-hearted and generous, and contained some inner reservoir of fascinating if improbable stories which would gush forth indefinitely. At some Bloomsbury parties she used to perform turns, dressed in a nightgown and a blonde wig, which consisted in singing nursery rhymes or even hymns (*Onward Christian Soldiers* was one), with a wealth of expressions and gestures that made them highly obscene as well as bringing the house down. Boris Anrep was a great admirer of these performances, and once arranged for her to appear at a smart evening party given by Samuel Courtauld,[1] with Julia as accompanist. The conventional audience was appalled and the affair was a complete flop. Marjorie was a keen chess player, and took lessons from Miss Menchik. When she retired to a cottage in Surrey she taught her little maid to play chess with her.]

[1] Art collector and founder of the Courtauld Institute.

April 30th. We had arranged to meet the Brenans in Hungerford, and all go together to try and find the Pasque Flower on the downs above Streatley, where Gerald had seen it thirty years ago. He sat beside Ralph in the front seat giving directions, as the car waddled up a deeply furrowed chalk track marked 'Impracticable for Motors', and on to the highest summit of the downs. Here we felt very conscious of our altitude; shoulders of pale downland stretched away in all directions, dotted with clumps of trees — it was warm and thundery, with no wind. In front of us we saw the long grass track called the Fair Mile, where the Pasque Flower is supposed to grow. Two shepherds were standing there talking, and Gerald got out and pranced ahead to ask if they had seen the flower. I saw their arms waving and pointing; then Gerald came running towards us with a look of boyish excitement on his face. In recent years the plant had apparently moved across a shallow valley, but there we found a large patch of the purple and astonishingly exotic-looking flowers and buds coming up in the homely English grass among their silky grey leaves. A marvellous 'botanical sight'.

May 4th. I quite often look back at the pleasures and pains of youth — love, jealousy, recklessness, vanity — without forgetting their spell but no longer desiring them; while middle-aged ones like music, places, botany, conversation seem to be just as enjoyable as those wilder ones, in which there was usually some potential anguish lying in wait, like a bee in a flower. I hope there may be further surprises in store, and on the whole do not fear the advance into age.

Mouse-quiet day, working and reading. I got so enthralled by *La Prisonnière* that I couldn't go to bed until Albertine really had left Proust. I still take the unpopular view that it is one of the best volumes in the book, and I read on and on, hour after hour, breathless and with a beating heart.

May 5th. Ralph to London to the dentist. I have sprained my ankle so cannot go with him, but as the years pass I *hate* being parted from him even for an hour or so; I feel only half a person by myself, with one arm, one leg and half a face.

Warmer, softer, sweeter day: the birds sing very loudly and the pollarded trees on the road to Hungerford station seem to be holding little bunches of greenery in their fists.

September 9th. To Aldbourne to lunch with Hope Johnstone[1] (the Brenans are away). He is a curiously unreal sort of man, who looks at the food on his plate with more interest than he bestows on his visitors. He told us some remarks of Henry James's. About golf: 'Golf, my dear Frank, what is it? Some beflagged jam-pots sunk beneath the earth at long but varying distances; and then, a swoop! a swing! a flurry of steel! a dormy — ' To H. G. Wells he said: 'And how do you find you can endure the daily entombment in — and disinterment from — the Underground?'

Hope Johnstone's own contribution was almost in the same

style about the delicacy of babies: 'Yes, they certainly make a gallant effort to avoid surviving,' he said.

¹An old friend of Gerald's, an eccentric bachelor. He had once given lessons to Augustus John's younger children, and was still known to some as 'Tutor'.

September 12th. Campbells and Connollys to tea arriving through the rain in a hired motor; the jeep being too bleak was left for Robin to drive our new hens over in. I was touched by his solicitude for their happiness and comfort.

With his long bobbed hair and smart South of France clothes, what does Cyril look like? A china pug on a mantelpiece perhaps? He doesn't snub Lys, even when she tries to 'produce' him: ('Oh, that must have been wonderful, Cyril!' or 'Oh, do you know Cyril was remembered by the waiter at the *Chapon Fin* who hadn't seen him for twenty years?') Cyril was friendly and often very funny. He wanted to see the upstairs, so I took him up and showed him the library. He has a 'second spouse' complex — he talks to Mary about Philip Dunn¹ as 'your husband', and to me he spoke almost exclusively about Carrington. I didn't get the impression the Campbells and Connollys were very happy together; Mary in particular wasn't quite at ease with him.

¹Her first husband, before Robin.

November 8th. I have been writing little because we have been through a very anxious time about poor Burgo's unhappiness at school. He is now a boarder at Millfield in Somerset and we feel almost able to bank on his remaining there until the end of this term.

Lunch with Mary Campbell just back from Paris. 'Cyril was there the last few days' she told us, 'and I had words with him. He asked me why I was antagonistic to him, and under the influence of a high temperature I told him.' She feels he is an enemy to marriage. Did we think it was possible to live completely united to your mate and yet be spiritually and mentally independent? We both said No.

November 24th. A short visit to London, staying with the Kees at Sussex Place. For me there was the Memoir Club, where Leonard read aloud an enthralling, brilliant extract from Virginia's diary, stopping now and then to say tantalizingly that the next paragraph was 'quite impossible'. Several names of suggested new members were mentioned, but Duncan said: 'I shall have great pleasure in blackballing them all.' I find this exclusive and unadventurous attitude of Bloomsbury's deplorable.

A lot was crushed into these days — a party at Karin Stephen's, lunch with Clive, a visit to the library and an evening with Robert and Janetta at the Gargoyle Club, where we ran into Julia and Philip Toynbee. He, poor fellow, is very unhappy because his wife is leaving him, and was making a token gesture of giving up drink for her sake, and resisting the cry of 'Do let's go on to the Coconut Grove or *somewhere!*' — a last resort of the unhappy. On the whole I dislike the ambience of night clubs. Ralph goes further and says that 'everyone in London is on the assembly line and daren't step off it for a moment,' also that 'London talk is scatty, and slides over the surface, and only in the country can a subject be pursued to its bitter end'.

We are left with a lot of other people's problems to brood over and discuss, and a desire to hold out a helping hand to various distressed persons, but no certainty how to do it.

November 28th — Ham Spray. Noel Sandwith arrived in darkness and fog, his train over an hour late. We spent most of the morning profitably, discussing various botanical points, and then stamping out to the Little Wood in gum-boots, where we succeeded in digging up several fine *Ornithogalum* bulbs. They are to be flown out to Portugal for experiments. 'Lucky things,' said Ralph.

After Sandwith had gone we walked down to Ham through ever-persisting mists, in spite of which it came over me in a sudden wave how much I still *love* being alive and particularly when I am alone here with Ralph and now that, for the time at least, Burgo has assuaged our gnawing anxiety about him.

December 3rd. Walked to the village with a pot of honey for the Christmas draw. A wild, grey afternoon; the children were just coming out of school. They do seem to lead a queer bleak existence. In the desolate square of cement which is the school playground two little girls were holding hands and whirling round and round with sad, abstracted expressions. Is this all the fun they have? I wonder.

1949

January 1st. The New Year arrived with shouts, bells and the voice of Robert Donat on the wireless. The whole hullabaloo was senseless and missed the mark completely. Not so the deep boom of Big Ben, whose voice is the nearest I can imagine to that of God. Impossible not to be moved to some extent by a new year, to listen as if for the sound of a huge body turning over in bed, or the creak of an un-oiled wheel. Ralph and I were standing before the fire, and we clutched each other in a sort of panic, as if the days, weeks and months to come formed a long steep slope tilting downwards, and we were off, rolling down it and couldn't stop.

The morning post brought a pleasant surprise — Burgo's school report, all of it good and the first thing that dropped out of the envelope being a book token marked 'First Prize for Progress and Industry in this group'. Burgo was as amazed by it as anyone.

January 3rd. To the Campbells for a drink before lunch. Robert and Janetta were staying with them; talk was stimulating and lively. The dachshund puppies cantered in and out on short elephant legs, their claws clattering on the polished floor. Mary looks at her most sympathetic when, as today, her hair is unbrushed and she wears corduroy trousers with a hole as large as a potato in the heel of each sock.

Burgo and I have begun acting *Henry IV* Part I on the model theatre. He has become a stickler for detail: dead soldiers (lead) lay before the walls of Orleans, while the plasticine corpse of Henry V was draped in a white shroud. Sometimes I see the miniature world with such infatuated eyes that the delusion takes over and becomes real.

Ralph is up in the library writing something about human credulity, a subject that has always fascinated him — and me too. At dinner we talked of various irrational beliefs: in ghosts, Father Christmas, etc. Burgo thought that when people believed they had seen a ghost, it was really a symbol of fear, and that fear was the worst thing one could be afraid of, so it was really better they should believe in ghosts — rather good, I thought.

January 9th. Arrival of Raymond [Mortimer] yesterday evening in specially high spirits has cured us of our slight hump of yesterday. Talk about Charleston and its affairs. Laughing heartily, he told us how Lydia [Lopokova] said to him: 'Oh yes, of course Vanessa likes you very much. She says you are a "nice old thing".' This morning he has retired into the little front sitting-room to write a review; sighs and groans ring through the door.

The Campbells came over with Philip Toynbee, whom they have kindly asked down to nurse his broken heart. Robin has a quiet subtle style of conversation, but loves an argument. Mary claims not to, but in fact her contributions are usually very much to the point and can bring a generalization out of a wash of general chatter. Philip taps a rich vein of comedy. Starting with homosexuality and whether one would mind one's child becoming 'queer' and if so why, we went on to free speech and Fascism. Philip and Mary held that Fascism was evil incarnate and should be stopped at any price. Robin believed in free speech so passionately that he was prepared to suppress it forcibly in those who were against it. Ralph and I alone cried for tolerance and true freedom of speech, and were gloomily struck by the distance all our three friends had come from the attitude of the Oxford undergraduates who voted against fighting for king and country before the war.

January 14th. Quentin and Julia for the last weekend of the holidays. I asked Quentin, who is secretary, what was the result of the latest election for the Memoir Club. He said: 'I'm afraid there will only be one new member — Angelica. Sebastian and Julia very nearly got in and it's just possible Clive may withdraw his black-ball on Julia.' A wave of irritation passed over me at the occasional *stuffiness* of these old Charlestonians! Lovely of course to have Angelica, but we should have had some new blood to mix with this almost exclusively family party. I think Quentin agrees. He also told me about Charleston's indignation at Roy [Harrod]'s biography of Maynard. He had been bold enough to go there for a night to receive their criticisms and told Quentin they were not as bad as he feared, but Quentin admits that the truth is that none of them, particularly Vanessa, can bear to have anything said about themselves at all.

There are, however, several ingredients which make this weekend a failure in my eyes. One is the approach of Burgo's departure for school, and our inability to do special things with him because of Quentin and Julia. Julia has always been a demanding influence in the house, and this time, poor thing, she is sad and wants to take me off on walks and talk about her troubles. In spite of which she has entertained us all amusingly, partly with an attack on Cyril for being what she calls the 'High Priest of Smarty Literature' and a disagreeable character to boot.

January 18th. As I sat sewing a name-tape on Burgo's sponge-bag I tried to pierce his aloofness by telling him something of my own recollections of going to school and how quickly the strangeness wore off. Then he gave me a very delightful smile and said that it was nice to think it was such a short time to half-term. At our early lunch he grew livelier — having got so near zero hour he evidently wanted to be up and over the top. To Newbury with school trunk, bike, etc. Several other boys on the platform. The idea that boys are unattractive, misproportioned creatures is quite untrue — these at least were mostly good-looking, well-built, with bright eyes and the bloom of peaches on their cheeks. We said goodbye to Burgo and drove back to Ham Spray feeling like flat bicycle tyres. And very pianissimo did the evening trickle by.

January 21st. To the sale of Dr Hemsted's effects. He and his wife died together a few weeks ago. It was somehow pathetic to think of the good old Doctor with his bulbous bright blue nose, gentle voice and sympathetic eyes, who would come out in the thickest snow to see a sick child and has done so much for these trampling hordes of sightseers who were ready to pick his eiderdowns, his milk-jugs, his very bones to pieces. A table was covered with small objects lovingly accumulated through a life-time — sea-shells, field-glasses, Indian idols; and in the garden was a 'Wendy House' where his children must have played, slept and cooked scrambled eggs. The utter disappearance of the human feelings that had collected these objects or given them to each other made them seem like boulders in the path of an avalanche.

February 6th. We have again visited Euphemia and collected butter and a chicken. The barking of the fourteen dogs mingled with the non-stop chirruping from an incubator full of chickens hopping up and down like sand-fleas in a corner of the beautiful kitchen, lined with pale blue and Persian tiles. Her doctor son Christopher Turton was there, a specialist in the mad who works in a mental hospital at Bristol. He says the analytical couch is quite superseded by 'hard' talks, or electric or insulin shocks. Ralph asked him whether it was really possible to give drugs to people which would make them confess to crimes they never committed. 'Oh yes,' he said, 'perfectly easy. You can reduce them to a state wherein they can't resist any suggestion made to them.'

This evening after much cogitation I began reading Madame de Sévigné's letters. I am so tired of reading bad books, and books Connolly says I ought to like and I don't. It is heaven to embark on these fourteen stout volumes of reality.

But what, I have been wondering, is the prop which sees the rationalist through acute misery and stress? For Madame de Sévigné it was religion, but for the atheist what? I can only think that he clings to love and friendship; not that these are the only things that make life worth living of course, but that they are the most unifying, coherent influences, unless he has an absorbing ruling passion for work — painting perhaps or scientific research. In personal terms, however, even when I am abjectly miserable I know that I love Ralph and Burgo, and by clinging on to that thread I can probably scrimmage through whatever morass I am in, which is not far from Morgan Forster's religion of personal relations.

February 19th. The Kees for the weekend; the weather delicious; we felt proud to have provided it for them, with sun hot enough to sit out in, snowdrops and dog-tooth violets under the beech tree. A walk to the Netherton Valley: having traversed its smooth green basin we sat down on a bank where flints rose out of the complicated texture made by winter shoots and mosses mixed. Here we were when a grey van drove by, turned and stopped. Out stepped Euphemia, holding a basket containing a huge pat of yellow butter, two pieces of meat and some cream. All 'black' of course. There was something so like a witch in a fairy-tale about this encounter with a beneficent but amoral being that no wonder the Kees thought it a pre-arranged meeting and couldn't believe it was pure chance that made us pick on the Netherton Valley for our walk.

February 26th. For Burgo's half-term we had taken rooms at Bath. We got up early and anxiously and were on our way soon after eight, driving through the cold morning, laden with jams and cakes and picnics. As we travelled West we saw some primroses in the hedges, it grew warmer, and our nervous temperature rose a little. But suppose he says, 'I can't bear it, take me away'? This is the first time we have collected him from the upper school at Millfield, and the first moment of seeing him would probably give the key to his mood. There he was waiting in the drive, case and mac in hand, a little keyed-up but smiling and friendly, not doubting us. He seemed perfectly at ease with us and there was plenty to say. I asked him if he liked the Upper better than the Junior School, and he said 'Oh *miles* better. Edgarly was *awful*, really it was, and it felt like going back to something childish.' So far so good, but it is horrifying to think how much has *not*, at times, been said.

What to say about the future? I feel I have very few securely-based hopes about anything, either Burgo's having a happy life in this dismal war-haunted world or ourselves being free from increasing infirmities of various kinds.

But if one faces these gloomy truths, surely it is possible to be happy by means of taking what comes, expecting nothing, and above all not feeling 'now our troubles are over and we have got into calm water again'. There's no such thing as calm water in life in any sense more permanent than there is in the English Channel. And somehow or other we have now reached an age when people suddenly die for no reason, so that I think we both expect to do it ourselves, or perhaps Burgo's anxieties about our deaths have made us conscious of the possibility, as Ralph remarked when we set off to Somerset, and he resolved to drive carefully.

March 2nd — Ham Spray. There was a good chance for turning one's eyes outwards and observing other human beings when we went yesterday evening to a house-warming party given by Philip Toynbee in the cottage he has rented from the Campbells. Beside the Campbells, only Julia Pakenham and her husband

Robin Mount were there. Julia has the Pakenham bloom and charm, and the soft husky lisping voice. She is in fact very pretty in spite of having an outward squint, so that one of her eyes seems to be flinging itself skywards in amazement or abandon while the other looks straight at you. The effect is quite fascinating in a curious way, like a permanent gesture. She is very intelligent.

The evening was immensely enjoyable. We talked without stopping, drank just enough to stimulate the mind without fuddling, and that was quite a lot, laughed a great deal and carried on some quite dense arguments. Very shortly after this Philip suddenly melted like a candle in the fire, his features softened, and he gently draped himself round the neck of Julia Mount. When he tried to stand up he nearly fell down again, and when he began a melancholy monologue about his loneliness and how lucky we all were to have mates, we saw it was time to go. He is a touching figure, and he was hospitable and sweet to us all. His new lady doctor friend, Ruth, comes down at weekends, meanwhile there he is alone with an absurd white poodle, shaven all over except for a mushroom of curls on top of its head. This creature somehow symbolizes and externalizes the clown element in Philip, and I feel that by laughing at it and guying it he is able to laugh at that part of himself.

During dinner he told us about his schooldays: how he was expelled from the Dragon School for a start.

'What for?' asked someone.

'Collecting money for Dr Barnardo's and keeping it myself.'

His bewildered parents took him to Dr Crichton Miller, who sent him to work on a farm for nine months, though he was only ten or eleven. The farmer was a slave-driver and worked him desperately hard, and at length he could bear it no longer and persuaded the bailiff's son Jesse to run away with him. They covered some eighty miles, when they were stopped by the police who sent for the farmer.

'Now you've always been a truthful boy,' he said, 'tell me the truth — you and Jesse did something dirty behind a hedge, didn't you?'

Thinking he wouldn't be believed if he said 'No' (which was the truth) Philip said 'Yes, we did,' and of course Jesse said 'No'. All this must have made a deep impression, for he told us he went back to the farm a few weeks ago to look at it.

[I never knew Philip Toynbee well, and have no right to do more than try to describe the impression he made on me. The first thing one noticed was his very deep, dark and beautiful speaking voice. In appearance he was tall, dark-haired and loose-limbed, and could have been good-looking but for the ruggedness of his features and complexion. An occasional missing tooth, as he grew older, blotted the attractiveness of his wide crocodile smile — a smile that revealed some of the complexity of his character: warm and ready affection combined with destructiveness and a good deal of the *enfant terrible*. Highly intelligent, well-read, romantic, gregarious, a buffoon capable of outrageous behaviour but who would not hold the recipient's reaction against him and whose friendships tended to be lasting, a sensitive literary critic.

It was during his tenancy of the Campbell's cottage at Stokke that we saw most of him, both there and at Ham Spray, on picnics and bathing parties. He loved arguing, particularly on abstract or political subjects, and so did we. He was good at the game — that's to say he listened to his opponent and returned the ball into his court.

A Communist at Oxford, by 1949 he was merely left wing and against most things. Ralph foretold that he would end up as a Christian, and this is exactly what he did, as anyone who read him to the end will know.

Much later I wrote him a fan letter about one of his books and he wrote back:

Thank you for such a very warming letter, it made me nostalgic for the all-too-little that I saw of Ham Spray. . . . I wish I didn't like money so much. No, not even *like*, which would be something, but *fuss about*. Perhaps I shall take scrip and staff soon and appear bare-footed in Wilts, a wandering friar ready for *instant* corruption at the first gleam of a cocktail-shaker. . . .]

March 11th. Hope Johnstone came out from Gerald's cottage to lunch and tea today. I picked him up in Hungerford High Street, where I found him pacing up and down, looking foreign and pathetic and wearing a small dusty beret Basque. But he has something of the distinguished American senator about him, with his neat yellowish features and the smoky blue of his hair and spectacles making a curious colour combination. He was eager to reward us for our hospitality by a volley of anecdotes. One has the feeling that he has loaded himself up before starting, with a belt of machine-gun bullets, and as soon as he gets into the warm and has his glass of sherry he presses the trigger. Many are about Henry James, and involve imitations of the voice of the Master. There was one about an artist's model who used to sit to Sir Charles Furse, 'and Sir Charles used to put my armpit in with a bit of cadmium', she said.

Sitting at lunch he was seen to be as blind as a bat and had to bend right down with his nose in his plate to cut up his food. Yet reading must be almost his only occupation. He has been to almost every country in the world — Bali, Persia, the United States, Turkey and Greece, lived four years in Istanbul and talks of settling in a Greek island for the rest of his life. A happy man in fact. I envy him all those parts of the world I shall probably never see, and am ashamed to think it may be so, for not to go everywhere possible is like living in a house and never going into some of the rooms.

March 19th. Ralph brought Julia from the station, and on arrival they remained in the car earnestly talking instead of coming indoors. Ralph has a way of launching straight away on to the chief theme in a visitor's agenda, which is tantalizing for me. It was easy to see some important topic had arisen — yes, it was Lawrence. But there was much more talk about books and writing. She was anxious to listen to Robert, who was taking part in a wireless discussion called The Critics, and prepared to be disapproving. 'Why should *Robert* get such a job?' she wanted to know, 'he was much too young anyway.' The truth is, I believe she is jealous because of the enthusiasm Ralph and I show for him. But she has been very much herself on this visit and given us great pleasure thereby. The two Pritchetts came to lunch. V.S.P. was immensely encouraging to Ralph about his writing, saying he is 'by far the best journalist now writing on biographies and history'.

April 13th. Burgo is home for the Easter holidays. We met the Campbells for a picnic lunch at Oare, where Serena and Nell were riding in a children's gymkhana. We ate among the cars in a high wind, surrounded by horsy bun-faced little girls in jodhs,

their horsy mothers and dogs — an uncongenial lot. The Dunn
children unfortunately failed to get their plump ponies over a
single fence and were feeling horribly humiliated. Philip Toynbee really saved the situation by his jokes and clowning,
climbing on to the saddles of the ponies, loping off incessantly to
the Gents, drinking all the port brought by Philip Dunn and
spilling the Campbells' beer — a genial old buffoon. The
Campbells have now taken Philip into their hearth and home,
unable to stand the pathos of his lonely muddling life; it is an
arrangement which does them infinite credit but seems fore-
doomed to disaster. We stopped there on our way home. Ben
Nicolson was staying, and Mary's mother Lady Rosslyn, and
above all dogs — three house dachshunds, Philip's comic poodle,
and a huge wet spaniel from the village in love with one of the
dachshunds. All these creatures quarrelled, copulated, yapped,
chased the ducks and dragged their bones over the human beings
who sat about on the lawn.

April 25th. To London to see Janetta and her baby[1] at Queen
Charlotte's Hospital and to go to *The Marriage of Figaro* at Covent
Garden. Janetta was asleep when we arrived and looked so
touchingly and completely exhausted that we felt guilty for
disturbing her. Robert's mother also came in, very handsome if
rather conventional in appearance.

   Next day I lunched at Kew with Richard and Noel Sandwith,
and walked with Richard through the gardens and glasshouses,
dividing my attention between the tropical plants, tall palm trees
with London sparrows twittering in their tips, and pools from
which water-lilies raised their blue, pink and yellow heads — and
the dramatic confidences and 'problems' which Richard was
pouring into my ears.

[1]Georgiana Kee.

May 16th. Ralph and I converged on Sussex Place, where we
found Janetta, Robert and the baby in her pram in the garden.
Robert is mad about her, and enters into her feelings so
thoroughly that he cannot bear her to cry for an instant. 'Do you
think she *knows* how much we like her?' he asked Janetta
anxiously. He has a plan to leave *Picture Post* where he has been
working for some time and set up as a publisher with James
Macgibbon.

My evening was with the Memoir Club. After supper, in Duncan's room in Taviton Street, Vanessa read a short memoir of Virginia as a child, and then Virginia's own account of her early days. Enthralling of course. It aroused in me a desire to know more about their brother Thoby, adoration for whom appeared to have been the great emotion of Virginia's youth — and who was so important to many others also, yet like a large grand mirror his image only emerges as the reflection of all these violent feelings. Though Vanessa read until nearly midnight the paper could not be finished as Desmond was so obviously ill, and had been seized with fearful wheezing while ascending the steps to Duncan's flat. Dermod drove him, Leonard and me home. Desmond sat frozen by breathlessness, with the muscles of his neck standing out like cords. Dermod was all kindness to him; while he escorted him upstairs Leonard and I sat in the car discussing the relation of Brain to Mind.

May 17th. An incredible collection of masterpieces from Vienna is now on show at the Tate, including Tintoretto's Susanna, so long admired from reproductions, and seen in reality a perfect knock-out. Duncan, Vanessa and Angelica were there; we saw them again this evening at Lytton's *Son of Heaven*, where also were the Bussys and James and Alix. Dorothy Bussy was beaming with pleasure over the success of her book *Olivia*. I saw Vanessa talking to the producer of the play Vera Bowen; their heads moved closer and closer together until they finally touched. 'Who have I just kissed?' she asked us in her deep resonant voice. Alix said she had never been less bored in her life than at present, when she is writing a book which she hopes never to finish.

It was interesting to remember the old amateur production of *The Son of Heaven* at the Scala long ago while listening to Lytton's words spoken by professional actors. I thought the play was moving and astonishingly good, but for one or two blemishes which could easily have been removed.

May 21st — Ham Spray. All yesterday afternoon I picked and arranged flowers till it was time to go and meet Saxon. Over tea we pressed him with questions — what had he thought of *The Son of Heaven*, and how had *Siegfried* been last night? But you could take a corkscrew to Saxon when in an obstinate mood, and hardly a drop of satisfaction would you get.

The Kees arrived for lunch today, which consisted of one of Euphemia's fat chickens with new potatoes and carrots. Little Georgiana was laid out under the trees in her wicker cot, and our table was set beside her. Saxon has been exceptionally cheerful. Someone ought to paint his sensitive, beautiful face.

May 28th. Having Raymond and Helen together was a bit of a gamble but it went quite well. Raymond has just been in America. He described sitting next to an old lady at dinner one night: she was tall and angular, wore her hair in a high grey pompadour and ropes of pearls round her neck. She suddenly bent towards him and said: 'You know, Mr Mortimer, I'm just an eerie little person.'

At dinner last night Helen told us about her life years ago in Paris, when she first met Henry Lamb, Augustus John and Dorelia.

'Henry must have been very attractive — were you rather sweet on him?' asked Raymond.

'Sweet on him? I was desperately in love with him for years!' A gallant avowal. She went on to say that Henry and Dorelia fell madly in love at sight, in the picaresque manner of those days, and 'walked off into the mountains trailing her two small children behind them' but that Augustus came storming after them and brought them back.

July 8th. To Hungerford early with produce for the market stall, which is eager to sell our fruit and vegetables for us. It made a charming continental scene this hot morning — the stalls had been set up in a cool archway, and small quantities of tomatoes, currants and sweet peas kept arriving and being handed in to the fairly efficient ladies who were keeping shop.

The post brought a bombshell from Richard containing the news that Lane means to publish our Volume I at *five guineas*, and is doubtful to say the least if he can publish any more volumes after it.

July 9th. I staved off the thoughts which were bound to follow from Richard's letter last night, but of course the moment I opened my eyes they were upon me like a swarm of bees each bringing its sting in the form of a puncturing reflection. After half an hour of this I got up and went out into the unearthly warm morning and took communion in the form of a solitary silent bathe, then padded about on the dewy lawn until it was time to cook breakfast. I can't say my thoughts were very profound, but I was facing the fact that if I have to be divorced from my work and its constant place in the future as well as the past it will be like parting with a piece of myself—a kidney, say. I have the feeling I have anticipated the operation and reconciled myself to it — but am not really sure.

This was the hottest day so far, 88° in the shade. Mary rang up and came to lunch in her jeans-and-jeep mood — candid, sharp, full of good-will and life. We lay panting under the beech tree most of the afternoon talking hard, and every so often one of us, talking as they went, would go off to the pool and dive in. Tassel, the dachshund puppy, was glad to suck some ice. Mary told us about the difficulties of life with Toynbee — much as we supposed: the worst drawback was his abandonment to drink. 'I've taken to watering the gin,' she said.

After tea I forced myself to go up to the library and do some work on my poor book, which will almost certainly never see the light. I am sad but not at the moment agitated. The work I am doing on it has become detached from thoughts of publication.

July 26th. First day of the school holidays. A large party came to bathe in our pool — Campbells, Philip Dunn, Lady Hardwicke with two children and governesses. The Philips (Dunn and Toynbee) got into an argument on their usual subject — the upper classes v. workers, which brought out a tough businessman's side of Philip Dunn's character. The discussion finally congealed into the question whether there should be 'bidets for peasants', a phrase which resounded through the hot afternoon like an often repeated refrain in a popular song.

August 1st. The Campbells gave a dancing-bottle-party two nights ago. Everyone was rather drunk when we arrived, particularly Philip Toynbee (lachrymose) and Robin Mount (comic). Others present were the Pritchetts and Julia (neither of them at their ease), Virginia Tennant, Lord Bath ('*Bath's* the name, not that it matters'), the Kees, Janetta looking lovely in a dress of grey watered silk.

Tonight's cocktail party at Tidcombe Manor[1] was a sort of continuation of the Stokke one which had been going on spasmodically ever since. Julia told me that Philip Toynbee had been drunk and threatening suicide all the weekend. Even the subjects of conversation persisted, for apparently both Philips (D. & T.) returned to the old theme, which under the influence of drink became 'Peasants for bidets' instead of 'Bidets for peasants'.

[1]Home of middle-aged friends, Paul Cross and Angus Wilson.

[I heard much later from Julia that at breakfast that morning one of Robin's little boys said: 'What was that shot this morning?' No explanation was forthcoming, and it wasn't until she and Philip Toynbee were in the train for London that he told her he had got out his gun and had been 'thinking of committing suicide but not having the courage to, when it went off through the ceiling, bringing down plaster and making a large hole'. It seems incredible that no one heard it except for Robin's boy. Julia gave Philip a piece of her mind. 'I told him, "If you want to commit suicide, commit suicide, but don't make everyone's life a misery as you have this weekend."' She then advised him to go to a psycho-analyst. He hasn't forgiven her for her unfeeling attitude.]

August 6th. I've been re-reading some of the diaries I kept during the war, and asking myself how different is the frame of mind in which I write now. *Then* the public world and its horrors were constantly in our minds, seen through a sort of dark-room window reddened by our passionate rejection of the things that were happening. We closely followed the thread of the often nightmarish events we read about or listened to on the wireless, and spent hours analysing and arguing about them with each other, or held debates on pacifism with imaginary opponents, whom I can remember trying to convince while I carried out boring practical tasks — spouting a silent speech, for instance, into a washbasin I was cleaning.

Now we have lived through three years of total peace; we still have rationing but don't fear it getting worse (as we did then); there have been political crises and alarms for us to read and talk about *ad lib*. The chief change is that today our minds are much more often full of the books we are reading, the work we are doing, and above all the vicissitudes in the lives of Burgo and many friends whose troubles are very much our concern.

In the early years of our life together Ralph and I used to read aloud a lot to each other, taking turns. Especially was this enjoyable on holidays abroad, and I can remember taking eight volumes of *Clarissa Harlowe* in our rucksacks to read aloud in the bedrooms we stopped in. Now it is more likely that each will tell the other about the book on hand — this has the advantage of being like reading two books at once, and of course often leads to an exchange afterwards. Beside the many books from Lytton's collection kindly left with us for the present by James, to whom he bequeathed them, heavy parcels travel to and from the London Library.

August 11th. To London for the day. I lunched with Richard and then went with him to a meeting at Allen Lane's office. Its huge black leather armchairs (from the German Embassy) were suitable supports in which to receive the news that, in view of the Slump, Lane didn't see his way to publishing our book, the first volume of which is entirely in proof, with Richard's plates looking very charming. I consider we 'took it very well' and I think Lane and his secretary thought so too, but his innocent air of candour covering a businessman's astuteness faintly sickened me. All is not definitely up, since the attractiveness of the first volume might possibly produce a sponsor, but I have decided that if it is really to be the end of our enterprise I should try and squeeze some financial compensation out of them. It hasn't so far occurred to them to offer me a penny.

September 26th — Ham Spray. Ralph is very much set up by the fact that Chatto & Windus have asked him to write a book on Broadmoor and Dr Hopwood is entirely in favour of the idea.

October 1st. Ralph drove over to Broadmoor and spent the whole day there. He came back full of stories, in a state of great excitement and fruitful activity, bringing a lot of papers about the relation of insanity to crime; we spent the evening poring over them. With my flower book in its parlous condition, I naturally feel envious but not, I hope, jealous.

Raymond came for the week-end and Sebastian [Sprott]
dropped out of the skies at the last moment. What's more on
Saturday we had a great lunch party, with Pritchetts and
Campbells added, to eat a Michaelmas goose. I love the way
Mary warms one with little blazes of apparently candid affection.

Next day we whisked Raymond over to see Euphemia — a
great success; they took to each other at sight. Euphemia put on a
magnificent performance as the eccentric ex-courtesan. One of
her old lovers, Morty Sands, was staying with her; he contrived
to look gentlemanly even in very long shorts and a jacket fringed
with old age. Euphemia brought out some of her Inneses and
Johns and propped them on a chair one by one, including a very
lovely drawing of her head as a girl, by Augustus. She told us it
had been drawn for one of her lovers, Turton, who took it to the
First War; he was killed and it was picked up on the battlefield.
'Augustus did it the day before Christopher was born,' she said, 'I
looked very nice when I was pregnant.' Many of her stories are as
improbable as this one.

Followed by a little cortège of bouncing pekinese puppies she
now led us into the garden, which was in a state of total Irish
neglect, with waddling geese and a long vista of tangled
Michaelmas daisies stretching up a slope. Raymond tactfully
praised it. Euphemia was delighted.

'Yes isn't it lovely?' she said. 'I never stop admiring it. It's
always perfect. I never have to say "You should have seen it last
week," like Ruth Draper. And would you believe it there used to
be beds and flowers and rose-trees, and a gardener — *awful*.'

An evening talk with Raymond about the age at which
buggery declares itself. He thought it was decided long before
school, and also believed that no buggers can throw balls or
whistle. I'm not sure that I agree with him on any of these points.

October 4th. With Raymond leaving us, and the glorious weather
remaining, I could wish I either had an incentive to go on
working at my flower book or else could eradicate it completely
from my mind, and stretch myself out on a rug in the sun under
the still blue sky. But I am too restless.

The great heat has at last started the leaves turning brown, and
they were fluttering down through the morning mist as we drove
in to Hungerford. I suppose the well-known feelings of melancholy that human beings are prone to in autumn may well come

from some analogous physical fact — perhaps there is a little rush of decay in one's physical frame, bringing with it a desire to let go the twig and float down oneself.

The 'Tidcombe boys' invited us to a farewell party before they go to Jamaica. They gave us nothing to drink but champagne. I don't remember getting tight on champagne before — I rather dislike it — but it has left me with a dreamy autumnal vision of the firelit Tidcombe drawing-room swooning in pink electric light, and Robin, V.S.P. and I carrying on what appeared at the time to be a brilliant triangular conversation, an impression probably caused by the effort it was to make any sense at all. Nothing remains of it at any rate but a recipe for risotto given me by Robin. (Absurdly, I hear his voice saying: 'Take two onions, fry your rice lightly', and so on.) Meanwhile V.S.P. looked hunched and alert. Then Paul put on a Monteverdi record and decoyed me out into the garden to listen to a somewhat vainglorious story of personal success. Yet I'm sure that amusing things were said, there were illuminated moments, gaiety and spasms of friendly communication. What a pity such a wretched little collection of grounds is left in the saucepan!

October 7th. Looking back to the first things I can remember, this still and lovely morning, they seem an *eternity* away (and that is probably no further than babyhood appears to a child of six). However much more of my life is left, I want to extract the most out of it, and feel a useless regret for all those moments spent mechanically, unconsciously — sitting in buses for instance, brushing up crumbs, merely *waiting* — more regret than I do for those instants extended by the elastic of anxiety or physical pain. The fact is I don't know how to reconcile my long-standing hedonism with the value I set on being as conscious as possible, which is not to exclude nebulous, dreamy or atmospheric states of being, but only 'killing time'.

October 11th. To London for several days. In the train we met Gerald with Miranda,[1] whom he was taking up to buy some clothes, so we arrived having already had quite a dose of social life, and went almost at once to the Ivy to meet Clive, the Colonel and the A. P. Herberts. The poor old Colonel has become almost too absurd. He still wuffs like a dog or seal, but all too patently hasn't heard what he is supposed to be wuffing at, and his innocent boasting about the titled people he knows is really rather distressing. I was amused by A.P.H. and very much liked Gwen his wife, who has a charming and original appearance and much character.

Later to a cocktail party given by Macgibbon and Kee[2] — a terrific crush filling the Kees' two large sitting-rooms. I talked for a time to Peter, current wife of Bertie Russell, a Lamia-like woman with an expression of widely distributed hostility. Buttering up was what she appeared to need and I did the best I could but she only thawed at all when talking of her son of twelve who was 'brilliantly clever', 'told her everything' and 'never wanted to go anywhere without her'.

[1] His daughter.
[2] Publishing firm formed by Robert in partnership with James Macgibbon.

October 13th. Ralph and I went to Cameo Corner this morning to buy me a ring. I had a delightful time there, having out all the cases and selecting those I liked best, making my choice at leisure. And what made this easier was that Ralph angelically insisted on my having not one but *three* rings! All three seemed beautiful in the shop, and yet more beautiful when I got them home, with new previously hidden beauties. I resolve to try and keep my hands worthy of them and wear them constantly.

Before catching our train we went to see Robert and Janetta at Sussex Place. They were just back from a strange wedding-party: Sonia Brownell had that afternoon married George Orwell in hospital where he lies seriously ill with T.B. He is said to have a fifty-fifty chance of recovery, and as he is much in love with her everyone hopes the marriage will give him a new interest in life. After the ceremony Robert and Janetta, Sonia and David Astor had a bridal lunch at the Savoy, without the bridegroom of course. The curious halo of emotion which invests weddings still lingered in the room, and the Kees had obviously been much moved by the event.

October 15th — Ham Spray. Saxon is here. His perversity is something to marvel at; it half maddens, half delights me. Ralph took trouble to find a brace of young grouse in London, and these I roasted for our lunch. Nothing could possibly have been more delicious, they melted in the mouth, and neither Ralph nor I

could keep from exclaiming how good they were. Not so Saxon;
he maintained a rigid silence, and later on in the day mentioned
that he had had grouse at the Ivy last week, as if to show it was no
treat to him. Yet one can't really feel he means to be ungracious;
he likes in many ways to give people pleasure. I think perhaps he
feels trapped into inarticulacy, just as children sometimes are, by
the mere consciousness that a word of appreciation is expected of
him.

Then he complains a good deal of failing health and feebleness,
and indeed looks distressingly pale. But when we solicitously
enquired about his feeding arrangements he replied that he never
draws his milk or meat ration, never buys fish, vegetables or
fruit, and hardly ever eats out. His breakfast is a cup of tea
without milk and a little bread and jam. Lunch and tea are non-
existent, so far as I can make out, unless he buys a bun, and supper
is bread and cheese. We tried to suggest various means of getting
some food cooked for him, but all in vain, he stubbornly rejected
them all. He really *is* like a child refusing to eat in order to draw
attention to itself. And on top of all this he spends the major part
of his income on backing horses that never win, sometimes even
backing so many horses in one race that it's impossible for him to
win. He is always reproachful to me because I have given up
following races at all, says he 'is sure I used to be lucky' and that
being very unlucky himself he wants to follow someone who
isn't. I get the feeling that he thinks all the money he loses is in a
sense my fault.

October 16th. Saxon stays in bed for breakfast, so we have it alone
together without being interrupted by having to be polite. There
is no time nicer in the whole day. Having been half asleep during
baths and the cooking of eggs and coffee, the mind now begins to
stretch itself and expand into strange shapes like Japanese flowers
and slip easily into conversations, usually without a very strong
thread which would be alien to the drifting morning mood.
Today I think we began with the aesthetic theories held by artists
themselves — or sometimes the surprising lack of them. Then on
to the attractiveness of characters with something androgynous
about them; and finally to the sort of reading we both went in for
in our youth. We both remember being rather conscientious
hard-working readers, often of books too difficult or boring to
us. Now with the wireless and cinema, the young can't be

bothered with that. Paradoxically, they read bad books for a good reason — pleasure, while we used to read good books for a bad reason — wanting to show off what we'd read, add them to our personality as it were.

October 18th. Many people regard the Orwell marriage cynically and remind one that Sonia always declared her intention of marrying a Great Man. I see it principally as a neurotic one, for a marriage to a bed-ridden and perhaps dying man is as near no marriage at all as it's possible to get. She has had a great many admirers; the Pritchetts were indignant that she refused [G. W.] Stonier,[1] who came to them for sympathy and tried to cheer himself up by saying 'Sonia Stonier! I suppose it would never have done.'

According to modern sexual morality, some would say that a girl should never allow herself to be taken out by any man unless she is ready to go to bed with him — a drastic limitation of the range of human pleasures, so it seems to me; but then I'm all for as much variety in human relationships as possible. So hurrah for homosexuality and also for the happy friendships between buggers and women, and vice-versa.

[1] Author and critic.

October 21st — Long Crichel. Somewhat in tune with my last entry, we set off today on our first visit to the four tenants of Long Crichel House — Raymond, Desmond Shawe-Taylor, Eddy Sackville-West and Eardley Knollys. Dinner was delicious, and so was the wine. Afterwards we listened to some of Desmond's records. Alas we were put in separate bedrooms, and my mind, teased and stimulated by the new environment and ringing with music, refused to relax into sleep.

[I look back on my first visit to this most hospitable of country-houses with gratitude and affection, nor can I think of any other where I have spent so many happy times both with Ralph and during my later, lonelier life, right up to the present day. And I feel towards that handsome welcoming house, its garden and the surrounding country a warmth such as I hope some of our guests may have felt towards Ham Spray — because though it fell far short of Long Crichel in creature comforts it too had personality and charm. A house can't of course be thought of apart from those who live in it, and over the years the cast of Long Crichel has been altered perforce by two much-lamented deaths and one departure, so that at present the only member of the original quartet still to be found there is Desmond, yet as a household it has still astonishingly and persistently retained its delightful atmosphere. It would be fascinating to analyse (as surely some day someone will) exactly what contribution each of the original four made to the total very special flavour.

Raymond's was certainly not the least dominant. I often remember him in terms of the warmth and the surprising depth of his speaking voice, the softness and beautiful colour of his beloved 'woollies', or a suit of dark-brown homespun tweed, the amusement in his twinkling brown eyes, the despairing sighs that rang through the house when he was at his typewriter. The little daughter of a friend once remarked to her mother: 'Mr Mortimer is a very *cuddly* man.' She was quite right, but woe betide the would-be cuddler who let drop an incorrect date or a fault in pronunciation or grammar! A debatable point would send him in hot haste into the next room, where he would be found down on his knees, consulting one of the stout volumes of the *Oxford English Dictionary*. Long conversations on these themes led to Crichel being nicknamed 'the Prose Factory'.

If Raymond was the cello in the quartet, Eddy was the first violin — at times poetical and mellifluous, at others wailing or strident, always exact and confident. Perhaps it was the effort it had cost him to overcome the many serious illnesses of a delicate youth that had given him in the prime of life the strength of steel wire, the agility of a gibbon. One of my mental images of Eddy sees him elegantly dancing round the drawing-room to pull the curtains or put a log on the fire (he was ever-attentive to his guests' comfort), or — my favourite of all — jack-knifed into a scream of delighted laughter at someone else's witticism. No one could be funnier than Eddy himself and laugh more infectiously. No one could on occasion look more *pained*.

Eardley was the most practically efficient of the four, the one to be relied upon to make decisions about planting trees, or to seize his gun and shoot a pheasant straying on the lawn; while Desmond has always contributed boundless high spirits, optimism, volatility, and interest in everything that comes his way. In one of my photo albums I have a picture of these two which always makes me laugh, by capturing their contrasted characters so perfectly. They are arguing a point in croquet — have indeed been at it for ages — but whereas it's plain that Eardley will hold to his position until kingdom come and nothing will budge him, Desmond is obviously on the verge of desperation.

But to return to our first visit, it struck me at once that what made the company of the four members of the Long Crichel quartet so highly enjoyable was that each played his individual and very different part in delighted awareness of the other three — as of course every good quartet should. And another element in their guests' pleasure was provided, like a sort of counterbase, by an overlapping series of large, soft, affectionate labrador dogs, who rushed to give visitors a gratifyingly enthusiastic welcome, filled the hearthrug with their outstretched, golden bodies, or fixed one with doe-like eyes pleading for a walk.

More visits to Long Crichel will crop up again in what follows. I realize that I was rather intimidated by the brilliance of my hosts on this first occasion, but also that the more I got to know it and them, the more I loved and felt at ease with them.]

October 22nd. By the admirable house convention we were left to ourselves during the morning, while the others were at work in their own rooms. I persuaded Ralph to come for a brisk walk along the lanes to Crichel House, now a girls' school. Here we walked beside a wide stream running under stone bridges and bordered by a hedge of tall pampas grass, handsomely outlined against dark green shrubs.

The standard of comfort here puts ours to shame. There is warmth, elegance, the attentions of a stout butler and his wife, not to mention two other maids. Conversation is lively, easy and flowing, and about almost everything except politics.

I wish I didn't feel absurdly apologetic for my female sex. Looking at the visitors' book I see that almost no women visitors came in earlier days except mothers and sisters. When a marriage is discussed it is generally a marriage of convenience, for some good practical reason like companionship, care of each other's orphaned children, rather than love. I am hopelessly outclassed by Raymond's high standard of feminine 'chic', Eddy's '*nice* women', and the elegance of the bosomy Edwardian beauties in an album lying about. Nor do I think they would agree with Ralph and me in preferring (as I have lately written) a touch of androgyny in both sexes. But really! I am ashamed of such idiotic thoughts! I think they must have arisen as a result of our segregation from each other in single beds in separate rooms. The one allotted to me will eventually be Raymond's — it is grandly furnished with wallpaper of wide khaki-coloured stripes and gorgeous *boule* furniture. I slept beneath an immense old master in a massive gold frame. Our hosts have been unfailingly charming to us and we have enormously enjoyed our stay.

October 24th. Leaving Crichel, we stopped off at Tarrant Hinton to lunch with the Wests, where we heard from Anthony's own lips his reasons for wanting to ship his whole family off to America. They seemed understandable at the time, although I rather think that his quarrel with Rebecca [West] over the advance advertisement of his book in the *Times Literary Supplement,* describing him as Wells's son, may have had something to do with his decision. There has been no follow-up to this so far. Anthony talked as if he meant to write his father's life with very little mention of Rebecca. He will go first to spy out the land.

October 28th — Ham Spray. Ralph has a pile of books from the London Library to help him with his researches into Broadmoor. Last night I plunged into one written by two sane and sensible Scots, and ploughed my way enthralled through the neuroses and psycho-neuroses, recognizing myself at every turn. Not having congenial work, say the Scots, is a great source of neurotic symptoms, and I see grave dangers ahead if I can't find some new occupation.

I went to meet the Kees on the morning train. The station was quite deserted, and I was walking up and down the platform to keep warm in the frosty air when I was brought to a sudden standstill by the unexpected sight of a chaffinch hopping on the railway lines. Seeing its beautiful little shape and soft colours so close forced its appearance vividly through the layer of practical thoughts which all too often lies, like butter on a pâté, on the surface of the mind.

Robert was blanched with fatigue and spent most of the afternoon asleep. Janetta and I took a chilly walk under an eiderdown of little clouds, but our visitors are very unexacting and seem to require nothing much beside food, warmth, books and comfortable chairs.

November 1st. A beautiful crisp day, the edge of its brightness just taken off by a faint autumnal haze, but as fresh as a Cox's Orange Pippin. The Kees have been replaced by Gerald, who has lately surprised himself by a recrudescence of thoughts about sex. He looks and says he feels years younger all at once, and has gone back in various ways to the moods and thoughts of long ago. Even his voice now ranges between low, poetical and romantic tones and a husky, ironical shriek. A good deal of this mood is due to the vicarious pleasure of seeing his daughter Miranda grow up and become a young woman; but we talked little about her, and rather more about Dr Johnson. Departing, he left behind the last bit of his diary (1927–32), covering several abortive love affairs and the death of Carrington and Lytton, none of which we had seen before. It was a just account, painful and touching. We both read it and it provided food for a long conversation between Ralph and me.

Now Ralph is up in the library writing. I had been happy writing letters when there suddenly came into my head some childhood memories that might make material for a paper at the Memoir Club should such be required of me. I amused myself jotting them down and found — as always — a flotilla of other little memories swimming behind them.

I sit writing with my back to the log fire which crackles softly and flicks tongues of light into the outer fringes of my field of vision. The frost has made Minnie very skittish, but she has tired herself out and lies glossy and extenuated on the sofa, while Ralph is taking notes for a review about Nelson. Happiness.

November 5th. We chose Sidmouth for this half-term holiday. Burgo's letters had given us no cause for anxiety, nor did his company. As soon as we saw him, looking splendidly big and strong, we felt sure that things were going well. Indeed he was very ready to tell us so. The time had 'whizzed by', he likes his work (particularly history), has started physics, and described arguments in the dormitory about such subjects as patriotism, in which he enjoys taking part. He is the only one of seven who doesn't say his prayers every night, hates games, and is delighted that Ralph has got him out of the corps, which no one likes, on grounds of family pacifism. Yet we don't get the impression that he is too odd a fish for the rest of them.

The sun came out as we drove into Sidmouth, a sweet little

Early Victorian town with a short esplanade filling the gap between two tallish red cliffs. The rough sea tossed close beneath the hotel dining-room windows, and sent up fountains of foam against the low sea wall when we took our afternoon walk along the front. After dark the people of the town gathered on the beach, where a huge Guy Fawkes' day bonfire was lit and fed with old chairs, prams and the hull of a boat. We could see the waves rolling in reddened by the glare, and a great twisting turgid coil of black smoke full of fiery sparks surging out over the sea.

Our hotel is comfortable, warm to suffocation, and even in this wintry season almost full of permanent residents — Ralph says retired Anglo-Indians, come to end their days in mild South Devonshire. It might be a section in some anthropological museum, so homogeneous and remote from modernity is the life going on in it. All round us sit white-haired couples on whose faces one sees traces of long-gone beauty and persistent gentility; behind us are a touching pair, the old gentleman cutting up his food for his blind wife — under her eyeshade her old face is clever and humorous. They all speak in educated voices and dress for dinner each night, the ladies with fur tippets over their long dresses; the old gentlemen, some with woolly pullovers under their dinner jackets, hurry forward to open the door for their wives with old-world politeness. They were keeping up the standards of gentility for all they were worth, and though these are not what I am often taken by I couldn't help admiring the discreet elegance with which they did so.

Burgo's return to school was not this time at all clouded by gloom.

November 9th. Alix and James are to spend the winter in South Africa. They stopped to lunch with us on their way to Southampton, looking mightily distinguished, two erect ageing figures well wrapped up in thick fur-lined coats, and Alix wearing a fur-trimmed hat like a Greek soldier's helmet, specially designed to keep her ears warm. They came in a hired car with an elderly chauffeur, and appeared to enjoy the rich, creamy and sweet repast we gave them. For two thoroughly analysed people, it struck me that they are swimming off into a world of fantasy — and fantasy of grandeur. They have 'introductions to General Smuts and others given us by our friend Princess George of

Greece.' They hope that they 'will not be *made* to sit at the Captain's table' (though they will obviously be disappointed if they are not *asked* to), 'as we might be mistaken for the Food Minister'.[1]

[1]James's cousin, John Strachey.

November 14th. A day in London, partly to do a little Christmas shopping. Hamleys was a seething palace of toys; egotistic children were dragging their elders towards expensive things they coveted, while others just lay back in their push-chairs and bawled. Grandparents lovingly stroked the silky fur of monster Teddy bears. I felt stifled, and hurried away to a very different atmosphere — an exhibition of paintings by Francis Bacon, a friend of Richard and Denis's whom I met briefly last summer. His pictures were impressive, completely original and absolutely terrifying. They reminded me of the thoughts and images aroused by the books Ralph and I read all the time now about the Criminally Mad. They represented nebulous grey curtains fastened here and there by a carefully painted safety-pin through which figures could be dimly glimpsed — faces whose wide-open mouths expressed the ultimate degree of horror and fear. I was very much fascinated by these — less so by some of pink penises tipped by little grinning mouths full of crooked teeth. All seemed to personify the Id, and I took the safety-pins and veils to stand for the inadequate forces of suppression. The artist is said to live alone with his Nanny. I couldn't help wondering what she thought of them.

From there to the [Heywood] Hills, where I found Anne and the two little girls having pandemoniac nursery tea. Further excited by the appearance of a stranger perhaps, they stood on their heads, jumped off chairs and brought me their favourite possessions to admire, all in the friendliest way and greatly to my enjoyment. (Adults often do the same less directly and less successfully.) They all walked with me to Paddington through the foggy darkness, to 'have a nice breath of fresh air,' as Anne said. She described a farewell party she and Heywood had given for Eddie. He and Bob [Gathorne-Hardy][1] started a quarrel with Bryan Howard, which was still going on when she came down from bed hours later for a glass of water. It went something like this:

Bryan to Bob: The trouble with *you* is you're a most fearful old
           bore.
Eddie to
    Bryan: Well *your* old friends can't bear to see you any
           more. Julia says you make her *shudder*.
Bryan to the
    brothers: Look at *your* friends — Kyrle [Leng] for instance
           is so middle-class he might as well be a Swiss!
Bob to Bryan: I'm a success, you're a failure. I used not to be
           able to write, but now I can. *You* could write
           once, but now you've forgotten how.
And so on.

¹Anne's brothers.

[The brothers Eddie and Bob Gathorne-Hardy were so alike in
some ways that they might have been twins — in others very
different. Both had been at Eton and Oxford where they early
developed intellectual interests in such subjects as bibliography,
botany and archeology; thereafter they joined the same antiqua-
rian booksellers and became well-known figures in literary
London in the Thirties, swiftly going their rounds together, each
with a monocle in his eye. Each had an excellent memory and was a
natural highbrow. To see them, as one sometimes might, standing
side by side at a party, glass in hand, going off into bubbling
fountains of talk and rockets of laughter, was a very comical sight.
   As for their differences: Eddie, the elder, was something of a
rake and idler. He made short work of a legacy he received at
Oxford, spending it on silk shirts, good food and wine and first
editions of Jeremy Taylor. He was amoral and selfish but
disarmingly affectionate and gloriously funny. The words 'My
dear' in a confiding tone frequently interrupted his speech ('Do
you know, my dear, what the taxi-driver said to me, my dear? He
said, my dear. . . . '). One had only to look at the way he held his
hands to see how impractical he was, but he knew how things
should be done and could instruct others. Compared to Eddie,
Bob was domestic, unselfish, practical and an energetic gardener;
unlike him he could sometimes be boring. Anne Hill was their
only sister.]

November 16th. Last night the subterranean stream of melancholy
which had been flowing beneath my happy secure life broke

through its banks and I sat before the fire giving way to it. Lord knows I have little cause — only one in fact, the frustration caused by the collapse of the flower book. I can no longer fork through the subject in the way I loved to, and discuss it with Ralph as we do his Broadmoor. The result is my confidence is badly shaken. If this book is to stop I *must* find something else to do. But what? The question haunts me. Feeling relieved by having brought this discontent to the light of day, I put it as it were into a mental rack labelled: Questions to be settled in the near future, and passed the rest of the evening very pleasantly.

November 18th. Richard, Denis and Sebastian (who hadn't met them before) for the weekend. 'Any news from Penguins?' I asked Richard. 'None whatever,' he answered.

It was gloriously fine all day and warm as summer. The brilliance of the virulent green lawn and blazing red trees dazzled the eyes, and the birds cackled and reeled among the branches in a sort of autumn hysteria. Much of the morning I had spent picking and arranging chrysanthemums from large mop-heads to tiny daisylike filigree ones of dusty pink.

Interesting conversation about Francis Bacon and his paintings. Denis supplied some biographical details: he loves gambling, luxury, and the company of rich tycoons, and has a project for decorating a luxurious drinking-club in the City for big businessmen to meet in. Sebastian and Richard got talking about mutual Norfolk friends, and seemed to like each other very well. An after-dinner conversation about human credulity, a subject about which Ralph and I think exactly alike. Sebastian charged us with not wanting to believe, and said that he preferred to sit on the fence and keep as many doors as possible wide open. 'Very well,' I said, 'but you can only achieve "knowledge" by shutting some doors and leaving only one open.'

November 23rd. Last night a debate on Conscription was broadcast from the Cambridge Union. We listened to it all, I for one hoping for some signs of anti-war feelings from the young men who are most concerned in it. What a disappointment! In feeble, woolly terms all the speakers assumed that we must prepare for war and only argued how best that could be done. So much for the Second War to end war.

December 2nd. A visit to London, and nothing much to remember it by, except for a remark of Desmond McCarthy's during an argument about Capital Punishment. He thumped the table and cried: 'YES, yes, two wrongs DO make one right!'

In this last month we have been made aware of the many stresses and strains experienced by friends, money troubles and ill-health also, of older friends like Desmond and Molly slipping gradually into increasing feebleness. Sometimes it's as if everyone was struggling out of a bog or plodding along in some ghastly spiritual retreat from Moscow. Human beings value their power to bestow life — but is it also such a boon? So far, goodness knows I have found my own a thousand times worthwhile. Who knows, though, what is in store? And there are the lonely deserted wives, or those who never found a mate and fear it's now too late — they seem to be playing some horrible children's game like Twos and Threes, each longing to be one of a pair and dreading to be the odd one out. Just as waiting for death — which is bound to get us all in the end — is like that other awful game, where the gym mistress swings a rope with a hard leather pad on the end, round and round, higher and higher, while the children jump till they can jump no more, and the rope twists itself round their legs and catches them.

December 7th — Ham Spray. To Euphemia for supplies: we walked straight into a scene going on in her blue kitchen. A handsome young farm labourer was talking to her.

'John wants to go off with Jimmy O'Hagan the boxer,' she said, and as John left the room she shouted after him: 'Don't you go to any more disused sites!' And then, the door having closed behind him: 'You see he and Jimmy went to a disused site at Southampton together. His mother came to see me about it, said "his father didn't like it." I told her all the men who'd been in love with me were that way, and they were a very nice lot. She said: "Go on, Mrs Grove." I think I'll put him in the Merchant Navy, he'll do very well there.'

The Wests arrived at tea-time in a large grand car, each in their different way like a bird in fine plumage — glossy and lively. Anthony went off with a typewriter to finish his novel in the music-room, but was always ready to interrupt himself by a sudden flare of animation, becoming all flashing white teeth, snapping black eyes and rumbles of suppressed amusement.

Later we were joined by Boris and Maroussa. With her tinted spectacles and swathed turban, her cigarettes in a long holder, and a foreign accent too good to be true, Maroussa is so much a thriller-writer's picture of a female spy that I wasn't surprised to hear of all their difficulties in getting through the Customs. Boris is monumental, magnificent.

We made it a gala night with smoked salmon, a Virginia ham, pineapple, two bottles of wine and Calvados to follow. I don't know why the subject of religious belief cropped up at dinner, but Maroussa reacted against our tone by bringing out a beautiful little ikon which she carries everywhere in her bag. It was much more surprising to find Anthony on the same side, confirming a suspicion I had got from his book, though I only half understood it.

December 11th. A bright and lovely morning. The trees, now as bare as they will ever be, stretch their twigs in a clear blue sky. We were able to sit out and read on the verandah.

Maroussa had her breakfast in bed with the curtains drawn and the room full of tobacco-smoke, looking as Russian as possible and reading Robert's novel. What a contrast with Kitty, with her very white skin, light hair and attractive yellow eyes, her jerseys well-washed, her figure like a little girl's.

I have now nearly finished reading Madame de Sévigné's Letters, and was moved by my heroine's thoughts as she approached the grave: '*Il me semble que j'ai été trainée à ce point fatal ou il faut souffrir la vieillesse; je la vois, m'y voilà, et j'entends une voix qui dit "Il faut marcher malgré vous."*'

Ralph is hard at work on his Broadmoor book, and comes down from the library with his mind happily full of it. My thoughts are turned towards Burgo's return on Friday.

December 16th. Burgo back this morning, enormous and apparently grown-up and sensible. While we made Christmas cards we had a conversation about life. Burgo: 'Time is whizzing by so fast. And the world is so terrible. But now I realize how terrible it is, I can face it and enjoy myself as a result.'

F: 'What is so particularly terrible?'

Burgo: 'Oh — that it's an uphill struggle all the time. And all the awful things that are going on, like the atom bomb. But I feel that everything will end when I do, because someone will manage to blow us all up. Then human beings are getting more and more like machines; soon their hands will just be pitiful stumps fit for pressing buttons or pulling levers, and they'll even have machines for minds, that can only react to what happens in one way.'

Yet he seems quite cheerful, if rather dreamy, and when I said he seemed to have had quite a lot of fun at school he agreed.

1950

January 24th. As 1949 dragged to its end I got the senseless feeling that it was a bad old year, which had made a faulty start and gone on developing all awry, and that 1950 might well be quite a different affair — its very name had a better ring to it. But now that three weeks of it have flashed past I am not sure that I was right. I don't remember a time when other people's troubles came more closely hailing and snowing around our shoulders, nor when our ears were so deafened by the cracking up of the personal relations of our friends. All these earthquakes have made Ralph and me infinitely thankful for the stability of our own, and rejoice in the harmony of our days and nights together. Burgo too, rapidly enlarging his personality as well as his physical frame, *seems* — thank goodness — to have got over his unhappiness of last year, and went back perfectly serenely to school whence he has written us one sweet and friendly letter. Now, at fourteen and a half, his problem will be to complete his detachment from us, and put down stronger roots outside the seedbed.

Anthony rang up to say goodbye as he was sailing tonight for America, not at all sorry to go as he says, but wishing he was taking Kitty and the children. There has been some difficulty with H. G. Wells' executors about the papers being taken abroad, so it sounds as though he may give up his project of writing his father's life. His telephonic style is thoroughly unbuttoned, and he talked a good deal about what he hopes to get out of American social life. He particularly likes their superficial geniality.

February 1st. We are plunged in the full Reports of the Commission on Capital Punishment which are of absorbing interest. Went to bed at nearly one, feeling haunted by my long companionship with murderers, either in the condemned cell or witnessing their twilit transit thence into eternity. Humane as all the prison governors, doctors and chaplains appear to be according to their lights, they are one and all against abolition. I must say there is something both ludicrous and macabre about giving attention to such questions as: Shall the condemned man be allowed a wireless (strictly expurgated) in his cell as well as draughts, chess and cards, when all the time you are preparing to take his life away by force? Or, on a more plaintive note, testifying to the dreariness and monotony for prison officers 'on death duty' when they aren't allowed to smoke, and 'the prisoner shows not the smallest desire to play cards or draughts, but gets continually more morose'. Perhaps it's natural that the clergy come out of it best. They become more intimate with the prisoner, and one is impressed by their sincerity when they say that they have seen men hanged who should not have been hanged 'because there was something on which to build'.

March 9th. A night in London, chiefly to hear the afternoon session of the Capital Punishment Commission, at which Stanley Hopwood was the sole witness. With his long amiable face, large strong teeth, flabby handshake and very short legs, he is an endearing figure, who looks at one with a dispassionate gaze which has made acquaintance with two thousand murderers. The Commission was held in a stately first-floor room in Carlton House Terrace; the Commissioners seated at a horseshoe table, and we — the public — at the back, whence we could see Stanley's short legs in white socks tucked touchingly under his chair like a schoolboy's, while his calm elderly face confronted his questioners like a figurehead. Many of the chosen ten were old men with faces deeply engraved by experience and natural cleverness. I don't know why it was so fascinating: probably because it was manifest that these various minds were trying their level best to arrive at Truth, sometimes through strenuous efforts and subtle analysis. Often the crucial issue seemed to be contained in a little knot of sentences, hard for the layman to unravel. It was all of course to do with the McNaghton Rules, or suicide pacts or uncontrollable impulses. Afterwards Stanley took us to his club, where we ate rich cakes, sitting in sumptuous chairs among one or two youngish cads entertaining beautiful and smart girls.

Dined with the [Craig] Macfarlanes,[1] where we met the Noel Blakistons — he, an old Etonian and early love of Cyril's, is a handsome man with greying hair. When we mentioned where we had been he said: 'Oh, but do you feel strongly about Capital Punishment? I'm all for it. And flogging too. How else can you deal with these thugs? It's the only thing they understand. I hit my daughter at breakfast this morning because she was being so stupid.' Giana, his wife, adores cooking and foreign travel. I liked the way she described her pleasure in peeling a carrot, and also in reading books about Afghanistan. In fact liked them both very much.

[1] Our solicitor and an old friend.

March 12th. Back at Ham Spray, with Richard for a week. We were promised sleet and cold this morning, but going out on to the verandah with Minnie I found it cool and sweet, with innumerable birds keeping up a high-pitched whistling chorus like the boys in Britten's Spring Symphony. It has rained in the night and enormous drops were quietly falling from the honeysuckle. Last night we went to have drinks with the Campbells, Ben Nicolson[1] and Freddie Ayer.[2] I was interested in Ayer and wanted to hear him talk, but out of some sort of diffidence I withdrew to a secluded seat on the sofa next to Ben, so that while enjoying talk with him about Lawrence Gowing and Antwerp, I saw and heard a lively spate of words of the sort I most love flashing from Ayer's animated face. Mary scored a general laugh by saying, when asked why she believed in Capital Punishment: 'Because it's the only way to keep the population down.'

[1] Art historian.
[2] Sir Alfred Ayer, philosopher.

March 24th. For the last weekend we had Molly MacCarthy and old Saxon — an unplanned combination which turned out very well. Molly amused us a great deal; Saxon was talkative for him, and a visit from the Campbells put him in the seventh heaven of being able to hold forth about racehorses and Spanish towns to his heart's content.

Molly's stories:
Of little Hugh hating his sister Laura. Rachel asked him to kiss her good-night. He replied: 'Well, I *will*, but she makes my blood run cold.'

Of a lecture Molly went to by Nansen, who described their dreadful polar adventures, 'And then we had nothing to eat for four weeks but penguin meat, and I dare say you can imagine *that* wasn't very nice. . . .' Or again, 'the wind was so strong it blew our huts over. And I dare say you can imagine *that* wasn't very nice.' So it went on until the end of the lecture when Nansen described their return home, 'and when the ship entered harbour there was my wife waiting for me.' A voice from the back of the hall: 'And I dare say you can imagine *that* wasn't very nice.'

[At first sight Molly MacCarthy might strike the unknowing as a conventional and possibly slightly irritable member of the 'Upper Middle Classes', and how very wrong they would be! Fairly generously built, she dressed unnoticeably in good safe suits rather long in the skirt, and shoes with low heels and long pointed toes. Her straight grey fringe came just over her eyebrows and her dark eyes were small and bright. But the first conversation revealed at once that here was an original personality and a fantastic, witty mind.

Her deafness was a dreadful affliction for her and an obstacle to her friends. She tried every device to surmount it, including a box needing batteries that were always running out and a pair of small tortoiseshell horns which gave her a comic appearance that she was the first to appreciate. She spoke in the soft voice of the deaf, but in quick little runs of words, with frequent emphases, spontaneous and unexpected. She was a natural comedian, mimic and raconteuse, and whenever she came to Ham Spray, or we went with her (as we sometimes did) on some outing such as a day on Brighton pier, there was always boundless *fun*. Molly was indeed the arch-priestess of fun; she used to invent it out of other people's remarks and it made the tears run down her cheeks. At Bloomsbury parties she would sometimes perform a turn. Once, for instance, she dressed up as a dwarf fortune-teller, and read the hands of fellow-guests disconcertingly, but acting so well that not a single one recognized her.

Social life was much curtailed for her through deafness and she kept away from the smart dinner-parties at which Desmond was a particular star. To use a favourite word of hers she could be 'censorious', but in the company of old friends she was happy, and warmth itself. Both Ralph and I loved her dearly and I think she was fond of us. She invented a 'little language' full of family phrases which figured often in her brilliant letters, written at speed and with many deep underlinings. They were a joy to get, and bring her to life again unfailingly.]

May 4th. Last week we went to the Broadmoor dance, one of four attended by men and women Parole patients, though as there is usually a serious shortage of women Dr Hopwood says: 'any woman who can put foot to floor is roped in'. Richard came with us. After his first visit to a dance, so he told us, he lay awake in tears thinking about the poor lunatics' miserable imprisonment. Well, I couldn't kid myself that any of them would be any happier for dancing with me: and I felt a certain alarm at the thought of *having* to dance with any madman who asked me, however repellent. So I dressed myself unfestively in my green corduroy suit and rubber-soled shoes, with the idea of sitting watching among the doctors' wives. This we did. I talked to an enormous doctor's mother with many pendulous chins, who pointed out some of the more famous patients, like Mrs T., a slight girlish figure with a piquant little heart-shaped face and red hair. 'It's terrible to think what those little hands have done,' she said, obviously relishing doing so intensely. Soon I began to get requests to dance, and finally stood up with a very lively red-faced old man in a dinner-jacket, and had two dances with this old reprobate, whose speciality was raping little girls. He taught me the Boston two-step, remarking that he 'hoped he had given me something to think about when I went home'. Another exceedingly courteous old fellow taught me the La Rinka, and an elderly female known as Ivy told me how she loved taming birds and squirrels, and couldn't bear seeing the boughs of fruit-blossom broken by the snow. 'After all, they're life, aren't they?' she said with rather a sly smile. But my nicest partner was a charming and apparently quite normal young man who spoke with cheerful anticipation about the flower shows, cricket and concert parties to come. Stanley told me he was an airman who had cracked up under stress of the war and killed his girl. 'He'll go out soon, but is sensible enough not to want to till he's quite well.'

All said and done I was glad to have taken part, but ashamed to realize how little insight I had into these abnormal minds. No alcohol was allowed naturally enough, but there was a moment when a glass containing orange juice was dropped and broken and a sudden complete silence fell on the packed room, which gave me more idea than anything else of the fragility of the crust of normality overlaying seething emotions. I noticed also that when we arrived home in the small hours and I got sleepily out to open the gate, I breathed in the freshness and sweetness of the garden air with thankful relief, it contrasted so sharply with what we had left.

May 16th. Janetta and Robert have been here for a warm spring weekend. We saw the Campbells, had the Pritchetts to dinner and picnicked by the Barge Inn at Honey Street, a very romantic disused canal, where drowned barges lie entangled in a welter of reeds — a sight which in its way symbolized the impression made by certain symptoms shown by the Kees that have revived a buried disquiet. Why aren't they happier together, I wonder? Complete satisfaction may be too much to expect at their age, but to hear them talk it seems that a lot is wrong with their life, and Robert has returned to his sad old habit of denigrating Janetta for incompetence, or what she herself calls her 'legarthy'. Her confidence is shaken and she defends herself half-heartedly, as if her chief aim was to avoid annoying Robert. This ghost train running along old railway lines is very disturbing. If Robert goes on writing down her character she will go off with someone who thinks her wonderful and tells her so, and there are plenty who will.

May 30th. On Whit-Sunday we walked with Heywood and Anne Hill, our weekend visitors, to see the new Inkpen Gibbet being installed on the site of the old. I had a feeling it would be worth looking at, but didn't guess in what way. It was unexpectedly grim and dramatic. We came over the shoulder of the down just as it was half-way up: the new gibbet is a stout oaken affair with a longer cross-bar at the top, so that it looks rather like a great crucifix, and as it sloped against the grey windy sky it reminded me of Tintoretto's masterpiece in the San Rocco in Venice, in which one of the thieves is being elevated to his position on the cross. Add to this a silent crowd pressing round about it like a swarm of bees. It was easy to imagine that we were looking at a human sacrifice, the retribution of the people against a guilty individual, or an execution in the French Revolution. As we got nearer the effect was broken by seeing the crowd more closely —

the usual country lot, children on ponies and hundreds of cars drawn up beyond; Victor Bonham-Carter in the middle with some BBC men and his microphone, and just under the brow of the down the Inkpen Silver Band in full cry. When the gibbet sank down into its socket the spell was quite gone, and a sense of anti-climax was produced by three feeble cheers being given and blowing away in the high wind. The band then set up a maundering tune more suitable to a village fête on a drowsy August day than to this bleak windy hill-top, and the crowd rapidly dispersed, we with them and on to take an immense walk by Combe and home.

June 5th. Back from half-term weekend in Dorset, finding Burgo well and happy. We saw Abbotsbury in an eerie sea-mist through which the hissing, flapping swans moved like ballerinas; charming litle grey cygnets were floating in a kind of nursery pond — and we even saw one break its way out of the egg-shell and lie resting, like a weak, damp snake. To Fleet in honour of *Moonfleet*, which Burgo had been reading. We were shown round the church by a cheerful little negro boy in a scarlet jersey, who must have dated from the American army's local presence in 1944. We had tea in the Manor House of the book, now a hotel, a plain white building unpretentiously pitched beside the waters of the Fleet, and then walked along the shore through a rough field and a small wood full of 'roast beef' irises. The sun made a poetical moonlike appearance through the clouds, and the Chesil bank was a faint ghost across the water. Kitty West was with us all day long. She has heard no more from Anthony since his cable telling her that plans were altered and she and the children should not come to America. We were full of admiration for her courage and resilience. All Sunday we roasted on Charmouth beach — it was thick with people. Lovers lay entwined behind the shingle bank; children trotted briskly about muttering obsessionally to themselves; balls were thrown, dogs ran and barked, and here and there the mountainous hip of a recumbent housewife reared itself into the air.

June 6th. What an odd lot the members of the Memoir Club looked, gathered together outside Olivelli's restaurant. The day had been a fizzer — 88 in the shade, but in the basement restaurant whose walls are papered with photographs of film stars the air was cooler, and the Italian proprietress, though she gave us a fierce, measuring look, soon brought asparagus and chilled Orvieto. Bunny beamed out upon the rest of the company from within a warm blanket of absorption in his own affairs — his new venture as partner in Rupert Hart-Davis' publishing firm, his cows, Hilton and the boys — the four little girls were mentioned chiefly as nuisances. Across the table Oliver Strachey, dressed in a pale green Palm Beach suit, glared at me rather sourly. 'One of the things about growing older,' he volunteered, 'is that one discovers the true character of one's friends.' Oh dear, yes, I thought guiltily, we didn't do enough for him in his time of illness and trouble. I turned to Clive, who was anxious for news of Kitty and Anthony.

After dinner we walked in a body through the hot dark night to Duncan's rooms, passing James standing on his doorstep in Gordon Square, a splendid figure in a white silk suit. It was as if all London had shrunk to Bloomsbury and was peopled only by these human portents. The papers read were by Angelica (a beautifully written account of her stay in France as a girl of sixteen), and Dermod, about sex at school. His paper led to a discussion as to whether school-boys should be beaten.

'Oh YES — of course one must beat boys,' said Desmond, and Oliver joined him. It seemed priggish to attack this fashionable swing of the pendulum, but honesty obliged me to. Only Vanessa took my side. Sitting on an upright chair with her hat on, she pondered for a moment and then said conclusively in her deep voice: 'I see *no* point in punishment myself.'

[When I first got to know David Garnett he was a young man in his thirties — well-built, broad-shouldered, fair-haired and blue-eyed — who seemed ill-suited to the nickname 'Bunny', given him no doubt in childhood by his fond parents. I am glad also to have known that remarkable pair, Edward and Constance, even slightly. Indeed I stayed more than once with Constance in her improbable Kentish cottage, where she led a self-contained life among her pumpkins, giving little away of the brilliant intelligence that had made her one of the earliest Greek scholars at Newnham before she took to translating the Russians. I saw Edward more often, for he used to visit his son's bookshop, Birrell and Garnett, where I worked as an assistant. He was a tall stooping man with a thick crop of yellowish-grey hair crowning his ugly, amiable, pleated face. Both Bunny's parents peered through the thickest spectacles imaginable, with the questioning, but unseeing gaze of fish in an aquarium. Only when he was grown up and ambitious to become a writer, did Bunny get to know his father on equal terms, so he told me, and when he consulted him as to how to prepare for his career the answer he got was: 'Read, read, read.' The outstanding success of *Lady Into Fox*, based on a course of Defoe, caused great jubilation in the bookshop, but quite naturally led him to leave it and devote himself to writing in the beautiful, unbelievably cold Queen Anne House, Hilton Hall, where he lived with his first wife, my sister Ray, and their two sons, and later with Angelica and their four daughters.

In the First World War Bunny and his partner in the bookshop Francis Birrell had been Conscientious Objectors, and worked either on English farms or in reconstructing French villages (as he well describes in one of his best — if least known — novels, *Plough over the Bones*). However, when the Second World War came along he accepted an invitation to work in the Air Ministry with the rank of Flight Lieutenant. There was a side of Bunny that entered enthusiastically into what he was doing, down to the details of dressing up for the part. As owner of a bookshop he for a while wore a bowler hat and carried a rolled-up umbrella. As a countryman he took an innocent delight in his bee-keeping and salmon–fishing outfits: so that it was not surprising to see him happy in his R.A.F. uniform.

When Bunny wanted to look at someone it was characteristic of him to turn his whole head and blue gaze swiftly towards them, until his chin touched his shoulder. This, and the purposeful stride with which he would cross the bookshop, take out a book and hand it over to a customer all in one movement, showed the extrovert energy and decisiveness concealed in a temperament that was superficially genial and deliberate. The tempo of his talk was thought by some of his Bloomsbury friends to be very slow and they teased him about it; but though a conversation with him might start at a leisurely pace and be interrupted by long pauses, it usually burgeoned into a lavish growth branching in unexpected directions, for he had an excellent memory for what he had read or experienced. His cornflower-blue eyes might twinkle in silence for several minutes while he hatched his next remark, but then out it came with a rush of sudden fantasy or maybe firmness.

His other activities had the same quality — his letters talked in his own voice. When he learned to fly a light aeroplane with dogged determination rather than aptitude, a visit to Ham Spray from the 'Rabbit in the Air' was a nerve-racking experience. The time to leave had come, but he seemed quite unable to get the machine to start, and paced round and round it, swinging the propeller with a deepening frown. Then a slow smile dawned — he had forgotten to turn on the petrol.

Bunny's absorption in his own affairs was sometimes amusing. When I returned from my first visit to Russia (a country I knew he loved talking about) I was longing to talk myself about peacock-blue churches with gold spires, but he didn't ask me a single question about it: instead I listened to a detailed description of his failing to catch salmon in Wales.

As a friend he was first-rate — staunch, warm and appreciative. He always gave careful and wise advice when it was sought. France was his chosen country, and he spent his last years there in a remote valley lined with box trees, near Cahors. Here he could be seen sitting out of doors under a large straw hat typing out his manuscripts, going to market with his beret pulled well over his eyes, bottling his wine. Here he entertained his family and friends with food he had lovingly cooked himself. The athletic figure of his youth retained considerable dignity even in his eighties, though his movements had become deliberate. He was still ready and eager to dive into a pool of cold water or go looking for wild orchids in the limestone hills. He was a happy, remarkably sane and lovable man.

Ray died of cancer during the Second World War. By 1950 he was married to Angelica Bell and the father of four daughters.]

June 12th. I live for pleasure these days, and find no difficulty in filling my days and nights with it — reading, writing, eating, sleeping, gardening (mildly), looking for flowers and butterflies, listening to the wireless, talking, thinking, playing my violin, being with Ralph — there is no end to the delights. And what do I do for suffering humanity in return? Or for anyone else except Ralph, for that matter? I do believe in some form of Social Contract, so no wonder my puritan conscience stirs uneasily in the depths. This state of things cannot last for ever and is too good to miss a moment of, so if my conscience can be stifled I mean to stifle it. All the same I do quite seriously envy people who feel they do some good in the world. Ralph never stops believing that if one is not doing *harm* one can congratulate oneself, and such is the conclusion of many of our ethical conversations. Yet, in my opinion, one of the signs of present-day decadence is that 'do-gooder' has become a term of abuse.

June 14th and 15th. Staying two nights at Broadmoor with Stanley in the Superintendent's house. The drawing-room is a perfect replica of an Edwardian parlour as seen on the stage. Over the fireplace a complicated overmantel rears itself, its shelves holding ebony elephants and Japanese vases; like the cushioned 'love-seat' it is painted a horrid matt peach-cream, with inset panels of a blue jazz design. Numbers of tiny occasional tables stand about the room, ready one would think to tip over when Crook the clumsy spaniel flounders about the room, but not actually doing so. We sleep under a violently glossy orange eiderdown, and a faint smell of escaping gas scents the room. All night long I was aware where we were, and that a narrow if high wall separated us from the Parole Block of male lunatics.

Ralph and I are falsely bright and ill at ease with Stanley; and I haven't yet learned to wait when given a drink, and then tip it back in unison with Stanley and Ralph, saying 'Cheerio!'

On our first day we went to the Sports for the Better Male Blocks. A cold drizzle was falling but everyone felt that the eager children taking part must not be disappointed; so, along with the doctors, the chaplain and some wives, we descended the broad steps down to Avernus while the lost souls gathered for each gate in turn to be unlocked by the angels (or fiends?) in dark blue. Dressed either in thick institutional black coat, cape and peaked cap, or the working orange corduroys, or even in running shorts, I suppose three-quarters of them looked pretty mad. Some were restlessly moving to and fro, talking or laughing to themselves, singing a little. One man had his hands permanently held as if bicycling.

A young fat boy came up to the doctor to whom I was talking and began muttering, '*Very* HUNGRY. I'd like some more *cake*. Not enough to eat.' 'Good, good,' replied the doctor, 'so you've written to me about it? Good.'

The sports were being organized by the 'Blackheath Murderer' (a kindly looking man), and Ronald True, who exactly resembled his portrait in the Famous Trials series. I shook hands with both these famous monsters.

Next day the Bad Blocks had their sports, a function that had never been held before and was therefore an experiment. Stanley seemed to expect some 'scenes', so I was not allowed to attend. It's true that strangers affect the patients a lot; one can never look at a crowd of them without finding many pairs of mad eyes fixed on one. So I took a walk across the famous 'moor' with Crook and my botanical vasculum, and became ludicrously rattled. There were long straight rides of yellow sand running between pines as far as the eye could see. I soon began to feel lonely and depressed, and even frightened, and when far off I spied a bicyclist approaching, wearing pale corduroys like the Broadmoor patients, I simply could not bear to wait for him to catch me up, so I turned down a side track into a little dell, where I went through all the sensations of being attacked and strangled in my imagination. After which I returned, hating the moor and wanting none of it.

June 21st — Ham Spray. Crowds of people at the weekend. To stay: Noel Sandwith, Janie [Bussy] and Olivier Popham[1] (a new visitor whom we like very much). To tea: the Kees, Nicko [Henderson] on leave from Greece, with a friend of his called Donald Maclean. The Pritchetts afterwards for a drink. A strange thing about Maclean — we were asked of course about our visits to Broadmoor, and led on to talk. Then, walking on the lawn with Janetta afterwards, I heard from her that he had been a member of the Embassy at Cairo, but had just been sent home because he tried to murder his wife.

'No, *really?*' I said. 'Yes, really — and another friend got his leg broken going to her rescue. It happened because he got fearfully drunk with Philip Toynbee.' He has not been sacked from the Foreign Office, but sent home for psychiatric treatment. He's a tall, very good-looking man, friendly and smiling — charming in fact.

Noel Sandwith's enthusiasm for plant-hunting made his eyes sparkle so behind his spectacles that I felt my own sparkling too. We all drove with him to a bleak stretch of downland near Bordon Camp to look for *Astragalus Danicus* ('a glorious thing with reddish flowers'). After tramping through the long grass like a herd of buffaloes, with many interjections from Noel of '*that* looks a bit funny', we at last found the rarity — an insignificant squalid-looking plant with blue flowers.

Janie, told that we were planning a trip to Spain, said: 'Oh, I couldn't do it. Too much unavenged blood there.' Meaning, we supposed, that a further drenching would improve matters?

[1] Now Mrs Quentin Bell.

June 29th. Our dear daily, Mrs Hoare and her family have recently been turned out of their house and are at present occupying the nursery wing. A breakfast conversation between Ralph and me which almost became heated began from my saying how odd was the effect of our life and the Hoare's running side by side. I often wondered about their life, surely they must wonder about ours? And if they wondered, must they not envy certain things? Our having more money, our freedom, our power to trundle the car out of the garage and be off? Ralph couldn't accept this, and clung tenaciously to the idea that they envied us nothing. We agreed that there were morbidly envious people in all walks of life, but I cannot agree with Ralph that the 'average man' is completely satisfied with his lot. From here we moved on to the differences between asking people to do things and telling them to. Ralph would no more think of *telling* Wilde[1] to do a thing than I would Mrs Hoare, but small children are certainly told, and punished if they don't act accordingly. Is discipline only valid for the immature in age or capacity?

[1] The gardener.

July 8th. I put my question about asking and telling to Raymond and he said it made him livid with anger when people refused to be told things: that all work involved taking and giving orders. When I asked him whether he liked being called 'Sir' by younger men, he replied with vigour: 'No, but I do like being called Sir by the lower classes, servants and chauffeurs.'

This occurred during a sunny weekend at the Bothy,[1] when we lay and walked by the Thames, watched crews practising for Henley Regatta and were taught to play Canasta. I caught a beautiful and rare moth with the enchanting name 'Scarce Merveille du Jour'.

[1] Raymond's country cottage.

July 10th — Ham Spray. War has broken out in Korea and for several days loomed larger. Yesterday the first British casualties were announced. It is inevitable (but depressing) to what a degree it has revived feelings from 1939, and nightmare images also, such as being in a small boat slowly but inexorably moving towards Niagara Falls. Yet a sort of excitement seemed to possess our weekend visitors, Judy and Dick [Rendel][1] and Quentin, at the thought of the bravery of soldiers in wartime. Talk is quite openly anti-foreign: all Germans are monsters impossible to shake by the hand, the Italians beneath contempt, and the French and Russians as bad as the Germans. Nor is this by any means meant as a joke. Benjamin Britten is a 'bloody man' (and *therefore* a bad composer) because he went to America instead of fighting the Germans.

[1]My sister and her husband (ex-Colonel in the regular army).

[A week later we started on a holiday at Deva on the north coast of Spain, with Vicky and her mother Esme as companions.

Waking in our wagon-lits at Hendaye was 'as delicious as it always is. We were still in gentle motion, gliding through the fresh morning air, and behind us a good night's sleep, broken as with commas and semi-colons by harsh voices crying "Poitiers!" or "Bordeaux!" into our dreams. At Irun we were decanted to fend for ourselves among the pungent Spaniards. Reached Deva by two little trains, the last of which ran screaming across a bridge, whence we saw a beach with a gay row of sun-umbrellas. The sky is a soft grey, the charming landscape very green, with conical haystacks and intersecting valleys.'

Deva turned out to be an elegant resort, where the rich and smart took refuge from the summer heat of Madrid. We went to the beach every morning: 'The colours worn on the beach make up a beautiful palette of clear Matisse pink, grey and yellow, with one or two stronger blues and reds. The children are enchantingly pretty with their big lustrous black eyes and gold rings in their ears; they wear crisp cotton dresses trimmed with frills, scallops, tucks and broderie anglaise, all looking as if they had just come out of the wash-tub, also large straw hats or starched white bonnets: and are in charge of nurses very chic themselves in aprons with crossing bands and white lace caps.'

Everyone told us it was madness to go to Loyola on the day of the Fiesta of San Ignacio, but we were obdurate: 'Before our crowded train started a lady sitting next to us shrieked from the window "JESUS!" When he appeared he was an immaculately dressed man of kindly appearance, who took a fatherly interest in us all day. Pilgrims were pouring into the great church and the Saint's birthplace next door, stopping to drink water gushing from the mouth of the "holy fountain" — a metal lobster. The interior of Loyola's birthplace was lavishly and opulently furnished with gold, silver and mosaics, giving an impression of outrageously materialistic values where spiritual ones might be expected.'

The bull-fight: 'From now on the day passed like the onset of a fast-mounting fever. Burgo and Ralph made off for the bull-ring. I was thankful not to be going; as it was I found almost intolerable the crescendo of hysteria and noise, steadily working up to discharge itself on this scene of blood and death; and when two cars drove by in which sat — well back and erect — the dignified Madame Tussaud dummies in their black hats and gold-embroidered suits who were to figure in the ring, a hoarse deep roar of "*Los toreros!*" went up from the crowd.'

Later on: 'A door leading into the ring opened, and out trundled a cart drawn by two bullocks, on which lay the carcase of a huge black bull, leaving a trail of blood in the street. Vicky was more affected by the sight than I was; partly because she wished she had seen the corrida. To me it was just a dead animal like one in a butcher's shop, but I knew that what would have horrified me was the transition from an active living animal to a dead one, and all that led up to it: the cornering of the desperate creature, its teasing and tormenting by the banderillos, the futility of its frantic efforts to defend itself.]

September 19th — Ham Spray. Holidays over, we return to find ourselves once more deep in the problems of our friends, far the most agonizing being a new and it seems possibly final breach between Robert and Janetta.

[During our absence in Spain the situation between the Kees had grown intolerable, and finally Janetta took wing to France. To us she wrote saying that she hoped never to return to married life, while a letter from Robert asked us to come to dinner and 'talk, talk, talk'. Such a break between two much-loved friends is as shattering as the sound of splintering glass in a road accident; Ralph and I both felt the tragedy bitterly, and despite our aversion to 'taking sides' in matrimonial troubles, it was natural to try and give support to the person in most pain. While we were away I believe this had been Janetta, but she was now out of reach, abroad with no address, whereas Robert was urgently needing someone sympathetic to talk to, though he admitted that he had even felt a certain relief when she left — until, that is, he got the fatal letter saying she was never coming back. Then he followed her to France and talked to her for hours, but she was still 'adamant'. Turn and turn the facts as we might, Ralph and I couldn't extract a favourable prognosis from them. According to the fiendish law that governs human emotions and makes what is unattainable much more desirable, Robert now desperately wanted Janetta back. Hearing all this, not once but many times on the telephone was, so I wrote, 'unspeakably harrowing. I said what I could, which was little, begged him to come round and see us (but I don't think he will), and went off to chop onions in the kitchen trembling so that I nearly chopped my fingers off in horror at the human capacity for inflicting and enduring pain.' Meanwhile life had to go on.]

September 20th. To London. Met Richard [Chopping] at the Society of Authors, to discuss our position with their cool, kind grey-eyed lady barrister. Richard still hopes to get another publisher, or rather is confident we can. I am not nearly so sanguine, but it seems I may get some financial compensation for my five years' unpaid work. Ralph and I went to Eliot's *Cocktail Party* in the evening — a bad play, badly acted, but thought-provoking. Next day to the National Gallery to see a magnificent late Rembrandt on loan there, and lunch with Clive and Raymond. In the evening the Memoir Club, one of the nicest meetings I remember. After eating the tenderest of ducklings cooked with cherries — a great improvement on our usual fare — we repaired to Duncan's rooms, and listened to two excellent Memoirs: Clive's on losing his virginity and Bunny's on getting to know Indians at school. Just as in near darkness Clive was describing the crucial moment on the sofa with Mrs Raven Hill, and his anxieties and doubts whether he could properly carry out what was expected of him, a feeble knock was heard on Duncan's door, and Marjorie's silver head poked in, saying in a faint, hoarse whisper: 'Duncan are you in bed?' 'No,' replied Duncan, in an equally subdued tone.

'Well, IS there any competent male present?' A roar of laughter greeted this; it came so aptly to Clive's reading.

'The fact is I'm very frightened.' Her expressive face left us in no doubt of the fact. Quentin rose gallantly to his feet, and left the room, to come back in a few moments, saying: 'She was unable to twist the cock.' There is a gas strike at present on in London, by means of which the flow is reduced so low that panicky people think it has gone out altogether. Marjorie must be one of the most alarmist of these, and she had been trying to turn it off at the main.

September 25th. I spent much of the morning writing to Janetta, now that we have an address for her in Paris. I was overflowing with things I wanted to say, but my main object was to keep contact with her. Then out into the garden to pick some of the purple and yellow September flowers, the reddening leaves, which inevitably led to thoughts of autumnal decay and then death. Fuss though we may against Capital Punishment, we none of us escape the execution shed into which we must at length be driven whether we like it or not. We must just hope not to face it too cravenly.

September 28th. A day of tidying and putting away, and of tactile pleasures: sorting through drawers and handkerchiefs, gloves and beads, for instance, with their different textures — soft, velvety, silken, hard or bright. Then cooking and bottling our home-grown tomatoes. Skinning them I felt like a surgeon, with sleeves rolled up dipping the hot fruit into cold water, seeing the thin skin come off like red rubber gloves. A bird was singing piercingly in the garden and a cloud of gnats danced outside the kitchen window. And all day the telephone went on ringing like a motif in an opera.

In the afternoon came a fat letter from Janetta. She doesn't seem to have resented anything I said in mine, and almost all of hers was about Robert. There is no mention of other people in her life. She talks of perhaps going to Rome, looking at pictures and 'being un-domestic'.

Saxon has been here for a few days. His stock is rather low with Ralph, and I felt I must make up by listening to a long account of all the various parts of his person — eyes, teeth, rheumaticky hands in turn, with their weaknesses, recent history and future prospects very carefully gone into. We walked to the village together, while he ran over the names of some French and Spanish towns asking: 'What was that *other* town I wanted to go to?' Or 'Where did that painter live?', as if these were what Freddie Ayer calls 'significant questions'. (I have been reading *Logical Positivism* with great pleasure and interest, and now want to go back to earlier favourites such as Berkeley, Hume and Mill and sort out my beliefs.)

I've started typing Ralph's book.

October 5th. The cheerful voice of Mary Campbell came over the telephone at breakfast time. They are just back from France and had been told by the Pritchetts about the Kee tragedy, which she said had upset her terribly and given her nightmares all night. Then she read me part of a letter from Philip Toynbee announcing that he was 'as good as married and tomorrow would be as bad as married'.

Drove to Oxford to fetch Robert, who had been doing some work there. The beauty of the pale green rolling downs on the way was quite blotted out on our return journey by my intense absorption in conversation with him. We might have been driving through a long tunnel for all I saw. With his violent life-instinct it is impossible for him to sit back and await developments patiently. In this he is very unlike Janetta who, when trouble strikes, folds her head under her wing and sinks to the bottom like a stone. But Robert is already swimming vigorously, and much that he said this afternoon was greatly to the credit of his candour and sense of reality.

October 7th. We have exchanged Robert for Raymond and Janie, the shadowy side of whose genial character is suppressed bitterness, but she is excellent company. I don't think Raymond, amusing and full of ideas as he is, can be called a very good talker (some *do* think him one as a matter of fact) because his conversation too easily gets on to a well-worn track or even a slightly modish tone supported by such words as 'dazzling', 'rewarding', 'riveting'. The really good talker's response to life

is too original and inventive to rely on catch-phrases. V.S.P.,
Julia and Gerald all have the good talker's gift, and it magnetizes
attention. But what a strange thing it is, this ectoplasm spouting
endlessly out of mouths, and usually carried off into oblivion.

October 9th. How busy I feel now that I have nothing to do! And
how on earth did I fit my flower book in? It's not only prep school
boys who abandon a craze for conkers and take up stamp-
collecting instead. I'm well aware of fickle attention, whirling
round like a lighthouse in the darkness, illuminating one thing
after another — flowers, moths, Henry James, music, philosophy — everything by turns.

    After lunch we took the train to London. I went off to the
Opera Club with Saxon, where we saw two short operas: a
Milhaud, which began with the heroine singing loudly 'Are you
fond of dancing?', and the hero singing in reply: 'In a *way*, yes.'
And secondly a very jolly Donizetti called *The Night Bell*. Back at
Oakley Street I found Julia sitting over the fire with Ralph like a
nice domestic cat, and we had a very cosy chat. Her view of the
Kees is that they are both so handsome, talented and above all
lucky, that they will soon be quite all right and there's no need to
be sorry for them. (Julia's version of the world includes a premiss
that everyone but herself is lucky.)

October 12th. We lunched with Robert in a Swiss restaurant. He
seems to be doing very well at his process of reconstruction, and
the Life Force is hard at work; but the children are a problem, and
Robert is worried about Georgie, who is still in the charge of Mrs
Brenan, their daily. Noticing that she was walking oddly he took
her to Selfridges to buy new shoes and found that the ones she
was wearing were indeed much too small. Robert continued:
'Georgie suddenly made a most fearful mess on the floor. I asked
where the lavatory was and when we got there of course it was a
Ladies and they wouldn't let me in, "but we'll have the little
chap". I said "She *is* a lady," and had to let her go in alone.' This
story illustrates in concrete form something that is worrying
many of the Kees' friends. It's clear from her letters that Janetta is
missing her children badly, but she has made no mention of their
missing her. Ralph and I have been discussing the possibility of
going to Paris to see her, but only if she seemed to want us to.

Above: Ralph and
Richard Chopping
at Ham Spray

Right: Robert and
Janetta

Ralph and Burgo at Lugano

Above left: Burgo at Lugano

Right: Vicky Strachey

Left: Mary Campbell and girls with Philip Toynbee at a point-to-point

Below: Frances, Vicky and Burgo in France

Mary Campbell and Raymond Mortimer

Eardley Knollys at Long Crichel

Ralph in the Dordogne Valley

Richard Chopping and Sebastian Sprott at Ham Spray

Robert   Janetta

Above: Janetta, Robin Campbell, Frances and Ralph at Buis

Left: Janetta at Buis-les-Baronnies

Breakfast at Ham Spray. Ralph and the Hendersons

Mary Campbell with Nell Dunn and Robert at our château in Vaucluse

Above: The four Garnett girls at Hilton

Left: Straffen in the dock, drawn by FP

October 19th. A little pepper was thrown over the morning by a letter from Allen Lane saying he had been approached by another publisher about the Flower Book. I felt flustered by this almost certain red herring, and also by the knowledge that I can't really ask Ralph's advice because he has all along been defeatist, and said my contract is worthless and that I shan't get a penny of compensation. I taxed him with this, and he admitted in the most surprising but honest way that he thought he felt jealous of the book, and especially of my cooperation with another man, namely Richard! I asked him if he would have been jealous if Richard had been a woman, and he said he thought so.

October 22nd. A letter from my heroine, the Society of Authors' barrister, telling me that Lane had agreed to pay me £1,500, and we are free to take the book elsewhere! I try to stretch the jaws of imagination to swallow this enormous *bonne bouche*, but find it very difficult. I have begun to consider whether a spring trip to North Africa or Damascus or Italy would be nicest. Ralph is very pleased too.

November 3rd. A visit to Christopher Turton's asylum outside Bristol. We were taken to the encephalographic department where he was working, and given station tea in very thick cups, while he brought out graphs to show us, each with its several black wiggly lines and one red.

'This is an epileptic having a fit' (a wild series of up and down jerks), 'and here is an unepileptic schizo — quite normal.' In the next room was the machine itself — a fantastic affair as big as an Aga cooker but covered with switches and knobs in brilliant colours. Very soon the first patient arrived, one of four epileptics from the Incurables department of the asylum. She was an old lady, who hobbled in and without any fuss prepared to lie down on a bed in a small ante-room. I was surprised and touched by the docile trusting manner of all four patients, but also shocked by the fact that they obviously didn't realize they were mere guinea-pigs, and thought they were being given some form of treatment. One asked, 'Will it hurt?' but took no convincing that it wouldn't. There in turn lay these shapeless sacks of old womanhood (one had twisted-up toes like the Dame in a pantomime) while a sort of hairnet was fixed over their heads and a rubber sponge under their chins. They were then wired up to the machine itself round which we and the doctors crowded, watching rows of mechanical pens inscribing with incredible delicacy on a moving strip of paper the actual life of the brain. What a sight! A series of small waves sometimes worked itself into a crescendo of alpine peaks. The doctors ignored what looked like a large variation from the normal, but pounced eagerly on some tiny zig-zag. 'That looks significant! Oh yes, I think we could almost go to court on that.' Most of the things they said might have been in a foreign language, they were so humiliatingly unintelligible. The old women were made to open and shut their eyes, subjected to flashing lights, and all the time the pens went on inexorably writing in their awe-inspiring way the actual language of the brain. Then Christopher would say, 'Shall we *trigger* her?' and yet another machine was brought into play, with the fiendish purpose, I gathered, of getting each patient as near having a fit as possible. I was struck by the intense happiness, as well as detached absorption expressed on the research workers' faces.

Christopher took us to other departments, where among retorts and test-tubes were more workers, all with the same dreamily happy intellectual faces, peering beyond the obvious surface of things into an enthralling hinterland visible only to them. In another laboratory white rats, scarred and painted yellow, were moving about apathetically in cages. 'They were operated on twenty-five days ago and they're still alive,' said the research worker in charge in a tone of faint surprise. In yet another a huge and miraculous glass construction stood near the window catching the sunlight, while some liquid dripped from bulb to bulb of a glass tube — a most poetical sight. 'What are these?' we asked pointing to a glass bell containing what looked like potted shrimps. 'Oh just some bullocks' pineal glands; we hope to have some fun with them.'

We left, immensely impressed by the happiness of the research workers and the moonlike eeriness of modern science. All the complicated and expensive apparatus we had seen made up, to my eyes, a voluptuous Haroun-el-Raschid display more staggering even than the glitter of gold, glass and mosaics we saw at Loyola.

Arrived home in a state of great stimulation, and found my cheque from Penguin books awaiting me, also a short, sad letter from Robert.

November 30th. A flying visit from Boris and Maroussa. She is living in a state of constant terror, surprising in view of the courage with which she stood the bombing in the war and the escape from France. Now it is burglars she chiefly dreads: as ill-luck would have it the pub next door to them was broken into and she lay in bed paralysed with fear, hearing them take away cases of drink and terrified lest she should betray her presence to them. She daren't go to the cinema, her greatest pleasure, for fear of being attacked, and when Boris goes out she gets quietly drunk to calm herself.

Boris' doctor brother Glyep has had the most ghastly experience. His wife was bitten by a rabid dog, in Egypt I think it was, but some distance from the nearest Pasteur Institute. She was whisked off and injected, and when the danger period came to an end they went to a ball to celebrate. When they returned that night Glyep looked at the place where she had been bitten and saw to his horror that it had swollen up, showing that she had taken the disease. It meant a certain terrible death, rather than which he took her to hospital and killed her.

December 1st. Soon after the Anreps had left we set off for a visit to Crichel. The air was sharp with frost, and a pale greenish-blue sky lay reflected between black leafless twigs in the still ponds we passed on our way. Not long after our arrival more visitors came to tea — Lady Juliet Duff, Somerset Maugham, and a rather colourless female described as 'a *nice* woman' by Eddy. I sat next to Somerset Maugham at tea and was charmed by him. He belongs in the reptile house, a chameleon by choice, with his pale deeply furrowed face, sunken glittering eyes and the mouth that opens deliberately and sometimes sticks there — as he has a distinct stammer.

A delicious dinner, much jolly talk and Canasta. After Eddy had gone off to bed very tired, Raymond pushed his chair suddenly from the card-table, knocking over and breaking a lamp made of glass. He appeared to be quite unworried, and Eardley said 'Good. That was the only unpleasant object in the room.' However, at breakfast next morning Eddy looked delicately distressed. 'Yes I know,' he said, 'I've got over it now, but I was *terribly* upset. I nearly burst into tears when I heard about it. It was almost my favourite possession.'

It's a great pleasure being at Crichel. Of all our three hosts

(Desmond is away) Eddy is the most attentive. His exquisite sensitivity to his own feelings in no way prevents him being aware of those of other people, and I was several times struck by the diverse range of those he talked about with interest and affection. So long as they don't rise above the Plimsoll line of his distaste — by having dirty fingernails for instance — he enjoys his friends to the full. He delights one by the quality of his personality, much as Boris does, but oh so differently; his charm comes out in the rather medieval beauty of his face, his sudden laugh and quick pungent remarks. Eardley has just taken to painting with enormous enthusiasm. He took us to see his pictures in a studio over the garage.

It was a beautiful morning, steely and fine, the lawn powdered thinly with frost or snow. I took myself for a solitary walk, and set up a snow-white pheasant crouching in the ivy on the bank. Went into the churchyard to see how the house looked through the tombstones, and disturbed a little wren in the vestry. Somehow such poignant moments contrast with the mainly indoor life of this household; if anything is lacking it is the farmyard warmth of family life.

An exchange: Eardley: 'When Raymond goes to Paris I shall read *Madame Bovary* — in English.' Eddy: 'Don't you mind *me*?'

December 8th — Ham Spray. While Ralph was working away steadily in his library I squelched my way through the sodden leaves in the Snowdrop wood, pulling my rubber boots out with difficulty one by one and thinking of what? Burgo and Janetta, and as usual Death — and the contradictory sensations of security and precariousness one gets from its being *there*, round the corner.

The more philosophy I read the more I am amazed by its inexhaustibility. Though the cleverest minds of every age have been considering its problems for centuries there has never been a question of settling any of them once and for all, yet by their very nature they force one to think that they have the truth concealed in them, possible to find. Going on looking into them seems at times to be like trying to apply scientific investigation to the infinite series of reflections in the opposite mirrors of a restaurant.

December 10th. Pouring with rain again, yet at breakfast our spirits were high and we talked about enjoying life. Who would have expected when young that in middle age there is such intense excitement to be had just from being alive. That is justification enough, Ralph said, for having brought a child into this wicked, frightening world — no need to seek further.

Psycho-analysts can be very crazy. I have been reading a clever Miss Sharpe's collected papers, largely about Shakespeare. It is really too absurd to talk of King Lear as 'His Majesty the Baby' just as in *The Nursery World*, or toss off a remark that his Knights, who made such a lot of trouble in the houses of Goneril and Regan, were of course *faeces*. Any airs, winds or blasts from hell became farts, and jaws of the tomb the womb, and so forth. It's so easy, for everything *is* rather like everything else in some respect. I am enormously impressed by the profound truths discovered by Freud, and believe him to be one of the most important thinkers of the century; but then up pops the stereo-typed language of the Id, Ego and Super-ego, seen by people like Miss Sharpe as concretely as Punch, Judy and Jack Ketch. (In fact she would probably have equated them had she thought of it!) Anyway I found the book stimulating as well as quite ludicrous.

[Christmas was fast approaching with all its connected problems. We had invited Robert to bring Georgie to Ham Spray, and at first he said he definitely would; later he qualified this by saying that if Janetta wanted to come and see Georgie then, he would absent himself. The reasonable thing would have been for Georgie to stay with us long enough for her to be with both parents in turn. But it was hardly a question of reason by now and events conspired to make this impossible.

On December 13th Robert telephoned to say that Janetta had been seen in London, and from the Campbells came the first news that Derek Jackson was pressing her to marry him. On the same day Burgo came back from school ill; feverish, and depressed because he had had a return of his 'worries' last term. Two days later Janetta rang me up (the sound of her voice, low but calm, was what had been lacking all through these long tortured weeks). She told us she would like to come and see us in January, but there was no grain of comfort for Robert in what she said. On the 21st Sonia Orwell telephoned to say that Janetta had gone back to Paris and Robert to the Campbells at Stokke.

Writing now, some time later, my impression is that the

nightmare colouring of the beginning of the holidays (because of Robert's tragedy, Burgo's illness and the piercing cold) persisted through Christmas. To take the place of Robert and Georgie we invited Lawrence and Julia, and they seemed pleased to come.]

1951

January 2nd to 4th. We left Wiltshire under cover of thin snow. It grew thicker and thicker as we travelled east, and by the time we were on our way to the Ivy for lunch with Clive and Isobel Strachey, enormous flakes as big, round and flat as halfpence were lying quite unmelted on the coats, hats and umbrellas of Londoners, as they trudged through the deep slush like absurd Father Christmases.

I had arranged to meet Janetta that afternoon at our hotel, the Great Western, and as I sat waiting for her my heart beat quite fast with agitation. She has been so long the unseen and unheard focus of our thoughts, conversations and conflicting feelings, that it was I suppose inevitable that a certain unresolved sediment remaining from all the pain and anxiety, lay as it were before her door, and she must needs kick it over to come out. She came in looking very charming, and more like the Bohemian of past days than I had expected, unconsciously affected probably by thoughts of Derek Jackson and Claridges. She was wearing nothing but a little short green corduroy jacket over camel's hair trousers, in spite of the bitter weather. We went up to our bedroom and talked and talked until Ralph and Burgo returned. I think she was afraid I would 'take sides' — and not hers. When she had finished her account of the last months she asked 'Do you still hope I will go back to Robert?' It was true that we had hoped; now, seemingly, it was no longer possible. In any case we could only have *wanted* what made her happy. I don't think any harm was done by our talk. She has promised to come to Ham Spray in a few days, and after we had had tea with Ralph and Burgo sitting in the portly green leather hotel chairs, I saw her slip off into the night looking very defenceless against the cold and toughness of life, pale, thin and with a ghastly cough. I was left understanding more, and loving her as much as always.

Charlie's Aunt on our first night, *Traviata* at Covent Garden the next, and on the 4th we returned to Ham Spray with Janetta and her two children. We saw them arrive in the obscurity of Paddington Station, flanked by a supporting figure — Derek Jackson. He greeted us with effusive embarrassment, and the hardly remembered flavour of his personality came wafting across: the over-excited manner, muffled speech, small bright intelligent eyes. He is not without a good deal of charm. Little Georgie was fussed and inclined to break into wails. Janetta looked even more ill than before, and very anxious.

January 5th to 10th — Ham Spray. Child-life was dominant, but talk went on in its intervals. Georgie is a charming little being, whose physical presence (so like both her parents and therefore tangible proof of the unity that is lost), is moving in a special way.

The impression left by these five days is that with that gentle indomitableness that is so characteristic of her, Janetta is pulling herself out of a morass. Derek seems to be the main figure in her life, but I would guess that 'love' is not what she feels for him at present. She and the children went to London one day to do Nicky's school shopping — she is going to boarding school. Next day Burgo went back to Millfield.

January 12th. Back they all came, Nicky — poor little creature — intoxicated by her school clothes and the vista of life that they evoke. What pleases her most is her school tie — a horrid shiny green striped one — and she insisted on putting it on at once. When I was reading aloud to her tonight I couldn't resist adding a school tie here and there to the characters ('the sailors were all dressed in smart blue uniforms *and school ties*') for the pleasure of seeing Nicky double up, turn pink and say 'Not *really*? No, you're *teasing*!'

Janetta has been wonderfully successful in restoring Georgie's sense of security, and I think is very happy to have her with her.

Tonight the Campbells brought Cyril and his new wife Barbara [Skelton] to dinner. Though Mary mistrusts Cyril she was anxious to make the weekend 'go', and she is a great one for rising to occasions. The evening 'went' pretty well I too think, though I feel faint resentment at the way everyone lays out the red carpet for Cyril just because he seems to expect it. Nevertheless I exerted myself to cook a reasonably good meal and please and flatter him, because I knew Mary, Robin and Janetta all wanted him kept happy. I got the impression he disliked me, and was amazed when Mary said afterwards that he had said he liked me very much and 'not had such an enjoyable evening for weeks'. He has become quite humpty-dumpty shaped, his egg head backed by a wild tangle of hair and merging necklessly into the larger egg of his body. Barbara his wife is pretty but aggressively silent; she absolutely refused to be drawn into the conversation.

January 19th. Janetta returns tomorrow to Sussex Place with five days in which to finish Nicky's shopping, pack her off to school, arrange for Georgie to be put on her passport (which needs Robert's consent and he isn't back from Mégève), and leave for Paris.

January 20th. I sat all day over the music-room fire trying to stifle a cold and reading with intense pleasure *Tristram Shandy*, surprised to discover that one of the world's 'masterpieces' is so obviously masterly.

Listening to the news a wave of war-memories came over me — how, in particular the encircling darkness used to represent the menace and hostility of all those dismal years. *Could* one ever bear it all again? Ralph, who wasn't unduly concerned when the Korean War began, is now inclined to think we may be in for a third world war; but he talks and presumably feels rationally about it and I'm not sure that I do.

A call from Janetta who is doggedly straightening out her life. Robert is said to be due back today, having left Mégève earlier than he meant to. Hearing of Janetta's plans to take Georgie abroad he wanted to see the *bonne* who has been engaged to look after her.

February 14th. Just before ten pm some days ago the telephone rang, shattering our peace. Ralph went to it and I heard him say 'Oh my God,' and immediately guessed who it was. It was Meyer, Millfield's headmaster, to say that Burgo hadn't been seen since tea-time. For half an hour we sat in the dining-room in a state of unnatural calm, drinking whisky and trying to prepare ourselves for a night of no news. Then the telephone rang again. It was Burgo saying, 'I've rung to tell you I'm all right.'

'Where are you?'

'I shan't tell you unless you promise not to take me back.'

Ralph promised he wouldn't do so without Burgo's agreement, and we set out to fetch him from the Bear Hotel, Devizes. The journey there passed in thoughtless relief, the journey home in gloom. Next day I had a talk with Burgo, who was sweet and grateful. I tried to discover what was wrong, but all he could say was that he was in despair, couldn't stand the other boys, they were so 'animal'. In the days that followed a new plan was hatched — by me, because Ralph had been floored by the whole affair and, though managing with a supreme effort to behave reasonably to Burgo, he is filled with what I can only call wounded pride. No one could call him conventional, yet in some way he identifies with Burgo and would like him to be a credit in the eyes of the world. It is I think a typically male attitude — or am I being unfair? The situation would almost be easier if he and Burgo didn't deeply and intensely love each other. I don't know that I can analyse my own feelings clearly yet. I can't of course see the faintest change in my own love for Burgo nor my desire to do the best for him, and there seemed so little choice that I am not gnawed by anxiety as to whether I *have* done that best. I say 'I' all the time, but Ralph has really thrown in his hand for the present.

I must describe what the 'plan' is: he is to have a room at Isobel and Charlotte's[1] in Oakley Street and go to a London tutor to work all day. He has seen Dr Glover, who approves and said that Burgo had come on and grown up no end since he saw him, and was now virtually 17½, two years older than his real age. But having been used to rely so completely on Ralph's support for most things in this life I have found it unbelievably strange to have to take all the decisions and carry them out unaided — go to Millfield and fetch Burgo's clothes, interview tutors and Glover. And although when Clive and the Hills came to stay I don't believe they noticed anything, the fact remains that Ralph and I have been living together for over a week like strangers for the first time in our lives. Not quarrelling — that might have been easier to bear.

[1] Isobel's daughter, the same age as Burgo and an old friend.

February 15th. Yesterday had the character of convalescence between Ralph and me, quiet, gentle and kindly. Perhaps it was a relief to write down all I did. This morning there came from Burgo a touching little list of accounts, plainly showing the struggle he had had to keep within his allowance. The pathos of it moved Ralph more than anything heretofore, and he is writing to tell him he needn't scrape so. For *of course* as I full well know he loves Burgo most tenderly. (But alas where there is love there is usually jealousy.)

February 19th. Recuperation, convalescence, thaw. I begin to see Ralph's point of view more and he mine. We have seen various friends and their light on our problem is salutary. 'What would *you* have done?' I asked the Campbells. It is a good way of disarming criticism because no one can think of anything. Nobody so far has suggested ruthlessly returning Burgo to Millfield. The Stones[1] thought it a promising sign of character in him. Gerald took the line that children were a fearful nuisance and the less one saw of them the better. Gamel, meaning to be tactful but not succeeding, told us how some really horrible boy she knew eventually turned out very well! Julia has been far the most consoling:

['I'm quite sure there's nothing to be worried about,' she wrote. 'As regards Burgo himself I feel strongly that his behaviour, though inconvenient, is very healthy and normal, and it shows he has character and spirit and sensibility in my opinion. Of *course* the schoolboys he sees are barbarous animals; I don't doubt it; and if he is upset by this — well, all honour to him say I. I wouldn't have it otherwise. You know Burgo has developed into the most charming, sweet, intelligent fellow, as I observed with my own eyes and ears, and just because he *is* so intelligent and emotional he is very naturally causing trouble in these difficult years. I hear from Isobel that he is turning Communist and is taking her to a Communist meeting!']

[1] Reynolds and Janet.

February 24th. We spent three days in London this week and they have certainly cast a new light on Burgo's démarche. We had lunch with him on arrival, at a tea-shop near his tutor's; I looked out and saw him crossing the road through the pelting rain and felt sure his morale was good. He strode along in a purposeful manly way — there was none of that cornered, hunched appearance that sometimes greeted us on collecting him from Millfield. Later we saw him at a cocktail party of Isobel's and next day we took him to supper and a Mozart concert. I was glad to learn that he had thanked Julia effusively for asking him out to tea, and taken the trouble to ring up Saxon for giving him dinner at his club. His emotional steam is, oddly enough, provided by Communism, and he buys the *Daily Worker* every day. This produced digs from Ralph but he took them good-humouredly.

We lunched with Robert one day, still sad I fear and rootless. He came back with us for a weekend of reading, writing, music and lots of talk. His spell-binding quality never seems to desert him.

February 28th — Ham Spray. I feel rather like a bat hanging upside down in the dark, and even when devoured by fleas putting out small hook-like claws and clutching surrounding objects — such things as a wonderful little group of yellow dwarf irises spotted with black that has sprung up outside the dining-room window in a miraculous fashion. True I planted them there, but I never expect what I plant to grow, nor does it generally. And there is the frenzied early morning singing of the birds.

Ralph has been to Broadmoor again, and brought back a mad letter which was pressed upon him by one of the patients with an air of special urgency. It was written in a niggling, tiny hand. There was an immensely complicated date ending 'C Period'; and it was addressed to 'Lady Neta Dece' and signed 'Baron Sir Pammell Herod, Imperial Monarch and Emperor, Herod.' Ralph takes what I can only call an affectionate delight in his lunatics' eccentricities.

March 13th. This afternoon I had another go at Hume's *Treatise*. I think of philosophy as a great forbidding house of large rooms, which I hesitate to enter. I walk round, go up the drive, even ring the bell and retreat, before I actually enter the cold interior, where there is the same chill grandeur. Step by step I'm seduced in, and begin studying the pictures and furniture; only my mind wanders off and I wake up as if from a dream and find I am staring at a shut door. That's the *difficulty* of it — as for the pleasure it is much like that of reading music. How amazing that those black inverted match-sticks on the page can be translated into movements which magically produce the very sounds which ran in Haydn or Beethoven's head. But though the printed words bring one in contact with the thoughts of Hume, it's no good just knowing their meaning; an active process of interpretation is needed, requiring a drastic mental effort.

Easter Week-end. Olivier Popham came last night and Quentin this evening. They seem to like each other — what a pity they shouldn't make a match. The Campbells, Julia, Anthony Blunt and Ben Nicolson to dinner. Olivier is the easiest and most companionable of visitors, but I noticed she didn't join any discussion, such as one about vulgarity and another on aesthetics. Burgo was home for the weekend, rather thin but giggly and cheerful, talking of everything including Communism. We had a walk on the downs flying his kite, the poetry game and quite a lot of fun.

March 29th. Mary rang up to say she had heard from Derek Jackson that Robert seemed to be objecting to a divorce 'under instructions from Ham Spray'. As no one has even mentioned the subject to us we were quite annoyed.

Later, however, Janetta rang up, in a much more confident and happier voice, sounding as though she would like to see us when we came to France. She then wanted to speak to Ralph. Would he ask Robert to divorce her? For legal reasons she couldn't do so herself.

Ralph: 'Does this mean you want to marry Derek?'

Janetta: 'No. I don't want to marry anyone. I never do.'

In the odd way that convictions have of settling on one suddenly like birds perching, I remember that as the car turned into the drive this morning the sense of the pathos of human beings overwhelmed me with a surge of emotion. For the most part *they only want to be liked.* Yet what do they do? Spend all their spare moments rending each other's characters into shreds, or pouncing eagerly on small defects and weaknesses.

[*May 9th to 19th.* A short holiday in France in the company of millionaires.[1] Ralph, Robin Campbell and I took the train to Valence, and thence to the little town of Buis-les-Baronnies, where Janetta's mother Jan had spent the war after she was banned from the coast by the Germans. Janetta was keen to see it and arranged to meet us there, and Mary (who was travelling with Philip Dunn and their two girls, Serena and Nell) was to pick up Robin. A complicated and not at all easy set of combinations.

Buis stands in a charming valley full of fruit-trees, with Mont Ventoux in the background, snow-capped, and yellow tulips, grape hyacinths and narcissus in the foreground. The village centres round a small arcaded *place*, and is full of fine crumbling old houses with beautiful wooden doors.

We stayed in the inn where Jan had taken refuge and helped in the kitchen. The André family had been very fond of her and were longing to see Janetta. She and Derek arrived for two nights in a nine-seater Ford, and soon afterwards came the Dunns in a brand new monster with a wireless spouting *Mrs Dale's Diary*. After they had all gone away Ralph and I talked with amazement and I must confess disapproval of their way of foreign travel. Robin was the only one who wanted to soak in his surroundings, walk about the village and into the fields. The others were perfectly content to sit in cafés all day long drinking endless pernods, talking loudly, seeming to expect local admiration and certainly getting it in the case of their cars. Derek kept up a good deal of buffoonery with imitations in French — sometimes funny, sometimes not. The Andrés welcomed him and Janetta most warmly and brought out old photos and books which Jan had left behind. I think she was much moved by this revival of Jan's ghost. She was looking very pretty in extremely short shorts, but thin and tense; smiling and friendly however. Everyone wanted to make things 'go' and on the whole I think they did.]

[1] Derek Jackson and Philip Dunn.

June 2nd — Ham Spray. In the morning I had a drink with Mary in the Shalbourne pub. She was at the top of her form, set up by a visit to London 'in my new blue chip hat' to go out with an old flame, an American, who gave her unlimited caviare and good wine. They came to see us later in the afternoon, as she rang up to say Robin was disgruntled and 'clamouring for Partridges'. He was reacting by becoming aggressively highbrow to Mary's immersion in the worldly pleasures of the Season (in order to 'bring out' Serena), and took a comically stuffy line about Gilbert and Sullivan.

Ice-cold, wintry weather, dark grey clouds under which the tender greenery lies like a mockery. I have been suffering rather from world depression, and liable to pitch into the abyss when I read about all nations frantically devoting themselves to making lethal weapons. But I have developed a technique rather like that of the Euston Road painters — 'point to point realism' they used to call it — by which (like a fly) I crawl from one material objective to another, not looking further afield than is necessary.

[*August and September*. We took a second longer holiday, with Burgo, in Ibiza to join Darsie Japp and his family who had rented two little houses there. Flew by unpressurized aeroplane to Palma, and thence by sea to the small pyramidal town of Ibiza, where a crowd stood waving and shouting; and suddenly we saw that we too had our welcoming friend, for there was Darsie Japp, and a weak cry of 'Ralph!' floated up to us. He drove us to our hotel: it was like a set for a Somerset Maugham play about life on a tropical island, and kept by seven German-Jewish refugees, known locally as the Seven Dwarfs. The Japps have made quite a few friends — in particular Eduardo, a painter from Ecuador, and an aristocratic Spanish couple who speak English when alone 'because of the servants'.

The warm pellucid sea, the beauty of the persons and clothes of the natives (long plaited hair, much gold and silver jewellery, silken skirts and shawls), all this was truly marvellous. When they danced, the girls scuttled round with small hither-and-thither steps and head and eyes demurely cast down, while their men approached them in what seemed like an excess of sexual frenzy, and without actually touching them kept up a continuous wild high kicking and leaping. This violently male behaviour applied to the marked modesty of the females had a very erotic effect, as did the monotonous Moorish music on pipe, tom-tom and castanets.

We met the Japps every day to bathe; Darsie entertained us with his stories. One was about the wife of Max Ernst, who was a great hypochondriac. One day she remembered about the cramp got from bathing too soon after a meal, and rushed out of the sea crying '*Max! Max! La congestion, comment ça commence?*' '*Avec la mort!*'

In the aeroplane going home a little girl of six took up her paper bag and tentatively put her face into it. Her brother: 'Look, she's going to be sick!' Little girl: 'Do I put my eyes in

it?' Her father: 'No, don't put your eyes in.' Little girl: 'Then I
can't do it.' And she didn't.]

[Darsie Japp was a painter of the school of Henry Lamb and
Augustus John, a particular friend of Henry himself, of Boris
Anrep and Faith Henderson. I remember him first in the
Twenties when he was living not far from Ham Spray with his
Spanish wife Lucila and their two daughters, in a prosperous-
seeming country house with a large garden and ponies for the
two girls. The rumour was that he had once been rich and even
owned one or two race-horses. If this was so he probably cared
little for money, or else was reckless with it, for they lived later
on modestly in Chelsea. The family came over to Ham Spray one
memorable evening when an impromptu dance was held; Darsie
and Lucila were both beautiful dancers and they gave a display of
the tango and tried to teach it to us all, including Lytton.

I never knew anyone who could resist Darsie's unostentatious
charm: he had exquisite manners, much interest in people and a
certain debonair, dashing quality which he retained into old age.
Yet I suspect that there was a layer of melancholy deep in his
nature. He told me he often lay awake half the night reading.
'What do you read?' 'Usually poetry — sometimes *Don Quixote*.'
His growing deafness must have caused him sorrow, and in old
age it became a serious bar to what would otherwise have been
fascinating conversation. His visitor would bellow some complicated and tedious remark in foghorn tones only to be greeted by
Darsie's folding back his jacket to reveal a little machine modestly
tucked away beneath it, and dumbly asking for it to be repeated.
(This predicament was amusingly described by Julia Strachey in a
sketch called 'Cosmic Toes' in *Julia by herself and F.P.*)

Lucila and the younger girl, Juanita, shared the same Spanish
vitality and practical efficiency. Juanita married Euphemia
Grove's doctor son Christopher, and we saw quite a lot of her.]

December 4th — Ham Spray. All three to a concert in Newbury, of
wind instruments played by Denis and Leonard Brain and others.
Like circus ponies in tight bearing-reins, like the Dong with the
luminous nose they sat nodding in their chairs, transmitting their
airy music for our delight. Beside the weightlessness of the
sounds they make, they have a human poignancy; especially was
this true of the Horn, marvellously played by Denis Brain (a sleek

seal-shaped young man); its notes seemed to come straight from a human heart.

December 8th. To London with bad toothache — once in the lee of the G.W. Hotel I had no desire to leave, but we had tickets for *Billy Budd*, 'a queer's heaven' as Robert calls it, and it is true that not a woman appears on the stage (rather as if a composer left out the violins in his symphony) not even a boy's treble, and only homosexual emotions figure. The climax comes when Captain 'Starry' Vere and Billy Budd, condemned to be hanged, are shut together in Vere's Stateroom. A spotlight plays on the door (as in *Peter Pan* — 'do you believe in fairies?' Do you indeed?) And thirty-four triads, to which the critics have referred in surprise, punctuate the space of time when the sentence is being conveyed to Budd. The imagination can deal with this as it chooses. But what makes the drama to me so unmoving is that Budd is a tiresome prig, the good boy who sucks up to the headmaster and even when doomed to die is oozing with hero-worship.

After the opera we went to the Hills for red wine and cheese. Here we found the painter John Nash, a charming small birdlike man, with prominent eyes and an unusually high voice. Back to a night made hideous by toothache, and an awakening with my face swollen out like a vulgar postcard. Draw a veil.

December 11th. Face going down steadily — what a relief. Ralph and I lunched with Robert at the Étoile. He has come to terms with his life — or so it seems — and resembles a comet shooting among new skies and strange planets. However, he is still the same charming, funny, fiery Robert. He describes Janetta as having become very firm and decided; this is probably the front she deliberately presents to him.

To Francis Bacon's private view — only six canvases, three being of Popes in purple robes, shouting, declaiming or simply glaring, each from within a shadowy glass box. No one can deny his impressiveness.

December 15th — Ham Spray. All to Aldbourne to lunch with the Brenans, who leave tomorrow to fly to America where one of Gamel's brothers is dying. Success has set them both up like a tonic: Gerald's *Face of Spain* has had an excellent reception, and Gamel is delighted by good reviews of her Spanish translation,

The Spendthrifts by Perez Galdós. What a pretty old lady she will become! Gerald, as at all moments of excitement, was looking positively Chinese, his black eyes reduced to slits by intensity of feeling.

[In 1930 when Gerald Brenan invited us to meet the girl he meant to marry, we went to the encounter full of curiosity. What would she be like? The previous objects of his love had been too various, from Carrington onwards, to give us a clue. We found a young woman whose appearance was arresting; one saw at once that Gamel Woolsey had a beautiful face, though rather pale and sad, noticed next that she held herself badly and with a sort of apathy, an effect enhanced by the 'arty' clothes she was wearing — shapeless purple silk embroidered with bright coloured wools.

Gerald had been Ralph's earliest friend and always confided in him. He soon told us how he had found Gamel in Dorset, staying amongst the Powys family of writers, and actually involved in an intense but difficult love-affair with Llewellyn Powys, whose wife was her best friend. Before that she had lived in the American deep South, suffered several attacks of T.B. and spent her time lying on a sofa reading poetry and writing it, surrounded by the easy-going civilization of a plantation, and with devoted negro servants hurrying to pick up a dropped handkerchief or do her least bidding. Gerald thought an income of £350 a year was enough to marry on, and Gamel agreed, but emotion brought on a haemorrhage and she spent the first months of their joint life in a sanatorium. All in all the start of their 'marriage' (it was legitimized later) was fraught with unreality. But Gamel had plenty of character as well as a good mind with a sharp edge of irony to it; she set herself valiantly to lead the life of a poor man's wife in a small Dorset cottage.

When Gerald returned to Spain and began to achieve success as a writer Gamel blossomed as 'la Señora', of whom hardly more was expected than to give a symbolical stir to the marmalade oranges and snip the dead heads off flowers. She developed an individual taste in dress and was the centre of a little salon of admirers; for Gamel was a poetess, who had published one slim volume, who had an air of great distinction, and loved to talk about poetry. As well as her translation from Galdós she wrote an excellent account of the Spanish Civil War from an expatriate's point of view, *Death's Other Kingdom*.]

December 31st. What can I say about the last ten days of this old year? Burgo went to London for a party at Charlotte's and returned dead beat having slept not at all but obviously enjoyed himself. The party broke up at five, when it turned out that four other boys and young men were all expecting to sleep on the same sofa as the one he had been promised. 'We spent the night groaning,' he said, 'and everyone got up every few minutes. I had the broadish arm of the sofa, and was lying half on top of the son of the inventor of the jet engine.'

On the 22nd came Robert and Georgie, a dear little girl with a gentle voice and Janetta's lovely grey eyes and long black lashes. When Robert is about she makes a bid for spoiling, so that she ends up most meals on his lap with him feeding her. Anyone else was rejected if they offered assistance, but when left alone with me she was as good as gold, trotting to and fro on her own devices. Robert had brought with him trunks full of toys, and he pondered deeply over her stocking, which was one of my longest stuffed right to the top. No wonder that she burst into tears when all the opening was over and her emotions deflated. Starting manfully as nursemaid, poor Robert found it an exhausting task and to see him wrestling with it wrung my heart, although he got great pleasure I think from her dependence on him. Georgie shows one sign of her background having been disturbed — a tendency to reject all offerings at first blush: 'No-o-o. DOO-O-ONT *want* it.'

I have felt harrowed by having Robert here, and that he is still a deeply unhappy man. He agreed that his philosophy of life is that it is hell, but that one must and could extract one's own happiness from it. According to the Third Programme this is the message of Francis Bacon's painting, and also (according to Robin) the Existentialist's philosophy. Strength through Misery, it might be called.

1952

January 1st. I start the New Year with some courage and a sort of philosophy of life. There is a lot of friendliness circulating in the passages like the warm air from our new radiators. Ralph, too, seems to be manfully turning over *his* new leaf by working steadily in the library.

In the evening all three of us had a talk about financing Burgo in London; Ralph is giving him a bank account and he is delighted. After which we set off for the Campbells where we spent a delightful evening in that warm friendly atmosphere, along with the Pritchetts, drinking some glorious wine — a present from Derek.

January 19th. A lovely cold blue day, sparkling and clear, with a N.E. wind — but not too strong to spoil our morning walk to the windmill on Ham Hill, though we had to forge our way against wind and sun together, leaning into them, blinded, exhilarated and drenched by them. Then turning, we had sun and wind at our backs and peace reigned, while an incomparable light only belonging to winter shone on the landscape, bringing out the texture of things like so many different stuffs — tweedy thatch, the velour of grass, and ivy leaves polished like mirrors. Our long shadows lay on the road ahead of us, and all round was a delicate grey tracery cast by the bare trees.

Much of the time we talked about how we could describe the *Zeitgeist* of today — sad, embittered, afraid, disillusioned with the scientists, who once seemed about to dispense what religion no longer gives — faith, but have not done so. Theirs is the great betrayal — '*la trahison des scientistes*' — by deliberately applying their brains to destruction. It is a joyless age too, an age of gin-sozzling and drug-taking even by school children; and of over-riding preoccupation with material things like television sets.

Burgo's new London lodgings seem to be a great success. Jane [Ainley], his landlady, writes: 'Burgo fits in very well and we all like him immensely. He is most kind and helpful about the sitting-in.[1] We had a small party for the Hinchingbrooke girls who are about his age, and everyone liked each other. Burgo was most amusing at dinner.' Music to our ears!

[1]For her two small children.

February 6th to 11th. What a surprise! As I was cooking lunch I heard Mrs Hoare's steps thudding along the passage and down the kitchen stairs. 'Have you heard the news? The King's dead! He died last night in his sleep. Isn't it *awful?*' My first reaction was to think 'Lucky fellow, to die so peacefully.' Then came the implications: a young Queen, new stamps, court mourning — only faintly interesting, but certainly not 'awful'. The wireless has entirely failed to rise to the occasion — first it shut down everything but news. Now all three programmes jointly broadcast the silliest, most nondescript items in their repertory, punctuated by bulletins of thunderous gravity and richly revelled-in emotional unbuttoning. One note they strike is the 'Three Mourning Queens', another is that the late King's devotion to duty is what killed him. Richard Dimbleby made a bold bid to coin a name for him in the history books, by several times calling him 'George the Faithful'. The whole effect is of 'ham' acting; and a lot of nonsense is being talked about 'the relief necessary to our tortured feelings'. What the public is feeling is a sense of great drama, not at all unpleasant; the magnificent sight of a coffin surmounted by a crown and draped with the royal standard carried on the shoulders of enormous guardsmen. (What if they dropped it, muffed it, or let the crown roll on the ground! My word!) Well then of course death is a subject deeply moving to us all, and the King perfectly symbolizes these feelings, especially with the grandeur of the public obsequies, the black-veiled Queens and so on. But to talk of personal sadness is absurd. When a great actor, artist or writer dies, one feels sad for what one will miss. (Should Max Beerbohm die it would be very sad to know that that charming personality would no longer express itself on the wireless). But the *King* is after all at once supplanted by a *Queen* who will I'm sure do just as well; and though he was probably a good, hard-working man there are plenty other such.

In fact I feel a craving for a little realism, and a talk with someone like Alix say, who is capable of being interested in this great tide of public feeling without swimming along in it.

This morning at breakfast Ralph suddenly said how feeble and old he had felt this last year, and he didn't want to be 'livened up' and made to 'hop about'. I am seriously worried about his thus giving up and accepting old age before he is sixty. Perhaps he really isn't well I thought as I drove into Hungerford, and — oh dear! — perhaps I do not look after him well enough. I resolved this morning to exert all the energy I possess (and at the moment I have quite a bit) in trying to support and sustain him and making him happier. Looking after someone so dearly and devotedly loved is after all the greatest possible pleasure.

February 14th. Off to London for three days in Barbara Bagenal's flat, two of them on my own. In the train I was alone with an erect grey-haired lady, who opened fire:

She: I must say I'm surprised at the Duke of Windsor coming over for the funeral.

F: Oh really? It seems to me quite natural.

She: Well, perhaps he's begun to see reason. He's a *quitter*, that's what he is. Wanted to have his cake and eat it, like everyone else these days.

F: Well perhaps he realizes his brother would be a better King than he would. Did you read his Memoirs?

She: (sitting even more bolt upright). No I didn't. The fact is I've no patience with him. *I'm* not one to shilly-shally!

The last remark left me speechless.

I found Percy Street immersed in an odd perplexity: Barbara's lavatory is out of order, and Sonia Brownell in the flat above dislikes hers being commandeered. The sudden importance of our excrement is a trifle ludicrous. Call on Saxon who was padding round his dusty cluttered room like a melancholy old goat dressed up. Then to see Burgo, in a nice warm cheerful room at Jane Ainley's.

Dined with Janetta at the Ivy: she looked happy, her face ironed out of strain, and was friendly and charming. It is probably true that I miss the girl of sixteen — my goodness how lovely! — who trudged round with her cloak and her stick and her 'disrespect' (a famous remark of hers was 'I disrespect you for what you've just said'); but I know that is senseless. Derek telephoned while we were dining, and asked us to join him and Sonia at their restaurant. This we did, and drank brandy among a smart crowd in funeral black and arm-bands. I still can't help thinking of Derek as a little boy, though a brilliantly clever one. His mind whirls like a mill-race but sometimes on little-boy things, and little-boy jokes amuse him. Sonia was keen to 'go on somewhere', so on we went — first to the Gargoyle and then to Claridges, where the 'Jacksons' were staying *en route* to Khartoum, with a packing-case of scientific instruments, for Derek to do experiments on the total eclipse. At the Gargoyle we ran into Francis Bacon, lit up with drink, reckless, charming, giggling wildly. He joined us at our table, and turning to me asked, 'Don't you think Derek is the most marvellous person you know?' Next we were joined by Lucian Freud, who began a serious conversation with Derek about Art and Science, Derek's contribution to which was eager, amusing and paradoxical. Champagne was ordered and when Sonia, Lucian and I left Claridges it was two o'clock. Outside the front door two handsome, well-educated policemen were standing, to whom Lucian remarked, 'I suppose you're here to prevent all the Kings getting assassinated?' (There are seven Kings and Queens here for the funeral.) The policeman looked down his nose and didn't deign to answer. We three took a taxi to Percy Street, but even at her door Sonia couldn't give up and they left me and drove on 'somewhere else'. When we were at the Gargoyle, Sonia tried to describe to me a little Connemara bay that had charmed her, and something lit up in her eyes, though it was tragically imprisoned by inarticulacy, due not so much to drink as to deep despair.

February 15th. The King's funeral day; the problem was how to get across the path of the procession so as to lunch with Burgo in Kensington. My bus decanted me at Selfridges, and all at once — like a bucket emptying its contents on me — I saw a horde of human beings advancing towards me. The procession must just have passed as their faces distinctly showed traces of a cathartic experience, like blackboards after a teacher had wiped them. I slipped between two files of soldiers and there I was across the frontier, in the milky sunlight of the park. The ponds shone like pale tea, and equally pale was the gold on the Albert Memorial.

February 16th. Ralph arrived last night in time to go to Quentin and Olivier's wedding party in remotest Canonbury. Luckily ran into Quentin himself crossing the road in search of a corkscrew.

The party was extremely jolly, the vitality of the Old Blooms-buries comparing well with the world of the Gargoyle, and being so amusing, so light of touch and stimulating. Afterwards we dined with Bunny and Angelica, Julia and Lawrence.

February 29th — Ham Spray. A flying visit from Phil and Phyllis Nichols. He told us what it was like to walk in the King's funeral procession — all the preparations beforehand for the gruelling ordeal, like soaping the inside of his shoes. He walked between M. Schumann and M. Stikker of Holland. They were all told to go to the lavatory at Westminster while they had a chance, because at the last King's funeral there was almost a stampede when they reached Paddington, with guardsmen nearly drop-ping the coffin and rushing off into corners. But this time only one old gentleman failed to stay the course. The word went round that Signor B. was in difficulties and he was ushered to the kerb, where five doctors sprang up and smuggled him away.

The Brenans are back from America; Gerald came to dinner last night. He looked like someone who had just been shot off a machine in a fun-fair, still whirling and dazed and unaware where he was. His eyes were nearly closed with the violence of his emotions and the number of impressions needing to be got off his chest, which spurted forth in an inchoate stream of talk. By the end of the evening he was quite hoarse and we had gleaned: that Americans were much stupider than Europeans; that they were just like Anglo-Saxons; that they were years behind the times; that Gamel's brother was a wonderful man; that he was a pro-Nazi and a monster; that Gamel had cut quite a figure in America; that he, Gerald, had quite eclipsed her; that her family were rich, grand and erudite; that they were of no account whatever. There were also some good Geraldisms — e.g. 'Parents have to learn that they are to their children what a lamp-post is to a dog.'

'Why have them then?' asked Ralph.

'Because in spite of all it is an experience not to be missed, and one gets some sort of animal pleasure in their company.'

Of girls, he said he couldn't resist any who made themselves agreeable to him, in spite of his age. 'I'm just a Sir Walter Raleigh tearing about putting my cloak down in puddles.'

I dreamed we were at Crichel and Eddy was dreadfully upset because Ralph and I didn't say 'Frencheon' instead of 'French' (like 'luncheon' for 'lunch'). What absurd things the unconscious coughs up!

March 23rd. So hot was the sun that Ralph and I lunched on the verandah at my table, vowing that we would often do so again, and were the luckiest people alive to be able to sit here looking out at the beauty of the March view, with its purity of line unfuzzed by any foliage. It was unthinkable to go indoors all afternoon.

I'm reading Veronica Wedgwood's life of her uncle Josiah, which starts a train of thought about the change in the intellectual outlook since 1900. *Then* work was paramount. Intellectuals were also idealists, optimists, enthusiasts; they believed in progress, freedom, justice, integrity. Their desire to improve their minds and the lot of the masses was boundless. Against this must be set some lack of irony and proportion, heavy over-seriousness; puritanism (or shamefaced suppression). And *now* what? Since the Twenties play has become more important than work, but instead of optimism there is disillusion and pessimism, cynicism, frivolity. Pleasure eagerly pursued, wit and gaiety are all to the good, but less good is addiction to time-killing activities, anything for 'amusement'. Does it add up perhaps to decadence? I believe it does, and that it started in 1918 as a result of that beastly war, and has stamped its pattern more indelibly since the last beastly war.

In spite of the tragic demise of the Flower book, my interest in the subject has not declined. Going for walks with Ralph my eyes drift to the hedge-banks, covered as they now are by the intricate mosaic of springing leaves. And each year is different; just as the great Parisian couturiers produce each spring new points in their fashions. This season wild Arums are being worn in profusion; dark and glossy, with their wicked-looking blackish spots, they burst in positive cascades down the banks.

[The Campbells had for some time being trying to entice us to go shares with them in renting a house — a battered château rather — in Vaucluse for a fortnight. They told us that Robert and his new friend Oonagh Oranmore were in Paris and might drive down and join us there. In the surprising way such plans consolidate (especially when fired by the positive enthusiasm of someone like Mary), Ralph, Burgo and I duly set off, by sea and road on April 5th, arriving a few days later at the outskirts of a castellated, semi-ruined village of yellow sandstone, perched on a narrow rock. After winding our way up alleys so narrow that the car sometimes scraped both sides between tall houses with vestiges of Renaissance architecture, we finally reached the terrace of an imposing château with windows thrown wide open, and here we found Robin, Mary and Nell sun-bathing.

We soon settled in. Mary held the Common Purse, a visible bulge in her jeans. We shopped in the village, filled up our bottles from the incredibly cheap local wine, and picked asparagus running to seed and greener than the French like it, in the sand by the river. We bathed, read, went on drives and sat in cafés; Nell and Burgo went for milk and bread every morning and breakfast was on the terrace. The evenings were sometimes rollicking with wine, talk and laughter.

A little later Robert and Oonagh arrived in a large hired car. Oonagh looked like some veiled Eastern woman in her enormous black glasses. Her small fragile and elegant body, her tiny hands loaded with huge rings hardly promised co-operation to our housewifery, nor was it wanted, but I found her tragic expression and air of being lost rather worrying. Her rare contributions to the conversation were often strange, for instance, 'I used to carry the Bible about with me *every*where, and read it *all* the time, but people were so horrid to me I had to stop'. And after several days in our company she leaned across the table and asked me 'What *is* your name?' When I told her, 'And what is your husband's?' But her English chauffeur, Teeder, was a constant source of amusement to us with his efforts to carry standards of English upper-class life into this large but uncomfortable house, with its quantities of yellow dust, its shortage of water where wanted and plentiful amount leaking where it was not, and his disapproval of everything French was obvious. All females were addressed as 'Milady'. When he disparaged French food Mary exclaimed 'Shame on you, Teeder!' 'Oh, it doesn't matter, Milady,' he replied, 'I manage quite well somehow.'

After all the others had left for home, Robert stayed on with us Partridges, and a new more adventurous form of life began. Robert, best of companions, excellent with Burgo, steered us up the Gorge du Régalon, a stony cleft between two giant cliffs that almost met overhead, out into a hillside thick with miniature daffodils and irises, and persuaded us to climb the Luberon. By the time we started for England a violent storm had transformed the valleys, lining them with luscious grass and wild narcissi, loveliest and most intoxicatingly scented of flowers. Arrived back at Ham Spray to bad news. Burgo's tutor had had a stroke poor fellow, and couldn't possibly take him next term.]

May 1st. Burgo and I took train to London, and while he went off to stay with Jane Ainley in the Isle of Wight I interviewed and engaged a new tutor for him — Alan Tyson, a clever, nervous young man with bright blue eyes, Oxford double-first, training to be a psycho-analyst. Perhaps that will come in useful, as I have just agreed to index the complete works of Freud for James's translation.

May 26th. The papers have recently been full of a ghastly incident when a young Broadmoor patient called Straffen escaped, and though only out for a few hours managed to strangle a little girl (the same crime he was originally put in for.) Tremendous indignation has been aroused, and there is an outcry for tightening up security at Broadmoor. It is hard on the poor little Super, who was away at the time looking for a house to retire into. Today, on the spur of the moment, Ralph and I jumped into the car and drove to Reading to attend an enquiry into recent escapes.

It was merely a hearing of local protests by four Commissioners and should have been boring, yet somehow was not.

The policeman at the door put his finger on his lips and we entered on tiptoe. It was Alice in Wonderland. Or the most stagy and unreal of Crime films. Three of the Commissioners were sunk in apparent apathy, the fourth was actively picking his nose. When we came in a series of witnesses were giving evidence. Mrs Barnes had seen Straffen cross her garden — he had even stopped and picked up the cat and fondled it. In all he had been seen quite a dozen times before the little girl was murdered. Mr Johnson said: 'Just to show you how we all feel, my wife cannot bear to let our youngest child out of our sight *even in our garden*.' I wonder what the effect on the little girls who have read the staring headlines in the papers, and whose parents react thus to the tragedy, may be.

May 28th. This morning I fell to clearing my botany table of all its sad and derelict deposits to make way for my Freudian indexing for James. So that is that, and I have now cut the last knot tying me to botany as work, and put it in its place as a hobby.

Mary invited us to dinner to meet Janetta and Derek, adding that Janetta was radiant with happiness; she added that she had mentioned Robert's name to her and saw she had put her foot in it by the lengthening and greenification of Derek's face. She was saying in effect: 'Come to dinner. Janetta wants to see you. But do behave properly to Derek — and leave Robert out of it.'

The expression of happy relaxation was there all right — the only sign of imperfect adjustment was that everyone depended so much on hard liquor. No one was without a glass in their hand all evening. We quite enjoyed ourselves by dint of getting into the same parboiled state, talking freely if somewhat incoherently and swimming along like fish in the alcoholic tide — a dreary state where nothing is exact and where ideas that have come into one's mind with a certain pungency lose their definition before ever they reach one's lips. It isn't our way of life and somehow we felt we were in an alien camp.

June 16th. Weekend at Crichel. We were sitting over the fire with Raymond and Eardley discussing our reactions to the modern world when Deverell the butler came in with stately tread and announced: 'I thought you might like to hear the news. Sir Desmond MacCarthy has died at Cambridge.'

[Everyone found Desmond MacCarthy irresistible. Even the sharp pen of Virginia Woolf described him as 'my dear old friend Desmond', 'tender and vague', 'sympathetic, humorous, reminiscent and perhaps melancholy in a happy sort of way.' I believe this irresistibility depended less on his Irish charm and wit (great as these were) or his social gifts, than on his extraordinary power of sympathetic understanding. To understand other people one must want to know about them, and Desmond's curiosity and interest were boundless. In many ways a lazy man, certainly one who could never answer letters or despatch his reviews until the very last moment (and to whom posting a parcel would I'm sure have been impossible), where there was a friend in sore grief or a young person in need of a hoist on the literary ladder, he would put himself out to help them with the utmost sensitivity and imagination. At one time he even gave a job in his house to a burglar. I do not know if the plan worked out well.

I called his wit 'Irish', and so it seemed although he was one quarter French and one German. It was not of the lightning-flash sort, however, but expressed itself largely in anecdotes told in a way entirely his own, or in sudden swoops from the particular to the general — such as 'Oh YES, two wrongs DO make a right'.[1] From photographs of Desmond as a young man it would appear that it was his interested, quizzical, responsive expression that charmed, rather than his good looks. When I first got to know him he was middle-aged, squarely built, with few but telling gestures, careless of his appearance and dress. (Lytton Strachey unkindly described him as looking like a seedy actor.) Could he perhaps have made a distinguished career on the stage? He has many of the necessary gifts — and here there comes to my mind the way he once made us laugh by the rolling sonority with which he read aloud what he described as 'the *snobbish* chapter in the Bible' — the passage about the Dukes in Chapter 36 of Genesis. He enjoyed many things beside conversation — games and swimming for instance — and his great appreciation of the comic, whether in situations or other people's remarks, emerged in chortles of laughter that still had a boyish ring when he was comparatively old. Yet the vein of melancholy noticed by Virginia was certainly there, and I feel sure it came from the realization that many of his early literary projects would never materialize, while at the same time he underestimated the value and influence of his outstanding contribution as a critic. And he never, I think, found it easy to deal with the material world. His wife Molly described how some small ailment or frustration would throw him quite off course. 'Then he flings up his arms and gives up *every*thing, groaning aloud "This life is so *terrible!*"'

Desmond appreciated receiving a knighthood. 'One doesn't enjoy being honoured unless one knows it has also given pleasure to one's friends,' he wrote in answer to our letter of congratulation; but he went on more characteristically: 'I am asthmatical — and my goodness old and dry in heart. I can tell you this; it is not easy or pleasant modulating into old age. And that reminds me of Burgo. Lay your hand on his head and give him my blessing. He has a nice long run in front of him.']

[1]See p. 107.

June 23rd. David and Rachel [Cecil] to Sunday lunch. We talked of Desmond's death and the question where Molly should live.

Someone mentioned the newspaper tributes; 'Oh, I do hate *tributes*' Molly had said. With her candid eyes wide open and her face full of feeling, Rachel described the funeral ceremony: 'If one had the courage to *force* oneself to look down into the grave and see the coffin lying there I found it looked so peaceful, and that was very consoling.' Janie Bussy, who went to the memorial service, told us that after it was over Desmond's friends gathered outside St Martin-in-the-Fields and stood talking together, and that an impromptu party atmosphere spontaneously generated itself, which seemed entirely appropriate.

July 11th. Social life has kept us on the hop. Darsie and Lucila [Japp] came for the weekend, driven over by Henry and Pansy Lamb. Hot on their heels came recently widowed Faith [Henderson][1] for a week. She is so intelligent and interested in other people that a certain lack of vitality is easily forgiven. Conversation was easy and spontaneous between the three of us. Today was the first day of Burgo's exams, and we were half expecting to hear that he hadn't gone to it. But a railway strike gave me the excuse to ring up Juanita with whom he is staying, and she gave us the welcome news that he had gone off perfectly cheerfully, adding that she 'adored him, and loved having him there'.

[1] Her husband was Sir Hubert Henderson, Warden of All Souls.

July 21st. Burgo's exams went on all the week, and he says he enjoyed them. This morning was the last. Robert came back for ten days with us. Today he and Ralph went together on Press tickets to the trial at Winchester Assizes of Straffen, the escaped Broadmoor patient who strangled a little girl, and returned full of it all.

July 22nd. As Robert had work on hand, he offered me his Press ticket for Straffen's trial today. We had an early breakfast and a drive of great beauty in all the freshness of a day that was to become blazing hot.

What follows is being written inside the court-room in Winchester Castle, where an effect reigns as of several pageants having got accidentally mixed together. Arthur's Round Table on the wall, the tip-staffs with their absurd fringed lances and counsel whisking by, bird-like, with the little grey tails of their wigs flapping as they turn their heads from side to side. Everyone seems to be acting a part only moderately well but with confidence: the jurors patently enjoying a feeling of importance, one of them (a small fat cad in sandals and tie-pin) flirting with a handsome jurywoman.

From the pew-like seats where we are I can look back down the dark passage leading to the cells where a policeman is combing his few strands of hair and talking quite affably to a silhouette which must be Straffen. The 'Boys' of the Press now squash in beside us, bright as buttons, or blackbirds on the look-out for a juicy worm. A few rows behind us sit Straffen's mother and sister, a couple of debased sheep-faced women. 'What *can* they be feeling?' I whisper to Ralph. 'Rather proud,' he replies.

There is a long delay. Clearly the main requisite in submitting to the Law's operations is *patience*. Some of the Boys hurry out — to telephone presumably, saying out of the sides of their mouths, 'Think there's a hitch somewhere.' I believe I'm the only person in court who can see Straffen, the downy outline of his head, his bent knees, and official boots placed side by side and tapping gently. This stifling atmosphere of waiting drowns all realization of what is happening — a man being tried for his life, a woman waiting to hear if her son is to die.

At last! Enter with all paraphernalia the owl-like judge, seats himself beneath the royal arms and proceeds in a soft but distinct voice, in small *chunks* of words, regularly to tick off the jury. One of their number has talked about the case, and the result must be a re-trial and a great waste of money and time. The jury, lately so self-important, now look pictures of embarrassment and guilt, and file out to the back of the court while a new jury is sworn. By now Straffen has entered and taken his seat at the front of the dock. The Clerk of Indictments — the only man who wears his wig as to the manner born — in clear tones introduces that lucid and impartial note expected of British justice. The judge wears an engaging expression of tolerant scepticism, emphasized by the thick raised bands of his eyebrows.

Straffen sits only a few yards away from me. He is tall and narrow, dressed in his black Broadmoor suit and a white shirt. His head is very abnormally shaped, a high thimble, microcephalic and with no back, his fair hair is cut in a short bob ending suddenly above his long neck, like an Italian baby. His forehead high, intellectual; fairly good features except for a foolish mouth and bad teeth; his neck so thick that his head seems a mere extension of it. The effort of connecting this wooden figure, staring ahead, with the events counsel is describing is beyond me.

Witnesses are called and some of their evidence is very dull and involves much rustling of paper. The judge is like a sophisticated and humane participant at a dinner party, or an intellectual parakeet.

The lunch interval follows. The Boys of the Press are waiting to pounce with false geniality on Mrs Straffen; outside in the sun the camera-men wield their weapons. We gather somehow that the guilty juryman had expressed the view that the child's step-father, not Straffen at all, was guilty of the crime. The bad jury then retired, leaving the good jury grinning all over their faces in smug satisfaction.

Straffen's case was resumed by policemen giving evidence of finding little Linda's bike and corpse; unlike the jury they do not seem to be human beings at all but blocks of oak, standing awkwardly stiff and mechanically going through statements they have learned by heart. One wonders why they aren't allowed to read it out of their famous 'stubby notebooks', which would be more convincing. The afternoon is grilling hot. The great swarthy face of counsel for the prosecution gets shinier and shinier, and his little wig is slipping off the back of his head. Various witnesses now give evidence of having seen Straffen: Mrs Kenyon, very much the lady, sits slouched in the witness-box like a provincial actress imitating Cathleen Nesbitt. Miss Saxby, a tiny gnome with a white face under scattered grey hair, eagerly turns her face to counsel. This is her big moment for Straffen actually *spoke* to her. 'And I said it's ten miles, and he said Oh.'

Linda's mother is quite young and attractive. She is the star of the cast, and her demeanour and charm are not entirely artless, though her grief is of course genuine; but the atmosphere of the court is so remote from emotion, so sterilized and clinical, that I am shocked to find in myself little human sympathy — only intense interest. The sinister step-father follows, with his un-trustworthy face, his head shaped like a top-heavy pear. The next witness refers to Straffen as 'a gentleman', quickly corrected by counsel to 'a man'. 'Can you see him here?' The witness looks wildly round at the High Sheriff, the judge, the marshal and

seems as though he would never light on Straffen, when counsel
says helpfully — reminding me of a game of Hunt the Thimble,
'Look in the middle of the court'.
More interchanges:
Judge: This is all very confusing. The witness keeps talking
about 'down the line'. What does this mean? Perhaps you mean
'lane'?
Witness: Yes, *line* Sir.
Judge: *Lane?*
Witness: Yessir, *line.*
Judge: Oh, I see, *line — lane*, I mean.
A pretty blonde describes being spoken to by someone on the
fatal day: 'I think it was the gentleman in the dock.'
A legal battle of a highly technical sort follows as to whether
we are to be allowed to hear the crucial dialogue between the
prisoner and the police at Broadmoor after the murder. Objec-
tion over-ruled. We are! And here it is:
Police: We should like to know if you got into any mischief
while you were out?
Straffen: I didn't kill her.
Police: No one has said anything about being killed, injured or
in any way attacked.
Straffen: I know what you policemen are. I know I killed two
little children at Bath — but I didn't kill the little girl with the
bicycle. (The bicycle hadn't yet been mentioned.)
Police: Why did you escape from here?
Straffen: I did it to prove I could be out without killing little
children.
His face, as he sits in the dock, looks slightly more aware of
what is going on, but his chief expression is one of lost, abysmal
sadness. Counsel for the Defence stands with bent head display-
ing his grey sausage-roll curls, like an elderly lady fresh from the
hairdresser; his cross-questions are maddeningly slow. The
judge's face displays boredom. He bursts out irritably, 'It doesn't
matter where he lives. It doesn't matter TWO STRAWS'.
Later, as counsel drones on, 'That is the — ' the judge
intervenes: 'End of all *that!*'
And so it was. We adjourned after six, dead beat. Personally I
couldn't have taken much more.

July 23rd. Ralph took Burgo to the trial today, leaving Robert and me alone in the peace of the sunny garden — with much talk about the case, delectable summer weather, raspberries, swimming, deck-chairs, and only enough breeze to stir the long green curtains of the willow tree arbour. Burgo was pleased and excited that Ralph was taking him, and dressed himself carefully as one of the Boys of the Press.

July 24th. Julia went to Straffen's trial with Ralph today. She can be counted on to react differently from anyone else, and returned saying that he was 'marvellously good-looking, though of course I took a purely abstract interest in the legal proceedings'. In the evening came the Campbells with Wynne Godley, and Lawrence to fetch Julia, and we all sat out by the tuft of pampas grass until the sinking sun at last deserted us.

July 28th. Alix and James have been and gone, leaving me full of admiration for Alix. She is the most intelligent woman I know, the best conversationalist, the most fluent and logical thinker — I don't feel she has received enough recognition for this fact. Then her long serious face from which her grey dispassionate eyes look out, set in a series of flattened triangles, should really be perpetuated by some master painter.[1] Throughout the weekend hearing her talk was pure joy. She listens, what's more, usually calmly, to what others have to say, surveys it with detachment, sets to work spinning from it a threat of ratiocination — and ends in a conclusion that is often fantastic, wild! James too was very entertaining in his laconic, puncturing style. I was interested to see them with Robert; they got on very well, and he and Alix even have something in common — a desire to go swiftly and ruthlessly to the point, say, as well as a streak of the Red Indian, a fierce look under dark thatches of hair. Yet in sheer intelligence Robert was outmatched.

We talked a lot about Straffen, who has been condemned to death; whether the sentence will be modified we don't yet know. Alix thought it might be necessary for him to be hanged so as to satisfy the bloodlust of the public — which if left unsatisfied might produce more serious results. The old question as to whether savagery and violence are increased by being fed or starved came up once again, and was tossed about for a while.

[1] The best portrait of her was by John Banting.

August 6th. Ralph, Burgo and I have just passed a week in Ireland, our first stop being Mullingar where Derek and Janetta have rented for the summer a fine Georgian house in the middle of a spacious park, with mown lawns, clipped Irish yews and formal flower-beds, all very charming. Indoors — every comfort, and the days starting with breakfast brought to us in our soft beds. The country is too flat and featureless for pleasant walking, yet we eat and drink so much that we feel the need of it. Gradually we get the hang of the ideology of the house, which is Derek's, but if he is a dictator he is certainly a genial one. All animals get high marks for being dogs or cows as the case may be. Games are 'not socially O.K.' The red rags which turn him temporarily into a bull are the Labour Party, God and the Royal family.

'Do you know, Burgo, what are the three most important things in life? Be rich; *be rich*; and BE RICH.' And: 'Don't you agree that the point of making money is not to spend it but to make more money?' Is he teasing? I'm not sure. Burgo loves it, and Ralph is quite good at finding bridgeheads on which they can meet and agree. I am the least at ease with him, but one can't fail to respond to his friendliness; the trouble is that we don't *want* to be as rich as he is. Janetta seems happy and very relaxed.

'You've said several awful things this evening,' she said one night to Derek without a trace of malice, 'and I'm not going to forget them.'

On the way home we were to stay a night with Oonagh Oranmore at her house Luggala in the Wicklow mountains, where a rollicking party for Dublin Horse show week was just ending. There was Robert of course, Francis Wyndham, Lucian Freud and his wife Kitty with her huge dark eyes, perfect teeth and soft cooing voice; Claud Cockburn, tall, dark, ugly and animated. Everyone was eager to tell us the story of Lord Powerscourt's recent ball to which the whole Luggala party had been invited. They turned up in force, no less than three with black eyes; however it was Lucian's tartan trousers that caused the trouble. 'You can't come in here dressed like that,' said the doorman, and this was backed up by his Lordship saying, 'I'm not going to have any drunks here.' And 'If you don't like it you can get out!' Daphne Bath tried to mend matters by saying as she left, with her attractive stammer: 'Thank you for the most b-b-beastly party I've ever b-b-been to in my life.' To which Lord Powerscourt replied, 'I'm so glad you didn't enjoy it.'

We had met our fellow-guests in Dublin and driven to Luggala with them. Incredible beauty lay before us as we climbed the last ridge before dipping into the valley — range upon range of mountains spread around us with their tops still golden in the setting sun, and the deep, green, lost valley below. A big loch of brown peaty water with sheep browsing round a small formal temple, and beneath the domed forehead of a crag the house itself — a fantastically pretty white building in purest Strawberry Hill Gothic style. The front door was opened and we were at once in the hall-dining-room, where a huge fire blazed and an oval table laid for dinner filled nearly all the space. What a magical atmosphere that house had, charmingly furnished and decorated to match its style, dim lights, soft music playing and Irish voices ministering seductively to our needs. In the drawing-room stood Oonagh with her hair down her back, and in her short diaphanous dress looking exactly like the fairy off a Christmas tree.

Ralph and I were borne off to our little bedroom where yet another roaring fire was being lit and our things unpacked. The prettiness of the room itself, the humble bathroom next door where the softest dark brown water smelling of peat awaited us, all made up a work of art whoever was responsible, and a contrast to many of the houses of the rich where one may find a single match sticking out of its box as if one were too weak to take it oneself, and inadequate heating. We were led through another room where Tara, Oonagh's youngest boy, was ensconced in the bath. Gareth aged thirteen, with a husky breaking voice and a passion for wild flowers, had appeared during dinner with some friends carrying autograph books in which we were all told to draw or write something *very* funny. When we climbed into bed I for one felt soaked through and through in this pleasant Irish atmosphere.

[I first met Derek Jackson when he came to Ham Spray as the fiancé of Poppet John, daughter of Augustus. He was a lively, spontaneous young man of quick speech and winning ways, whose slanting eyes (half-closed when he smiled) gave him a fawnlike appearance. Some time later Ralph and I ran into him lunching with Bryan Guinness, and I wasn't impressed in his favour by hearing him say excitedly, across the huge round dining-table: 'I hate Mozart — I absolutely LOATHE Mozart'.

However I don't think this incident had any part in what now seems a somewhat biased impression of him given in these first diary entries. To be honest I believe that jealousy was partly responsible — a jealousy with regard to Janetta that had been completely absent in Robert's case, but then he ranked (they both did) among our most beloved friends. Almost a stranger, Derek carried Janetta off into a world of very different values from our own, and during her years with him she appeared to Ralph and me to be less 'herself' than at any other time.

What then did I leave out? I have not made it clear that he had a brilliant if specialized brain, nor was this obvious during ordinary meetings. It was true that he set what seemed to us a greatly exaggerated value on the possession of wealth, but it is only fair to say that he was much more generous with his own than any other rich man I have known, both by coming to the rescue of friends in trouble and by giving presents of cases of superb claret to those hardly more than acquaintances. His work as a physicist was what occupied the centre of his life, and his chief extravagances were a spectroscopic laboratory in France, race-horses, good wine and French Impressionist paintings, of which he had a fine collection.

After his divorce from Janetta I naturally saw much less of him, until their daughter and his only child Rose began to grow up. During the later years of his life he evidently had a happy relationship with her, he always visited her when he came to England. I met him at her house a number of times and grew to like him more and more and appreciate his geniality and comic style of talk.]

August 13th. A brilliantly fine morning for our journey home; and time to dash out with Robert to the rippling edge of the lake, walk up to the waterfall which tumbled over mossy stones and under a bridge behind the house, and drink in with a gulp of agonizing brevity the astonishing beauty of the place. Everyone was leaving in different directions and by different means, but Oonagh's butler, the genius of the house, saw that they signed the visitors' book, collected their coats, keys and passports and got off at the right time. This perfect butler is the one of whom Oonagh is supposed to have said when her husband left her: 'Never mind O'Hara' (or whatever the butler is called), 'didn't ever like him much.' This morning the first thing we heard was the maids' Irish voices counting dirty sheets: 'A hundred and wan, a hundred and two' and so forth.

August 16th. Back at Ham Spray we discussed Luggala with Lawrence and Julia. Is it illogical we asked, to be bowled over by the impact of this eighteenth-century life, full of material splendour, recklessness, dash and style, which is of course supported on things none of us approves of — like the assumption that class distinctions are insuperable? What can all those servants feel about the indulgent, selfish display of their masters' goings-on? 'Intense pride mixed with intense pity,' was Lawrence's excellent answer to this question. Julia, more disapproving, suggested that the output of such lives was *nil*. My remembered picture of life at Luggala is mainly attractive, even romantic, and such shadows as it possesses are thrown by childishness, insensitivity and competitive drinking. And after sojourning in other civilizations, it is very pleasant to feel alive again in our own.

Ralph on war: It is important, he says, to remember that killing your enemy in war is assassination (it's no use both sides thinking they are acting in self-defence) and that in theory one should prefer being assassinated to assassinating.

September 8th. At breakfast on the last day of a visit from Isobel and Charlotte Strachey the news came that Burgo has passed his exam in all subjects. What a relief! I think I subconsciously believed he had done so, and he admits the same. We are sliding into the assumption that he will now get to Oxford. The next step is a tutorial establishment called MacNalty's where he will work with other boys. Charlotte has become extremely pretty as well as funny and charming.

October 11th. Hot, still, beautiful autumn weather. As I sit at my verandah table it would be impossible not to respond to the deep appearance of calm. The lawn is emerald green and sprinkled with dry leaves; the orange trees in the park are blotted with purple shadows. Minnie lies beside me looking out with half-shut eyes and the distant sky is full of the subdued chuckle of rooks. Every now and then there's the bang of a rifle — partridge shooting.

I thought what a strange role conversation plays in human life: just as a bird has to keep flapping its wings to stay up in the air, so when human beings meet others they have to keep themselves afloat with words and when there is a very long gap they begin to feel uneasy. But though speech must have started from something like a child's cries of 'Mummy' when it is frightened or 'Water' when it is thirsty, from these basic cries of need an aesthetic creation is produced by what are called 'good talkers', as enjoyable and stimulating as any other form of art. (I am struggling — as I often do — to frame a biological basis to a theory of aesthetics.) Then what of the web of thought that lies behind the web of conversation? Perhaps it is a first means to an end — a step by which human beings use their intelligence to get what they biologically need in its modern, infinitely complex shape.

It can become a disease to be so bent on keeping high standards that one never does anything for fear of not doing it well enough. We jeer at people who force their bad pictures and bad books out into the world in the happy conviction that they are artists. But there is danger in the opposite, too critical and therefore too passive attitude. Bloomsbury's fastidiousness has prevented some from 'competing'. Raymond, full of appetite for life as he is, gratifies it by constantly absorbing works of art — a wonderful occupation — but *something* is missed by being a sea-anemone eternally stretching its tentacles for more and more aesthetic food rather than launching out on one's own.

October 25th. The telephone rang. 'Gerald speaking,' in the low hoarse tone of a sea-monster just arisen from a deep plunge. 'I've stopped smoking,' he began. 'I don't *want* to smoke ever again, but the trouble is it has also stopped my writing. And I can't read either' (this on a higher screech). 'I don't do *anything* except read thrillers.' I said something to him about his *History of Spanish Literature*, and how absolutely brilliant, lucid, sensitive, perceptive, profound and penetrating it seemed to me. (I have just finished reading *Don Quixote* in Spanish, and I wasn't flattering Gerald — all was truly meant.) He told me he had been asked to lecture to undergraduates, but it was impossible. I said, 'I think it's almost your moral duty to go, as you have such a power of spreading enthusiasm and understanding.' 'Oh no, no, I can't possibly. I can't talk to people; it makes me too aware of my own existence. I love life, but I don't want to remember my *self*. When I'm alone I can be happy and forget I exist. When I talk to people I can't think who and what I am. I say silly things — and then afterwards there's the remorse! I suffer terribly from remorse. Gamel too — we are both full of remorse.'

October 27th. To lunch with the Brenans today. Gerald has begun to smoke and write once more. He is writing his autobiography and has just got to the arrival in his life of Hope Johnstone (who is living in his cottage at present). He fears he may have gone too far, as lately Hope Johnstone, who was titillated at first, has 'fallen strangely silent'. Gerald's object is to convey to the reader the absurdities in Hope's character without making them apparent to Hope himself.

More talk about remorse. Gamel said in her driest way: 'I'm so eaten up by remorse that I have no energy left over for anything else'. Gerald talked with scarcely disguised satisfaction, of the approaching end of the life of Poffet their cat. 'He has vitamin H deficiency which makes his fur fall out. *Poor* Poffet; we think he will soon have to be put to sleep.'

After lunch the Brenans took us for a walk up the hollow in the downs below Snap to see a group of horn-beams — very beautiful trees with their sheaves of papery bracts. As we came home in the twilight it struck me that (though I don't altogether like the look beech trees have of being red-headed persons) they were mysteriously moving, standing there with the blood of their fallen leaves below them.

November 6th. A day in Oxford, Ralph's sister Dorothy having invited us to a concert by Segovia. I enjoyed the concert, though the music — perfect in its way — made quite a tiny pluck at one's sleeve. All round sat the highly educated, eager audience, and in the centre of the round floor this glossy, stout, bespectacled Spaniard nursing his guitar. It seemed rather a selfish, introverted performance at which we spectators had no right to be present, and this was stressed by the desperate or resigned gestures with which Segovia deplored the interruptions made by passing lorries, banging windows, and even a lady who fell in a faint or fit! He managed to make us feel guilty and ashamed, though surely we weren't responsible?

November 12th. To London for the night to go to *Porgy and Bess*, with Craig Macfarlane and Burgo. Burgo had been with us about an hour when I said, 'Well, isn't there any London news? Has nothing been happening?'

Burgo: 'No, I don't think so. I can't think of anything — Oh, well, I *was* nearly arrested for murder last week!' Then the following incredible story came out: (I must preface it by saying that there have been sensational headlines about a young ex-public school boy arrested for pushing both his parents over a cliff). It seems that last Saturday Burgo left his rooms in Tite Street to buy a newspaper. Just as he was opening the front door on his return, five men in mackintoshes appeared from nowhere, and pushed him into the house saying with very fierce expressions, 'We are police officers and we are armed'. 'Then they asked my name,' Burgo went on, 'and they obviously didn't believe it, so I showed them the name-tape at the back of my shirt, and one of them took off his hat to squint down my neck. They asked me if it was my car outside, and I said, 'No. Shall I go and see if it belongs to anyone upstairs?' They said, 'You are not to communicate with anyone in this house.' After a while they let me go for a walk, but one of them followed me at a discreet distance. Nothing more happened until midnight when a taxi drew up; the police appeared in scores and hustled out the young man inside it — the murderer himself, of course. The car had belonged to his dead parents, and he drove up in it to visit his girl, who lived in Tite Street.' The description, even the photograph of Gifford fitted Burgo to a T: 'A very dark young man, with hair worn long, wearing a green sports coat, greenish trousers and a pullover'.

We were all amazed at Burgo's sangfroid about this episode.

November 27th. To London for an evening party given by Mrs Maud Russell in honour of Boris's new mosaic pavement in the National Gallery. What a Proustian scene! The heads greyer, the faces marked by age, but not much the worse for that I couldn't help feeling. The belle of the ball in fact was Vanessa — so bewitching she can be if she wants to, and for some reason she did.

December 21st. Some good sayings of Robin Mount's — at least I like them:

On Derek Jackson, 'It isn't so much a question of whether his drinking will interfere with his work as of whether his work will interfere with his drinking'.

Of marriage: 'When it comes to marriage there's no difference between one man and another.'

And best of all: '*Never marry a man.*'

1953

January 3rd. Last night a young people's ball was given by 'the Tycoon' (Philip Dunn), for Serena and Nell, to which we went with Burgo, Isobel and Charlotte Strachey, after an evening spent ironing and dressing up in a fizz of expectation. Burgo looked very fine and what Charlotte described as 'Byronical' in his new dinner-jacket, in spite of very long hair and woolly socks. We collected the Campbells and their guests on the way — Paddy Leigh Fermor (high-spirited and friendly) and Joan Rayner (beautiful and shy). I sat in the back of our car with these two, discussing the structure of the human face, and I remember that Paddy declared that he had strong feelings about the runnel down the centre of the upper lip. 'I often think about it,' he said. Wynne Godley and a young sweet-faced Michael Rutherston were also of the party, and tended to form a somewhat bohemian gathering talking animatedly, with Charlotte and Burgo, in a corner of the ball-room.

January 12th. Robert has gone to Geneva on a new job, and the Brenans back to Spain, leaving us with melancholy gaps in the ranks of our friends. The drama of Poffet the Brenans' cat grew more and more Wagnerian towards its close. They insisted on fixing the date of execution as the very eve of their departure, and all the while the atmosphere of wakes, keening and candles grew more intense. Gerald told us that they had been indulging the poor condemned creature with such rich food that he refused to touch anything but chicken or turbot — thus making it quite impossible to change their minds and reprieve him as no one could afford to keep him.

After the dreadful day was over Gerald wrote a horrified letter to Ralph, blaming himself bitterly, saying that they had 'buried Poffet in silk because he had lived in silk', and that one should never keep pets because it was so terrible that one had in the end to destroy them.

Occupational therapy is at the moment my panacea for all ills; I have started working on the Index to Freud, and found it such a boon and blessing that I am resolved never to be without work again while I can totter about or wield a pen. Poor James! A fearful disaster has befallen him. After months of planning for their winter in Ceylon they set sail, but he suffered a slipped retina in his good eye on the voyage and after seeing a specialist in Colombo they took the next boat home — a dismal journey, ending in a desperate attempt to save his sight by operation. He lies now in Middlesex Hospital waiting for the bandages to be removed. What happens to Freud I cannot think — it might mean no more work for me.

Two pieces of human news: Anthony West has married his American girl-friend Lily. And Janetta is pregnant.

February 9th. Our first visit to London for some time, though its object was not particularly cheerful — to visit the afflicted James and the equally afflicted Bussys. We went straight to Gordon Square, and I received a wave of nostalgia for its dignified façades and the tall plane trees with their dangling bobbles of fruit in its spacious garden.[1] Up in the Bussys' flat an overpowering smell of gas nearly stifled us. The whole family has had to fly back from La Souco because Simon has either had a stroke or become suddenly senile. Dorothy at 87, intelligent, charming, sweetly girlish, enjoyed her first flight in an aeroplane; but poor Janie looked worn almost to nothing, her face no bigger than a bead, emerging from Alix's fur coat. The flight had been far from enjoyable for her. She couldn't tell the air hostess that Simon was off his head or they would have refused to take him, and he didn't take kindly to any restraint. All went well for a bit, then he rose to his wobbly little legs and made as if to open the door. Janie managed to subdue him by saying in an impersonal voice 'It is forbidden to leave the aeroplane,' and giving him some chocolate.

If there is a comic side to the Bussy tragedy, there is none whatever about James's. Alix looked pale and haggard, and said she found drink a considerable help. We took her to lunch at the Ivy, and then Ralph and I went by instalments to visit James where he lay flat on his back at the Middlesex Hospital like a wonderfully distinguished marble effigy, waving one long beautiful hand. His eyes are bandaged, so all expression is done by hand movement. Ralph said he anxiously asked how Alix was looking — how poignant that he has to ask! There's no knowing yet what the result of the operation will be, and partial or total blindness cannot be ruled out. Yet so wonderfully calm, serene, even gay did James manage to be — and in her way Alix too — that I begin to see how courage can turn horrible events into inspiring ones.

¹Ralph and I had begun our life together there in 1926.

[The marriage between Lytton's second sister, Dorothy, and Simon was in some ways a strange one; but since at the time of poor Simon's decline it had lasted fifty years it must have been solidly based, even though it had united a highbrow English-woman of nearly forty and a penniless French painter, reputed to have sprung from humble origins. True, he was a friend of Matisse, and was steadily gaining a reputation for the originality and accomplishment of his own paintings — many of them of birds, fish and animals, but also including charming landscapes, and portraits of his wife and daughter, of André Gide and Paul Valéry. Dorothy's father, Sir Richard, gave her a fine villa on the Riviera (La Souco, Roquebrune) as a wedding-present, and it was for many years a refuge for members of the family (and friends) in trouble or convalescence. An odd feature of the marriage was that Dorothy (like most Stracheys) was loth to speak French, although reading and understanding it with ease, whereas Simon never learned much English — indeed his conversation consisted largely of grunts to which he contrived to give a rich variety of meaning. Whenever we saw them (and they used to stay with us at Ham Spray, once a year at least) Dorothy spoke English and Simon French. Dorothy must have known French extremely well, however, as she was much admired for her translations from the French — particularly for those of Gide's Diary. I think she was in her seventies when I first got to know her: her grey hair was cut in a neat bob, with a long fringe reaching to the highly intelligent brown eyes that shone through her spectacles.]

February 10th. I am having my first Spanish lesson with Lucila Japp tomorrow. It suddenly occurred to me that if I got good enough, translation was something I could do for the rest of my life; so I have begun working at it quite hard and eagerly. Modern novels so often fail to grip the attention; one comes out from them shaking off clotted humanity with a faint sense of disgust, and feeling that the author has worked like a caddis-worm to make his characters out of conglomerations of material objects — cuff-links, cigarette-cases and fishing-rods for upper-class men for instance. So that it would be a rare pleasure to be able to transfer an old masterpiece into English. All a daydream no doubt.

Last week we drove to Seend to lunch with Clive's brother the Colonel, and bring Clive back to stay. There was a third Bell present — a raw-boned, reddish sister, with Clive's combination of rather coarse skin, clear-cut features and yellowing teeth. We ate in the hall which Violet, the Colonel's recently deceased wife, had tried to make snugger by lining it with stalls and a gate from the stables, and behind these we sat like horses munching hay, waited on by a silver-haired stage butler. Afterwards the Colonel took me round the garden and touched me by the way he spoke of the taste and hard work his wife had bestowed on it, telling me he thought it was lugging heavy water-cans to her plants in a drought that had killed her.

March 2nd. A new visitor this week made a great impression on us both — Freddie Ayer, a clever man as well as a delightful guest, and it was a good idea to have him with Raymond. Each was glad to meet the other and appreciated the other's different kind of brain. From Freddie's opaque and very dark eyes gleams out what seems like an affectionate nature and a certain vulnerability — a desirable ingredient in every human character. I'd expected him to be more metallic and armour-plated — but no: he showed a simple pleasure in the prettiness of our crocuses and a boyish eagerness to be the first to solve the lights of a crossword. We very much liked him in fact.

In the mornings he sat down with paper and pen at the table in the music-room. 'Wouldn't you like to be more private if you're working?' I asked. 'There's another room, you know.'

'Oh no, I can only think with other people about — that is if you don't mind.'

'What is it you're writing?'

'Something I've been working at for some time about our knowledge of other minds. I think I'm almost able to prove that we *do* have knowledge of them. Starting, of course, on the principle of analogy, that because we scream at the pain of our teeth being extracted, when we see and hear other people do likewise it's reasonable to assume that they also feel pain.'

'So, if you can do that, you can definitely disprove the truth of solipsism?'

'Yes.' He walked busily to and fro as he talked and sometimes rearranged the logs in the fire with his foot. He told us about Max Newman's Mechanical Brain and the lengths in problem-solving it had been made to reach.[1]

'Can it play chess?' we asked. 'After a fashion. It's quite good at the end-game, but there are too many possibilities at the start. Then if it's losing it cheats sometimes; there's a device by which it can flash the words "My turn" and "Your turn", and sometimes when it's getting the worst of the game it flashes "My turn. My turn. My turn".'

Ralph remembered with pleasure how one of the Brain's guardians said that he thought it might soon be induced to appreciate poetry, 'but it would probably have to be poetry written by another Mechanical Brain'.

[1]Newman's 'Colossus' was the earliest programmable computer in opposition to the German 'Enigma'.

March 5th. Alix rang up to say that James is sending me another volume of Freud to index, probably just as we start on our motor tour to Spain. Could I take it with me? Under the attack of this gentle voice, so undemanding yet fraught with the importance of the task, I very nearly agreed, but good heavens! An index on a motor tour! So I wrote to suggest working flat out before we go.

Saxon and Burgo for the weekend. On Monday Burgo has to take the Christ Church entrance exam, which produced a certain tension. Saxon is concerned entirely with betting on every day's races. It's strange to see this frail but still elegant and distinguished man, who has spent his life reading Pliny and listening to Mozart and Wagner, giving all his elderly attention to fat brown books on racing form.

To drinks with the Campbells and Ben Nicolson. Mary made the perfect remark about Burgo's exam: 'Oh, I know people who've got into Christ Church who could hardly put a cross against their name.'

In the night the poor fellow was dreadfully sick and came down looking green, having had hardly a wink of sleep. Oh dear!

March 16th. Up early and drove to Oxford. Burgo tense, but able to laugh at jokes and looking a lot better. After leaving him at Christ Church we spent the morning with the Cecils, and Ralph fetched him back to lunch with us there. 'Not too bad', was the verdict on the morning's paper, though it looked atrocious to me. Little Hugh Cecil, coming back from the Dragon School, slipped into the seat opposite me; I watched his small school-bound face.

'How was the Dragon?' asked David.

'Oh, all right. Lambert's decided to stop his feud with Hodge-Brown.' These are two friends of Hugh's. It seems that Lambert is nettled by the thought of Hugh's aristocratic background, and inclined to boast of 'coming of good yeoman stock'. Hugh is going to act as page to his uncle, Lord Salisbury, at the Coronation. When he was told the news all he said was, 'That'll shake Lambert.' David's sister[1] is Mistress of the Robes, and has discovered to her horror that she will have to practically dress and undress the Queen in the middle of the ceremony. She is very short-sighted and dreads being unable to manage the hooks and eyes. Can she wear her spectacles?

[1] Dowager Duchess of Devonshire.

March 20th. Good news! Burgo has passed into Christ Church! Both Ralph and I are absolutely delighted and we hope Burgo is too. A success pleases everyone and bounces back like reflected light. His tutor Mr MacNalty is pleased; so even was Wilde when Ralph told him. How nice to go to Spain with this in our pockets.

[Our holiday in Spain and Portugal lasted until nearly the end of April. We took Pippa Strachey (Vicky's sister, in her twenties) as companion to Burgo and extra driver. Our first Spanish stop was at Tarragona, where Ralph and I spent a happy week many years ago. An old haunt revisited is either what you expect (and clicks into place) or leaves you seeing double, with two incompatible pictures side by side. Tarragona seemed the same place as before, and I felt it was no more than a week ago that I had last been sitting picnicking with Ralph among the scratchy scented shrubs under the aqueduct, looking up at the birds wheeling round its honey-coloured crumbling arches under a deep blue sky.

Arrived at Malaga, we checked in at the Hotel Cataluña opposite the Cathedral and drove up to call on the Brenans at

Churriana in the late afternoon. Their garden was a paradise scented with roses, stocks and arum lilies. Once again I admired Gerald's marvellous taste, shown above all in his choice of Spanish plates and jugs. As dusk fell, the hills beyond Malaga sank into folds of velvety softness and lights shone from the town and the lighthouse. 'I never get tired of watching the lighthouse,' Gerald said. 'It never says No; it can only say "Yes."' Pippa rapidly fell for the Brenan way of life, and particularly for Gerald himself.

Leaving Malaga we drove through Tarifa to Cadiz. In the woods wild arums were growing, and everywhere was the great white cistus with a blood-red blot on each petal. Then came lagoons where storks were flying, salt in white pyramids, and the strange flat-roofed villages that lead to the peninsula of Cadiz. Here we saw the Museum of Zurbaráns, but at Seville we were told 'Franco is here' so we were only allowed to gaze at the outside of the Alcazar, where he was in residence. We hung about and were rewarded by the sight of a bus full of Moorish officers in gorgeously gaudy dress. Then the sleek black car of Facismo rolled out of the gates and the fat hand of Facismo was seen waving within. The onlookers sent up a feeble cheer and the newspapers reported that the Generalissimo had everywhere received 'an enthusiastic reception'.

In Portugal our best 'sight' was a crowd of students from Coimbra wearing their long black hooded cloaks draped around them with great style, floating out of the windows of cars or drifting behind them down streets, so many clever and alert Hamlets, their cheeks abloom with youth and health.

Back in Spain for Altamira, and to the Dordogne in France to see Lascaux. We waited for a party inside to come out; and when they did, surely there was something familiar about the uptilted head whose spectacles flashed in the sunlight? Why yes, of course, it was Morgan Forster with two American friends! Meanwhile we had been talking to a young man who told us it was he who had discovered the cave. Asked if he was trying to find more he said it was impossible without money. 'What? Do all these visitors you speak of bring in no money?' 'Ah, that all goes into the pocket of the landlord.' 'And who is that?' 'The Duc de la Rochefoucauld.' 'And isn't he interested in prehistory?' 'No!' in a tone of fierce indignation, 'only in his bank balance. *Il est snob!* The next time I find a cave I shall keep it to myself!' He went on to the war in Indo–China, and said how much better it would be to spend the money it cost on better things — like prehistory.]

May 11th — Ham Spray. We have been back just two weeks. Ralph's *Broadmoor* came out on the day we arrived, and has had nothing but praise from friends and reviewers. Burgo is back at work in London, our garden is green and smiling. News of friends: Robert is still in Geneva, but writes that he can keep his job no longer. He has been seeing Melinda Maclean, who has heard from Donald since his disappearance.

May 13th. I was dandelioning yesterday afternoon near the empty swimming-pool when I saw a dead hedgehog lying curled up at the bottom. I shouted for Ralph, who came and took it out, but had great difficulty in jumping up from the empty pool; an upsetting conversation followed, one of those that lay a chilly hand on the heart and bring about a discord between the significance of the words spoken and the fresh green of the beech leaves, the narcissi, the pale blue sky. The two refuse to merge and their co-existence is painful. It seems that poor Ralph has been feeling so feeble as to become seriously anxious about his state of health. I blame myself exceedingly for not seeing what I didn't want to see. It shocks me that there should be any water-tight doors between two people as intimate as we are. In getting him to come to London tomorrow and see a doctor I hope I am not forcing him to do something he always avoids when possible; but in this case I don't think so. It's my belief he is glad to have made the decision.

May 14th. The doctor was pleased with Ralph's check-up but we await the result of further tests.

Lunched with Clive and Raymond at the Ivy off gulls' eggs and salmon mayonnaise. Last Sunday Raymond reviewed André Maurois' book on Georges Sand, and before setting out to praise the book itself (which I'm now reading and think very good), he devoted a third of his review to saying how wicked and treacherous Maurois had proved himself to be at the time of the fall of France. I tried tentatively to put the general question as to whether this was relevant to a purely literary article on a purely literary subject. Nobody, surely, thinks that the fact that

Marlowe was probably a police spy and a disagreeable character has a bearing on the excellence of *Doctor Faustus*; but all Raymond would say was that his conscience wouldn't have allowed him to praise the book without this reservation.

Goodness, London looked drab today: just enough of the Coronation decorations are up to have a fussy and sad, rather than a cheerful effect. Regent Street was particularly disastrous, decked in enormous pink waxy-looking Bedalian roses, through which the grey faces of the houses are anxiously peering.

[On May 16th we received a bombshell from Ralph's doctor. The tests we were awaiting had come and revealed sugar, which meant that he was in some degree a diabetic. To find out what that degree was and how to deal with it he was condemned to spend a week in the London Clinic having further tests, while I stayed with Juanita and spent all my days with him. We went for walks in Regent's Park, admiring the rose garden, and experiencing that strange calm that comes from having no doubt what ought to be done and concentrating on doing it. At least that was what was my prevailing mood and I believe his, too. He was in any case amazingly philosophic and resigned, showing neither irritability nor depression, and remarking among other things that his new diet would give us an excuse to prevent Mrs Hoare putting flour in the gravy. He was given a pocket set to test his own urine by boiling it furiously and watching it turn any colour between navy blue and deep orange (which was bad). How strange that the human body could express its abnormal function in these vivid terms of colour! Preferable to other forms of reaction, such as pain, however.]

May 19th. Dorothy and Janie Bussy for the weekend — Dorothy as fragile-looking as something made of matchsticks, and as alarming to be with as a very young baby. One moment she is completely on the spot, sharp as needles. The next she says 'Indian' when she means 'Chinese' or begins telling us who Beckford was, till Janie (irritated beyond control) tells her '*of course* they know'. There was a conversation about Raymond's article on Maurois. 'Do you disapprove of the book?' I asked.

'*Yes*'.

'Of the book or the man?'

'The man. I haven't read it.'

I thought as much. Yet Maurois turns out to have been quite an old friend, and Janie went so far as to say she 'didn't think he had been so very wicked'. Her case, perhaps the best that can be made, was that a treacherous or false streak in a character must come out in his artistic products. I suspect that to both Bussys, politics are the ultimate touchstone of everything. Dorothy said how shocked she was that Cortot[1] had been invited here to play in a concert and given an enthusiastic welcome. When I said I thought the consideration when inviting a pianist to play was how good he was, she merely smiled and said, 'I would much rather have had a German', as if this was being very audacious. 'But of course have a German too, if he's good enough,' I said. To Janie intellectual activity that is not founded on politics is worth very little — 'academic thinking is dead, out of touch with what's going on'. And just look, what *is* going on in the world! War after war, violence, bitter building up of hatreds, righteous resentment because old hatreds are dropped. It is morally wrong to do so, the Bussys would have us say. On the same note there has recently been an outburst of indignation because the Crown Prince of Japan is arriving for the Coronation. Could anything be more futile?

[1]Alfred Cortot (1877–1962) was the foremost French pianist of his time. During the Second World War he was appointed to an official position under the Nazi régime and after the war was forbidden to play in France for a period.

June 4th. The Coronation has come roaring towards us like a lorry heard approaching up a steep incline, and now, thank God, has roared away again. There has been an almost maniac note of mass hysteria about it all — culminating in the high-pitched screams of false excitement of the BBC commentators. We walked to the village in the afternoon to see how Ham's Coronation was going. It might have been a hundred years ago. Outside the school some of the children were dancing round a decorated maypole, while opposite them sat the village old folk doubled up on kitchen chairs and perfectly silent. All the ages between had gone off to somewhere livelier, I suppose. The little girls wore pink paper roses in their hair, and when the dance was over they lined up and sang *Land of Hope and Glory*. Ramshackle sports began in a rough field next door, organized by the 'Italian prisoner from Mr Hudsons'.' No other representative of the 'gentry' being present, I was appalled to be asked to give away the prizes, and beat a hasty retreat.

The last item of this great day was a firework display at the Romillies — very pretty as they burst over the water and dropped into it. Here we met Eardley and Eddy from Crichel, the Campbells and Connollys. Dora and Bunny [Romilly] tried on their coronets of red plush, fur and gold balls for our benefit, looking both splendid and absurd.

I suppose it has meant fun for a great many people, though I allowed myself to be momentarily overcome by dislike for the mumbo-jumbo of the service, with its 'holy oil' and the rest, as well as the noisy way the English always pat themselves on the back and say how well the monarchy 'works'. It's just harmless, that's all. Burgo of course is violently against it.

June 10th. Drove to London for two days, lunching with Molly on the way, in the fresh peace of Garrick's villa. She advanced towards us shaking her scarves, her hands, and the small pallid jowls which flank the ironical hyphen of her mouth. To me she said, '*You* look well. The whites of your eyes are clear. I always like to see clear whites.' Then she told us about the savage rape and murder of two young girls somewhere along the river, quite close — a maniac's murder, it was thought. Molly said, 'It's not nice for me you know having all these maniacs about. I met one the other day in Bushey Park. They always *love* a *park*.' We walked in the eighteenth-century garden shaded at one end by two magnificent Spanish chestnuts probably planted in Garrick's day. On through a grotto tunnel under the road, to the bank of the tame brown river with its few floating swans.

June 12th. To Benjamin Britten's Coronation opera, *Gloriana*, which we enjoyed a good deal more than *Billy Budd*. Apparently the aristocratic but unmusical first night audience were bewildered by the music and took the sight of Joan Cross as Queen Elizabeth I without her wig as a deliberate insult to Queen Elizabeth II. Met Heywood and Anne [Hill] in the pub opposite where we saw the musical world working away like yeast, and many familiar faces including the interesting Celtic one of Myfanwy Piper framed in its curtains of straight hair. On the way home we stopped at Bob Gathorne-Hardy's to pick up Eddie to stay the weekend. He combined well with Noel

Sandwith who came on Saturday. Eddie has become something
of a caricature of his old self — in appearance a great fabulous
bird, in character a mountain of pretty ruthless egotism, yet
lovable and good company none-the-less. Though he never
puts himself out for anyone else and is determined to have his
own way, he is a genuinely affectionate, wicked, charming old
monster. He is one of a good number of characters whose butter
of affection is spread wide but thin, who is fond and appreciative
of a great number of friends, but very deeply of few. Conversely,
we see the narrow and deep type in Vanessa and Pansy Lamb.

Now we are alone again and must think very seriously about
Ralph's health. I am impressed and moved by the uncomplaining
patience with which he takes it all. A change of diet doesn't — alas
— seem to be enough and he will have to take regular insulin,
which it was hoped he might avoid. At the weekend there was
talk of the Missing Diplomats and whether Donald Maclean was
ever a homosexual. 'Oh, yes he was. I've been to bed with him
myself,' said Eddie.

July 23rd. Back at Ham Spray after London and the Memoir
Club. Somehow or other, but only just, I got my Memoir
written in time, the effort leaving me electrically charged and
thus ready to enjoy lunch with Clive, Freddie Ayer, Bunny and
Angelica. It was enormous fun, and the contrast between
Freddie's birdlike quickness and Bunny's soft deliberation was
amusing to watch. At first communication between the two
seemed impossible, the pace of one having no beat in common
with the other. But after some preliminary skirmishing they got
going — four semiquavers of Freddie's to one crotchet of
Bunny's — and the resulting harmony seemed to satisfy them
both, and was principally concerned with the Russian anarchists
Bunny had once known. Angelica and Freddie, seated opposite
each other, exchanged searching glances but hardly any words.
When we left, Freddie and I got on the same bus. 'What did you
think of Angelica?' I asked him. 'Striking but not beautiful,' he
replied, to my surprise, as I thought she was looking marvellous.

I saw the Garnetts later on at the Memoir Club meeting, which
took place in Vanessa and Duncan's new flat in Canonbury.
Angelica was in a mood of apparent abandon, tossing back her
wine, with flying hair. I talked to Leonard about his selection
from Virginia's diaries, *A Writer's Diary*, which he has recently

brought out, saying how immensely I admired and enjoyed it. What principles of selection had he followed? 'On the whole I kept to what concerned her work, her writing and reading. Of course there's a very great deal more, and of that a great deal which would cause acute pain to living people.' 'Yes', I said; 'so I imagined, and was rather surprised you left in that amusing but unkind bit about X.' 'Oh is X still alive?' Leonard said. 'I thought she'd been dead for ages.' I told him how tantalizing it was to know of this hidden gold-mine, asked whether he meant to publish the whole eventually, and if so when? 'Do you think I shall live to read it?' He looked me up and down. 'I *think* you might just about manage to', was his reply. An argument about the Bloomsbury aversion to accepting honours followed, something I have never understood. What is wrong about such an acknowledgement of their achievements? Why should writers and painters not receive the same ornaments or grace-notes as scientists and surgeons? But I was in a minority, Clive and Duncan being particularly averse to the idea, and seeming to imply that by so doing they would forfeit their independence in some way that I cannot understand.

My Memoir[1] had a surprising, and of course pleasing success; they are I must say an appreciative audience as a general rule, and laugh wherever it is possible to do so. Bunny insisted on carrying it away, saying he 'wanted his sons to know about the Marshall family'.

[1]Foundation of the first chapter of *Memories*.

[One thing I always enjoyed at Memoir Club meetings was a chance to talk to Leonard. Otherwise our paths now seldom crossed. In the days before the War I would see him sometimes in the bookshop where I worked, or dining with Clive, and I was occasionally asked to dine with the Woolves, or Ralph and I boldly invited them to Gordon Square.

I know from the stories told me by Ralph and other workers at the Hogarth Press that Leonard could at times fly into irrational rages. To me he always seemed as gloriously the same as some well-loved monument: there was the melodious, quavering voice that never altered its timbre nor lost its note of confidence in being right in an argument; the deliberate movements, the slow charming smile, the deeply grooved face, the steadfast gaze from his blue-grey eyes, the hair that still stood up in tufts like a schoolboy's even as it grew greyer. Much of his admirable *Autobiography* was derived from papers read at the Memoir Club — I can still hear his voice saying firmly, 'I was exceedingly intelligent.' I tremble to think that I argued with him more than once about G. E. Moore's *Principia Ethica*. As well attack the Bible to an Archbishop.

I remember a pre-war evening when the Woolves were dining with us, and Virginia was giving an astonishing display of trying to charm the company and make us look ridiculous at the same time by her usual attack on 'the younger generation', and certainly succeeding in the first. In the latter, however, she was worsted by Alix's logic, and Leonard took her by the arm saying 'Come on, Virginia, don't disgrace the older generation'.

It was easy to see what rocklike support he gave to that brilliant, uneasy mind.

Whatever she wore, and sometimes it was very strange, Virginia could not help looking infinitely distinguished, with her thin beautiful face, deep-set eyes, and the accompaniment of a remarkably low-pitched, electrifying voice.

I only once or twice visited the Woolves at Rodmell, and then it was generally from Charleston. One occasion gave me a chance to see another side of Virginia's character. It took place soon after the deaths of Lytton and Carrington and she showed her sensitive kindness to me in ways I shall not forget. How glad I am I have survived to read the whole of her Diary for I believe most of it to be her masterpiece.]

July 31st to August 4th. A weekend with the Nicholses at Lawford Hall, lunching on the way to Essex with Janetta who is in London to have her baby. Beautiful mellow weather took away from the somewhat haunted melancholy I sometimes feel hanging about that handsome house and its romantic garden, with the huge tulip tree, the reedy pond and the pleached apricots and plums. All the children were there, friendly and happy, Anne being tutored for Oxford by Marjorie Strachey, who added a good deal to the jollity.

August 29th. Raymond arrived last night and this morning the three of us are to begin on our drive north for the Edinburgh Festival, leaving Burgo in charge of the house, chickens and Minnie's forthcoming *accouchement*. 'My motoring friend' (a fellow-student from MacNalty's) is coming to stay while we are gone.

[Because it altered the course of Janetta's life entirely, the distressing fact must here be recorded that on the very same day that her baby, Rose, was born, Derek telephoned to say that he had fallen in love with someone else and intended to throw in his lot with her, leaving Janetta still weak from the birth and completely shattered by this cruel desertion. Ralph and I felt very far from clinically objective about this harrowing situation, and it was some time before the seed of relief that the marriage was over could develop into a thriving plant. We had never happily accepted it. Of course we did our best to support and sympathize. Janetta told us that she thought Derek broke the news as he did out of a feeling that if one is going to be beastly one had better be *really* beastly. With amazing fortitude she wrestled with the practical problems confronting her, moved into a furnished house and sent for Nicky and Georgiana from France.]

September 1st. Our drive north was taken gently and well-furnished with 'sights'. Raymond chose Kedleston and Chatsworth — Adam's Kedleston is proud without any hint of a warmer attitude to life, its nose (figuratively speaking) well up in the air; Chatsworth more splendid, with its fantastically beautiful gardens set in a wide valley, great sheets of water, fountains, pollarded avenues and metal trees spouting water from their twigs.

My recollections of the Lake District were so vivid that I feared it might prove a dreadful disappointment. But no, our drive along the shores of Windermere and Ullswater brought back in rich and exact detail all my earliest pleasures in nature. Green and glistening after rain, fresh-smelling, clear as crystal yet with floating scarves of mist, the emerald grass tightly drawn over knobbly limestone, streams rushing downhill between clumps of ferns — leaving this beautiful landscape was like leaving childhood for a second time. We arrived at Heriot Row, Edinburgh, that evening, to be warmly welcomed by Colin and Clodagh [Mackenzie].

[The high-grade musical pleasures of the Festival were well suited by the noble architecture and pure air of the town. We listened to the Virtuosi di Roma, *Idomeneo*, a recital by Irmgard

Seefried, and Bruno Walter conducting Brahms. Much social life included a champagne supper party given by the Mackenzies.

The sophisticated manner of a little Lord Binning aged twelve who was also staying with the Mackenzies, and 'very precious heir to the Earl of Haddington', amused us a good deal. He disapproved of the clothes of the Ghost in *Hamlet* 'being made of that stuff with holes in it that ladies wear', and cast down his dark eyes on to his plate at lunch, saying in a soft sad voice that he would have no more pudding 'because in point of fact I don't like it much'.

Off after breakfast on September 10th, awash with gratitude to our incredibly kind hosts, and leaving a touching tableau behind us in the drawing-room, where Clodagh's female pekinese, suddenly indisposed, was reclining on a red cushion having ultra-red ray treatment and looking round at us all with speaking eyes demanding sympathy, while beside her — watchful and solicitous — sat her husband.]

September 12th — Ham Spray. Back by tea-time, finding Burgo smiling and apparently pleased to see us, having put flowers in vases, seen to Minnie's *accouchement* and the execution of superfluous kittens, and enjoyed his visit from 'my friend', who had left two days earlier. Our Scottish stay was an interlude of pure pleasure. After so much spoiling I am reluctant to start scrabbling back among the knobbly pebbles of daily life.

September 13th. Visit from the Cochemés.[1] He has got the job he wanted and they are off to Amman in a few days. I love his vivid phrases and charming French accent. Of Wynne he said, 'I like the albuminous look in his blue eyes, which seems to have lasted over from babyhood.' And of crayfish: 'They go forwards slowly and then much faster backwards — like a very nervous, very clever young man.' Burgo made himself agreeable to the visitors and offered to help me in the garden. Why then did he say suddenly in the middle of a game of croquet: 'I can't enjoy anything'? And how could it fail to give a blow to one's spirits? But Philip Toynbee, at dinner with the Campbells gave him the right foretaste of Oxford in a most amusing style.

[1]Jacques, a biologist and native of Mauritius, and Joan, painter.

September 15th. In London for the day, I visited poor Raymond, prostrate after yet another operation and 'three of the worst days in my life,' and Janetta, so deeply sad that Ralph and I agreed all words of consolation left us. Burgo and Ralph went off to buy his Oxford trousseau — the most cheerful episode in our day.

September 30th to October 5th. What a treat to have Janetta with us at Ham Spray for five days, during which — gradually at first, but then (in a tongue-loosening session of blackberrying along our laden hedges) more easily and completely, I think and hope the old position of mutual confidence was restored.

October 8th. A new era begins. Today we drove Burgo to Oxford to be installed at Christ Church; some anxiety of course there was, but as the day wore on it seemed that Burgo was welcoming his new life, advancing towards it where he has often shown signs of retreat. We saw with relief that he began to take command of the situation as soon as he found his name in white letters painted over the door, and even more when his scout appeared and said 'Are you Mr Partridge, Sir? I shall be looking after you now,' and went on to produce a lot of useful information. Burgo's rooms (two of them) were large and sympathetic if bleak, their furniture and decoration that of a past age, when a civilized life was more esteemed. I went happily to sleep that night, glad that Burgo was launched on the ideal life for a young man and at a suitable age — seventeen. However Ralph was reminded too vividly perhaps by our glimpse of Oxford of its stresses and strains, and had a restless night worrying on Burgo's behalf.

October 12th. Burgo's first letter from Oxford was an antidote to spectral premonitions: 'I have got to know two other people on the same staircase. Everybody seems extremely friendly and nice. The room is not at all cold once the fire has been lit. There is plenty on my bed, anyway kind Rachel [Cecil] has given me a hot water bottle. I have repulsed the Rugger and Soccer canvassers fairly easily and ordered *The Times*.'

Driving to tea at Lambourn today Ralph and I got out and spent a few moments in a wood where dark moist ivy made a carpet beneath tall horse-chestnut trees, whose yellow leaves drained of sap hung like the great blunt-fingered hands of workmen. I got back into the car with a chestnut in my hand, so sweetly glossy and giving such a pang of voluptuous pleasure that I wondered whether it is these particles of sensation rather than cerebral activity that makes life worth living. But what would Freddie Ayer say, who thinks the emotions are equivalent to inarticulate screams?

December 4th. Burgo back from Oxford. So now I must see if I can keep up my conversation with these ruled pages through the Vacation — as it now has to be called. Is it a mere habit that makes me do it? Or is there really some salutary effect in the mere expression of thoughts and description of events in words? An entirely selfish one at all events.

[Breaking all past habits, Ralph, Burgo and I spent the Christmas of 1953 in Paris. We had intended to fly (it would have been only the third flight of our lives), but a dense white fog and a strike of security staff at Le Bourget forced us to change to sea and train, and we chugged across the Channel lulled to sleep by the soporific hooting of foghorns. It was the first time we had spent more than one night in the grey spaciousness of the city since the war. Our hotel was the pretty little Beaux Arts where Oscar Wilde died, now kept by a distinguished-looking elderly lady with a stick; its liftless spiral staircase led up and up to an elegant round skylight.

Boris and Maroussa called for us that evening. Instead of imagined burglars, Maroussa has now a real horror to contend with — she has to have an operation for cancer. Strangely enough, this has given her fresh vivacity and she is as brave as a lion. With them we went to the Deux Magots and the restaurant called the Cochon de Lait, where we dined off sucking pig with buckwheat and other indigestible Russian accoutrements. Next day we went to see them in Boris's studio in the Boulevard Arago, the centre where his creations have for many years taken shape. It looked as though it had remained the same, and nothing in it had been moved or dusted, for fifty years at least. On the vast studio table lay a mosaic in progress and some cartoons, while variously coloured little cubes of marble and glass lay all around, spilled on to the floor or were heaped in sacks like Ali-Baba's jewels. The high walls, on which hung pictures by Henry Lamb and Man Ray and more cartoons of Boris's own, led up to a gallery where he and Maroussa slept.

We had a day at Versailles, a morning at the Louvre and a good deal of shopping, Burgo laying out a large sum on ties from Sulka.

Returning to the hotel next morning with *The Times* Ralph told me that dear Molly had died. We feel intense sadness and disbelief that we shall see her no more.

Our last dinner in Paris was at Laperouse, an old-fashioned restaurant of high quality and restrained dignity, recommended to us by Derek. Our menu was *Oeufs Laperouse*, followed by 'the' chicken in 'its' tarragon sauce and a Grand Marnier soufflé, during which we had quite a lively conversation about values. Both Ralph and Burgo appeared to think their place could be entirely taken by cold reason and attacked me for 'highmindedness'. All right, reason is the sausage-machine but whence comes the meat to be passed through it? I defended myself as best I could by saying that it was priggish and puritanical to shun values out of fear of being too priggish and puritanical.]

December 28th — Ham Spray. Arriving home we found the saddest postcard *d'outre-tombe* imaginable awaiting us, written in a quavering hand:

> Darling Ralph and Frances, I am very ill, and sad to be writing that soon I expect it must be my farewell. Perhaps you know it may not be quite at once and so then it will be what is called the beginning of the end. So with all my love to both dearests and all my thanks for the lovely times I have had with you, your most loving Molly.

We shed tears of sorrow, and bitterness too — for before we left for Paris, hearing that she was gravely ill we had ordered a very large bunch of flowers to be delivered at Garrick's villa. It would have been a small comfort to think we might have given her the tiniest last pleasure, but those brutes Harrods, hurrying with the mince-pies and turkeys, deprived us of it by arriving too late.

1954

January 6th. Janetta came to us for the New Year week-end. She is back in trousers, she is back in her original self. An appetite for life is returning to her, but is not much stronger than her appetite for food, which probably symbolizes it. She is very thin, even fragile-looking and seems to have a pleasure in doing without things like sleep or food, which reminds me alarmingly of Jan. One day, awakening from a short nap on the sofa, she began talking about the importance of loyalty to people you were fond of, especially if you were aware of their failings and that not everyone liked them. She applied this to Sonia [Orwell], who had given her immense support but been accused of battening on disaster by several. She admitted that Sonia had been bent on separating her from Robert. I expect she knows that we like Sonia as little as she likes us; Ralph believes that it is the neurotic side of her character — and the unhappy one too — that damages her friends.

We went over to Stokke one evening, where the Connollys, Freddie and Joan Rayner were staying. Mary was dressed in her new 'Top' covered with pink sequins, a present from Robin. 'Oh, is that your top?' said Ralph gallantly, 'can't I see your . . . er. . . ?' Cyril and Freddie were both vain enough to enjoy the suggestion that they might have been included in the New Year honours. Cyril and Barbara went early to bed and the rest settled round the fire. Visual images were the subject of discussion. I asked Freddie — who rejects them — could he not visualize Mary's face when she wasn't there? 'I know it's round and pink, with blue eyes,' he said, 'but those are concepts.' 'Well, how do you think of blue?' Freddie was now inclined to say that we who believed we had visual images were mistaken, that if we had them they were not coloured, and that the same went for dreams. I find it quite extraordinary that so clever a man can say such things, but perhaps he is colour-blind, as he described Barbara Connolly's coat as green when in fact it was red! As we left he bid us goodbye 'to your coloured dreams'.

When Freddie was at Luggala, Robert — a little piqued at having driven him through acres of wild and beautiful scenery without getting a response — asked him, 'Don't you enjoy looking at all this?' 'Not really,' Freddie answered. 'When I see those sheep grazing on a mountain I at once start wondering what they are thinking about — or whether indeed it's proper to say they *think* at all.'

A return visit by the Campbells and Freddie next day, full of complaints of the Connollys. They had insisted on bringing their coati but it was not allowed to sleep in the nice hutch lined with straw prepared for it and had to share their bedroom, where of course it shat on the coverlet. Barbara sulked in her room and refused to come down to meals. She had asked to be taken to the early train on Monday, which meant getting up at seven.

When Monday came and we drove Janetta to the station, we found the whole Stokke party pacing up and down the platform, their faces lavender with cold. Robin told me in tones of stifled horror that they had got up at seven and called Barbara, only to be told by Cyril that she was sleepy and had decided to take the *next* train. So here they were, but Barbara refused to get into it, saying she had left some kind of basket behind at Stokke. 'She's going on the 1.17 though,' Robin said between clenched teeth.

January 13th. Euphemia to lunch. She has become extremely deaf, so that the only possible reply to her rather exhibitionist talk is to send her back her own remarks at the full pitch of one's lungs, after some time of which one feels like a pelota player, arm aching from sending the ball as hard as possible against the back wall. She talks as if it were only yesterday that she was a lovely girl, winning all hearts as she loped round Paris. Her stories are incredible. One told how when Dorelia went off with Henry Lamb, Madame Maeterlinck urged her (Euphemia) to go and kill Dorelia.

'I told her I didn't want to kill anyone, but she dressed me up in workman's trousers and a cap, and sent me off with a huge Swede, a friend of hers. And a knife to stab Dorelia with. Then Augustus arrived and found me lying asleep under a caravan, so he lay down beside me. The police came and arrested us, and put us in prison for being homosexuals. Then I said I thought it would be a good thing to show them I was a female, so when the police next appeared I took off most of my clothes and my cap, and let down my hair. So they shook hands with us and set us free.'

She went on to talk about Ida John. 'She was a wonderful woman. When Dorelia came to live with them it wasn't such a perfect arrangement as some people said; but Ida decided that she would rather have hell with Augustus than hell without him. She always behaved perfectly to Dorelia. When Henry was born, she was terribly ill. I went to an English doctor and asked him to operate, but he wanted the money in advance and we had none. I got a *sage femme* for her, but she was dirty and infected Ida. Her hair turned quite white in one night and her head shrank until it was as small as *that*' (pointing at Minnie in my lap). 'Augustus came, and she drank a glass of wine and said: "Here's to your past and future loves!" and was dead.'

January 21st. Yesterday I began re-reading Gibbon. I had forgotten the delight of swimming out into so large an ocean — and everything in the current world is illuminated by it. Militarism appears as the most destructive force even in peacetime, and porphyrogeniture difficult for any individual to survive.

January 26th. It was a surprise to see the garden covered in snow when we pulled back our curtains. Already it was two inches deep and still falling. While we were in the bath the electricity failed, which always raises a ghost of impotent panic; then comes the positive physical pleasure of making a quick blaze in the dining-room fireplace and seeing a frying-pan with eggs and bacon on it. Round the garden to look at the humped vegetables and prettily outlined trees and bushes. Needing an indoor task I started sorting the great trunk of letters to Carrington that has lain for a long while in the flower-room. They made me dreadfully sad: such feelings of poignant loneliness or ill-usage were set down on the fading pages, and all of it over, and many of the writers dead though their voices go on screaming silently. I was struck by how good many of the letters were — Alix's for one; they had the touch of deliberation and formality more often found in the best male letters. The scrabble-scrabble, spontaneous, gushing female type of letters (Dorothy Brett or Phyllis de Janzé among Carrington's correspondents) are nice to get but unreadable later. By evening, I had thrown away whole mounds of parental love and scolding, or girl-friends' meaningless high-spirits, and was feeling rather like a murderess; but only by such destruction could life be given to the rest, in neatly docketed heaps or boot boxes full of frustrated love and other emotions. I found it gruelling and ghastly, and was near tears when I sank back relieved into the world of the Emperor Julian and the Aryan Controversy.

We are supposed to go to Crichel for the weekend tomorrow, but I fear it will be impossible in this weather. A faint smattering of snow has fallen, and a small cold wind is raking the frozen world. Each day I put out crumbs for the birds and a saucer of water which rapidly turns to ice.

January 31st. Last night was the coldest yet. Going to fill my hot-water-bottle at midnight, I was horrified to find a 'Moujik's moustache' (Ralph's name for water frozen to a *double* drip when the tap is turned full on), and though I stood beside it for twenty minutes no greater flow appeared. The electric fire burning all through the night cast its friendly glow on our walls, but this morning — total lack of hot water. Wilde went up into the roof. No go. Plumber telephoned for. No go either. My hands ached with cold before breakfast was cooked. Later the cold water joined the hot, so we are without a drop, and worst of all there is none in the lavatories. Over all stretches a sky as cruelly blue as that on a Swiss wintersports postcard; on the verandah icicles two foot long sparkle in the sun. Wicked old Minnie thought fit to lie on my bird-table among the crumbs. The mind freezes like the body, and becomes incapable of any but the most prosaic reflections. Mary telephoned, 'Can we come and have a bath? We've been frozen for several days,' and though we had to disappoint them they gallantly said they would come to supper. It was delightful to have company in our igloo over a makeshift but piping hot meal.

February 4th. The water is 'through'! Long may it be so! The plumber has been, and our pipes are now cased up in wood and sawdust; yesterday evening I revelled and wallowed in a hot bath, emerging soaped, scented and invigorated. This morning I measured the longest icicle on the verandah — it is nearly *five feet* long, strong and ribbed, and tapering to a fine point.

February 8th. The thaw has come, and we set out for London in
steady rain, driving through water over sheer ice. How we
enjoyed everything! — the warm railway carriage; the intellect-
ual-looking fellow passenger who put in suggestions for the
crossword puzzle, and raised his hat with a polite 'Good
morning!' on leaving us.

Left our things at Janetta's and went to lunch with Julia and
Lawrence. The crisis at the Tate Gallery fills their thoughts. Julia,
cooking away in the background, explained that her watch was
an hour slow — and lunch indeed appeared about two. Meanwhile Lawrence flapped out of the bedroom wearing a jacket and
pyjama legs; he is put to bed by Julia at every moment when the
Trustees are not meeting, fed with glasses of milk and carefully
ministered to. When we got back to Alexander Square Janetta
had just arrived back from Paris. We spent the evening with her
and Robert oddly enough, as Janetta had asked him to a drink,
thinking 'we would like to see him'. Freddie Ayer had been
invited to dinner, so it was natural to ask Robert to stay on, as he
did, though 'natural' is not the right word. Their manner to each
other was friendly, even polite, but controlled, only once sending
off a spark on the quite impersonal topic of whether the new
magazine *Encounter* was anti-Communist propaganda, run on
American money, or not. Robert thought it was, and that it
attacked Communism for all the wrong reasons, 'for improving
the lot of the lower classes, instead of for *not* improving them'. I
do not see the faintest chance of these two coming together again
— though neither of them is easily eradicated from the system.

February 9th. We were about to leave the restaurant last night
when I said, 'I expect the waiters are longing for us to go,' and
Robert came back quick as a flash and suddenly savage: 'Oh well
then — let's *not* go.' Freddie supported me, saying he didn't enjoy
thinking he was making people miserable, but the truth is that a
nucleus of 'desire to cause pain' lies within every living soul. I'm
well aware of it in myself and bitterly ashamed of it, especially in
view of my pacifist and anti-violent beliefs. There it lies like a
wild animal crouched inside one, ready to leap out if the door is
left a crack open, but unlike a wild animal it can only be shut in,
never killed.

February 20th — Ham Spray. A happy morning, turning into a day that sparkled like a diamond. Saxon was with us, and we sat out until lunchtime. Ralph accused Saxon of not eating enough.

'Perhaps I don't eat enough,' he said. 'But you see I don't really want to go on very much — except when I look at something like that view.' It's about the most intimate remark I remember him making to us, and certainly the saddest. However I was thinking very different thoughts — that I was glad to be alive, that life still held much to enjoy.

After lunch we drove to the Gibbet Hill and walked along the downs. The beauty of the day, the soft clear distance visible so far in every direction, had brought out a mixed bag of fellow mortals — country gentry with their dogs, two Irish priests (bigoted-looking, blind-eyed) and a covey of schoolboys. I left the other two and walked home alone. The dewpond was full to the brim with yesterday's rain, reflecting the blue sky among its golden rushes. When I turned through the gate towards home, I entered a silence so utter that I could hear the voices of the cowman's children in our farmyard. It was four o'clock, the light softened, the trees grew feathery and pigeons wheeled above the corduroy fields. My huge shadow stood like Napoleon on the brink of light and darkness, and then paced downhill ahead of me.

Saxon in very good form this evening, talking about various objects of his love — Plato, Spanish towns, Kubla Khan.

February 22nd. Saxon left us, pathetic to the last, and tragically reminding us of the predicament of old age. With the conviction that we made him a little happier over this weekend, we sink back into our own slots.

February 26th to 29th. Children's weekend. Nicky came for half-term and Robert brought Georgie from London. They are both I think quite happy with us, and of course they freshen a room like bunches of primroses.

March 8th. Janie has been here talking a lot about two who were (and very likely still are) her heroes: T. S. Eliot and Gide. Of Eliot's strange ménage with John Hayward,[1] she said that she thought he was paying a debt by looking after John — pushing him about in his wheel-chair and allowing himself to be silenced in all conversation — as atonement for his deep sense of guilt over putting his late wife in an asylum. Where, Janie says, she certainly belonged. It had been a queer marriage: he picked her up on Brighton pier.

Gide's marriage is a stranger story. He had had no sex of any sort until he was twenty-three, when he went to Egypt and 'almost accidentally' went to bed with a boy. Soon after this he met Wilde and Lord Alfred Douglas and took to buggery with enthusiasm. Meanwhile he declared his love to a beautiful, clever female cousin who adored him. They married, but he decided that she was much too pure to want sex, it would be an insult even to suggest it, and with no previous explanation the marriage began and ended in perfect chastity. He said he was not 'in love' with his boys, only with his wife, but she was horrified by his homosexual affairs, longed for a normal married life and children, and was most deeply hurt of all when he had a brief passage with another woman to whom he gave a child 'as a sort of present'.

[1]Writer and biographer, suffering from a degenerative disease.

March 11th. Eardley [Knollys] described a Crichel visit that went wrong in the excellent phrase 'there was no love in the room'. I thought of this when we returned from Bunny and Angelica's Anniversary party at Hilton, where the reverse was manifestly the case. We had wondered if we were mad to drive right across England and spend the night in an inn in St Ives, but how glad I am we did. There were quite a lot of 'good grey heads' and white ones too hinting at the last volume of Proust, but also a large ingredient of youth. Of Bunny's boys, Richard is newly engaged to beautiful and sweet Jane; Angelica's four little girls, wearing their party dresses and highly excited, revolved among us with dishes of caviare and smoked salmon. Looking down one saw an angelic face looking up enquiringly from waist level, munching hard. There was music: William and Angelica played an oboe sonata: Leslie Hotson[1] sang American songs; the little girls played solemnly on recorders. Duncan and Morgan [Forster] greeted each other like survivors on the same raft.

Now we are back again. Ralph looks well and cheerful, and has had a good report from his doctor.

[1]American professor of literature.

[When early in their married life Bunny and Ray Garnett were looking for somewhere to settle in the country, they saw and fell in love with a picture of Hilton Hall, near St Ives, Hunts., in the pages of *Country Life*. It was a three-storey, seventeenth-century house, neither large nor pretentious but beautifully proportioned, facing due north through handsome tall iron gates. It was Cromwell country, and the pretty cottages making a distant ring round the large village green seemed hardly to have changed since his day; in fact, when Bunny bought one of them to save it from destruction the men working on the job found frescoes portraying Moll Cutpurse, highway-woman of the period, while on the green itself was an inexplicable old maze. One usually entered the house through the back door into the busy, untidy kitchen where one or two Siamese cats would be prowling and wailing. Many of the rooms had panelled walls; the ground floor was paved with flagstones covered in Kelim rugs, and a staircase of dark wood led up to the bedrooms. A collection of bronze and stone heads stared through blank eyes at the visitor from the hall or the garden wall; most were the work of Stephen Tomlin — there were Bunny himself, Duncan, Vanessa and Virginia. The vast beamed fireplaces in drawing-room and dining-room gave out virtually no heat at all from their log fires in winter, even at close range. That was the snag — Hilton was the coldest house I have ever spent a night in, and I used to smuggle an extra eiderdown in the back of the car to help suppress its penetrating chill. There were lovely things — early paintings by Duncan, Bunny's fine library supplemented by his father's and mother's books, Angelica's piano, harp and cello. She was always adding beauty in the form of patchwork curtains and covers, and my two nephews built on a panelled writing-room for Bunny with astonishing proficiency — yet there was no denying that Hilton had at times a sad atmosphere. Was it the dank East Anglian climate, the knowledge that cabbage fields stretched away in all directions over the perfectly flat land? I remember cheerful days in summer, playing bowls or badminton in the back garden, where there was also a big old pigeon-house and a home-made swimming pool and where the four charming little girls and their step-brother, William, were usually enjoying themselves. Ralph and I spent many weekends at Hilton and there wasn't a soul in it we weren't delighted to see; but it was a house of moods, and at times a mute hush could stifle the Garnett family's natural animation.]

March 16th. Robert for the weekend. I lay awake for some hours thinking of his views on bringing up children. He believes that adults should devote themselves entirely to their children's happiness. 'Then,' said I, 'you would have the paradox of each generation focusing on the next and never leading their own lives.' 'Ah, but it's never been done,' he said. 'It would be well worth giving it a try for two or three generations.' He is violently against schools and their stereotyped constriction.

Next day Burgo came back from Oxford, lively, talkative and seeming interested in his work, friendly to Ralph and me.

March 17th. What do *I* care, I said to myself reading Gibbon, how, when and where the Norman invasion of Sicily began and ended? Why on earth bother to read about it? And went on reading entranced.

Ralph has been going to the Winchester Assizes to hear the trial of Lord Montagu and others for buggery. It was not a very moving tale that he had to tell. The two little tarts from the R.A.F. made a pitiful showing in the witness-box, saving their skins at the expense of their three victims, Montagu, Pitt-Rivers and Wildeblood, who sat with folded arms in the pillory. Wildeblood is the most to be pitied. Ralph thinks he will get a stiffer sentence than the other two; he has admitted to being 'in love' with one of the cadets. It may ruin his promising journalist's career, hard cheese indeed when no one can conceivably be said to have suffered in the very least. James Macgibbon has suggested Ralph writing a book about homosexuality. I wish he would, but doubt it.

March 19th. Ralph is still attending the Assizes; today Burgo and I went for an hour. The proceedings seem to have a natural sluggishness of their own, and at first I was afraid that it might become intolerably boring waiting while the barristers swayed on the balls of their feet pondering their next question. But I am fascinated by the formality of the scene — though it tends to act like a bandage hiding the human element. Then this suddenly gushes out like blood, and with a start one realizes what a crucifixion it must be for the three educated, personable young men in the dock to have their most intimate feelings dragged around the court by hostile, mocking, aggressive Counsel before a mass of indifferent faces. Poor Wildeblood is sensitive, nervous, emotional and intelligent. He clasped the edge of the dock with long thin fingers and listened intently to every question before quietly and thoughtfully replying. A clever grammar-school boy who got a scholarship to Oxford, he was obviously the pride of his parents and had a very good newspaper job. I was appalled at the cruelty of these proceedings, which seem morally wrong as well as painful, in the way that seeing stones thrown at a negro because he is black would be painful. But since it happened I am glad I went.

March 23rd. Just lately the Atom bomb has refused to be ignored — the Hydrogen bomb rather, which the Americans (in the course of letting it off in the Pacific) have found to be about twice as powerful as they expected. Ralph has for some time been calling to me to 'think about the Atom bomb', and I have stubbornly plunged my head into the sand. What use to think when there is nothing we can do? What use to think when thinking must perforce reduce one to despair? Better to go on living as best we may on the last feet of mossy turf on the edge of a precipice, enjoying its texture and softness but never looking over the edge. Yet Ralph is right of course. The human spirit revolts at not facing facts, is not content to be shut up in a lunatic asylum happily conscious of being Catherine the Great, any more than it shuns all knowledge of such outrages as the Montagu trial. So yes, we *must* think about the Atom bomb.

April 14th. Why, I wonder, did I wake in the small hours of this morning to one of those unexpected and acutely painful 'moments of truth'? In a flash I saw the precariousness of happiness — of mine, of Ralph's and Burgo's, of the world's existence, and saw it very very clearly. Impelled by some strange impulse I got up quietly so as not to disturb Ralph, and crept downstairs to the music room, where I now sit amongst last night's débris, with Minnie still folded in sleep on the back of the armchair. I saw the start of another perfect day through the window but it gave me no pleasure. I thought that to be a practising hedonist was an enormous gamble; happiness to him fulfils the same role as faith plays to the Christian, and loss of happiness is like loss of faith. The Christian says, 'With my body I thee worship' in the marriage service. The hedonist is all the time saying, 'With my happiness I worship the world', but when it fails him he is clueless.

I took a life of John Stuart Mill out of the shelf and began reading with growing interest.

April 16th. Julia and Lawrence are at present holidaying in Stokke, and came over with the Campbells to dinner. Lawrence was amusing us all by brilliant mimicry, but he put on an inscrutable look when Robin (who is much influenced by John Berger at the moment) put forward the view that art cannot ignore its social surroundings, but must represent them in its content. I cannot see why art must be a communal — or Communist — affair, and I set up as an Aunt Sally for Robin the suggestion that it could be entirely personal in its reference, getting a groan from him of, 'Oh, you're such an old-fashioned individualist. I was just telling Julia at breakfast . . .' and here the conversation slid off amongst Universals and the Absolute. Lawrence said, 'Generalizations sprout from the sub-soil of Ham Spray.' On Ralph's side of the table the Atom bomb gave place to homosexuality. Both Julia and Lawrence are full of praise for the Campbells' kindness and way of life, but deplore the lack of vitamins in the diet. Julia fusses over Lawrence's health as though he were her son rather than her husband — I have never seen him rosier or plumper.

April 23rd. Julia and I went up to London together for the Memoir Club, leaving our husbands to entertain each other. I hoped Ralph might discuss his plans for his homosexuality book with Lawrence, but he told me later that he had taken no interest in anything but his own problems. I can say the same for Julia. I listened to her complaints of men in general (for never doing things that bored them) and of Lawrence in particular, while I reflected that she would never darn a sock or sew on a button if she could pay someone to do it for her. I lunched at the Ivy with Clive, Barbara Bagenal and Harold Nicolson, and in the evening to the Memoir Club. A rather small gathering; I talked mainly to Bunny who read an admirable paper, partly about his relations with Duncan, Lytton, Frankie Birrell and Clive, due for his next published volume, and partly some unpublishable episodes illustrating his attitude to sex.

There was an amusing story about the bugs in Duncan's studio in Fitzroy Street, which used long ago to be lent to Bunny to take his girls to. He noticed the bugs were increasing at a great rate — one day he killed thirty-six on the wall. The two of them decided to try and kill them while Duncan was away for a week or so, and Bunny consulted a friend of his who was chief entomologist at the Royal College of Science. A poison was recommended which they laid down in saucers, carefully closing all the cracks, even the keyhole. 'I hope the people downstairs will be all right', Duncan said as they went away. This was an Italian family, including a little boy of seven who practised all day on his violin. 'The odd thing was,' Bunny's story went on, 'that when we returned the bugs were all gone but the Italian family had completely vanished also. There was no sign of them whatever.'

While Bunny was reading I had been watching Duncan's face with great pleasure: his expression kept shifting, smiles giving way to blinks. Now he interrupted: 'Oh but don't you remember, Bunny, we met a coffin coming down the stairs?' '*No!*' 'Oh yes, indeed we did.'

'What was the poison?' asked Dermod MacCarthy, who is a doctor, 'XYZ,' replied Bunny, 'that couldn't kill anyone, could it?'

'Oh, yes, certainly it could. They might not die at once, you know. When did you say this was? 1916? Yes, then it could probably be taken for kidney disease. How much did you put down?'

'About a pint I think.'

'Good heavens!'

Every face in the room wore a look of comic horror. But Duncan said serenely, 'Well, it wasn't my fault. I *did* say I hoped the people downstairs would be all right. Personally I blame the entomologist from the Royal College of Science.'

May 8th — Ham Spray. Janetta came last weekend. She, Ralph and I spent an afternoon of watery sunlight walking in Collingbourne Woods, among huge primroses, bluebells, violets and anemones; following a trail of animal excrement to a badger's lair, and picking up globular flints in the hope that — like a little local boy — we would find one containing a cache of ancient coins. Later at Stokke, I thought how quickly one would be charmed and interested if one saw Janetta for the first time, standing as she now was in front of the fire in her thick white sweater and tartan trousers making her characteristic clawing gestures in the air with her hands.

Next came Robert, and both have been entirely delightful companions. Wherein, one cannot help asking, lies the gap between them? Robert seemed in good spirits, working hard, full of conversation, realistic, entertaining us with his imitations, collapsing into giggles. He was summoned to the War Office last week to be interrogated about his acquaintance with Melinda Maclean, and confronted with a photostat copy of a letter to her from himself. As she has now re-joined Donald in Russia, Robert thought it probable that they were combing her 'contacts' for possible Communist agents, but the idea that they might suspect him of being one evidently doesn't alarm him.

May 13th. Not long ago I got a letter inviting me to join the Newbury Orchestra, and I accepted with joy, since there seemed little chance of any more quartet playing. Yesterday I went to my third rehearsal — the last before the long summer break. I had found them absorbingly interesting and exciting, but alarming also, because although I can read fairly well, the Brahms symphony we are playing is much too difficult for me, so I am tempted to sit by myself and make as little noise as possible. This time, however, I shared a desk with a prim young schoolmistress from Downe House School who was about my level. I had been practising quite arduously and all at once began to feel I was getting a grasp on the music, certainly I love it. The sensation that one is minutely contributing to this massed sound, this combined tweedling, fluting, thrumming and hooting, is intoxicating. I am determined to go on with it if I possibly can.

May 29th. To Oxford to see Burgo, and after lunch to watch the Eights-week races among crowds of variously elegant and dandified young men, many wearing beautiful snow-white flannels, straw hats and huge button-holes. There was a great feeling of youth, high-spirits and promiscuous élan; also a lot of pretty girls with peach-like complexions and ugly clothes. Drizzle fell sparsely, the river glittered like tin under a grey sky flaming with sunlight at the horizon; the races created intermittent moments of excitement and roars of 'House! House!' like a cheerful dog barking. Ralph wore his Leander tie, and in the boat-house we saw an oar with his name painted on it. An afternoon of youthful glamour and gaiety.

But soon after we had got home poor Ralph was seized by griping pains, which came and went and came again with such excruciating intensity that I managed to get him to go to bed and telephoned the doctor. He came out armed with morphia and confident of his diagnosis — kidney stone. Next day Ralph was perfectly comfortable, and saying that waking to find himself without pain was the keenest physical pleasure he had ever had in his life. Meanwhile I am still suffering from shock at seeing him convulsed with such fearful agony. There is no threat of the knife, thank God, but he is to have an X-Ray to investigate what is happening in his kidney. I dread the dawdling paraphernalia of medical reports. Among our friends Janie has been the most knowledgeably sympathetic, having nursed Gide through an attack when he was over 70. He said, '*C'est pire qu'une accouchement*', though I wonder how he thought he knew.

Simon Bussy has died in his loony bin.

June 5th. Ralph had his X-Ray yesterday, but we shall of course hear nothing for a while and must try not to behave like reasonable animals. Ralph observed that 'the radiographer was a grey-haired lesbian, taking every chance of paying Men out for what they had not done to her, and cooing sweet nothings to the pretty girl assistant.' 'We are told to cut the patient in half', she said, savagely tightening a strap round his waist so that he couldn't breathe. I sat in the tiny waiting-room watching the patients go in and out — a pregnant woman, a limping elderly man, a whimpering child. At last my particular sausage was ejected from the machine and we ate some belated lunch in the car.

June 14th. Ralph has had no pain for nearly a week and we both faced this morning's X-Ray report with some confidence. But standing on the landing while he spoke on the telephone to the doctor I heard him say 'Oh. So you think we had better not go to Sweden.' (We had a tentative plan to go with the Crichel boys to see the eclipse of the sun there.) Ralph is a good deal cast down, and suffering from regret in the form of a craving to put time back physically to a period when an unpleasant fact was *not* a fact. But the position is not it seems to be taken as serious, and for my part I cannot feel really depressed when Ralph says as he did today, that my being so extra kind to him had made his life more than ever worth living.

However, I am jaded today after two late nights and very little sleep. Janetta came here last night with Ralph Jarvis, an easy, pleasant, civilized man whose humorous vein reminds one that he is a relation of the Gathorne-Hardy family. Ralph and I both think he is greatly taken with her. Sat up till one o'clock talking, and got up this morning early to see them off. The night before we were at Stokke when Wynne and Kitty [Godley] came in after dinner with the light of battle in their eyes and fiery cheeks. Leaning back in his chair, Wynne said that they had been quarrelling because Kitty 'refused to hand up her friends' to him: 'If I like them they will also be my friends. If I don't she must give them up. I gave her *all* my friends.'

'Yes — but I like them,' murmured Kitty in a voice that brushed one's ear like swansdown. Wynne invoked his masculinity, and claimed that she must accept his view or do without him. Someone put in a plea for reason. 'I'm sick of reason!' said Wynne. 'I'm not rational man, I'm anthropological man.' I put in a defence of reason and Robin came up with his present craze for 'culture patterns'; Ben Nicolson added quiet and kindly support of women as deserving to be treated as rational beings — but to think it should be necessary! The argument was only about three-quarters serious and it now slid off crab-wise into Aesthetics.

We have had a letter from Alix describing various new physical troubles, and then continuing: 'life does become increasingly hospitalized as one gets on, and yet I like it better every day.' It is a magnificent declaration from someone who has just been through several medical horrors, who is getting old, never sees anyone but James, and whose sensual pleasures are moderate and circumscribed. I find it ringing in my head as I go about each day's menial tasks, and it makes me feel ashamed of myself.

June 16th. Mary rang up to tell us that Janetta had been taken to the London Clinic for an operation last night. A telephone call to the clinic was not very reassuring. 'Oh yes, she's had her operation . . . quite satisfactory . . . no, she won't be able to speak on the telephone yet . . . in a few days perhaps. . . . Are you a relation? . . . The surgeon is with her now'. All this left us much disquieted. Next day, before I could ring up again her own weak, quavering voice came sadly through. She had become suddenly very ill on Friday night with a high temperature and bad pain. 'Peritonitis,' the tiny tearful voice went on. 'They didn't know what it would be when they put me under — probably appendix, but they have taken *most* of my insides out. I thought I was dying and I didn't greatly care, and when I woke and found I had it all to do again I felt faintly disappointed.' Next day she rang again, better and voice stronger.

June 23rd. We've been to London to visit Janetta and spent over an hour with the sweet touching girl, who is mending fast.

Fetched Burgo from Oxford. Tea on the lawn; unable to leave the beauty of the evening, we sat out until the last rays of the sun had left the pampas grass and the long shadows were streaming over the surface of the hay field. I don't think Burgo feels he has failed in his prelims, but he showed me the papers — they look terribly difficult.

July 2nd. Ralph Jarvis motored Janetta down to convalesce with us here. We wanted above all to have everything calm (one of her favourite words) and welcoming; her bedroom looks very fresh in its new wallpaper of red rosebuds on a white ground. How maddening, therefore, that the electricity should suddenly fail. I was the first to fuss, Ralph followed, and then we fussed in unison, preparing to light a fire and cook the dinner on it. But ten minutes after their arrival the electricity came back, Janetta was looking pale but lively, and we are *so* pleased to have her. Put her to bed and after a meal of soup, crab mayonnaise and strawberries we all went and talked to her until midnight.

Ralph J. is more amiable and at home than ever, and has asked to come back and visit her. Goodness knows what he and she are in for. What a relief it is that perfect thought transference doesn't subsist between human beings; it's better far that we have to go on straining our mental antennae to read the signs of those curious clock dials — people's faces, whose hands are sometimes set to show the true time, and at others express deliberate disguises, and where the desire to communicate is often in complete conflict with the desire to conceal.

A telegram from Burgo who is in Oxford for Desmond Guinness's wedding: 'Seen Prelim results. Have passed. Returning six Monday.'

July 4th. Ralph J. came back, bringing his daughter Caroline, who is most attractive; she came and chatted to me in a very friendly way in the kitchen while I was making salads and she was watering her solid bull-terrier. I questioned her about the life of a Deb in the Season, which she is now involved in; she gave a vivid and intelligent account of its intoxicating pleasures (balls in houses like Petworth with beautiful gardens, bathing naked in the sea at Aldeburgh after her cousin Gathorne's coming-of-age dance).[1] Yet she hated and is ashamed of the marriage-market underlying it.

[1] She afterwards married him.

July 8th. Yesterday the Brenans arrived to stay. Gamel has dyed her hair a harsh metallic black, which entirely misinterprets her character; her pretty cream-coloured hands loaded with old rings, however, emphasize the passive elegance of someone who never makes demands but effortlessly arouses other people's desires to take care of her and spare her trouble. While Ralph drove them over to see the Pritchetts, I had a somewhat door-opening conversation about personal relations with Burgo, who returned from a London jaunt yesterday looking very handsome and as if he had had a good time, yet who wanted to know why life was so difficult? I suggested that love and hate tended to get entwined in his nature, and that sometimes he reacted with the inappropriate emotion. 'Well, perhaps, maybe — '

Rather like a clown in a harlequinade, I feel as if I had been juggling with different heavy objects — Burgo's moods, Janetta's health, the Brenans' comforts, and the telephone which never stops ringing. All Janetta's admirers have got on her scent.

Today broke hot and heavy with innumerable flies. Something of a Chekhov atmosphere brooded over our garden with ambulant couples stooping to study a flower. Venturing further, we took Gerald to see the orchids now blooming on Ham Hill — the Fragrant, Pyramid, Burnt stick, and even the Musk, which he had never seen before. Returned to the cool green arbor we have carved out of the weeping ash, where we had tea and discussed hospitality. Gerald said (truthfully) that he preferred receiving it to giving it; Gamel (untruthfully?) that she liked it the other way round; and both produced many reasons why with their five servants in Spain they found it impossible to have anyone to a meal.

Later came the Hills in Janetta's car. Anne has become a splendid old-fashioned bluestocking, and engaged us in a long gossip about Trelawney, Byron, Shelley, the Neapolitan child, et cetera. Burgo is now tapping on his typewriter upstairs; a heavy silence hangs over the fields and trees; even the flies are too sluggish to bother us.

July 12th. Janetta lay on the chaise-longue in the sun turning over her problems and helping us to turn over ours. Hers are the most pressing. Having tried every motor-drivers' examining board in turn to get herself a test, she has so far failed to find one, and after frantic telephoning ran out in tears to Ralph who was picking peas. She needs to have her car for her stay in the house she has rented for herself and the children in Cagnes, and constant jangling of hows and whys in her head have left her looking iller than when she first came to us. I seem to hear the rattle of wooden beads such as children have on play-pens, as we clicked the tangible segments of our problems to and fro, trying out different combinations to reach a solution. Ralph is already envisaging that he will 'have to' drive her down, something I refuse to pity him for.

Meanwhile Janetta has gone off for a night in London to go to a 'grand party decorated in jungle style with about twenty stuffed monkeys,' looking much too fragile in her best silk frock; and I have woken feeling stronger after a splendid sleep, and have got out the index box and made a start on the next volume of Freud which arrived two days ago.

July 18th. Burgo has gone off to stay with the Garnetts for the Hinchingbrooke ball. A slight breeze as to whether he should take his dinner-jacket or hire tails was settled by the news that white tie 'and decorations' were to be worn.

The Gowings are here on their way to Stokke. I walked with Julia up the downs. If it weren't such a nuisance her new craze for food faddism would be a matter of high comedy; she is quite obsessed with the vital need for green vegetables — turnip tops for preference. 'Do you think we shall get enough green vegetables at Mary's?' she asked me. 'I'm really very worried about it. Could I ask her if I might just cook myself a cabbage every day? It's so *odd* of Mary,' (I was vividly reminded of Julia's own Mrs Thatcham)[1] 'She ought to see those girls of hers haven't had the right diet by the shape they have become.'

[1] In *Cheerful Weather for the Wedding*.

July 22nd. To London for the Memoir Club and to see Janetta's new abode in Montpelier Square, an experience that has the effect of witnessing a rising temperature. By afternoon I was about 103° myself, after driving with her to Maples and spending over an hour helping her choose beds, mattresses and pillows. Back at Alexander Square, the telephone rang, rang, rang. Likewise the door-bell, and I let in Ralph Jarvis dressed as a city man in bowler hat and rolled umbrella. He took Janetta off to *Rosenkavalier*, and when I returned from the Memoir Club I found them munching in the kitchen, Janetta looking exhausted and with a headache but busy cooking eggs. I wasn't sure that Ralph was being as supporting as he might, or realizing that she must leave London as soon as possible — it's killing her. She had miraculously passed her driving test and could go next week, but obviously needs a companion to share the driving. Ralph's line was 'driving would simply *kill* you, and what would poor Nannie do then, poor thing?'

Memoir Club: Clive was sparring with Bunny about his autobiography. 'I'm sure Bunny's going to say all sorts of untrue things about me, he's so inaccurate.'

Duncan read a delightful paper about his student days in Paris and some letters, mostly between Lytton and himself, interrupting himself frequently with, 'That's not true, that *is* true'. Or, 'I shall have more to say about that later on.' Then: 'I'm afraid I can't *read* this — it seems to be written in what they call *vanishing ink*.'

Vanessa (sepulchrally): 'A pity *all* letters aren't written in that in my opinion.'

July 23rd. Eating breakfast with Janetta, the sun streaming through the window, we discussed the question of who should drive out with her. Robert? He had agreed when the idea was first put to him, but retracted next day, saying he couldn't undertake to go lightly as it were. She felt it would be bad behaviour to try to persuade him, so quickly withdrew. They have been meeting with apparent friendliness; all the same he said no, and work was the reason he gave and is now, I believe, his guiding principle. I was cast down to see this shining chink close.

July 25th — Ham Spray. Incessant drenching rain, beating and soaking. The madonna lilies lie prostrate; it is disgustingly cold. Lord what a summer! A call from Sonia Orwell, saying Janetta's last possible co-driver had fallen through. 'Just as I thought,' said Ralph, 'I always knew I should have to go.' He is inclined to preen himself on travelling with a lovely young woman who will be taken for his wife. 'More likely your daughter,' I say snubbingly. So it is now fixed. I hate his taking flights, going long drives without me, but I know that is absurd; it is the right thing for him to do and it is mainly my doing that he goes.

August 3rd. Ralph off to France and Burgo invited away for the weekend, I faced my odd lot of visiting musicians — Pippa Strachey, Alan Tyson and William Garnett — alone. We all, I'm quite sure, enjoyed it enormously. There was music, music, music all the time. Will (oboe) and Pippa (piano) were the best performers; Alan turned out to be pretty bad on the viola but kept us all laughing with his comicality and enthusiasm, as well as composing a Scherzo and Trio for our four instruments (the *Ham Spray Concerto*) which we performed to Ralph on his return. In snatches I was given some impressions of his lightning tour, amounting to a slightly piqued vision of it as a favour done to a somewhat *exigeante* princess.

August 27th. The pace of life this summer hasn't slackened, and like the Red Queen I race along, never quite keeping up with events and certainly never having the time for rumination which I know to be vital. The unspeakable weather goes on — rain, rain, rain, wind, cold. If it clears for an instant — flies! An Oxford doctor says that it has caused depression acute enough for several of his patients to consult him about it. V.S.P. on the telephone: 'Oh yes, I have my revolver always at my elbow.'

The weekend was spent at Lawford Hall arriving in the evening in a peachy glow which bathed the fine old house and its romantic garden in warmth and beauty. Phil and Phyllis are turning it from a melancholy Elizabethan showpiece into a growing organism possessed of beauty and comfort. Ralph and I have a palatial suite, furnished with taste, and our fellow-guest is our dear friend Eddy [Sackville-West]. As for the foundations on which Phil has striven to build it — they are a set of views and values as archaic as those of our grandparents, and Eddy's are just as bad. Phyllis? I don't know; I think she has accepted Phil's standards because it would be too painful to fight against them. Compulsory games was the topic at breakfast one day, and no word raised in opposition to them. 'What, even football?' I asked hopefully. 'Oh *yes*,' said Eddy and Phil in unison, 'boys like it, and anyway even if they don't they must be kept out of mischief. They have no idea what to do with themselves and they must have exercise.' I could hardly believe my ears, but was relieved to remember that Eddy spent most of his spare time at Eton playing the piano and reaching an almost professional standard; also that he must have been excused rough games from delicate health. At tea-time we got on to the importance of class distinctions, the Royal family, the Church and the supremacy of the English over all other nations. ('They are the only people with imagination'!!) Appalled and stifled, while the others trooped off to church on Sunday morning, Ralph and I walked down to the marshes, and along built-up grassy banks beneath which grey tidal streams crawled away towards the sea, trying to blow away the feeling of stuffiness, and enjoying the serenity of the mud flats coloured mauve with sea-lavender or blue-green with plumy rushes blown by the warm sweet wind.

September 10th. Richard and Jane Garnett came with dear old Saxon, blanched as an almond, fragile as old lace. He frightened us by suddenly becoming doubled up with cramp for a good ten minutes, hunched and speechless. A hot-water-bottle relieved him but he sank back panting, and for a moment I thought that death itself was with us.

September 13th. Desmond Shawe-Taylor had invited me to go to the first night of the Vienna State Opera's *Figaro*. Delighted at the prospect of such a treat, I went to London with Saxon and stayed at the Paddington hotel, feeling strange in my room there without Ralph, and afraid of losing my passport to paradise — my ticket. With the first notes of the overture the magic began; then the curtain went up to reveal a magnificent plunging view of Seefried's bust as she stood in her low-cut bodice. Jurinac was an enchanting Cherubino, Kunz Figaro, and Lisa della Casa a slightly breathy Countess. What rapture! At supper in Desmond's musical club I was fascinated to hear the critics' different views:

Desmond: Seefried top; Jurinac not at her best.
Andrew Porter: Jurinac sang everyone else off the stage.
Simon Mosley: Seefried superb, della Casa disappointing.
Jimmy Smith: della Casa glorious.
And so on. My word this has been a treat!

September 16th — Ham Spray. Day of Burgo's departure to stay in France with Isobel and Charlotte, and also of the arrival of a postcard saying that one of her sister's children has chicken-pox — a slight shadow on his anticipatory mood. Day also of the Newbury Orchestra's reopening. I have been practising hard and mean to hang onto it like grim death. After a recital I picked up Ralph and Burgo and his luggage and drove him straight to Southampton. We were both strangely moved to see our chick go off to his ship through the darkness. How do parents manage to despatch their sons to war?

September 24th. Here we are at home again after two visits to London. Is it the everlasting soughing of the wind and stinging of the raindrops that makes me feel so restless? Or the thought of being off to Italy in a fortnight?

My visit to *Figaro* has swivelled my attention in the direction of opera, and high time too. We went to Lennox Berkeley's *Nelson* with Juanita and splendid old Count Benckendorff, who did not much approve. He kept commenting to me *sotto voce*: 'It is aMORphous. A pity as the music is good. He understands how to make a certain tension.' Like all Russians he is wonderfully expressive and when words failed him he just threw out his hands and made an explosive sound: 'Pff!' This upset a young man in stiff collar and white tie sitting just in front of us, who kept turning round and looking at us anxiously. Once he even addressed us directly: 'The last act is the best of all. It beats *Peter Grimes* into a cocked hat.' The opera was well received, and it deserved to be. The music was really lovely, and the dramatic content would not have failed had Nelson acted better and looked less like an Aberdeen terrier. The Count drove us home in his small, noisy car, sitting square and bulky beside an empty space provided for the Countess's[1] harp or his double bass.

The next day to lunch with Janetta who is picnicking in her new house with a few sticks of furniture. I get the impression that she is essentially a loner at present, except for her children to whom she is more maternal than ever before. Coming home from Cagnes through Paris she lunched with Derek. He asked her not to divorce him, saying that he would only make a fool of himself — he was good for nothing but work and that was nine-tenths of his life. At some mention of their life together he burst into tears.

The second opera was *Don Giovanni* with Jurinac singing divinely, and next day we lunched with Clodagh Mackenzie, her charming father [Charles Meade][2] and Ralph and Coney[3] Jarvis. There was the ghost of a plot about this confrontation: a possible desire for us to see Ralph J. in the role of married man, not realizing perhaps that my Ralph and I take a purely passive part in Janetta's emotional relationships, now that her marriage to Robert has foundered. Coney met us with a guarded, rather strained expression, but thawed later. We liked her and found her very attractive as well as handsome — the position was made easier by our children, Burgo and Caroline, being friends.

[1]Maria Korchinska, professional harpist.
[2]Alpinist and writer.
[3]Mrs Ralph Jarvis.

October 4th. Last week Burgo arrived back from France, looking very brown and well, having 'managed' his travelling success-fully, and greatly enjoyed himself. He has been lively and friendly, though inscrutable as ever even in this expansive mood, and I try to keep the rules and in no way force his confidence. He made us laugh a lot with stories and imitations of Isobel at Cannes, has listened endlessly to my new records of *The Magic Flute* and has now gone off to Oxford several days before the beginning of term saying he wanted to do some work.

Our journey to Italy draws very close. I resolve to enjoy it to the top of my bent, and try and be half as nice to Ralph as he is to me.

October 8th. Dark is falling as we desert our Ham Spray ship. At Southampton total silence around the bulk of our solid boat; the harbour lights are reflected in the inky water. Eating our last English meal in the ship's restaurant a sense of liberation spreads like a warm glow from a log fire. The ship now becomes womb-like, and my eyes close over my book. We creep into our tiny cabin and lie like biscuits in a tin.

October 9th. Woken by a loud clattering about four. A faint drizzle, as if through the watering-can's finest rose, sprinkles us as we cross over into the customs' shed and recognize with delight the pernickety voices and ineradicably cross faces of the French officials. The six cars that crossed with us stand yawning their heads off while men peer into their entrails with flash-lamps; in a very few minutes we are off in the grey half-light through the ugly, shattered town of Le Havre. Everything continues hideous and wonderful. Why not start off with a really good breakfast at Tôtes, and my word it is! Perfect coffee and hot flaky dark brown croissants. All day we drive South, to arrive at a small village near Dijon and totter into a bedroom with massive wooden doors, steel-hinged, a floor covered with worn but polished red hexagonal tiles. It's an old house with a huge chimney down which came the pale glare of the moon. To bed, very happy.

October 10th–11th. Through rolling Burgundy, with great trees just tinged with brown standing in the still air as if in aspic, and autumn crocuses. Then we were driving along Lake Leman, and *suddenly* there was the huge silhouette of the mountain on the far side, smudged in in faint grey, while a single towering snowy peak rose out of its wreath of mist like a girl from her chiffon evening-dress. But the Swiss smugness and respectability made this vast natural panorama look like something indoors — a romantic scene painted on the wall of a second-rate hotel for instance. Next day we hastened on to the Simplon. A pass is an exciting thing, to be savoured and thoroughly understood. We breathed in the cold thin air, found some little starved alpine plants, including bright blue gentians among the woven grasses in earth soggy with melting snow, and plunged down — lacet after lacet — into Italy.

October 12th–13th. At Florence we had our first taste of sight-seeing. I had forgotten how like zebras north Italian churches are. (I had not been here for thirty years and Ralph never.) What must we see? The Duomo, of course. And the Baptistery and Giotto's tower. The first moments of looking at works of art are tentative and experimental. What exactly am I at? Do I feel anything? What sort of thing should I try to feel? Then it dawns gradually that what I want is to fall in love with these delectable objects — and that cannot be done quickly and at the drop of a match, although occasionally it can so happen. Both of us, for example, fell in love with the less famous of Donatello's Davids in the Bargello — there was something so stylish about his youthful swagger and grace; but it's as if one's hands were full of reins and at first it's hard to know which to choose.

A night and morning and then off through pale, dimpled hills dotted with nearly black trees and creamy oxen with enormous horns. Just as the light was fading the same evening we drove into Rome.

We take at once to the *Inghilterra*, our home for the next week. It stands in a cul-de-sac, is old-fashioned and spacious, with tiled floor and creaking lift. Our room is prettily furnished with antiques and the bed is as big as two. We look in on Henry and Pansy Lamb, also staying here and resting after sight-seeing, in a much less nice room than ours; and a note from Robert asks us to have a drink with him, at his 'swish' hotel. All evening the portentous — but as yet untasted — character of this amazing town stood waiting in the wings. What would it be like? Would we ever get the hang of it?

[Some while before I first met Henry Lamb, Ralph had described him to me as the painter who had fallen in love with the beautiful Euphemia Grey, married her and carried her off to join Augustus John's circle in France, where he had later become the lover of Dorelia. His famous painting of Lytton was not greatly approved by Carrington, though she was charmed and attracted by the artist himself; Ralph was inclined to feel that Lytton had been 'made a fool of' by Henry, not just by subjugation to his charms but because the result was his adoption of the bohemian disguise of large black hat, gold earrings et cetera, which was quite foreign to his character. For Ralph, Lytton's great qualities were his intelligence, integrity, affection and wit, but like many Stracheys he had a strong romantic streak and it was to this that Henry appealed. He was exclusively heterosexual.

I first met Henry when he and Dorelia spent a night at Ham Spray in 1925, an occasion referred to by Carrington in a letter: 'He has a most unhappy face but is amusing and charming. Of course he couldn't resist making up to F[rances] M[arshall] a little. She couldn't see a trace of his former dazzling beauty, she confessed afterwards.' Maybe not beauty but attraction yes; he was then forty, slightly built, his sensitivity and habitual tension emphasized by the penetrating gaze of his very pale blue eyes, and with a firm rather too thin mouth that suggested latent cruelty. I got to know him during the following years, and understood why Lytton had called him 'the most delightful companion in the world', though not why he had added, 'and the most unpleasant'. He talked with a quiet intensity as if his life depended on expressing exactly what he wanted to say — and it was generally original and very well worth listening to. I have never met a portrait painter who became so deeply obsessed by the characters of his sitters.

He married Lady Pansy Pakenham in 1928, and they had three children.]

October 15th. I've been all day in a state of electric stimulation but now we've taken our first bite of the vast meal, and have some glimmering of what we are in for. Last night I was a new boy — now I've fastened my snake belt and learned the way to the lab. This morning we went to the Doria Palace with the Lambs. Like us, Henry has never been here before, and is half out of his mind with excitement. I don't think he sleeps at all at nights. He puts on a rather loud check jacket, pulls a peaked cotton cap well down over his eyes and prowls along at a rattling pace, looking to right and left like Groucho Marx. Pansy walks with a rapt and thoughtful face, dressed in good English clothes and 'sensible' shoes. They are a touching pair and we love their company, but this afternoon we went by ourselves to St Peter's and the Pantheon. Dined with Robert in the Piazza Navona. He came here with Oonagh Oranmore in her car, but she has now left, and he works hard most of the day at his nearly finished novel. 'In spite,' he said, looking surprised, 'of a good deal of upheaval in my private life'.

October 18th. The Lambs and Robert have been brought together, and taken a mutual fancy to each other. Having driven the Lambs to the Villa d'Este and Tivoli one day, we persuaded Robert to take a whole day off with us at Ostia. The bathing boxes were all shut, and a single figure — an old lady with only one leg wearing a decolleté bathing-suit — lay on the beach.

October 19th. Now that we have fallen definitely in love with Rome we tried to remember what account friends gave of it — Julia, Raymond, for instance. Perhaps it was impossible for them or anyone to convey its immense distinction, beauty and loveableness. I hadn't guessed that not only the relics of antiquity but the fragments of it (which I have been prone to disparage as stumps of old teeth) are all harmoniously merged with baroque and modern Rome by being made of the same stone, whether silver-grey or honey-colour. Then the fountains everywhere, the display of splendidly gesturing arms, beards and Dolphin's tails of stone. And last but not least the personal beauty of the living Romans — their noble carriage, well-shaped heads and fine brows. The modern haircut which covers these small heads with neat but not too curly curls proves that here are still the faces of classical antiquity, as well as of Donatello and Raphael. In sober truth this visit is turning out so intoxicating that all energy is required for absorption, and none left for writing so much as a postcard.

While we were looking at Michelangelo's Moses today a young American said to Ralph 'Excuse me, Sir, but can you tell me why Moses has horns?' Luckily Ralph could, having just read it up in the admirable Baedeker. Called on the Lambs in their new hotel room — much better than the last but Henry has an appalling cold, which we do not want to catch.

October 20th. The buses of Rome are as special as everything else and we now make frequent use of them. You have to become like a piece of digestible food, leap in at the mouth, pass quickly through the teeth (a guichet where a man sits dispensing tickets) and then — taking advantage of all the peristalsis available — work your way through the whole length of the intestines so as to be ready to drop out of the arse at the psychological moment. The buses go so fast that it is a short sharp, profitable agony.

October 23rd. Last day of Rome. We are horribly sad to go. The Lambs wanted to know if they were going to see our 'nice Robert again', so we all ate together. We leave Robert after a great many companionable, gay evenings but there is a lot he has left unsaid, no doubt deliberately.

October 24th — November 2nd. For the first days of the homeward journey, we had the Lambs as passengers, ailing both but undaunted and enthusiastic. By Orvieto and Perugia we crossed the Apennines to Urbino in steady rain; there the sky cleared to a Piero della Francesca blue and enabled us to enjoy the splendid town to the full, and not only Urbino but San Sepolcro, Monterchi and Arezzo. The dreadful fact that we may never see these masterpieces again forces us to stare and stare, trying to imprint them on our inner eyes, polishing the memory so as not to lose its brilliance. Two more days in Florence, and at Pisa we parted from the Lambs. The sight of the shattered Campo Santo induced in me a violent sense of shame that our attacking aeroplanes should have so shockingly denuded it of the incomparable frescoes I saw in my early twenties. Then Lerici and Shelley's last dwelling. Leaving the coast we climbed the terraced hills in mellow golden sunlight, through morning-glory, maize, red and yellow vines and turquoise-blue spray — the last mouthful of delight before the plate is snatched away.

November 7th — Ham Spray. This Italian holiday has been our best for years. Every night I go back there in my dreams and Ralph says he does the same.

November 19th. Concert day today; quite a fizz. We had our dress rehearsal in the afternoon with our soloist Iris Loveridge and a stiffening of other professionals. I had time to drive home, change and bath and back to the Corn Exchange, with Ralph among the audience. I thought we made a *deafening* noise but we all enjoyed ourselves and anyway it was a new experience, a thing I always relish.

1955

January 6th — Ham Spray. Twelfth night already, yet not a thought recorded here so far. Not because I have had none — quite the reverse. I have simmered away among a fluctuating wash of them, about life, about death, about old age and where it is all leading? What am I at?

January 10th. Burgo's best Oxford friend, Simon Young, came with Janetta for the weekend. As the time approached he seemed to be silently saying 'do be nice to my friend', though goodness knows there was no need to do that. Even if we hadn't liked Simon I know we would have done our best to seem to, but we *did* like him very much indeed. He is a small clever-looking robin-like young man with a smooth sheet of dark hair falling over one eye, sharp-witted, quick to see and make jokes. He has read a great deal and sinks into a book like a stone. He had a dynamically stimulating effect on Burgo and revealed more of his Oxford life than we had glimpsed before. Simon obviously viewed him as rather wild and anarchical, also a comedian.

Janetta was low with a cold, and voiced sad views of life: 'I don't like it *one bit*. I don't mean that I don't enjoy quite a lot of the things I *do* — I do, very much, but I keep looking up and hating what I see.' We are beginning to hatch a plan to take a house jointly for several months of the summer, in Spain perhaps or Italy.

Sat up till one o'clock talking to Janetta about plans. Oh, how delightful she is to be with.

February 17th. Anne and Heywood are one of the couples we most love having to stay. They have made a great success of their marriage for one thing, and the house swallows them up pleasantly. Also as we do, they like reading and going for walks and Anne loves an argument. She is deep in researches into Trelawney. She brought down some chapters which I read and so did Heywood, who is a severe critic of her. As he read, he said to me 'we neither of us know any grammar unfortunately'. Anne, with a shriek, 'Heywood! Just think if Cecil Woodham-Smith's husband had gone on like that!'

Some time ago when we learned that both the U.S.A. and Russia possessed the Hydrogen bomb, and that these two monsters sit staring at each other across land and ocean, each with the means of destroying the globe in their paw, Ralph remarked how ludicrous it was that the generals still went on talking and writing about 'when war comes', in terms of tanks, infantry and air-raid shelters. Now, he explains, that recent tests have shown it to be so far more effective than they ever dreamed, those at the top are forced to accept the stark truth that the next war would in fact end war because it would end the world. There are signs in the papers and wireless that this realization is seeping down into the ranks of the general public.

February 20th. Gareth Browne, Oonagh's son, has run away from Bryanston. He rang up Daphne Bath (a friend of Oonagh's) saying that he was being driven in a taxi to her house in Cornwall. Would she encourage him?

Daphne: 'Oh darling, I couldn't do that — but if you do arrive I'll be delighted to see you.'

Half an hour later another call from Gareth: 'My friend the taxi-driver wants to talk to you. He's coming on the line now.'

Taxi-driver: 'Madam, it seems to me the boy's making a big mistake and is liable to blot his escutcheon. I think he ought to go to his mother.'

Gareth: 'Oh, I can't do that. She's at Brighton with Kee for the weekend. I don't want to spoil her fun.'

Taxi-driver: 'Well, I think it ought to be spoiled anyway. Brighton indeed!'

Later Daphne got a telegram: 'Browne gone to his mother. Thanks for your co-operation. Thistlethwaite, taxi-driver.'

February 24th. Up to London in snow and wind; the trees and grass in the parks expiring under the white sky, ice on the Serpentine, Janetta and her nursery low-spirited with colds in the head. I went to call on someone advertising Spanish lessons, and found that she was the Spanish mother of Rodrigo Moynihan, a sweet little plump penguin of a lady. In the evening to dinner with Alix and James. Alix's face was a mile long, solemn as a cathedral. She told us how angry she had been because John Christie came up to her at Glyndebourne and said 'Cheer up!' Talked of education, art, the proletariat — all the usual subjects. Alix wants to suppress Public Schools; she thinks it vital that everyone should have the best possible education. Accents must be eliminated. She declares she hears the working-classes whistling Mozart.

February 27th — Ham Spray. When we saw Robert in London the electric charge of his despondency was like thunder in the air. Evidently in a state of indecision and loneliness, he was, however — much to our delight — persuaded to come down for the weekend. His proneness to criticize life at Montpelier Square or Nannie, or Georgie's school, points to the source of trouble; but so marvellous are his qualities of realism and interest that once at Ham Spray he became like someone recovering from an illness, however temporarily, and we were pleased to have had a hand in it. With the Campbells, who came to dinner, he was suddenly social but also bristly and truculent. It was strange that after Ralph and I had commented to each other on the three Roberts: drifting and desperate in London, rational here at Ham Spray, and prickly with the Campbells — he should speak of himself next morning in almost identical terms, saying that he knew he 'gave off different emanations' and how hopeless it was to try to conceal an anxious or agitated mood even from Georgie. He had a good phrase about Mary: 'She gets through life jumping from tussock to tussock of treats, and is only at a loss when she can't see another coming.' He came down to breakfast telling of an unhappy dream. He had been trying to pour tea for some people, but nothing like tea would come out of the teapot. Then he looked inside and saw 'nothing but a horrible old osso bucco'. Too plain! He wants to produce love but its source is dry and leathery. Ralph complained of waking every morning feeling his worthlessness. Only I confess to waking in a state of senseless optimism.

March 4th. The third of three incomparable days with a sky as blue as our notepaper. Have been busy and happy at Spanish and violin.

A letter from Robert, who is — as we thought — fleeing the country on the very day that Janetta returns to it. He writes that as soon as he left us on Monday he was 'caught up and trapped in the thing one is constantly trying to get out of. I really feel I don't want to see anyone but very close old friends these days, with whom there is no need to do that awful acting we talked about. I can't put any conviction into my lines any more.' It is the saddest of stories.

March 5th — Long Crichel. Yesterday evening we drove to Crichel, over the rolling slopes of Salisbury Plain, and under a spectacular crimson sky marbled with purple. We kept exclaiming with amazement as we drove. Yet it was the sight of a sturdy little girl of six reaching up to put a letter in a pillar-box, with her straight hair falling backwards, rather than the incredible beauty of the sky, that brought home to me how interesting life is.

All four 'boys' were at Crichel. The evening began rather badly, with an emotive rather than persuasive argument about horror comics; but ended well with Desmond playing us his new records of Verdi's *Falstaff* all through. Today has been completely serene.

Conversation is one of the things I love to think about, but not while at it — then I feel excited and absorbed as if skating or dancing, while a retrospective glance afterwards is like looking at the dead embers of a fire from which nearly all the red life has gone. Conversation reaches a high level in this house, although I doubt if any of them except perhaps Desmond really enjoy arguments. (How few people do!) Both Raymond and Eddy admit that they often don't hear what other people say. At breakfast this morning Desmond suddenly burst out in comic desperation, 'Raymond never hears a *single* sentence I say, even if it's only three words long!' Raymond beamed sweetly but didn't deny the charge. What then does this 'good conversation' consist of? Sometimes it's like a lot of people building a sand-castle; one makes the tower, someone else decorates it with shells, another suggests a tunnel. Push it over and start again.

Raymond said he felt depressed, and the worst of it was he didn't know why. The extreme polish of Eddy's façade sometimes worries me — he keeps a sharply critical eye on superficial appearances, yet he can tolerate fools more easily than the others can — if only they pass that superficial test.

Eardley took Ralph and me and the two stout dogs for a lovely walk through woods just touched by spring, and later to his studio.

March 6th. Snow was whirling on the lawn when I got up. However Eddy was very keen for us all to drive into Somerset to see a recent portrait of himself by Graham Sutherland, so (wish-fulfilment coming to his aid) 'It's stopped snowing,' he said and no one said him nay. The portrait is a remarkable work and has a considerable likeness to Eddy, but there is something definitely unpleasant about it — whether its tints of mauve and lime green, or that it seems to depict him in the electric chair waiting for his quietus.

March 7th — Ham Spray. Nearly a quarter of 1955 has slid by on a basis of solid content, but — if one reads the papers and listens to the wireless — it can't be denied that the war atmosphere has imperceptibly crept up again like a stifling fog, and now instead of vague references to 'in the event of war' and 'the enemy', it is 'when war comes' and 'the Soviet forces'. *What* a world, oh God above! I was thinking, when (as if in mockery) the Creator spread a marvellously rosy glow over the western sky behind the spidery black trees. You see I can still do something pretty good; not such a bad world after all, eh? and I was inclined to agree, only that at that moment the piercing wail of the siren came drifting from Hungerford on the north wind. Only a harmless fire alarm, but it still has clinging to it the power to evoke the old horror, and because I was thinking about war it struck a cold blow to my heart.

March 24th. Two nights in London, the excuse being an invitation to Ralph to attend some medico-legal occasion with Dr Letitia Fairfield: our real reason being a desire to climb out of our rut for a little. I dined one night with Janetta and Ralph Jarvis, and whilst eating a late meal of consummate deliciousness a conversation about chaperonage got under way, set off by the question whether Nell Dunn should be allowed to drive to Italy alone with her Jeremy.[1] Said Ralph: 'Caroline went abroad with three young men and two girls and that was quite all right, but if she wanted to go abroad with one young man I should put my foot down.' Naturally both Janetta and I set upon him together, and he was quite taken by surprise and slipped into a lot of unfortunate phrases like 'people would think', 'there's a lot of sense in convention' and 'ruin her chances'. These were not let pass — oh dear no! When I told Anne Hill this she laughed very loudly and said, 'Well really that doesn't come very well from someone who in his youth seduced more perfectly respectable débutantes than anyone!' Her company [Anne's] was the best tonic I received in London — warm-hearted, genuine, intelligent and sympathetic.

As for London itself, its hideousness and vulgarity, and the *Antwerp* quality it sometimes displays were much in evidence. A greedy appetite for material things is on every other face; the rest look haunted by fear of boredom, now that the newspaper strike leaves them with nothing to read. I also noticed a great lack of elegance; streets full of prosperous elderly women had bird's-nest hair-dos with silly hats perched on them, legs swathed in bandages under their nylons, and squashy old fur boots.

¹Sandford, whom she later married.

April 2nd. We are still cut off from the world's doings by the newspaper strike. To me it matters very little. I listen to the daily abstract given us by the wireless — a little cup of concentrated Bovril — and get the impression that 'news' is not a real thing but an artificial imposition, a sort of false beard on the face of the facts. But poor Ralph is like a man choking for lack of air and light, and has eaten his way through a pile of thrillers which lie in a disconsolate heap round his feet. Shortage of absorbable material led to a long talk about activity-passivity, the difference between equality and sameness. If I don't look out I find myself pushed into an absurdly idealistic position, but this time I was almost disconcerted by the extent to which we agreed. For instance, about education, that though one should obviously aim at the best for all that doesn't mean the *same* for all, but technical education for the practically-minded and the most high-powered teachers for the brightest intelligences.

April 22nd. To London for the Memoir Club. Old Bloomsbury has been in the firing line. John Raymond has just launched a full-scale attack on them all, and Lytton in particular, in the *New Statesman*. He accused them of being 'vulgar', giving no reason for his view and showing his anger too plainly to be effective. So what would they seem like, I asked myself, this wood of old trees under whose shade I came alive myself? I thought there might be some talk of J. Raymond, but not a bit of it. There was the usual, really rather sublime indifference to what the world thinks of them. Then though they are getting old, and have been ill and had operations, they are still admirably adventurous. One and all were planning to take their cars abroad or hop over the Channel in aeroplanes. Bunny pounced on me, making it difficult for me to talk as much as I wanted to to Morgan on my other side. He [Bunny] said he had been writing a story about the 'amazing fact that young girls are always ready to fall in love with men of sixty-five', and would like to send it to me, 'as I value your judgement more than anyone's.'

The papers read were by Morgan and Duncan, and consisted almost wholly of old letters — cheating, really. Afterwards we repaired to Vanessa's, where Julia, who sets great store by manners, sinned against their rules in a manner possibly very wounding to her hostess: after a moment in her sitting-room she gave an exaggerated shudder, went and fetched her heavy winter overcoat and sat in it all evening.

April 30th — Mottisfont. We are spending the weekend in a new milieu — at Mottisfont, with Boris Anrep's friend, Mrs Maud Russell. We take to Maud at once; she exercises her function as hostess with great tact and skill. The party consists of Sir Maurice and Lady Violet Bonham-Carter and Caroline Blakiston (young and attractive actress), and by way of old friends Clive, Ben Nicolson and Paul Hyslop. This business of talking to fellow-guests for hours and hours on end belongs to a house-party technique I am not accustomed to. High marks to Ben for doing it successfully and yet always being himself. Not so high I'm afraid to Clive who got over-excited, boasted really too much about the cleverness of his friends, his Légion d'Honneur and being *tutoyé* by Picasso. The Bonham-Carters both exuded confident charm — he delightfully beaming, quietly interested in everything from birds to the Crusades. I didn't at first like Lady Violet, who had an off-putting mannerism of smiling at one from very close range with her eyes shut; but she was friendly as well as obviously intelligent. Impossible however to be unaware that beneath her social gifts lay a system of worldly and conventional values which set my teeth on edge, nor was I mollified by hearing her say to Clive that she would rather both her sons had been killed in the war than fail to play their part in it. Ralph and I had a three-room suite, the softest bed and smoothest sheets. But I felt a stranger in a world where it is assumed that 'we' are innately superior beings to those who minister to us, and deserve to have a better sort of life than they do. I cannot happily lie like a poodle on a fur rug being cosseted by an elderly grey-haired maid who is propping me on cushions and putting everything I could possibly need within my reach, not only because she received a salary for doing so, but because I have temporarily at least become a member of a privileged class. As she put down my breakfast tray one morning she gave me the latest news of the threatened railway strike, adding, 'It's disgusting! It's not British! I'm ashamed of my class, I really am!'

May 14th — Ham Spray. Ralph and I always enjoy telling each other about the books we happen to be reading. It is perhaps one of our greatest pleasures when alone. At the moment mine is *Education Sentimentale,* and though in some ways it is a failure I am finding it enormously absorbing; Flaubert's every sentence invokes the Frenchness of the French, and how brilliantly, how movingly he writes! Ralph made me laugh by beginning to shout about his author — Rousseau — this morning, although both our heads were actually on the same pillow. He declared this was because he 'didn't feel he had my entire attention'. (Quite untrue.) There are two causes of worry rumbling away in the cellars of my mind; one is that poor Ralph says he often wakes to sadness. This is all the more upsetting because he has hitherto rejoiced in such a marvellous fund of high spirits and power of arousing them in others — me, for instance. And I wonder about his health. The other is that we have heard nothing lately from Burgo.

May 24th. Burgo's silence has broken and on Sunday he brought two friends over from Oxford for the day — a great success and it made Ralph and me very happy. One friend was Simon Young. The other, Harry Graham, a whimsical character, made himself quickly at home and was somewhat teasing to our other guests, the composer Gerald Finzi and his handsome pre-Raphaelite-looking wife, who wanted to consult us about their son's conscientious objection. 'Musicians often seem to me such very *dull* people' murmured Harry rather outrageously. 'My sister is one and her friends are *terribly* dull.' Dullness is of course anathema to Oxford, though not to Cambridge.

May 31st. Three days of real summer have coincided with Whitsun weekend, making us grateful, replete and thawed, spiritually speaking. With wisteria and dusty pink clematis clambering lovingly over it, the dear old house seemed to crouch like a hen, while we chickens moved about in front of it, or sat for long hours reading or talking with the sun pouring its syrup over us. Raymond, Janetta and Janie were with us. Janetta 'turned her heart on' (a phrase Desmond uses for much-loved singers) for Raymond, and we were happy to see how she melted him. He and Janie had long, loud discussions of French matters — diplomacy, writers and the *résistance*, ignoring the rest of us in a way typical of Bloomsbury bad manners and reminding me of Julia's comment on her cousin Janie the other day: 'But good gracious, how the girlie *shouts*!'

June 1st. The railway strike clamped down on us on Sunday and has assumed a large threatening black shape, not to mention also that the dock strike is now in its second week. One is aware of industries closing down and echoes of war-time stoppages. The slight thrill of drama has all gone — nobody likes it now, as far as I can see. Ralph says he feels shockingly short of vitality. Oh dear, I mustn't lose my new philosophy of 'taking things easy'. I have an Index to do, *lots* to do in fact — and so far as that goes am contented. What I do dread — and hate to contemplate — is the possibility of advancing through space and time in a perfunctory or semi-conscious manner; for above all things I cling to the vital necessity of keeping awareness of one's surroundings sharp and clear, and not blundering along through a haze created by the frosted spectacles of apathy.

June 29th. I have been carried away on a giant racer of entertaining and other activities. However I think we got through something almost herculean in the way of a house-party with fair credit; at least our guests were fed, entertained and looked after. It was enjoyable while it lasted, and I again had the sensation of the house resembling a living thing, breathing softly like all the people sleeping under its spread wings. It began last Thursday, when poor Robin — who had been having trouble with his artificial leg — came for two days without it. Next came Burgo and Simon Young, fresh from the Wadham Commem. Ball. This meant inventing another bedroom, and I swept and scrubbed the little room on whose door Carrington long ago painted the word SERVANTS. On Friday the Nicholses telephoned and asked if Phil and Anne could come as well as Phyllis! New crisis. Burgo's room had to be made ready for Anne and he moved into SERVANTS with Simon. So we had three Nicholses and Craig Macfarlane — eight for dinner. Next day Martin Nichols and a school-friend were added to the party. The Nicholses left, but enter the Stones, just when I had gone to have forty winks. Five other guests invited themselves for the weekend but were perforce rejected. Today I felt as grey and limp as a fillet of plaice on Wyatt's slab.

July 9th. I have not mentioned the fact that we have rented a holiday house jointly with Janetta, in Galicia in the north of Spain. Our departure is approaching at full speed. Since I last wrote there have been lovely days of true summer — days when the beauty of the country has made me ready to weep, long though I've been accustomed to it. On one such evening last week Ralph and I motored over the downs to supper with the Finzis, returning under a soft and not fully darkened sky; the green slopes lay quietly under a bloom like pale green dust. Nothing more beautiful have I seen, I thought, in any country in the world. The Finzis gave us an elegantly set-out cold meal like something in *Homes and Gardens*, wholesome too. After-wards we sat out talking to the conscientious objector son.

July 14th. Marching towards the deadline of departure. One by one things get folded and tied in knots, in between bathing and eating strawberries, lying learning Spanish in the shade: my Index is finished, my last violin lesson over, the arrangements for our August tenants made. Janetta has not yet succeeded in getting a sea passage for Nannie and the little girls. 'Robert turned up this morning,' she told us, 'looking very bearish'. 'What about his coming with us?' we asked, and she thought it might be a 'good idea'. Poor Ralph Jarvis's stock is very low, but he still hopes to drive out with her.

I am amazed that life seems to get more and more interesting as one gets older — and also perhaps saner, serener, more tough. It is no doubt the Indian Summer before the hand of decrepitude strikes and health crumbles.

I don't understand Janetta's attitude to Ralph J. one bit. He has pulled strings and got passages for the children, so he is to be rewarded by driving out with her, but she made no bones (when she was here) about not looking forward to the Spanish adventure. Her presence in the house was like an electric dryer blowing our hair straight on end. Her desperate restlessness makes one draw short breaths and fail to sleep at night. From what we gather of life at Montpelier Square it has been beyond everything, with frantic lovers sobbing down the telephone and Cyril pacing her room all one night because Barbara has gone off with George Weidenfeld. Robert thinks her children show signs of lacking security, and that she should either centre her life round them or do something quite different. I think he is determined not to get drawn in again himself; he as good as said he would come to Galicia only if she didn't, and her own reason for coming is not very heartening: 'I've nowhere else to be.' Why on earth do I feel so sanguine?

Others who have been here have been the Gowings and Morgan Forster, who is as near to a Good Man as any I can think of, full of kindness and sympathy, understanding and tolerance, yet not at all dull.

[In Morgan Forster's company I have sometimes felt surprised that any personality could make an impression at once so distinct and so muted. For there was no mistaking the flavour of a single sentence of his talk, the voice it was spoken in, or a few words written on a postcard in his delicate, eccentric handwriting; yet these would be presented in a diffident, apologetic manner, so that the reader or listener might well be surprised to realize what a definite statement had been proffered, and with what resonant implications. Phrases such as 'Only connect' and opinions such as those on the relationship between friendship and patriotism are signs of the width of his influence even during his lifetime.

Yet he always chose to dress in almost aggressively dim grey clothes, woolly cardigans and cloth caps that would have merged easily into a London fog. I think this was because, like his close friend Sebastian Sprott (or Jack as he called him), Morgan felt much more affinity with the lower than the upper classes, and completely lacked ambition, envy and snobbishness. Starting with his mother and his aunts he spent much of his youth among middle-aged and elderly ladies — the prototypes of Mrs Moore of *A Passage to India* — and to such safe backgrounds he often returned after some bold episode in a rajah's palace, where a very different side of his nature was displayed in his obvious pleasure in wearing a turban and Indian dress. One such female confidante was my mother, with whom he lodged at Brunswick Square for several years during the Twenties. They got on well together, but I remember the complete lack of visual taste with which he furnished his rooms, and how he showed me with pride some crimson atrocities called Nell Gwynn candles, remarking 'they have a little womb, you see'. Morgan's conversation was interwoven with subtle humour, and his prevailing expression was one of gentle amusement, but he seldom laughed; when he did the sound was more suggestive of pain than pleasure, or sometimes resembled a sneeze. One often had the impression, when listening to his talk, that he was skating deftly between whimsicality and sentimentality.

Besides seeing him at my mother's house I used to meet him at the Memoir Club, and also in the early days of Ham Spray, where I sometimes played chess with him. He was very fond of Ralph, and continued to visit us after the deaths of Lytton and Carrington, showing particular kindness to Burgo in his adolescent troubles.

A little-known portrait of E. M. Forster by Carrington is in the National Portrait Gallery.]

July 25th. It's the last night at Ham Spray for many a long week, but this fact gives me, I must say, no great pang. I begin clearing and sorting and carrying things from place to place like an ant, to make the house ready for our tenants. Wilde and Mrs Hoare look reproachful — I hardly dare meet Minnie's eye.

Off to Southampton airport in the afternoon, Burgo looking very smart and smiling in a new café-au-lait suit. Among a row of people watching the take-offs I spot Desmond Shawe-Taylor's familiar silhouette. He is fizzing like ginger pop. (At Crichel they say, 'One can't play Canasta with Desmond, he's too excitable,' and it occurs to me he may be too excitable to travel by air also.) Considerable delay, owing to one or two aeroplanes 'proving unserviceable', not a very nice thought. We are off!

[Our plan to rent a holiday house with Janetta took shape when she
spotted an advertisement in *The Times* of the unforgettable San
Fiz, near Coruña. Later we found that it belonged to friends of the
Brenans and Japps: Natalia Jiménez and her husband who taught
Spanish at Oxford. But the most important member of the family,
who presided over the house from *outre-tombe* as it were, was
Natalia's father, Cosío, the greatest Spanish authority on El
Greco, as we were to be informed almost daily. As we approached
the village after five days motoring through France and Spain we
were full of speculations and excitement. (We had arranged to
meet Janetta and Ralph Jarvis at our destination, while the three
little girls and Nannie came by sea.) We were directed along an
appallingly sandy and bumpy lane, such that the car seemed to be
engulfed in huge holes, to arise again in a cloud of yellow dust
which must have stifled the passers-by. And now we were driving
between handsome iron gates up to the door of a tall seigneurial
house, and as it opened three figures emerged — the servants who
had been engaged to look after us, in view of the size of our party
and the fact that the house lacked such amenities as electricity and
plumbing, and that all water had to be drawn in buckets from the
well. They made us most politely welcome, telling us their names
— Dina the cook was a serious character, a little anxious, with a
slight moustache and prominent teeth; Carmiña a delicious
brunette, a Zurbarán with big black eyes and elegant gestures like a
crane; Maruja light-haired, vivacious and inclined to pout. They
addressed us in the incomprehensible Galician dialect, a cross
between Spanish and Portuguese. And now the moment we had
thought about for so long, the pin-point on the map, was tangibly
and visibly here and we saw at once that our house was *all right* —
better than our hopes, spacious and sympathetic. Ralph and I had a
big bedroom washed all over — even the ceiling — with copper-
sulphate blue, a massive wooden bed, and a little anteroom with
writing-table. The Sala and dining-room were furnished in
attractive, slightly moth-eaten Victorian style; there being literally no soft armchairs, Burgo and our younger visitors usually lay
on the floor. Behind the house stretched a big walled garden in
some disarray, but with arbours, a fine magnolia, a palm tree and
stone seats.

We had scarcely looked round when Natalia Jiménez arrived in
person and began spraying us with talk, flying from subject to
subject. She was handsome and friendly but dominating, and we

soon made out that *she* was part of the furnishings we had rented with the house! She was sleeping in the apartments of her sister who had had a nervous breakdown. So the mad sister and her housekeeper (mad also) were staying nearby and would be in and out and expecting to be looked after by 'our' servants!]

August 5th — San Fiz. Woken to a lovely blue morning with a multitude of civilities; we only understand half our three girls say. Breakfast in dressing-gowns in Janetta's room, coffee, an enormous round coarse loaf and honey. We took Dina with us into Coruña to shop; it's a magnificent town, very much alive and with its rows of *miradores* flashing in the sun. Natalia's descents on us are alarmingly frequent, and the trouble is we have many questions to ask her. But in reply to 'What time off do the girls expect, particularly Dina?' she at once tells us how lucky we are to have Dina, how everyone has put themselves out for us, and why has this miracle happened? Because 'everyone is so indebted to My Father'. As Ralph says, he dominates us like the Commendatore in *Don Giovanni*, and as we return to the house from a bathe or outing we half expect to hear his stone voice inviting us to supper. 'My Father' would in some odd theoretical way be 'so pleased' to know we are here, says Natalia.

August 7th. The sea-travellers miraculously arrive soon after two — Nannie pleased with everything; no little girl over-exhausted. After a certain amount of explaining and organization between kitchen and nursery we all went down to the beach. Nicky swims quite well, Georgie jumps up and down in a rubber ring made like a fish, Rose paddles hanging on to Nannie. We think the amalgamation of this new chunk into San Fiz has gone well.

August 8th. We begin to wonder whether Natalia realizes she has rented us 'My Father's' house. Today she suddenly came in unannounced with her sixteen-year-old cousin, who asked if we would like him to play us something on the piano? Nothing we would like less, but it was impossible to say so, and we were treated to a loud tasteless performance of tunes from *Tales of Hoffmann*. Not content with that intrusion she walked in later with the cod-faced English wife of a Spanish millionaire from Coruña, whom we could scarcely be polite to. Next, our bathing towels had disappeared from the line where they were drying.

When we asked where they were Carmiña brought them, but was followed closely by Natalia saying, 'My Father never liked to see bathing things in the garden.' Ralph and I agree that something must be done — a declaration of independence *must* be issued.

August 11th. And so it was. The first shot was fired when Natalia shouted down to ask had I arranged about the children's tea, and I shouted back, 'Would she please leave that to me.' It is all most regrettable, and as pacifists we dearly wish we could have gained our freedom by simple negotiation, but let's hope that's the end of it.

Very hilarious dinner, with Carmiña and Maruja in tearing spirits and fits of laughter over our difficulty in understanding the difference between a *pollo* [chicken] and a *gallina* [fowl] especially when Ralph said, 'Ah — I see — *un pollo es un hombre*'.

The post brought me the typescript of the translation of Carmen Laforet's *Nada*, which I am to revise for publication. Work! but I doubt if I shall be able to concentrate.

Ralph Jarvis leaves today and looked touching and sad in his smart travelling suit. He has been badly on Janetta's nerves at times, but is an endearing character. We are now waiting in something of a San Fiz for Desmond S-T. who is arriving no one knows quite when, on his way from Portugal.

August 13th. Janetta is a different person since Ralph J. left, much more relaxed and easy to communicate with. In any case one-sided love is a heart-rending spectacle. About one o'clock Desmond's car was seen in the drive guided by a village boy in a check shirt. A very lively new breath of air came with him, as well as civilized talk. He enters into everything inquisitively and with enthusiasm.

August 14th. All went to Coruña to meet Kitty West who was arriving by sea and train, but first we spent a delightful hour or so walking through the narrow streets or sitting in bars. Desmond constantly disappeared at speed, but was easily found because of the Portuguese shirt he was wearing, of enormous blue and green checks. Kitty was prepared to enjoy everything.

After dinner we all walked to a tiny fiesta in our nearest village, and Ralph and I whirled round for a little among the tightly-packed dancers. Each of us picked up a strange character —

Desmond a knot of boys, Janetta a very young man with a permanent rosy blush, and I a Spanish version of Tom Mix. Dozens of brown, eager, wrinkled monkey faces gazed at us from very close range in amazed curiosity; there was a powerful smell of sweat. Walking home was the best part, with glow-worms lining each side of the road, and — close above the packed dancers — a brilliantly-lit window full of women and children looking down as if from a box at the opera. Above them stood the tall trees in the lamplight under the black sky.

August 16th. This is the week of fiestas. Last night in Betanzos a huge crowd gathered in the Plaza to see the Fire-balloon go up. Suspended by a sort of fishing-rod to the top of the church tower, it inflated very, very slowly as the air inside it was heated, heaven knows how, taking quite half an hour, while the crowd watched enthralled. At last it had swollen to such a vast size that it almost covered the whole Plaza, then up it went, to shrieks and yells, and we saw that it was carrying beneath it a boat full of rockets exploding into the indigo sky — an intoxicating sight. Up and up it still rose, and then a sort of panic broke out in the crowd. I saw a little old woman's face close to my own, agonized and struggling. I was too thrilled to feel alarm, but Ralph thought there was real danger and began issuing military orders in a most impressive way.

Our three girls were dancing all night in shoes too small for them: they are hobbling about today.

August 18th. Today's fiesta took us up the river to a grove of trees, connected, Ralph says, with some ancient pagan festival. We piled into a boat with our three girls all dressed in their best, and joined the procession, Maruja and Dina singing in loud raucous voices. I never saw anything prettier than the stream of boats, some with awnings of green boughs and hy-drangeas, others with tables spread with white cloths, food and bottles of wine. And all along the banks of the narrow river — verdant green in the evening light — Renoir-like groups of old, young and children were picnicking, singing or drinking. Among the grove of trees there was great excitement — dancing and chains of rowdy young men and girls splashed with wine. We left our three girls to enjoy the fun and started home with our boatman.

August 28th. Unexpected arrival of Caroline Jarvis and Jonny Gathorne-Hardy,[1] excited and exhausted after a three-days' train journey. The Brenans are expected shortly. Jonny is interested in everything, starts general conversation going, has plenty of charm and is nice to the children.

We bathed today on a splendid Atlantic beach where huge rollers come racing in to shore. Only a few natives were encamped at one end, and when she saw us braving the enormous waves one black-clad woman suddenly rose up, very stout and square, stretching her arms as if crucified and shouting above the din of the water. I went up to her and saw that her face was contorted with anguish; she cried to me that there was *mucho peligro*, and that one of her *hijos* had been drowned there. The Galicians are a sturdy primitive race; everything is carried on their heads — earthenware jars, great big parcels, and today we even met a tall woman with a coffin on her head crossing the bridge at Betanzos.

[1] Nephew of Eddie and Bob, and Anne Hill.

September 6th. Arrival of the Brenans. I think Gerald feels that we are poaching on his preserves. 'Of course it's lovely here,' he says, 'but it's not Spain.' However, I can see he is surprised to find us managing so well. Jonny is a great success with the girls and addresses long remarks to them mainly in English: 'No, Maruja, *grazie*, I don't think I'll have any more tonight.' She laughs flirtatiously and calls him 'Yonnee!'

Gerald, lying on the beach beside Ralph, talked and talked about himself, telling him among other things that he has nothing whatever to say to Gamel, but couldn't possibly do without her. Meanwhile she was sitting on a rock not far away, like a mermaid, gazing at herself in a small mirror, as she often does, not so much from vanity as anxiety.

Janetta, Caroline, Burgo and Jonny have gone off on an excursion to Portugal in their car, leaving us — a much reduced party — with the Brenans and the children. The Brenans have paid Natalia a long visit; they think us idiots to have divorced ourselves from such a fascinating woman, who knows so much about folk-lore (but both Ralph and I detest folk-lore). Encouraged by our visitors, however, Natalia returned into our Sala talking to them in Spanish, which sounded beautifully clear and easy to understand after our Galicians.

September 12th. In spite of a certain buried irritation there has not been a single really difficult moment with the Brenans. One feels that Gamel must be treated like a blown bird's egg in cotton-wool; she told me she is sad and deeply frustrated to think that she has used so little of such talent as she possesses. Gerald conveyed the same thing more amusingly: 'I feel like a house that is wired all over for electricity, but the current has never been switched on.' They give us no idea how long they are staying. 'Oh, I never make plans,' says Gerald. 'I just do what I feel like on the spur of the moment and get on very well like that.' All too true!

September 15th. Janetta and the three young returned from Portugal, looking brown, handsome, and having had a wonderful time. Jonny is very good for Burgo; he is also, I suspect, mad about Janetta.

The Brenans criticize the way we deal with our servants.

'You allow them to rule you,' says Gerald.

'Well, at least,' says Ralph somewhat mortified, 'we do make them look after quantities of visitors, whereas *yours* won't let you even have someone to tea.'

'Oh no,' answers Gerald obliviously, 'that's *our* doing entirely. The servants love having visitors.'

September 19th. Drove the Brenans to catch their bus. Ralph and I look forward to having some time to ourselves. Our farewell dinner to them was lively and talkative under the starry sky in an outdoor restaurant, eating tender little chickens. One often feels specially warmly to friends who are leaving, and this parting was no exception. Nicky's sharp eyes had noticed Gamel's vagueness and *non sequiturs*: 'If I said, "Janetta wants to know if you'd like to come shopping in the car?" she would answer, "Mmm. *Yes* dear, *wasn't* it?"' Jonny liked Gerald enormously. Janetta had taken Gerald to Betanzos one day; they drank brandies and Gerald talked incessantly about himself, but his account to Ralph was: 'I got to know Janetta for the first time.' He spends a lot of time with his eyes turned inward, but when he suddenly transfers them to others they brighten like little black coals and his acute mind produces something much to the point or very funny, or both.

September 23rd. As our two months' stay in Spain comes to an end, tapering away as it were to a point, I try to sum it up. I feel it was the very solid creation of many hands. It even developed a sort of Frankenstein life of its own and there are many things we shall remember for a long time. Janetta asked last night how we would feel about doing it again. As Ralph and I walked arm in arm round the garden we talked of our sadness at leaving, how fond we had become of it. Two months? It's nothing.

September 24th. The girls were in tears as we left, Dina with a scarlet nose. Carmiña is the one I am fondest of, she has the Irish quality of always being sweet and kind, whether she feels it or not. All females were warmly kissed, even old Nannie; hand-shakes for the males. So goodbye San Fiz.

October 1st — Ham Spray. We have been back four days and are only just beginning to come out of the dazed stupor of return. First impressions are that England is very pretty, prettier than Spain. But what a remarkable difference between our reception at San Fiz and at Ham Spray! Wilde and Mrs Hoare had of course been told when we would arrive, and I half thought Mrs Hoare might be waiting to cook our supper. But no. We fought our way into an utterly cold, bleak house — not a fire burning nor a radiator turned on. No flowers; no pots in the jardinière. In the kitchen *nothing* except a few peeled potatoes in a saucepan of cold water. Goodness, how unimaginative! On the table was a grocer's bill which made me groan: margarine, Bisto, Quix. I groped in the dark garden for a lettuce, cursing. But next morning Mrs Hoare entirely softened me by her friendliness. 'When I asked Mr Wilde for some potatoes he said, "Will they want some?" so I didn't dare ask him for any fruit or vegetables,' she said.

October 12th. Of my two jobs *Nada* is done and packed off to the publisher, while tomorrow I start my next Freudian index. My 'life' is relegated to the numerous crannies between, and sweet-ened by loving companionship with Ralph and the summer warmth and perfect stillness of the weather. Every morning the lawn is pearly with dew and threaded over with spider-webs. A few mushrooms. The leaves have barely started to turn.

All is silence, except for our own voices. This morning we were considering the changing world. Ralph said we mustn't forget it is the next generation, not ourselves, who are making the changes. It is their world, and they have a much less permanent attitude to life than we did. Like gliders, they keep adjusting to new air-currents. One can see their attitude as adventurous, courageous and certainly pragmatic. Ideas are accepted as long as they work; marriages likewise. On the other hand the weeklies are very full these days of cynical abuse of *our* old Gods, the Bloomsbury ones, both of what they stand for and the characters themselves — Virginia, Maynard and Roger. I feel as certain as I am of anything that the journalists are wrong, and that one day it will be seen that they played an important part in the history of civilization. Not probably in my life-time, however.

Last weekend Janetta and Joan Cochemé met here. Joan was 'thunderstruck by Janetta, thought her almost perfect'. I must admit she glowed like the autumn days. I'm glad to say she feels, as we do, that San Fiz was a triumphant success. 'I tell everyone so. I hope you do too.'

October 18th. I wake like a sparrow on my twig, chirruping with trifling anticipations. But we have had two saddening glimpses into the lives of others: one was of Burgo at Oxford, feeling lost and lonely in his town rooms and missing friends who have gone down. The other was of Robert, who exhaled an unwavering air of desperation, as we both agreed, and this was made worse by his attempt to mask it with a large pair of pink-rimmed spectacles — a vizor of concealment and protection or a muzzle to prevent him biting? He left to return to Dublin where he works hard, sees no one and makes his own meals. A story of his about Georgie: Everything was nice in Spain, she told him, except the *gravy*. They were travelling in the underground at the time, and two black men sat opposite. 'They're not talking English,' she whispered.

Robert: I expect they're talking African.
Georgie: Do you think they like it here?
Robert: Oh, I expect they like some things and not others.
Georgie: Do you think they like the *gravy*?

October 29th. We've had three wet days in London, paddling through thin mud and enjoying the comfort of the G.W.R. Hotel. Nearly everyone we saw was hurrying and anxious, except Anne Hill, solid and splendid under a becoming powdering of grey hair. Poor Lucila Japp, a frightened bird in its cage, because her recent illness had been a terrible shock to her. Why not indeed? The first knock of Postman Death on the door is bound to strike a chill of horror. I notice that our generation talk a great deal about old age and death, because they have come within range and we talk about everything; but I'm not sure the young enjoy seeing us gesticulating and even laughing on our way to the tomb.

November 1st. Mrs Hoare is full of the news that Princess Margaret has announced that she will not marry her Group Captain. This drama has been going on before a world audience for weeks — it confirms my feeling that it is morally wrong to keep our Royal family like animals in cages, unable to lead their private lives. It is degrading to us who allow it, like Capital Punishment. Far better to do without them altogether. I had an argument with Robin on the subject. He declared they were 'valuable symbols', and went on, 'You're an iconoclast, Frances. Best leave things as they are.' I could only say 'Why?'

November 17th. A day in London, lunching at the Ivy with Clive, whose other guests were Harold Nicolson and Cressida Ridley,[1] whom I took to very much, liking particularly the combination of a pale handsome and intelligent face with spontaneous gaiety. Harold Nicolson is genial and easy to talk to. (I remembered Cyril's description of him as 'a professional human being'.)

[1] Daughter of Sir Maurice and Lady Violet Bonham-Carter.

November 21st. Another visit to London for Charlotte Strachey's wedding to Anthony Blond,[1] and a party given by Janetta and Joan Rayner. It was so long since I'd been to a party that I wanted to see if the style had changed. Not really. A great deal of champagne and whisky was drunk, yet no one was 'drunk'. In Janetta's long room the noise grew rapidly more deafening until it became merely a matter of guessing at other people's remarks. What's the point of talking under such circumstances, I wondered, even while doing and enjoying it. A lot of very interesting distinguished-looking heads were silhouetted against the dark green walls. Homosexuality was represented by Cecil Beaton,

Francis Bacon, Dicky Chopping; old age by Rose Macaulay; old friends by Mary, Heywood and Anne, Paddy Leigh Fermor, Cyril and Sonia. But when it was all done and we were back in bed there was less to ponder about than there is after a good evening's talk: just a noisy rush through a dark tunnel in a train with lights flashing past and quick glimpses of faces in other carriages.

¹Publisher.

November 30th — *Ham Spray*. Both of us in bed with flu. I'm reading Wildeblood's book, and find it thoughtful and interesting. Hearing the purple-jowled indignation of Counsel for the Prosecution against Homosexuality in his own case and comparing it with the same man's impassioned defence of it in the Croft-Cooke case, Wildeblood realized that barristers were purely actors, and that by the time they had been made judges they could have no feelings about right or wrong or anything else. I think this is true — why do we smugly accept this state of things?

My new records are a pleasure, the Brahms clarinet quintet for one. I am always moved by the strange voice of that solitary bird in the jungle, and the way it seems to keep trying to escape from the strings, but in vain.

December 15th. Clive and Janetta for the weekend. We were discussing Lawrence Gowing's appointment to be head of an art school. 'He's just a *civil servant!*' said Clive with unutterable scorn. 'Can anyone imagine Renoir giving up any of his painting time to become a civil servant?' This was at the end of dinner and he got up on rather wobbly legs and danced round the table in his purple spongecloth and black tassels saying, 'I'm drunk, I know I am, *all* the same I know that no artist should become a *civil servant.*'

Burgo went off to the Tycoonery for the night, with a lively party consisting of Nell and Jeremy, Caroline Jarvis and John Calmann.

December 24th. Christmas began today — no time to duck or groan. Isobel was driven down by Charlotte and Anthony in time for lunch, bringing a bottle of champagne. Robert came by the evening train; Burgo is back from Stowell so our party is complete.

December 29th. All over now, and Ralph even says it is the nicest Christmas he can remember. Robert and Isobel were a good mixture — it was they who entertained us. It is always a delight to listen to Isobel's drifting voice saying such things as, 'They say that if you keep on *fond*ling rats they grow very very *brave*.' Robert was obviously happier although still lurking behind his preposterous spectacles. He tells us that all London gossip circles round the Connollys' affairs, and that both Cyril and Barbara had been to see Edward Glover, who said he could help Cyril but do nothing for Barbara, who only wanted him to tell her what she wanted to hear. She is to be staying with Bill and Annie Davis at Malaga when the Campbells go there, and Cyril briefed Mary as to what she was to say to Barbara. When she asked him, 'What has she done to deserve such preferential treatment?' he said, 'Nothing, but please do.' However, Barbara has already left for Madrid. According to rumour it was to meet George Weidenfeld, but Cyril didn't know this, rang her up in her Madrid hotel and was told she was out. 'Gone to the Prado,' said Cyril to Robert. 'I told her she must.' Then, as an after-thought he asked the hotel receptionist: 'Is there a Mr Weidenfeld staying there?' 'Oh yes, Sir, just arrived. Do you want to speak to him?' So now Cyril has posted off to Spain.

Ralph says how Stendhal would have enjoyed the Connolly situation, and how Cyril would enjoy thinking of Stendhal enjoying it!

1956

January 2nd — Ham Spray. There can't be said to be much feeling of newness about this New Year. My love for Ralph, which welled up in a sudden fountain last night as I saw how much he was enjoying some gramophone records, is certainly not that. Nor is my frustrated longing to see Burgo more constantly happy.

We have Robert here, a pillar of support, for our other visitor Hester Chapman is quite a formidable steam-roller (though she makes one laugh a lot), or to change the metaphor she has a flavour like pickles, curry and Worcester sauce rolled into one. She was gratuitously unkind about her old friend Julia's last book: 'It was really shockingly bad, I thought.' (snort) 'Well, readable. Barely.' (snort). However she was worsted by little Nell Dunn, who came over one day. Hester took her for 'a silly little thing' and was determined to beat her on the blue-stocking level. Actually Nell was not only looking like a Piero della Francesca angel but in splendid form, speaking lucidly from a clear head and honest heart. From parents and children Hester moved on to how uninteresting the young were, and how much one wanted to be rid of them and 'get on with it'. 'Get on with what?' said Nell in bell-like tones. 'I don't even know what you do.' 'I write, as a matter of fact,' said Hester, closing her eyes with a snort, as who should say: 'Fancy not knowing *that*.'

Next day she asked me, 'Was I sharp with that charming clever girl? I liked her so much and thought her brilliantly intelligent.' For which, I suppose, she must be given due credit.

January 13th. I heard today from the Harvill Press that they are to publish the translation I have been doing of a Spanish story called *Little Andrés* which I have been working at for some time, egged on by Lucila Japp. They write that they are 'quite in love with it', and I like it myself but am positive it will drop like a stone. What with *Nada* coming out with Weidenfeld, it looks as if two of my translations might appear this year.

Two days ago I started reading Saint-Simon.

January 17th. Very sad news came in a letter from Boris today:

65 Boulevard Arago,
Paris XIII

Dear Ralph and Francis

I have the very sorry news to tell you Maroussa died on the 11th January on admission to the hospital. Her cancer developed in her lungs, and although she was with me sitting in the Studio till the day before her death sipping rum and smoking till the last moment when the ambulance people carried her away, there in the hospital her heart gave out and she dropped her head and was dead.

You were fond of her and she was very fond of you both.

The void is very great round me. I feel so confused and miserable.

My love
Boris.

It wasn't exactly a surprise, indeed we have been expecting it ever since her serious operation of a year or so ago, but her death makes us more melancholy than would that of many people we see more often and more intimately.

[There was absolutely nothing synthetic or imitative in Maroussa Volkova's very Russian character. Throwing my mind back to my first sight of her, I remember her at a party given by Boris and Helen when they were still married, in about 1926. Maroussa was quite young then, silent and shy, but beautiful in a very exotic way. Ralph told me she was a distant relative of Boris's as well as his mistress, and had come over from Russia soon after the 1917 Revolution. She seemed like one of the hangers-on who move silently in the background of a Russian novel. We learned later that Boris almost always had two chief women in his life. Not long after this party Helen eloped with Roger Fry, and Boris and Maroussa set up together, dividing their time between two studios — one in the Boulevard Arago in Paris and the other in Hampstead. Maroussa helped with the mosaics. From the Thirties onwards they came often to Ham Spray, and were among the most welcome of our visitors.

Maroussa's appearance was glamorous and distinctly foreign. Neat in her dress and her movements, she was compact in body and mind, from her small head (with the dark hair drawn smoothly back, the dark eyes that seemed to have no whites and the colourless complexion like cream-laid writing-paper), down to her feet in trim high-heeled shoes. She reminded me of some oriental figurine of polished stone or marble. Her smile was an attractive little snarl, her laugh was husky and low. I am sure she was completely devoted to Boris despite his infidelities; he called her his 'consort', always treated her kindly in company, and was proud of her courage during their terrifying escape from Paris at the beginning of the last war. Afterwards her nerve went, very probably because their Hampstead studio was badly damaged in an air-raid.

The pungency of Maroussa's character came out in her very definite views. 'Noa! that I do not like!' she would exclaim. She loved the cinema, and when we asked her what sort of films she preferred I remember her replying without hesitation: 'Sophisti-cated, sintimiental, fascinating.' And what foods did she prefer? 'Ah! I like such raice pudding, such ryed meat and such ryed wine.' Very occasionally, after some red wine maybe, she would become romantic and starry-eyed as she described pre-Revolution Russia, particularly evenings at the ballet or opera, with officers in gorge-ous uniforms, and women in evening-dress and brilliant jewels. One instinctively guessed at an efficient brain behind Maroussa's quiet presence; she had a head for figures and for chess, but never joined in highbrow arguments and was intellectually modest. She had few friends in London — a few White Russians, Faith Hender-son ('Faiff'). Ralph and I had the comfortable feeling that she was fond of us and that her fondness implied total acceptance.]

January 20th. Mary has dropped out of the sky from Malaga for a few days, and had many stories to tell us about Cyril's doings. He clamours for female company, but abuses his old friends like Janetta and Joan Rayner. He got on splendidly with Gerald one evening, but after the next declared that he was a fearful bore. Mary has been rather like a jolly red sun breaking through the clouds and illuminating a watery grey landscape. This morning we went in to Hungerford to see her off to Spain again, with two letters from us to the Brenans and two diminutive puppies blindly peering from a straw-lined basket.

More stories about Cyril: He had been making up to the pretty and amusing wife of Annie Davis' brother Tom Bakewell at a nightclub in Torremolinos, so much that Tom B. began to grumble. 'Well, hang it all, Tom,' said Cyril, 'I haven't had a woman for two months. You really can't complain of my just dancing with Carol.' Next morning Tom Bakewell drove up to the Davis' house and dashed upstairs calling 'Cyril! Cyril!' 'Oh, hullo, Tom, come in.' Tom had been to Malaga and found a nice tart for Cyril, and booked a date for him there and then.

January 31st. Janetta was with us for the weekend when a letter from Robert arrived describing an appalling fire which had almost completely consumed Oonagh's lovely little Gothic house in the Wicklow mountains, Luggala. The fire brigade were delayed by frost and snow, and Robert said the sight of it was so extraordinary that he stood spellbound watching it before he realized that all his belongings and money were inside, and started on rescue work. The letter ended with his saying, 'I was feeling in a very desperate state before this happened and was keeping it chloroformed with work.' Janetta said, 'I wonder *why* he's so desperate.' I deliberately dropped a pebble into the pool by asking if she thought it had anything to do with her, and she said she had been given no reason to think so.

February 6th. Winter has struck, and the cold persisted throughout a short visit to London, mainly to go to Vanessa's private view, where we saw Clive and Duncan, Angelica, Barbara Bagenal and Helen Anrep. It gave me a slight feeling of shock to see this noble-looking woman Vanessa (whose ageing face still has classical beauty) putting herself up for sale to all-comers. Surely it was a better tradition that the painter should not attend his own vernissage?

Afterwards we went on to that of Michael Wishart, whose charming wife Anne is Philip Dunn's sister and has become a millionairess through her father's death. This generally known item of news seemed to spread a wave of worldly excitement through the crowded room, where people stood with their backs to the pictures or actually leaning against them, jabbering their heads off.

Next day I lunched with Janetta and Robert at Montpelier Square, and I realized any idea that my 'pebble' had created a ripple was mere wish-fulfilment. They were perfectly friendly, much in the way that brother and sister are, and with an undercurrent of irritation.

I asked Janetta if her divorce from Derek was through yet. 'Yes, today.'

'And is it rather nice to feel free?'

'Well, yes, it is.'

Robert looked surprised, and said, 'But the trouble is you'll be in it all again in a minute,' and Janetta pulled a face at him. He then began to talk about Sir Roger Casement's Diaries, on which he is now working, and said he was going back to Dublin next week.

February 8th — Ham Spray. A very quiet grey day. The cows stand about in the field with the most peculiar appearance of apathy, their oblong box-like shapes fitting into each other but pointing in every direction like some obscure sort of puzzle. Looking at them I thought how like a huge enigma the visible world is, and how one gropes around for clues and sometimes feels the hint of a solution must leap out at one from among those pale quiescent shapes.

Janetta rang up and told us Robert *had* gone off to Ireland. 'He thinks of nothing but Roger Casement,' she said with a tinge of bitterness. I fear it's true, and I'm also cross with him because he's so pig-headed as to reject the ideas of Casement being a homosexual and that the Diaries are genuine, both of which Ralph and I believe to be as good as proven.

Burgo writes saying he 'wants very much to go to Cambridge this weekend with John Calmann to see Jonny and Caroline' and so won't be coming to us for the weekend. I'm delighted he should 'want very much' to do anything so agreeable.

February 17th. Up to London for a night, mainly to have a rest from battling with the cold but also to see a charming, 'sintimiental' René Clair film and go with Ralph Jarvis and Janetta to Rimsky-Korsakoff's *Coq d'Or* at Covent Garden, with splendid singing by Hugues Cuenod and Mattiwilda Dobbs.

This morning we woke in our hotel to find breakfast being wheeled in by a beautiful dark Irish maid, who brought us a paper showing that the Abolitionists had got a handsome majority. Ralph asked her whether she was for hanging murderers or not.

'Well, if it's to be in danger of being murdered I am when I walk the streets I'd rather they were hanged.'

February 25th — Ham Spray. The freezing cold has lasted nearly a fortnight, and it is as if all one's nerve centres were slowly going dead. The whole of Europe is in this icy grip, as photos of gondolas covered with snow in *The Times* remind us. An Italian postman has been devoured by wolves. We await Duncan and Vanessa's visit in something of a panic. The cold has made it impossible to get anyone to meet them.

February 29th. Our two Bloomsbury birds put us to shame by being the nicest guests and best company we have had for ages. They can and will talk about anything and everything with unfailing interest and gaiety. I must admit that Vanessa seems physically an old lady as one hears her bumping slowly down-stairs, but mentally and spiritually she is ageless; while having Duncan in the house is like having a young irresponsible undergraduate to stay, and I even felt a slight surprise at seeing him reading a solid history book. His hair is quite black still and there is nothing to remind one that he is seventy. Both Ralph and I were charmed by them. The only entertainment we provided was to take them to lunch with the Moynes at Biddesden. Vanessa afterwards compared the rows of faces of children (decreasing in size) around the dining-table to a scene from Mrs Molesworth. Bryan took us upstairs to show us a painting by Duncan, and didn't appear to mind when Duncan peered at it closely and said, 'I have absolutely no recollection of ever seeing it in my life before.'

[I sometimes wonder whether Duncan was the happiest man I have ever known. *Angst* and responsibility played a very small part in his scheme of things, and the rare state of serenity that resulted made him a very refreshing companion. With his remarkable good looks, bewitching Highland colouring of black hair and blue eyes, well-cut mouth curling in secret amusement, and voice as soft as cashmere, he must surely have been aware how pleased everyone was to see him, yet I doubt if he was vain.

Why should he not be happy, after all? Circumstances and his own desires had so arranged his life that he spent many hours of nearly every day doing what he liked best — painting. When I first got to know him, in the Twenties, he was enjoying considerable acclaim. It was very much to his credit that when his popularity gradually seeped away and his name became unknown to art students, he simply went on painting exactly as before, so that at the time of his astonishing come-back to fame he was able to bring up pictures from Charleston when more were clamoured for. The image of Duncan stamped on my memory shows him in the garden at Charleston on a summer day, wearing a broad-brimmed French straw hat, from beneath which his serious gaze keeps up a movement from subject to canvas, up and down. No sign of the vigorous blink that accompanied his talk when he was being fanciful or perverse — a vein that ran through all that I knew of his life. I sat beside him at a banquet given in honour of his ninetieth birthday by the Dufferins, and I'm sure he must have blinked as he murmured: 'I can't think *why*, with all this delicious food, I don't feel hungrier.' Long pause: 'Of course it's true I was taken out to lunch and ate two dozen oysters.' After Vanessa's death I saw him now and again. The straw hat — often with a feather in it — had become a fixture, he sat often with a rug of the Grant tartan over his knees, and a large beard had given him a resemblance to Monet which was noticed by everyone.

Many people said they found Vanessa alarming, but I'm glad to say I never did. From the first I felt great admiration for her, and when I got to know her better and love her the admiration remained. I see her most characteristically, standing bent a little forward from the waist, with a scarf knotted round her head and a crescent-shaped smile like that on a Greek statue of the archaic period curving her lips. Her movements were deliberate; when sitting she would be erect but relaxed, with her hands in her lap or darning a sock. Her voice was quite unusually melodious and deep — a true contralto. She wrote to me about the weekend I have just described that it seemed 'even more perfect and delightful when we returned to find not a drop of water in our pipes and the plumber as usual in a complete state of mystification. I think they ought to be taught that water runs downhill — doesn't it? — and escapes from holes and expands when it freezes. We think of all the delights of Ham Spray, the delicious food, the fireside, and above all sitting at ease and talking to you two.' Her last letter was written in March 1961, a few months after Ralph's death, and begins: 'Dearest Fanny,¹ we have just finished reading

Mansfield Park aloud and it's really impossible not to think of you. Not that you are in the least degree like that Fanny but you have the same name and perhaps I should think of you even if you hadn't.']

¹Clive gave me this name, which was used by some of his friends — and still is.

March 5th — Long Crichel. A week-end at Crichel followed hard on the heels of a visit to Ham Spray from David and Rachel, who rushed in talking till we felt quite breathless. I admire Rachel for her spirited attack on life as well as for her exceptionally warm-hearted character. She told me she is writing a novel. David, rather strangely, seemed to have no idea what the young Oxford undergraduates do and think, asked me about it and was shocked when I told him. 'I'm only a professor, you see,' he said.

All four 'boys' were at Crichel, and having come together from different directions were almost too excited by each other's company to have much attention to spare for Ralph and me. They made me think of a gramophone record they described to us but couldn't find, called the *Dogs' Cantata.* Each of our friends was eagerly bringing in his new bone ('Woof! Woof') some play or film seen in London or piece of gossip or book read, which he dumped on the ground, bouncing with pleasure at its characteristic reception by the rest. Desmond and Raymond barked the most excitedly; Eardley kept up a deeper slower 'Woof', doggedly pursuing a black rubber ball of an idea, while Eddy yapped on a slightly higher note — a note of complaint at the current dearth of really good new works of imagination or interest. Yet between them they must have mentioned at least fifteen that were 'brilliant' or 'riveting.'

By Saturday the members of the Dogs' Cantata had settled into their various baskets. Ralph and I had a walk up the valley towards Crichel Manor — very soft, mild air, sky a flannel grey, brown crumbled earth after the thaw. I am reading *Under the Net*, a novel by the Oxford philosopher Iris Murdoch, which arouses great expectations and sometimes disappoints them. The philosophical basis is there all right, though I should find it hard to plot its outline.

Sunday was brilliantly clear with a deep blue sky. I sat to Eardley in the greenhouse adjoining his studio, roasted by the sun and enjoying our conversation, while bees and butterflies fluttered on the glass roof.

March 7th — Ham Spray. When two people live together for thirty years as Ralph and I have done they must both have a clear mental map of their zones of agreement and disagreement. There are two dangers — not talking about the areas of disagreement because of the heat thereby engendered, and not talking about the overlap because it is thoroughly understood. This morning, however, as if we had been sitting in a boat at the edge of a lake and someone had given it a shove, we were suddenly afloat in the deeps; and a conversation began at breakfast and went on all morning. Ralph started it by describing a feeling of sadness and envy he had felt last night when I was playing the *Eroica* in Marlborough. I teased him about his idleness (which really sometimes worries me). He teased me about my belief in 'creative activity'. I tell him I am not and never have been capable of it, and that it is humble activity without the creation that I seek. His nature is much more 'creative' than mine. Then up came the Atom bomb, which Ralph claimed was the cause of his inactivity. I said he couldn't be *quite* sure we were doomed, and that even if we were there were only two logical courses — to commit suicide or go on as before, which is really the same choice to be made when you learn that you have a mortal disease. As we all have. Anyway that there were no grounds for a half-existence, and Ralph has such a capacity for enjoyment and interest, such an excellent brain and power of synthesizing the knowledge it absorbs that there was no excuse for it!

A new figure was washed up here yesterday in the person of Lady Ponsonby, widow of Arthur and daughter of Sir Hubert Parry, who was brought by the Finzis. She is at least eighty, bowed and bearded, with the ruddy cheeks of a gardener. I found her very sympathetic to talk to. How nice to agree on pacifism, socialism and being anti-Christianity and capital punishment. Her grandson Thomas has just been sent down from Oxford for failing his prelims which 'his tutors made no attempt to get him through,' and is now a fervent Labour politician. 'We argue a good deal because we don't hold the same form of Socialism. I'm rather more Communist than he is,' she told us.

March 10th. Two perfect days, the country glistening under blue skies and a brilliant flood of light; great blue splodges of shadow like marks of a giant's thumb on the flanks of the downs. In thick coat and scarves swathed against the cold wind, I made across to the little pond where we used to skate, which shone like bright metal under the sky. A flock of wild duck whizzed up just as I got there. I lay down on the grass stock still until I saw them very high up in the deepest blue part of the sky, saw the leader tumble downwards and heard the strenuous whirring of their wings as they turned away disgusted by my continued presence. Two tiny birds twittered on a topmost twig. As I lay there doing my bird–watching I felt some obscure internal amusement. When I had set out I hoped to think things out for myself, make some minor resolutions about how to deal with an occasional lost appetite for life, lost confidence in myself, lost heart. It's what Burgo often asks me, and *I do not know* the answer. A session of Any Questions would say: Stop thinking about yourself.

This morning we fetched Burgo from Oxford. How was he? All right. Had he enjoyed the term? Not really, but he had survived it.

March 12th. The Campbells are back from Spain, and we took Bunny — here for the weekend — over to Stokke. Philip Dunn, now Sir Philip and a millionaire, was there, no less uneasy than before as a result. Also Bill and Annie Davis, whose friendliness is cockle-warming.

Bunny's visit has been a great success: what one wants a meeting with an old friend to be like, with plenty of easy talk and warmth circulating. He got on particularly well with Ralph.

Burgo touches me by his sweetness to us and also by his sensitive, rather unhappy expression.

March 27th. Last weekend we had Simon — who always cheers up Burgo — Robert and Georgie. Georgie is in a state of development combining sensitiveness and courage. When she failed to fold up her Heads, Bodies and Tails paper properly she burst for a moment into tears. I was delighted to see Burgo come to her rescue most understandingly. She adores Robert and he her, but she is made of finer texture than he is. Thought and talked to Ralph a lot about his character. He was awfully funny, charming and clever. But he was bitter and tough when he talked about Janetta. She herself is bewildered. On the telephone she told me that before she went abroad he rang her up several times. Once he said he never wanted to see her again. Another time he begged her to put off her departure until he came and saw her. She did for several days and he neither came nor wrote. He stayed at Montpelier Square all the time she was away, and when she got home she found no sign, no message. Whatever the explanation it's an unhappy one.

March 28th. Rachel and David for dinner and the night. At dinner the subject of moods of depression came up and Rachel asked Burgo if he ever had them. He looked taken aback and said, Yes, he did, but was I think relieved to find others owning up to them.

David shares many of my feelings — particularly the torturing doubts whether one has 'done the best' for those one loves and longs to help, and the dread of putting an unsteady scalpel into a sore place.

April 9th. Had an interesting conversation about Robert with Janetta as we weeded my wild corner one soft damp morning. After he had vanished from Montpelier Square without a word, we had presumed that all was up. But apparently he returned a few days later and had been staying all the week. 'I feel like a sort of landing-ground; he zooms up, then round he goes and swoops down again. I don't know what he wants, do you?' She may join us in France for two weeks, and suggested he might come too!

April 25th. Robert is staying a week at Stokke and another with us. We paid a happy visit to the Campbells, where his typewriter could be heard clicking from an open window; croquet, Julia and Lawrence at their various activities. Mary's mother, Lady Rosslyn, looking nippy as a girl for all her seventy years, struggled heroically among the brambles with a secateur. A story about Julia's anti-draught fuss. She had asked if she might have *The Times* to sit on to protect her from the cold air that came through the holes in the cane seats of the dining-room chairs!

[From April 25th to May 15th we took our car to France. Robert finally decided not to meet us at Pau with Janetta: during his last few days at Ham Spray I could see him visibly turning against the project and at the same time his tragic expression deepening.

At Granville (a town of tall pale grey houses looking sternly down on a vast expanse of turquoise sea) we awoke to our first thrilling sensation of being abroad, something often forgotten. It's like sucking liquid through a straw. Home life is *in-out*, like the boat-race; abroad it's all *in*. Approaching Pau we first glimpsed the ghostly backcloth of the Pyrenees. There was a telegram from Janetta at the Poste Restante, and she arrived that same evening. 'Robert was torn by the desire to come till the last moment. He came to see me off, and he was quite dark blue in the face with wanting to come,' she told us.

After several days in sight of the challenging Pyrenees we crossed them by the Somport Pass and made for the little Spanish town of Benasque, recommended by Robin Fedden who had used it as a base for mountain-climbing. The Fonda was kept by a family of alpine guides; the dear old father had been up the highest peak, the Aneto, 400 times, and had the soft voice and air of restraint that I have noticed in all those whose livelihood is got from battling with Nature at her fiercest. We had one incomparable, unforgettable day, starting at about 3 a.m. when I looked out of our window and saw the pale light dawning above the pure line of the snow-covered mountains. We asked the dear old hard-working Señora for a picnic and she brought us hard-boiled eggs, raw ham, bananas — and then as a special treat positively *ran* to get us some *turrón* and rough white wine as well. We walked up into the heart of the mountains as far as we could go, finding narcissi just coming out and very small, sweet-scented white daffodils with narrow trumpets. The promise of flowers to come was almost unbearable; at one point the valley flattened out and was nearly black with the navy-blue buds of gentians. There were leaves of orchids and martagon lilies. 'We leave Benasque with that very special and rare feeling of being *in love* with it, and its extraordinary atmosphere of innocence. We mean to come back when the flowers are all out,' I wrote.

We made a stop on the way home at a village where a château once owned by Colette was reputed to be for let or sale. We asked the way many times — some had never heard of it, others said, '*Ah oui, je le connais, mais c'est pas bon là-bas.*' When we found it at last it was extraordinarily primitive, peopled by Breughel-like rustics speaking patois and the château had been sold; questions about its owner produced an affectionate smile. '*Eh bang, Madame Colette c'était autre chose. Elle n'était pas come tout le mang, vous savez!'* said a large fat bandy-legged woman half hidden by a vast mushroom hat, who might have come out of one of her own books.]

May 18th — Ham Spray. Ralph rang up Robert to ask him for Whitsun. Asked how he was he said, 'I'm BAD,' like the boy in the *Turn of the Screw*. Burgo is back from Oxford, facing his Finals bravely on the whole, and spending quite a lot of time in his study. Friends have been re-contacted and many sorrows have been spilled, leaving me feeling a tremulous quaking coward myself, distrait and confused, opening drawers and shutting them aimlessly. After all the Whitsun weekend passed off pleasantly, with Isobel, Charlotte and Anthony Blond.

May 28th. Robert has been with us ever since Whitsun, and Janetta joined us for the weekend. Before she came I had a long conversation with Robert, walking up and down the lawn. On the telephone he had said that he must stop floating and make some decisions about his life, but so far as his predicament emerged in speech it consisted in: Should he live in Dublin or London, and how could he earn some money. The question of with *whom* he should live was only skimmed over! He confessed to the ghastly difficulty he had always had in making up his mind. 'When you've bought something — a shirt for instance,' I asked, 'and are walking out of the shop with the parcel under your arm, do you wish you'd bought a different one?' 'Oh, YES, of course. Always!' It was the most revealing thing he said, except that he was quite sure he had been right not to come to the Pyrenees, much as he'd wanted to, because it would have 'begged the question and made the decision for him which he didn't yet feel able to make'. (At which rate, I reflected, you're not going ever to make any decisions at all. Why not a little more courage?) While we were talking, Janetta rang up to say she would like to come down, and asking to speak to Robert. 'Is that all right?' I asked him, 'or will you take to flight?' 'No, I'd like to stay till next week and do my deciding then.' I felt rather as if he were a Victorian young woman being pressed to give his answer to a proposal of marriage.

However, neither Ralph nor I were in the least prepared for what happened when Janetta was actually with us: we agreed afterwards that we had felt we should go away and leave them alone together, so obvious was their obsession with each other. It quite took us aback. Janetta's stream is clear and direct; there are all sorts of baffling currents going on in Robert's. Though he has more to lose and more old wounds to be reopened, it's Janetta at the moment I'm anxious about. On Monday morning Robert came down in his best suit and said that he had decided to go to Dublin at once, dispose of his flat there and move his things to London. But no sooner said than he began casting his eyes back at the shirt he had left in the shop, saying that it was impossible to write his book anywhere but in Dublin. 'If I could find someone to marry me and live with me there — an air-hostess, perhaps.' I said teasingly: 'Perhaps we're being unkind when we open our doors wide and say "Come back here whenever you like." We may be making your decisions harder; we ought to slam the door instead.'

May 29th. This evening has brought our own anxieties to take the place of other people's — poor Burgo rang up in a state of desperate gloom about his coming Finals, he was certain he couldn't pass and was afraid we didn't realize the fact.

May 30th. This is the sort of crisis which Ralph deals with brilliantly while I rely entirely on him. He flew into action on the telephone as soon as we were awake, and arranged among other things to go and lunch with the Cecils and Burgo. We are back from that now. I'm not sure Burgo was glad to see us, perhaps he felt we had betrayed his confidence to the Cecils. He had the tense preoccupation of someone who is about to face an ordeal the thought of which doesn't leave his mind for a moment; but he was pleased because Ralph took him some half-bottles of champagne to cheer him up. I only hope that when he begins writing tomorrow it will seem better. Lord knows we neither of us mind how he does, but it will set *him* up if he gets through. Meanwhile these next days have to be lived through by us, helpless in the background.

June 8th. Burgo has weathered his Finals, and no matter if he passes or not it is the greatest victory he's won over himself in his life. We heard nothing after the weekend, and I was like a cat on hot bricks till he rang up on Wednesday saying it was all over and he had had his first sip of champagne. Oh, the relief! And he was so pleased he had stuck it out, though he had a streaming cold and went back to bed at tea-time every day. Ralph and I feel very proud of him, if I may use that corrupt phrase.

June 18th. Janetta put me up for a night to visit the dentist. She told me that after their last visit to Ham Spray Robert had launched one of his great thundering depressing tirades against her way of life, her selfishness and how she brought up her children. She had been crushed and deflated by this wigging, and the worst of it was that he was not cross while delivering it, but seemed to be thoroughly enjoying himself. It reminded her of the old days with him and how desperate it had been trying to make a good, gay life under that withering fire, and I think it has finally convinced her that she could never join forces with him again. The odd thing is that were she Georgie he would see at once that a person can't live on criticism alone.

July 9th. Day-to-day events: Burgo came back cheerful from a visit to London and a party at the Nichols. We all three went to another given by the Garnetts at Hilton. Little Henrietta, most fascinating of the four girls, took a fancy to Burgo, and held his hand with a persistently romantic expression. A week later we celebrated his twenty-first birthday with a dinner-party at Ham Spray that was lively though put together in somewhat random fashion — the guests being Simon Young, Serena Dunn, Quentin, a great charmer called Christopher Arnander, and Rodney Leach (both from Oxford).

July 24th. Sudden overpowering heat as I got into the diesel train for Reading on my way to London and the Memoir Club. 'Whew! Isn't it hot? I'm dripping with sweat,' says a pretty girl to me. No one else speaks — they are too hot. Neither the American officer and his smart wife, nor the two plain schoolgirls with budding breasts, nor the young, dreadfully fat woman who has kept on her thick overcoat. I see with alarm her face turn slowly reddish purple and then this colour flood down her neck. London at last! It was full of summer frocks and tourists from abroad.

　　Geniality pervaded the Memoir Club, which was held in Saxon's old rooms now quite transformed by Vanessa and Duncan's magic touch, with large mirrors on the pale walls splashed with tomato and dull plum colour. But we are all getting

older, and the tendency for the human voice to make one drowsy
after food and drink on a summer's night is great. Not the old
only. Angelica subsided on a sofa with her head on Bunny's
shoulder and was nearly or quite asleep half the time.

August 2nd. Ralph and I are alone for a few days. Burgo has gone
to London for a party, and away for the weekend. The news that
he had passed his Finals, but with a Fourth, saddened me though I
hadn't expected more than a Third. The fact that Ralph took it
extremely well did a world of good to Burgo, who showed signs
of desperation and defeatism when he saw the notice in *The
Times*. Also his own niceness to Burgo has relieved the tension
that was building up inside Ralph and might easily have taken a
hostile form. Why, exactly, he did so badly is something one
can't just dismiss by saying he is 'neurotic', in view of his high
I.Q. and the opinions of some of those who taught him at school.
And yet it is as near as we can get to the truth. What above all
things I want for him is happiness, and that he should go on
developing the power to adapt himself which he showed in his
first two years at Oxford but less in his third. He is very much of
an individual and he made a lot of friends there. But I know he
does not find life easy.

August 13th. Two nights ago we dined with Arthur Koestler and
his pretty little 'Angel'[1] who have rented the Lacket, the Tom
Thumb cottage near Marlborough where Lytton wrote *Eminent
Victorians*. Sylvester and Pauline Gates were the other guests; he is
a fat, smooth clever man; I liked the spontaneous Pauline better. I
drank more than I usually do from feeling somewhat *dépaysée*.
The evening became rather uproarious, but I don't think the
better of Koestler after it. He is an aggressively male man who
likes to have subjugated, pretty women and fawning dogs about
him. After dinner he began lecturing us all on relativity in an
unconvincing and boring way, got Angel to bring in a kitchen
pot to illustrate his point and then did nothing with it. It was a
supremely arrogant performance. Then he embarked on ex-
trasensory perception, and when Ralph began to criticize Rhine
and Soal (about whose experiments he has read everything there
is to read, being fascinated by human credulity) he would brook
no disagreement, but held out a dismissive hand saying, 'Oh no,
come now Ralph — you may say such things about Rhine

Above: Burgo in his rooms at Christ Church

Right: Wynne and Kitty Godley at Ham Spray

Above left: Ralph
and Janetta at
Ham Spray

Above right:
E. M. Forster at
Ham Spray

Left: Carmiña,
one of our maids
at San Fiz, Galicia

James Strachey

Alix Strachey

V. S. Pritchett
and Freddie
Ayer

Above: Eddy Sackville-West with Ralph at Cooleville House, Ireland

Left: Pansy Lamb

Robin Campbell, Cyril Connolly and Ralph at Buena Vista, Churriana

Burgo,
Joanna
Carrington
and Gamel
Brenan in a
Spanish café

Cyril Connolly in the 'music position'

Rose Jackson

Janetta and
children at Ham
Spray

Desmond Shawe-Taylor and
Raymond Mortimer at Crichel

Robert and Georgie at Ham Spray

Nicko
Henderson
and Boris
Anrep
playing chess
at Ham Spray

Janetta with Paddy Leigh Fermor being
reminded of Piero della Francesca

Simon Raven

Ralph with
the Brenans
in Spain

perhaps, but Soal's results are incontestable. I will listen to you on Broadmoor but not on E.S.P.' A dictatorial man, impossible to argue with, and on this occasion rude. Yet like many ultra male men he has a vulnerable, little boy side to his character. What else did we talk about? The importance of brothels for one thing. Pauline disagreed, wanting 'everything to be romantic'.

¹Later his third wife Cynthia.

September 4th. Two copies of my Spanish translation arrived by the morning post. I was faintly sickened by the sight of them. Burgo has gone to London to join Anne Nichols, Caroline, Rodney Leach, etc. for a walking-tour in the Massif Central, a lovely plan which he is obviously looking forward to. Meanwhile Ralph and I are going to Ireland.

[An invitation to stay with Eddy Sackville-West in County Tipperary was the nucleus of our plan to take the car and explore the south-west, landing at Rosslare and setting off westwards near the coast. People are divided between those who are soothed by Ireland and those who find it maddeningly run-down and depressing. Both Ralph and I belonged to the first class. Irish voices were a joy to us, and we noticed the original way they use words as if they had never heard one before. We loved the rough little fields, needing a hair-cut and containing one donkey or cow, the fuchsia hedges bleeding their flowers on to the ground, the montbretias growing right up to the sea's edge, hydrangeas and tree-mallow vigorously on the march. We stopped at the charming village of Schull, where the streams were as brown as Guinness, and the aloe had run wild, even out on to a hermit's island in the sea itself. There must be something peculiarly rich in a soil that yields such vegetable riot.

Turning northwards, we rounded every promontory by Bantry, Glengariff and Sneem — a little town as pretty as its name, settled snugly among velvety hills; we visited the home of my Irish ancestors on Valencia Island in dazzling weather, and floated on the breathlessly still, gun-metal waters of Killarney. Thus we passed ten days of happy refreshment, rejoicing in our solitude together, before the first note of alarm about Ralph's health came to break the spell. As usually happens with such warnings we did our utmost to reason it away. (He had been on a controlled insulin intake ever since his diabetes declared itself, and looked rosy and well.)]

September 27th. The inn at Clohane, near Brandon, looked so unlike one that I went into the post office and asked: 'Will they have room for us, do you think?' The postmistress clapped me on the back: 'Sure they will — and be *charmed* to have you.' It was very nice, though simple; we ate with our two fellow-guests, an unattractive young Ulsterman with a rucksack and a heavy cold, and an intelligent lady from the Women's Institute, come to teach the villagers dress-making. Apart from upholding the way children are taught to speak Irish, which their parents do not understand, on the irrational basis that 'they ought to have a language of their own', she talked a lot of sense. We learned that Irishmen are loth to marry, confirming that as a nation they are undersexed.

After a windy night the sun came out in glory, and we decided to keep to our plan of climbing far enough up the flank of Brandon mountain to be able to see its celebrated cliffs, Ralph's reason being partly that Gerald had often given them a mysterious connection with Saint Brendan, and so with his own name. As we climbed the wind grew fiercer and the ground boggier. It seemed that a baleful force was shrieking at us, '*No pasarán!*' and I began to feel very anxious about Ralph, who had as usual forgotten to bring his emergency sugar-lump. 'Let's go back!' I said, but he wanted to go on; his face was red, and I knew that it went pale when exertion led to sugar-shortage. Though he is very good on the whole about keeping to the rules, he is admirably determined to lead as normal as possible a life while doing so, and he has a strong dislike of all medical precautions. Oh, how thankful I was when he agreed to give up the battle and return to Clohane.

But on the way to Limerick alas there was another nasty moment, when he hurried across a road to buy a newspaper and returned in a state of near-exhaustion, admitting to a pain in his chest. My problem is that he is fully aware of my tendency to worry intensely about him, and that if I make it too plain that I am doing so he will not tell me exactly what he feels. This horrible dilemma is, I feel sure, one that everybody who loves someone with a physical disability such as diabetes has to contend with.

September 29th — Cooleville House. Here we are at Cooleville House and civilization, with other people's feelings to consider instead of mountain roads, lakes, rivers. But I believe a good soaking in the natural world is a beneficial Turkish bath toughening one against human impacts — whereas (contrariwise) over-indulgence in sociability produces a form of sharp acid that erodes one's vital energies.

This square Georgian house has been painted apricot colour and looks over its lawns at the Knockmealdown mountains. Inside it is as comfortable as care and money can make it. The large drawing-room is papered dark red with stippled white roses at least three feet high all over it — very striking; carpet and covers are another sort of red; four maids wear red uniforms and Eddy put on a red velvet dinner-jacket for dinner. The house is in fact a beautifully constructed, smoothly working toy, but the little rich boy who owns it sits with great sad eyes, ringed round with ill-health, as thin as a sparrow and with spots on his poor face. Ralph and I agreed that it made our hearts bleed to see him look so ill and exhausted, yet force himself to be charming, amusing, intelligent and the most attentive of hosts. Elizabeth Bowen came to dinner; we both liked her *very* much. Horse-faced, with big hands and a clumsy body in a short black evening dress and flashing diamond corsage; she has an attractive stammer which makes her start words beginning with 'r' with a whirring sound like a clock about to strike.

September 30th. Drove over to Bowenscourt before lunch. It's a tall grey house with rooms, doors and windows on a huge scale only found in Ireland. It was full of lovely things that seemed barely kept together, and an endearing Irish ramshackleness pervaded it. Elizabeth has another Irish characteristic — she *adores* talking and does it very well.

October 1st. Eddy tells me he's worn out with being host, and longs to be a guest again at Crichel. I sympathized with him and told him that he entertains one unnecessarily, which is true. A tragic look crossed his face as he said: 'Oh, but I don't feel I can ask people to come all this way just to sit in the *rain*!' Yet it hasn't rained at all since we came and there's never been a dull moment. Though Eddy looks ill he's entrancing to be with, so gay and full of laughter. He rails against the state of things from a purely aristocratic point of view, and often declares his disbelief in, or dislike of equality, but here in Ireland he can live in a way that exists nowhere else, nor has done for about a hundred years. No two sets of values could be more different than ours and Eddy's, especially now that he has become a Catholic, yet very warm affection — mutual I believe — exists between us.

Most enjoyable evening dining at Bowenscourt, at a candle-lit table in a vast room full of shadows, servants waiting, and Elizabeth in a white evening dress and emeralds. Afterwards, before a roaring fire in the equally vast drawing-room we played Scrabble. Jim Egan, a friend of Elizabeth's known as the Kerry Bull, was very amusing, inventing outrageous Irish words like AMIDGIN [Imagine]. Our visit to Cooleville, taken all in all, has added its own very distinctive aspect to the view of Irish life we had been gathering on our travels.

October 14th — Ham Spray. We've been back over a week, time enough for the effect of our refreshing long drink to wear off and friends to reappear on the stage. Burgo has taken a room in Tite Street; Robert writes that he is 'in a terrific muddle. How *should* one live?' a question I believe (and hope) we shall go on asking ourselves until we die, and always with the feeling that we've almost got the solution, which remains teasingly round the corner. Robert added, 'How lucky you are down there in the oasis of Ham Spray,' and has been told to come here whenever he likes.

I have had a pleasant surprise in being asked to do a translation for the Harvill Press (French this time).

October 17th. We are sitting in the train to London, opposite an old woman sunk in the uncompromising egotism of age. What a waste of time for those plump, gnarled hands to bother to fasten strings of pearls round her spreading neck, or button herself into her expensive pink shantung dress — such were my unkind reflections; then she dropped her paper and when I picked it up for her she broke into an amiable, a really sweet smile. Good heavens, she's a human being!

The Bolshoi Ballet, the same evening, was a memorable experience, with Ulanova the most intoxicating element. The dancing seemed to me to be worlds away from the acrobatic performance of our English ballets, in which the dancers look like jointed dolls with each limb distinct from the rest. With the Bolshoi, movement flows into movement in a rippling stream, and the entire body — loose and limber — is given over to the dramatic emotion of the moment. Ulanova is a great artist, no bit of her body is out of the picture: expression of face, little fingers, the gentle curves of her arms, and the magic way she made Juliet grow from a child of fourteen to a girl in love. And she herself is forty-seven. Ralph, Janetta, Richard Chopping and I were so excited and moved that all four of us were at times in tears.

October 19th. Yesterday Ralph went to London to see his diabetic specialist, Oakley. He is worried by the pains he has been getting now and then in his chest when walking, although our Hungerford doctor believes them to be indigestion. Oakley at once said: 'You've put on too much weight.' He prescribed a strict diet and pills for the pain. 'Fat round the heart' is what he calls it. Ralph had pains on the way to Paddington station, quelled by pills, they came on again while he was sitting quietly in his armchair, and again — waking him up and frightening me into fits — in the night.

October 20th. Another bout of pain in the morning. I kept him in bed and sent for the local doctor (generally spoken of between us as 'Sawbones'), whose attitude alarmed me because it revealed his own alarm. Ralph was determined to get up, and at length was given leave, but with instructions to keep absolutely quiet. Worried to death, I ran like a squirrel from task to task. Sebastian and Raymond came in the evening, by which time Ralph seemed better and more cheerful. They were a welcome distraction to us both.

[Now began a time of nightmare and misery; but as everyone knows who has gone through a similar experience (and millions do), it was by no means continuous, and also we found it possible to live on two levels at the same time — one of anxiety and watchfulness and the other that of the outside world. It was much like walking over a rickety bridge made of broken planks. Every so often one of these gave way and pitched one into the river-bed below. Then up one scrambled again and struggled along as best one could, helped by a strange force which I can only call the life instinct — a fierce determination to exert every ounce of strength and thought to the preservation of our happiness.]

October 21st. Janetta came in the evening and sat talking to Ralph for a long time, which he loved, although she told him how hopeless things were between her and Robert. She has come all the way to meet him — only to get another of his periodic wiggings. Now she feels she doesn't want to see him again.

October 22nd. After driving Raymond to the station Ralph admitted to a slight pain. On Janetta's advice we telephoned to tell Oakley of the developments; were they possibly the result of his pills? He sounded alarmed. 'You ought to be in bed. We don't want you running into a thrombosis.' He evidently telephoned Sawbones, who came out later and told Ralph he must remain entirely in his room and do nothing, and that he was arranging for a cardiogram, etc. in Oxford early next week. How bleak these words are as I write them, and yet all the time my head is full of jangling alarm bells and my heart of love for Ralph.

Janetta left us. Robert came 'for refuge. Things are bad here,' he said. *So are they here, God knows.*

October 24th. The day of our journey to Oxford for Ralph's examination. Woke very early, brooding. Sawbones had told me I must do all the driving. 'I don't want to have to come and scrape you off the road,' he said. Oh, the horrible jargon doctors use! I wrote these notes as I sat in the central hall of the Radcliffe, waiting for Ralph to come back.

Living my own life no longer has any meaning, I notice with a certain surprise. My personal greeds are few — music, flowers, whisky, books, and my appetites so *un*-urgent that any strength I possess is available for Ralph's illness, though of course that *is* a personal greed, even without going into philosophical depths. I sit here thinking about fear and the way that a demand on one's courage causes one mentally to twist and brace to take the load. Then I think of Janetta's sensitive and helpful touch on Monday, how she always said the right thing and provided what Sawbones' waffling did not.

Meanwhile my task is to explore every cranny of the situation, however agonizing, and somehow come to terms with it as best I can. It is the combination of doubts about what *is* the best and everything mattering so desperately that is hardest to bear.

They are making poor Ralph run upstairs so as to see how his heart behaves afterwards — this, when he was told to avoid the smallest exertion on pain of death!

Through the heart of the hospital, where I am sitting, people are moving ceaselessly — visitors, stretchers carrying prostrate half-corpses off to be sliced up by one of those stalwart young butchers in white overalls, squat foreign ward-maids wearing absurd little caps like cuffs on their heads. An old man wheels in a barrowful of oxygen cylinders. There's no end to the flowing current, most of it so impersonal, in which one occasionally catches sight of a human face, with anxious eyes brooding over themselves or their nearest and dearest. A faint but definite sour smell pervades everything — the smell of fear, perhaps. So much of medicine seems to be just typing or scrubbing, while I'm aware of not being either a typewriter key or a cake of soap, but just an adventitious bit of grit in an eye. For in these great emporia where the commodity dealt in is human entrails, mind, feelings and thoughts are buried under a mass of tubes and switches.

I turn my mind deliberately to Robert and our conversation last night. The fact to be faced is that he is free from Janetta and from the conflict he was in concerning her, and as a result he is less fierce, calmer. It distresses me that he should reject something so valuable, but there is nothing anyone else can do about it.

Now Ralph came back, having run up several flights of stairs with only very faint discomfort; this was somehow reassuring, but we realized that the Oxford consultant would let us go without telling us *anything*.

October 27th. Sawbones came out to see us. 'I was wrong,' he said, 'it *is* the heart.' The cardiogram had revealed an abnormality of the heart muscle. (We both strove to understand him.) The pain was 'angina of exercise' and being overweight was certainly a part cause. He must take as much exercise as possible short of getting the pain, and go on reducing. There followed a silence, which was worse. This horse-faced man who sweats under the arms and has black fingernails must be the one to stab one to the vitals.

Campbells to dinner. I feel half-dead one way or another, and yet all too much alive, thinking and thinking.

October 30th. The nightmare quality of these days is only kept at bay by being constantly busy and as constantly exhausted. Thank

God for Robert; I do so hope he'll stay on with us; he has become the perfect companion as before.

I have said nothing about international politics, though there has been plenty of it to think about, and an extraordinary new crisis is blowing up now. Israel has invaded Egypt, as we heard last night on the wireless. Now an unbelievable step has been taken by France and England alone — a twelve hours' ultimatum to both to retreat to so many miles from the Suez Canal. *Or else.* We were at the Campbells' before dinner today listening to the latest news, and I was bewildered and almost shocked by the excitement of the three R's, and annoyed by Mary's tendency to exclaim 'Yippee!' at any bellicose item. Meanwhile Robert has been telephoned to by *The Observer* to go to Israel as War Correspondent, and he goes tomorrow. I'm very sorry, I was meaning to ask his advice, and it's been comforting just having him here.

Driving to the Marlborough orchestra last night through the darkness I felt terribly sad and lonely. I cannot forget for a moment my meeting with Sawbones yesterday outside the fishmonger's in Hungerford. I tried to avoid him but couldn't. *God,* how I hate that man, and his grating voice and his coarse red nose. With a grin on his face he told me straight out that he thought I ought to know that Ralph might die at any moment. 'Perhaps I'm being heartless,' he added. Useless to say, 'Yes, my dear chap, you most certainly are.' There flashed into my mind a phrase I had read years ago in a Western novel, and which had always puzzled me: 'When you say that — *smile!*' But this time I turned it round to: 'When you say that — *don't* smile!' I think he must have heard from Dr Oakley (who approves) that we thought of spending the coldest winter weeks in Spain. He — Sawbones — does not approve, and he chose this way of saying so outside the fishmonger's.

[I vividly remember how selfishly I minded Robert's going, just when I had made up my mind to consult him on an important aspect of Ralph's illness: did he think, I would have asked, that Ralph knew the extent of his danger, and if so, should I talk to him about it? For the fact was that I had been so used to confiding all my troubles down to the last grain to Ralph himself that I was finding it practically unbearable not to burden him with my anguish on his behalf. I knew no one who would give advice more truthfully and supportively than Robert.]

November 1st. Ralph listens all day to the news, looking sunk in gloom. Eden must be raving mad. We have started bombing 'Military Objectives' from the air. In fact we are *at war* again, and no one is on our side. America, even our colonies repudiate us. I feel extremely fatalistic about the whole thing — only a sort of contempt for anyone who holds the belief that you can solve problems by killing people. Ralph bought all the papers he could get. Today's had pictures of smug-looking airmen tucking into bacon and eggs after bombing some Egyptians. But nearly all the papers come out against Eden, and corny slogans like 'England and France stand alone' or 'Protecting our life-line' are few and simply *sickening*.

Burgo arrived in the evening, talking and thinking hard about the crisis, or war, or what Eden prefers to call 'Armed Conflict'. He was in Parliament Square last night where a huge crowd, mostly young, were shouting 'Eden must Go!' and being charged by mounted police with batons. Military veterans crawl out of holes and talk about 'pockets of resistance' and 'mopping up'.

November 4th. A visit from Bunny, bringing his two dear little girls, Amaryllis and Henrietta. He is very pro-Eden — the only friend we can say that about so far; but he was endearingly like a large slow, amiable bear. Life at Hilton, he told us, was like that of woodlice under a brick, crushed by material concerns and not in touch with the world of ideas: which I can only suppose was his response to the fact that we are more interested in public events than they. Bunny is a happy and very affectionate man, but a considerable egotist. He must have talked for nearly seven hours yesterday about his and Angelica's travels abroad — it was a bit too long. Among other things he said he would never go and see Berenson[1] again because he had been so rude about Vanessa. 'He said she was' (enormous pause) '*heavy*' (still longer pause) '*and dirty.*'

The two sweet little girls sat like birds on a twig, perfectly well-behaved.

[1]The art historian.

November 6th. Burgo came down in his London suit and paced about, Hamlet-like, but much loosened-up and mentally active. I wrote letters on the verandah in the warm sun, beside Minnie who was preoccupied with one tiny black kitten which she gave birth to last night. Ralph and I had a little walk in the fields in the golden light of afternoon, with no ill effects. I am developing a technique of slowing our pace, or stopping to look at hedgerow plants (which I am always only too ready to do) whenever I sense the least disquiet.

This evening came the welcome news announced by Eden in the House of Commons that a cease-fire has been ordered in Egypt. Ralph has had a friendly letter from Gerald, and we are seriously wondering whether to go out to Spain after Christmas. Cold is said to have a distinctly bad effect on Ralph's trouble. I have started translating the French book Harvill sent me, and read out my first chapter to Ralph. So quietly and pleasantly can the days pass when we are alone; but at night I often lie awake for hours.

November 10th. Dinner with the Campbells. I had a certain amount of argument about war with Robin. I raised the question with Ralph later: How much of a pacifist argument can one have with a man who lost his leg in the last war? Ralph thinks not much. I say it's paying him a compliment; anyway there were no wigs on the green last night. I tried to answer Robin's contention that death was not dreadful and anyway to be preferred to torture, which seemed to me to beg the question — for death is not the same as killing. Also when one nation sets about killing another, torture is generally involved, and just as capital punishment fails to decrease the murder rate, so does war fail to cure war.

November 20th. A wonderful ripe peach of an autumn day. Ralph and I took a walk along the top of the downs with no ill effects, which cheered him up a lot. Indeed I'm more than satisfied with his progress. His illness has completely expunged from my conscious mind all those infinitesimal selfish tugs and irritations which arise between two people who live so closely welded together.

Janetta came for a night. When I said I thought most of our friends were anti-Eden, as she is, she said, 'Oh no, I'm afraid we're in a minority,' but named no one except Cyril who takes his stand on snobbish grounds, being proud of the fact that he knows the Edens and dines with them in Downing Street.

This morning the papers announce that Eden is ill and has been ordered to rest.

November 21st. Both of us are feeling low this wintry morning. A breakfast conversation explored the aching area a little, but not to much purpose. Ralph told me he could not guarantee to report on all his physical sensations — life would be unendurable if he did. This of course I perfectly understand and sympathize with; it is one of the unimagined complications of the situation that I must suppress my anxious questions — or even looks — and wear a mask to which I am hopelessly unaccustomed. Secretly therefore I note down that I get the impression that he has felt less good lately. Noel Carrington wanted him to go and see his heart-specialist friend, Geoffrey Konstam, and he agreed to do so 'some time'. I feel at times as if I had been thumping along in the saddle for ages and long for nothing but sound sleep. But at nights I am beset by mosquito thoughts, and toss and turn for hours.

December 3rd. Burgo and Simon are here and have gone off for a walk. Their happiness together and youth are very consoling. Ralph saw Geoff Konstam in London two days ago and was thoroughly overhauled. He said he had definitely had a coronary thrombosis, but it had healed up pretty well and should continue to do so. On the whole the verdict was encouraging but it has left us both a little flat.

Notes written in Geoff's waiting-room: Here I am again waiting for the doctor's verdict; I can hear Geoff and Ralph talking through the thin wall: a big clock on the wall above me ticks loudly like the beating of a heart. Now there's dead silence from next door, and I sit like a worm at the end of a fishing-line waiting for the tug from the fish's mouth. I shut my eyes and pretend I don't really exist.

December 5th. Ralph has run out of tobacco and has gone in to Hungerford to buy more, raising of course the question of how much attention should be paid to Geoff's dictum that he should cut down on smoking and drink. The truth is I shall have to grit my teeth and watch him doing what is bad for him. He does make efforts but smoking in particular is one of his greatest pleasures. Janetta rather annoyed me by telling him, after our visit to Geoff, that it was monstrous to expect him to cut down on the drink.

Perhaps she couldn't herself but many people do it, and I see the two values balanced in imaginary scales — drink and life itself.

December 18th. Christmas is almost upon us. Last week in London we booked places on an aeroplane, thus committing ourselves to whizz through the night to Gibraltar in the middle of January. Is it madness? We both look forward, yet at times I feel sick with panic.

December 19th. A letter from Gerald. They obviously fear and dread our cóming to Malaga. 'Here, owing to cold, we just couldn't make you comfortable . . . we have been having too many visitors. I, you know, and Gamel too, need a lot of emptiness and calm.' I respect his honest *un*hospitality, although of course we wouldn't have wanted to stay with them for more than a night or two. And just as chilling as was Gerald's letter, a call from Janetta was warming. Ralph and I say to each other that she is our best friend. I certainly lean on her more than anyone else, young as she is. 'What shall I do with you away all that time?' she said. F: 'Why don't you come too?' J: 'I'll come like a shot.' If that's not friendship I don't know what is. I forgot to say that Gerald's letter went tactlessly on to show his readiness to take in Joanna Carrington.[1] 'We should both very much like to have her. She shall have my big room and I will see that she is comfortable.'

Nonetheless our morale is rather good. Ralph has been very gay and particularly sweet to me. But we admit to pique over Gerald's letter. Ralph said: 'If Gerald were in the Zoo he would have a notice on his cage saying, "This animal is dangerous."'

[1] The lovely young daughter of Noel and Catherine, who had been very ill.

December 31st. Rain has fallen all day. This horrid old year ends in a flood of tears. I believe that now our greatest pleasure is being alone together. We had Julia and Lawrence and of course Burgo for Christmas; ate a vast succulent turkey and drank champagne. But it was all slightly muffled. On Christmas Day it snowed and the telephone was down. Ralph was agitated by the responsibilities of Wilde's time off, and I made him sit by himself in the little sitting-room, behaving like a bossy hospital nurse when I really felt like a frightened mouse, isolated by lack of telephone. Burgo was angelically helpful, genial and talkative. Lawrence brought us a magnificent present — a picture; Julia made us aware of her criticisms and displeasure. I felt very sorry for her, a woman with nothing tangible to complain of yet so desperately unhappy.

Our only visitors were the Carringtons: they brought Joanna whose beauty filled the room like a glowing lamp.

1957

January 6th — Ham Spray. I started the New Year with a piece of paper on which I wrote: 'Problems to be dealt with' and 'Things to do'. One of the former is 'Cat and Kitten' (what to do with them while we are away)? This flimsy set of scribbles kept me writing cheques and letters all day, but the 'problems' floated in the air like barrage-balloons which I could neither forget nor puncture. Dined last night at the Moynes, where we met Laurie Lee and his wife Kathie. I sat next to Laurie, who is a great charmer, but more than that a very likeable man who wants to give pleasure and is quick and sensitive. Kathie is big and fine looking with a mane of thick tawny hair. After dinner we had some rather eccentric music — Laurie Lee played on Fiona Guinness's Amati, to my piano accompaniment, Bryan singing.

January 7th. Three letters from Spain: one from Gamel saying she had taken a *casita* for us belonging to a Marquesa, but there is alas, no room for Janetta. Another from Gerald was angry and bossy, saying that my letter announcing Janetta's arrival had just come, and it would make things most awkward with the Marquesa. On reading this, Ralph 'over-boiled' (his own expression) steadily for about an hour, which is the sort of thing he is forbidden to do! He says he gets no physical sensations from such irritable feelings, but they make me very anxious. Perhaps we'd better not go to Spain, I thought, if Ralph and Gerald are going to get so worked up with each other. Then we opened the third; it was from Annie Davis, inviting us all to stay a day or two at their house at Churriana, La Cónsula — this is really extremely kind as we have only met them a few times.[1]

[1] Annie was Cyril's sister-in-law. Both she and Bill were American. They died within a few hours of each other in May, 1985.

January 19th. The date of our departure swoops down on us like a great bird, and whenever I think about it I dissolve into unspeakable panic. The vet came and 'put' poor Minnie 'to sleep'. I kept well away in Hungerford feeling a little sick, partly because it caused me so little emotion. Her sweet black kitten takes up a lot of time, attention and love — rushing from wild antic to wild antic and then hurling itself exhausted and purring loudly on our laps, looking up with round beads of eyes and dropping instantly asleep.

Most of the time I am in a state of depression and lack of appetite for life almost equalling Julia's. I do wish I could find a little courage somewhere.

[My last entry was of course compounded of fears as to how Ralph would stand our journey. Might the altitude affect him? I had made enquiries about pressurization of aeroplanes and the answers were not altogether reassuring. And was it all a great mistake? Did he really long to be allowed to stay quietly at Ham Spray with no efforts required of him, with his *Times*, his books and his big green armchair? I had to guess, too many questions would only fuss him. Thank God, that obsessional, craven, dank state of mind really came to an end once packing was done, we had left the black kitten in her temporary home and said goodbye to Burgo. A curtain of teeming rain made England a place to get away from, with its scudding angry clouds, soggy earth, and the darkness settling down so early indoors.

On our way through London Ralph declared that he was going to the *New Statesman* to get a cargo of books to review, but it became suddenly obvious he would rather I went. Our night flight to Gibraltar was absolutely carefree; we were only fourteen souls where there were seats for forty-seven. So, after eating the beautiful slices of cold roast beef brought by Janetta, after looking down for a while through 25,000 feet of air as clear as glass to the map of Europe outlined in Christmas Tree lights below, we all stretched out on three seats and fell asleep. Gibraltar was moist, green and *warm*. We picked up our little hired beetle and made off along the coast road in excellent spirits. We had arrived!]

January 24th — La Cónsula. Awoke in our comfortable bedroom at La Cónsula, which contains at one end the Fiction department of Bill's excellent library. The house is all snowy whitewash and brown wood inside, with square white-covered settees and chairs, fireplaces full of glowing logs. In the dining-room a raised fireplace crackles and spits as handsome Fernanda cooks our *gambas* or grills steaks as big as Aberdeen terriers; wine and whisky gush into glasses, and I see it will be a job to keep Ralph to his régime. But this hospitality is so warm and generous; it is impossible not to be touched by the genuine friendliness of Bill and Annie. 'Thorough' is the word for Bill. All the books, all the music, all the food, wine and comfort a civilized person should require Bill provides.

The Campbells are staying here, and after breakfast Robin took us round the garden, where the trees are palms, mimosas and avocados, and oranges and grapefruit grow in Black Sambo profusion.

The Brenans came up to lunch, with Honor Tracy, a square literary lady with carroty hair *en brosse*. Ralph walked back with the Brenans. We are most anxious not to impose ourselves too long on the kind Davises but the problem is: Where shall we find a house?

January 25th. Springing into action, we have inspected and rented Buena Vista, a solid little house with plenty of beds and a sheltered patio, standing above the road from La Cónsula to Gerald's village, Churriana. There are too few blankets and no sheets or cutlery, but the Brenans have lent us the former and this afternoon we drove in to Malaga to buy the rest: sheets for all the beds — we got the man to cut them with his huge pinking scissors so they will not need hemming. Pillow-slips? A señora of the Casa could make them by tomorrow. *Con botones?* Yes please, *con botones*. So it went on. We were eventually fitted out, and the Brenans' Maria will come and work for us in the mornings.

Returning to the Cónsula we found two new visitors had arrived: Jamie Caffery is an American garden expert, a very friendly, rather comic character with something of the dog in his appearance and even more in his deep barking voice, whose resonance sends the lines grooving his face up and down as he talks. Jaime Parladé is a young, slender Spaniard, with an oval face and long-lashed twinkling eyes. The whole party except us and Robin went off to see the dancer Antonio perform in Malaga.

January 27th — Buena Vista. Yesterday we moved into our new home, dining however with the Brenans. Gamel gave us some more blankets, for the nights are cold, and an electric kettle to boil up our hot-water bottles. However, as soon as we plugged it in all the lights fused! So in utter blackness, lighting tiny wax matches and dropping them all over the place, we fumbled our way to our beds and crept between our new sheets in rooms which have the chill of having been shut up for weeks.

Today we drove along the Coin road to collect wood for our fires and fir-cones to light them with. The almond blossom is just coming out, and when we looked up from our task we saw the mountains beyond Malaga rumpling softly in the evening light and the snowy mountains far beyond. *Not* to live in a country where one soaks all day in such a bath of natural beauty sometimes strikes me as illogical.

January 31st. We all three took our little car further afield today, through villages dazzling with fresh whitewash, past brick-coloured hillsides dotted with olive trees. There were few cars but many more mules, on which their riders sat with that extraordinary style Spaniards show in everything they do, even to the exact angle they wear their hats, with which also they pull out their sturdy wooden chairs and sit in the sun, sewing or preparing vegetables, or tilt them back against the blue-white walls of their houses. As a nation they have remarkable good taste and are not prone to vulgarity, nor do I find, as Robin does, that the way they so often sing at work in the fields or as they walk to the well is sentimental and bogus — on the contrary I believe it is because they are happy or sad and like to express their feelings in their own individual musical idiom.

On and on we went, and up and up, until the sea lay far away below with the shadow of the American battleship which is at present in harbour lying unruffled beneath it. We ate our picnic lunch on the Pass of Leon, which is over 3,000 feet high and had snow below us and some small brown and green orchids around us, while far down in the valley were puffs of grey and pink smoke, which were olive and almond trees. A shout from Janetta who had wandered off (she had found big clumps of sweet-scented white jonquils) and another soon afterwards: 'Irises!'

February 10th. Ralph and I discussed the hard drinking habits of our friends and wondered what they are after? Drowning unhappiness, misting over reality? But none of them seems to be really unhappy, while someone like Julia (who *is*) doesn't appear to hanker after oblivion in drink. In youth, our generation used to take to it spasmodically as an accompaniment to dancing or something that downed the barriers and made people more sexually attractive. It doesn't go so well with middle age and conversation — drunken talk is usually (but not always) a poor affair. Then some drinkers plan their drinking day as seriously as writers do their writing days, which suggests it's a substitute of some sort. Is it a satisfactory one? Or is it more like trying to use spectacles for shoes than loving a pekinese instead of a person. Ralph thought that drinking 'bouts' were in the nature of Dionysian religious practices, and this was confirmed this afternoon when we walked over to the Cónsula and found last night's drinkers lying spent and deflated in the sun.

Gerald has been having flu, but called yesterday to say that Joanna Carrington *is* coming to stay. He sat with us for a couple of hours talking and talking, sometimes looking quite surprised at the words that came out of his own mouth. This interlocking world of expatriates seems to me rather like *South Wind*.

February 17th. The much-heralded arrival of Cyril at the Cónsula took place yesterday. He drove up in a barouche pulled by a skeleton horse straight from the bull-ring.

Ralph has been gaining strength and energy in a way I had hardly dared hope for, and Sawbones never gave us grounds to think likely. He even wakes cheerful. It is certainly the result of this celestial climate. We talk a great deal about possibly renting the house later this year and for a longer spell.

February 19th. Dinner at the Cónsula, and our first meeting with Cyril since his arrival. I was put next to him, and (determined not to be got down by his possible disapproval) I handed him a little butter about his broadcast, but resisted the temptation to lay it on too thick. The result was a conversation enjoyed by us both, I believe. But when we moved to the sitting-room and collected round the fire, Cyril, retired to a far corner of the room, flung himself back in a chair with his face parallel to the ceiling and his eyes closed, and remained thus for the rest of the evening. (Janetta christened this his 'music position'.) She said afterwards that his excuse for this ostentatiously rude behaviour was that he was 'desperately miserable'.

February 21st. We said goodbye to Robin, who leaves tonight, and went with Gerald and Gamel to see the English cemetery in Malaga. It is a very pretty place, and Gerald showed us round with an owner's pride. 'It's the nicest cemetery I know — but it's very difficult to get into now. We're going to the British Consul to book our places. I want to be in this corner here. The only thing that worries me is that I can't think of a good epitaph — it must be in Greek. Don't you think it's charming? It's got a lovely view — that's *very* important.' Feeling he was going rather far, I asked irreverently: 'To the corpses or those that visit them?' Gerald answered huffily: 'I don't think like that at all.' Gerald and I had become separated from the others and as we roamed among the tombs and the charming plants growing among them he let his mind run free about the domain of death, which he clearly found pleasant. I was only half-listening.

February 25th. On a morning that was still, hot and clear, we went with Janetta and Jaime Parladé to look at a possible house on the coast near Estepona, attractive but too small; we picnicked on the beach, and afterwards sat under a shady tree watching the beautiful day ripen into a golden evening. Jaime charmed us both by his intelligence and gaiety, and it's as great a pleasure to hear him talk Spanish as English.

February 26th. Though Janetta was subjected last night to a large dose of Cyril's pettishness and a good deal of the 'music position', she returned from dinner at the Cónsula very keen that we should invite him with the Davises to a ceremonial lunch at Martín's fish restaurant on the beach at Malaga. We are entirely agreed, as we shall not in a hurry forget Bill's and Annie's great kindness to us when we first arrived.

It took place today and 'went off' perfectly; Cyril was all amiability. But what an extraordinary object he is becoming! With his great round head passing necklessly into his body; his torso clad in a flashy American beach shirt, ski-ing trousers and fur-lined boots, he looked like some strange species of synthetic man or Golem.

[On March 1st we started on our drive back to Gibraltar by way of Cordoba and Seville. Ralph and I hadn't been to Cordoba for fifteen years and Janetta never; it is one of my two favourite

Spanish towns, the other being Salamanca. We went twice to see the Mosque. I received a shock of pleasure, interest and even alarm on entering that jungle of columns, gliding behind each other and continually making new patterns as one moved about; but the emotion it arouses seems to me more suitable to a cave or natural phenomenon than a work of art. Before reaching the strange coastal town of Puerto Santa Maria, with its flat roofs topped with croquet balls and its excellent fish restaurants, we stopped on a ridge with a superb view and an equally remarkable flora — tall orchids, a huge brilliant blue pimpernel, a faded brown scilla and many more, which I eagerly gathered, and contrived to get back to London safely, by putting them each night in our hotel wash-basin. The reason that I hadn't felt sadder when I thought of my stillborn flower book is that it left me a legacy of delight in wild flowers, a certain amount of technical knowledge, and contacts with botanical centres.

We took off in the small hours in a crowded aeroplane full of drunks, and got to London in a tepid drizzle.]

March 29th — Ham Spray. As far as Ralph's health is concerned the Spanish adventure was a great success and I am happier about him than I ever thought to be. Janetta, alas, looks neither well nor happy.

Two days in London yielded quite a lot of pleasure — an afternoon going to *Phèdre* with Julia, a visit to Burgo in his rooms, and another to the Natural History Museum, where I had left my flowers from Spain as soon as we got to London. On my first visit I saw, talked to and fell in love with a wonderful Dr Melderis, a tall, gentle, blue-eyed native of I don't know what foreign country, who presides over the European section of the Botanical Department. His domain is reached by a private lift leading up into a library and herbarium — all brown wood shelves and drawers, smelling deliciously of dried plants. On this second visit Dr Melderis was away, to my regret, but two assistants and a passing botanist treated my specimens with respect and even admiration.

But the most stimulating experience was the Racine. Ralph and I had read the play as well as various critiques coming up in the train. Some say that Edwige Feuillière is the best living actress, and her Phèdre sublime; others that it's a gallant failure. I thought neither was true. She's always the actress, you can't forget it, and at best you admire her art and notice it in operation. I never found her deeply moving — no clutch at the throat or starting tear; but is it possible to be moved by the horror of incest, when one doesn't in fact feel it? Ralph thought the love of an older woman for a handsome youth was in itself moving, as was any unrequited love. I agree and regret I didn't find it so. What enthralled and gripped me was the controlled concentrated emotion emanating from the marvellous music of Racine's words, acting exactly as do the libretto and music of an *opera seria* like *Semele* or *Idomeneo*, so I decided half-way through to give way to the poetry and cease to wonder whether the psychology was possible, or try to think Edwige Feuillière was really Phèdre, which did not prevent my feeling so much electric tension throughout that I could scarcely breathe.

April 3rd. My horrid French translation is packed off, the new Freudian Index not yet come — though I sometimes wonder if my 'work' is not the frantic leg-movements of a spider just before it hurtles down the run-away hole in the bath.

Ralph's health is still a source of pride and pleasure; he is very good about taking his exercise and not eating too much. Janetta has rented the Campbells' cottage, which is very nice for us. Our house is pretty trim; our black kitten growing into a charming companion, our staff fairly pleased with us, and Spain to look forward to in the winter.

April 20th. A visit to James and Alix on our way to East Anglia. They have reduced their womb, Lord's Wood, to some sort of order. A huge central-heating plant has been installed in the cellar, large enough to heat a battleship or blow up the house, and it makes the rooms far too hot, as even Alix allows, 'because the painters have stuck up the windows, so that I'm afraid none of them will open'. She showed us their Permutit water softener. 'It was very expensive, but filling it up takes two hours at least so we don't bother any more.' In this large house with a sitting-room for each (Alix's containing a frigidaire in case she should fancy a cold drink) as well as several communal ones, they lead a fairly ramshackle life, and feed off tinned soups and carrots. Alix does all the housework such as it is so the beds are never made, and she looked at the floor and said thoughtfully: 'I've not swept it for a month and I'm wondering when I shall have to.' Her book on psycho-analysis, the loving work of about fifteen years, has only had one review which began: 'This is an extremely bad book'. The only — yes, the *only* sign of her being a fully analysed person was that she told us that with a hearty laugh. I am not quite sure why the irrational life led by these two highly intellectual and rational people gives me such pleasure.

Back at Ham Spray, we have Julia for a nice long stay. She is in tip-top form, producing a stream of lively and fertile ideas, and conversation that is both interesting and fantastic. In between whiles she retires to her room to write her play, so that walks, talks and meals are mortar between the bricks. The secret of happiness is to have thoughts and exchange them with those of others — but the first is beyond one's control and it takes a lifetime to learn to do the second.

April 28th. Our landscape has been clouded by Ralph's twice feeling some 'uneasiness' or 'constriction' while walking. I feel dreadfully anxious, but must struggle not to show it; I just bow my head in ox-like acceptance of the blows of life, and bitterly regret that I am never, never as nice to him as I want to be and my love for him should make me.

An interesting jaunt this afternoon to the Rothschild rhododendron gardens.[1] It being a Sunday and the 'rhodos' (as they were actually called) in prime state, the public was there in full force; we were taken round by Leo Rothschild and his elegant mother, who had a heavy foreign accent and a marvellous memory for Latin names. The 'rhodos' made great cauliflower masses under the dark pine trees, or grouped round some black stagnant pools — in which sordid mirror Mrs Rothschild got us to admire their reflections. I have seldom seen anything more hideous. We were then taken to the orchid houses where the head gardener — a man so grand that he was said to have 'snubbed the Queen Mother' — showed us the nursery where seeds from orchids were incubated for seven long years in bottles full of warm jelly.

[1] At Exbury.

May 2nd. Up early and to London for the day for Duncan's private view. Many old friends were collected under the hot light beating down from the glass roof; very old they seemed, and dusty too, with the flash of false teeth and the glitter of spectacles. Vanessa stood beaming seraphically from under a huge inverted wicker basket. Marjorie Strachey like a swollen spider all in black. I came away feeling saddened. I'm well aware of what in Index terms I should call 'withdrawal of libido from the outside world', yet there are moments when something or other, some glue seems still to fasten me firmly to it. For instance, late tonight after our return I stood in the kitchen watching Dinah drink up her bedtime saucer of milk: the old scrubbed red tiles, the kitten's glossy black fur and the white milk, with the electric light pouring over them all from the ceiling and the quiet pattering of the rain outside sent a wave of peace, and acquiescence in the scheme of things, surging over me.

May 17th. A discussion between Ralph and me about Communism at breakfast. We had heard a debating society questioning a leading Communist on the wireless last night. It caused me to wonder whether one doesn't sometimes throw overboard a whole system of ideas just because some of them can be (and are) pushed to mad extremes — whether in fact Capitalism was necessarily right because so many Communist conclusions are wrong. Bound up with this is the dislike I feel at the thought of immense wealth in the hands of undeserving egotistic people, the height of whose altruism is reached by standing their friends large expensive meals of foods out of season, and who attach no responsibility to the power of money. (In contrast to Lord Nuffield and John Christie.) Ralph began to shout at me, and the effort to keep calm, and the failure, gave me an actual feeling of faintness. Later he admitted that he positively enjoyed the battling element in an argument, and when I said how much I loathed it we both became calm and interested again, and branched off into what was the foundation of ethical feelings.

June 3rd. The truth is I am suffering from all-pervading apathy, and though I know its cause all too well I don't know what weapons to fight it with. Some colossal mental effort, like heaving up a mallet and bringing it down on a peg? Where is my courage gone? It's lost, like my spectacles — and just as without my spectacles I can't see to look for them, without my courage I can't make the effort to grab it. If only a living being were like a motor-car and when he or she went wrong one could oil something or adjust the carburettor; but when the psyche is functioning badly, the mind won't get into gear and there's no psychological petrol in the tank there seems nothing to be done, no button to press or handle to swing.

This evening Ralph and I walked across the fields, and he came out of his usual stoical silence and talked freely about his troubles, the difficulty he had in putting up with the sense that his powers are failing or his clumsiness increasing. He made me feel ashamed, and when we got home I realized that something had clicked into place without my pressing any button or heaving mallets. I had found my spectacles.

June 15th. Persisting heatwave. In the evenings, after the midges have left us in peace, the wind drops and a great saucer moon sails over the downs. Were we younger and more enterprising this would be the time to go out, as Dinah does. When we were seeing the Campbells to the front door after midnight I was struck by the way the foxgloves stood up in the warm darkness, as if paralysed with waiting, like the paper hollyhocks in old-fashioned musical comedies. We had had a particularly happy weekend with Burgo the only resident; listening to the whole of the *Magic Flute* one evening, and all three walking along Rivar Down on Sunday morning.

July 17th. In London we went to Craig Macfarlane's[1] office to sign our Wills. Craig gave a very amusing description of travelling third class on the express to Rome: How a French lady got into trouble with her stays in the night and began to '*pousser des petits cris*,' how everyone co-operated to hold a screen of newspapers round her, while her husband hauled out what looked like yards of spaghetti, and at last she breathed a sigh of relief and sank back, touchingly grasping his hand. Then another lady had made several fruitless dashes to the lavatory, which was always occupied. '*Maintenant, allez vite!*' cried someone. '*Mais nous sommes dans la gare!*' '*Aucune importance, si ce n'est question que de faire pipi. N'est-ce pas, Monsieur?*' turning to Craig.

Memoir Club in the evening. Vanessa read some letters from Maynard — the dry husks of something that had once been dynamically alive and had stirred to the depths the emotions concealed behind those old masks sitting round the little room in Percy Street — Duncan's, Clive's, Vanessa's own. I let my eyes drift round at them all and felt moved, even while the crackle of deadness filled the air. As a Memoir it was non-existent, for Vanessa had contributed nothing. Then Angelica, looking very beautiful, read about her short career as an actress — interesting and vivid.

¹Our solicitor and very old friend.

July 27th. For some reason I can't define I'm counting the hours for the weekend to pass. I feel very tired at a deep level. Robert (here with Georgie) was the life and soul of yesterday evening. Just now, from the music room where he is typing, a melancholy voice rang out, loud and deep: 'When they heard of the death of poor Cock Robin!' Georgie was with me, and she burst out laughing and said, 'It's Daddy!' And who was Cock Robin, I wondered. Burgo, Simon Young and his sister are walking on the downs; Ralph writing a review in the library. Georgie has been writing a story about a King living in a golden castle, being attacked by another King, and returning home to find his Queen had had a baby. (Work that out in Freudian terms!) When the whole Stokke party came over for a drink, Paddy Leigh Fermor read Georgie's story and responded with enthusiasm. 'What shall I put next?' she asked him. Paddy: 'How about a tournament? Yes, I think you'll find that's your best way out — a tournament.'

Robert is now literary editor of *The Spectator*, offering high prices to reviewers to seduce them away from other papers. He walked with us this afternoon through grass sprinkled with harebells, wild carrot and bird's-foot trefoil — the autumn colours, purple, white and yellow, and down below us lay the ripe but still uncut cornfields between the green fur of August hedges. Lovely, I thought, but Robert was contemptuous: 'I've had it all. I simply hate it really. I think we're mad to put up with it.' It's touch and go how long he puts up with *The Spectator* and London life, and I suppose depends on whether he can raise a defence against loneliness.

August 22nd. Ralph wakes up most mornings disgusted with himself and feeling what he calls 'rubbishy' — this makes him very sweet to me, for having to live with such a rubbishy man. I'm more disposed to wake disgusted with the *world* and put the blame on the Creator. Once my eyes are open I tend to see some segment of the immediate future in exact detail, as when lying on a summer lawn one peers into the grass and sees the superhuman struggles of an ant to surmount blade after blade. At other times it's the insoluble problems I carry round — the black bag full of distressful secrets. A sort of thin horny development of the skin seems to have grown up to protect me, but at the first gleam of danger to what is vital to my happiness I become a quivering jelly.

Rosamond [Lehmann] and Burgo arrived together in her car. She was looking quite splendid, not a hair out of place and her bloom as fresh as ever. Last night she warmed up to pleasant old croneydom and we had a good talk about old friends and old times. When Ralph suggested she should write her memoirs, she exclaimed in a voice full of horror: 'But I've had such an *awful* life!' And in view of her beauty, sweet temper and success I suppose she has. I'm puzzled by Burgo. He has I think some schemes for living but doesn't want to talk about them. I can only applaud his independence and hope it is solid and secure. His instinct is right to keep a little aloof from anyone who minds everything that happens to him as much as I do.

August 24th. When we were alone again I pulled up an armchair in front of the fire and read steadily through the grey moist hours. Colette by her husband was my book. Impossible not to love and admire her, and it's one of those books that manure one's flower-bed. I really believe that reading books that don't do this in one way or another is a sort of addiction or mere time-killing. Colette was full of love, not only for flowers and wasps, but for things like food. When she was hungry she was *fiercely* hungry, almost growling with animal longing. She was a sensualist, and if she lacked anything it was — not hate exactly, but negative and critical reactions, something I miss in my friends when they haven't got them.

September 8th. We were bidden to stay with Kitty West to meet Anthony and his new wife Lily, this being the first time they had got together, along with the children. Lily is a tall girl with a fine figure and long limbs — almost a beauty and with a charming and responsive manner. Here were three people trying to do their best under fairly difficult circumstances, and possibly Kitty — who had suffered most in their joint history — tried a little too hard. On Sunday after breakfast on the lawn (delicious smell of coffee and sight of a bowl of figs, bananas and bright red apples) we were joined by Jimmy and Tania Stern. Jimmy is a gifted storyteller, a writer, and an Irishman belonging to the same civilization as Joyce and Beckett, of whom he had many memories. I had just been reading Joyce's Letters and not taken to their personal flavour. 'He seemed so uninterested in other writers, or anything in the outside world,' I volunteered. J.S. 'So he was, totally uninterested.' F: 'Was he a good talker?' J.S. 'He didn't talk much; he only asked questions. When I first met him he asked me questions for a whole hour about my childhood in Ireland. He was only interested in two things: Ireland and his own writing.' F: 'Forgive my asking, but have you read *Finnegan's Wake*?' J.S. 'Not a word! Wouldn't touch it.' Beckett, he said, was absolutely charming, but a very lazy man; he put off work as long as possible. In excuse for his lack of production he said to Jimmy: 'Ah, but you see I'm inarticulate.' 'I pleased him by telling him how much I liked the silences in *Waiting for Godot*,' said Jimmy, 'and he said, "*Aren't* they lovely?"'

Anthony's manner was very good, very dignified and restrained, and he was admirable with the children, if perhaps there were less of the satanic gleams and flashes of wit that I remember in the past.

Called at Crichel and on the Cecils on our way home.

September 16th. Robert was here over the weekend, and an argument about violence in the home arose as a result of news coming from Oonagh in Venice of a fierce scene of jealous fury, when a nose was broken and teeth knocked out. I knew Robert would defend this horrid outburst with the savage element there is lurking inside him, and so he did. It was quite unrealistic, he said, to suppose that everyone wouldn't do the same under pressure from extreme jealousy or sexual frustration. And anyway words were just as cruel. (He had a point there.) Ralph and I both said we had never hit or been hit under such circumstances; and I know this to be true not only of Ralph but of his contemporaries like Gerald. It is, I believe, a new and very disagreeable development in human relations. Can anyone imagine physical violence from an earlier generation — Clive, Leonard, Duncan? Robert obviously thought that we, and others who disapproved, were being pompous and stuffy, while we both found his arguments rather childish as well as terrifying.

September 23rd. The return from a weekend of restful comfort at Mottisfont to Ham Spray with its roughnesses, corners and chips is rather like stroking a wire-haired terrier after you have been fondling a Persian cat. For fellow-guests we had Boris, Clive and the recently-widowed Lesley Jowitt.[1] Clive was very genial and endearingly absurd, laughing as heartily at other people's jokes as his own. Boris, on the other hand, was unusually subdued. He told Ralph he had been quite ill after Maroussa's death. Lesley Jowitt was the novelty; over seventy, she's really pretty with the complexion of a baby and little blue curls all over her head, but her conversation mainly consisted in boasting. 'When the old boy was Lord Chancellor,' was constantly on her lips, but we also had her grandchildren, her charities, 'the Party', the House of Lords, the ships she had launched, and even the prize she'd won for a fancy dress on a cruise. She took no interest in anyone else and asked them no questions. However she told one story against herself which made up for all the rest. When leaving her butcher's one day she heard a customer say to him: 'Isn't that Lady Jowitt? She thinks everyone likes her — *but they don't.*'

The nicest thing we did was to go searching for fungi in a wood just as dusk was falling. The wide, dark glades were carpeted with a mosaic of shining leaves — it reminded me somehow of Turgenev: the *Sportsman's Sketches*, perhaps. Maud was wonderfully quick at spotting chanterelles, and we ate them for dinner that night cooked in a rich cream sauce.

[1] Whose husband had been Lord Chancellor 1945–51.

[Mottisfont had been converted from an ancient abbey and still bore many of its characteristics; it blended with its magically charming surroundings like some great rock or tree. The garden might have belonged to a French château. Besides a formal parterre entirely filled with heliotropes purple and mauve, flowers for picking were not much in evidence. Everywhere were smooth lawns intersected by water, and tall trees gesturing with low-slung branches. Crossing the widest stream by a bridge fenced with late roses, one entered woods full of the song of birds and carpeted with wild flowers. The large drawing-room, scarcely used except in the evenings, was a show-piece decorated by Rex Whistler with fanciful and delicate frescoes and *trompe-l'oeils* of white satin quilting, suggesting a set for a ballet or a fairy-tale. It amazed without altogether delighting the eye. Elsewhere one came across a mosaic by Boris.

Ralph and I spent several weekends there, and always enjoyed ourselves, although the ambience was so very different from our own, and in the end the comfort itself and the ministrations of man- and maid-servants had an anaesthetizing effect. But we both liked Maud very much. Though her way of life was conventional she herself was an original character, with something a little Oriental in her appearance and her movements. She had a great sense of humour and a low gurgling laugh. Also, though she put people at their ease and talked in a relaxed way herself there was a hint of the dark horse about her, a sense of mystery never quite cleared up.]

October 5th — Ham Spray. The chief piece of grit in our thoughts and discussions at present is Burgo's urgent desire to get a proper job, and his asking us for help in no uncertain terms. Ralph and I have both fired off letters to possible strings, containing S.O.S.'s veiled or open. We do not want to go off to Spain with the problem unsolved.

For once the News has produced something purely interesting and pleasant. The Russians launched an artificial 'satellite' about two feet in diameter, which is now hurtling round the earth at a height of 500 miles making a noise between a 'cheep' and a 'bleat', which has even been relayed to us in our drawing-rooms. Nobody seems to know what will become of this man-made object, whether it will disintegrate or fall to earth; but scientists all over the world are having a wonderful time listening to it and recording its path. Last night's wireless suggested a delightful idea: the *next* satellite will carry all sorts of elaborate machines including a camera which will photograph *the other side of the moon*!

October 15th. The divine beauty of these days is like the tolling of a bell summoning me to church to take part in some religious rite I don't believe in. Yesterday we walked on the downs above Hippenscombe, partly at the request of Mr Grose (who is compiling a *Flora of Wiltshire*) to see if we could find indications that it was the 'Juniper Down mentioned by the angry farmer of

Stoke'. The corpses of some dead orchids would also help, and
we did find several, only one — the Frog — being recognizable.
Such bits of fascinating detective work are an inheritance from
the poor dead Flower Book, but by no means the only ones. As
we walked home blue mist was collecting in the hollows between
trees which varied in colour from bright spring green to
vermilion.

October 17th. As we were driving to London I asked Ralph, 'How
would you define your chief beliefs?' 'About values or facts?' he
asked. 'Values.' 'I would say, I think, that it was vital to attach
oneself to someone or something outside oneself.' Rather a good
answer; and since he was too busy negotiating the suburban
traffic to ask for mine, I pondered them in silence, and decided
that '*Liberté, Egalité* and *Fraternité*' hadn't been half bad, but
needed a lot of qualification.

I telephoned the Natural History Museum and made an
appointment with Dr Melderis. He showed me my old specimens all beautifully docketed and pressed and then produced a
huge package of pressing materials — the 'flimsies' into which the
living plant goes, and the grey blotting-paper sheets that are to go
outside and have to be changed like a baby's nappies. It is the
most exciting thing that has happened to me for months, and I am
as proud of my 'press' and its webbing straps as I was of my violin
when I bought it. The good doctor really wants me to collect
everything I find in the south of Spain; they are short of material
for this time of year. I carried all my equipment away, glowing
and purring.

October 21st. We drove Raymond and ourselves across to Essex,
to spend a weekend with the Nicholses at Lawford Hall. My
opinion of Raymond went up even higher than usual when he
told us he still suffers almost constant headaches, which can only
be kept at bay by pills. And he was such a good guest, so
appreciative and stimulating. There was another person who
helped make it a particularly enjoyable weekend — a Dutch lady
of immense distinction. Her function was that of Director of the
Queen's Cabinet, whatever that means. About sixty and rather
heavily built, her smooth black hair hardly tinged with grey was
drawn back on either side of an impressively broad white
forehead and the features of a benign and amiable goat. Her

charming personality seemed to zoom out and fill the room, as she sat quietly knitting on the sofa. 'I only do it because I find it relaxing,' she told me and it was soon clear that her mind was extremely active. She is very musical and possesses all the records of Beethoven's Late Quartets which she loves better than any other music.

Phyllis [Nichols] is becoming more and more like the birds she so loves, who now hop in and out of her bedroom window and inhabit a maze of boughs and twigs inside it. She visited us one morning with a starling perched in her thick curly hair, showing in her bright eyes and rather stiff stance an affinity with her favourite creatures.

Then came Rosamond who descended to dinner in a dress of soft grey pleated stuff, looking so like a Greek statue that everyone gasped. Somehow the Monarchy came up in the conversation. 'I hear you're a Republican,' Phil Nichols said to me. 'You aren't really, are you? You mustn't be — you don't know how important the Monarchy is to the Dominions.' Rosamond declared herself 'a convinced Royalist,' and even Raymond accused me of 'wanting to deprive the typist of her daydreams.' 'Surely Marilyn Monroe would do as well?' I said, but the truth is, I am almost totally uninterested in the subject. Pacifism of course came next. 'I don't share your views,' said Phil. 'I believe there are worse things than war.' Maybe, but most of those worse things are fostered and manured by it.

Now we are back at home with Sebastian, the cosiest of fireside cats, and I think perhaps the happiest man I know. He tells us he has never taken a sleeping-pill in his life and didn't know what worry was. I *think* he implied that he had never been in love, but from one of his meaning 'ah's, I guess that he knows no difference between love and sex.

October 31st. In the bathroom today Ralph said that it was a little over a year since his first heart attack, and tried to convey to me what he felt about it. 'It's as if a finger or a hand was laid upon me here,' he said, pressing his chest, 'and came with me everywhere. I'm never alone, always accompanied. But I don't talk to you about it, though not a day passes when I don't think of it.' Nor, good heavens, for me either. I wish I was more certain whether I should encourage him to talk more about it. Oh, what a dunce I sometimes feel!

November 5th. It's tempting to connect the present sudden storms and freak gales with the news that on Sunday the Russians launched a second satellite much bigger than the first, with a live dog inside it! This and its attendant circumstances, such as the frenzy among dog-lovers, deputations clamouring on the steps of the Russian Embassy, or the word 'Satellite' heard from Mrs Hoare's lips, has made everything seem like a novel by H. G. Wells instead of the humdrum world we've been living in so long. As a background to this there is my own sense of feebleness at the approach of our journey to Spain, like two courageous but crazy old people about to walk the plank.

But my morning's post was full of interest: a letter from Kew asking me to collect specimens of *Dianthus* from Spain for them. A cheque for my last Freudian index, and a parcel of children's books to review from Robert. Such things give me a spurious sense of being a 'going concern'.

November 10th. I am writing in the corner of the same room where sit Eddy [Sackville] and the Godleys, our week-end visitors. Eddy has grown a small neat pointed beard, and (what with the bags under his eyes) has become unexpectedly like Edward VII. The first evening of their stay was spent discussing the Angry Young Men and the Establishment, and Eddy put forward extremely retrograde views, which dumbfounded Wynne. 'But I think you're appalling!' he said once. Eddy had been saying, 'I *hate* equality,' and that he didn't believe in education for the masses, the words 'people like me' and 'their proper station' occurring several times. He holds the odd view that the people he employs — cook, gardener, etc. couldn't do without him and that he is being somehow altruistic in looking after them. I ventured to say, 'But I suppose they look after you in a sense?' What, I can't help wondering, would have been Eddy's views if he had *not* been born in the purple? Luckily the argument never got out of the comic stage.

I love the Godleys more and more. Wynne enjoys his own cleverness; Kitty's intelligent sensitivity sometimes seems to worry her. She wears a haunted look at times, and one can't lightly mention the Atom bomb in front of her.

[Eddy Sackville-West, later Lord Sackville, was not exactly a clever man in the sense that his brain was a powerfully functioning organ, nor do I think it would have seemed so if his prejudices had disappeared and given it free rein; moreover he positively disliked argument or even discussion. I often thought that he cherished the illusion that all his friends thought as he did, and that the questions that came up when Wynne Godley was so shocked by his views had been settled once and for all long ago. Rather was he an artist and a scholar, whose special charm and originality lay in his imagination and invention. His humour was a delight, though these are pompous words with which to pin down his exotic butterfly nature. From childhood he had been delicate, suffering from bouts of asthma and being to some degree a 'bleeder'. When I first met him I was surprised to see him take out a little green bottle labelled 'smelling-salts'. Yet though his physical frame was slight he had iron strength in his fragile-looking limbs. Apparently in his youth he was an expert and fearless skier; he drove his car and even played the piano with the same determination and muscular strength.

Before he joined the others at Crichel he had lived in a Gothic tower in his family's great house Knole, and here Ralph and I several times visited him. He was surrounded by books, gramophone records and bibelots which he loved to collect. The piano had been his passion at Eton, and I believe he thought of making it his career. He seldom played in the Crichel days, but when he did I have to confess that I found his touch too steely for it to give me much pleasure, although he had such a great understanding of music; and his criticisms were brilliant, amusing and beautifully written, as were those of literature, backed by wide reading in several languages. He also published novels and a biography of de Quincey.

I once saw a photograph of Eddy as a marvellously aristocratic baby in his pram, and it struck me that the face looking out from the huge pleated bonnet had scarcely changed in forty years or more: there was the same fine rounded forehead, slightly tip-tilted nose and large sad eyes wearing a look of pained disapproval.

Later he became a Roman Catholic and bought a second house in Ireland, which I have already described. I do not think his religion solved the problem of his underlying unhappiness, which one could not help being aware of. Perhaps this was partly due to the fact that he tended to fall in love with people he disliked and disapproved of, as he once told me. But I shall close this

portrait of him by remembering his gloriously wild shriek of
laughter when amused.]

November 15th. We shall be off in a week, and I have been tying up
a lot of loose ends, one after another. The days are full of bumps
and hollows, yet if they weren't time would pass like a
gramophone record with no grooves in it and play no tune. I have
the horrors of the world on my mind again, though I feebly try
not to think about them. Everywhere the same ghastly unsolved
muddles are spread like slime — Korea, Algeria and the rest. The
Americans are deeply humiliated by the Russian success with
their rockets; meanwhile the dog in the second one is officially
pronounced to be dead. The *Daily Mirror* came out with a wide
border of black, and a great deal about soft noses and velvety eyes
up there in the stratosphere.

[On November 23rd Ralph and I set off for what was to be our
longest stay in Spain, in hopes that the mild weather of Andalusia
would benefit Ralph's health. Once again we rented Buena Vista,
the solid little house in Gerald's village of Churriana, where also
we now had our two more recent friends — Bill and Annie
Davis.]

November 24th. As we sped south I realized that Ralph had set his
heart on lunching at Bordeaux. And why not? I wholeheartedly
agreed — after all, it was his birthday, and the road was straight
and fast. Should we go to the Chapon Fin or Dubern? We chose
the latter, and also its two specialities: a smooth rich bisque of
écrevisses and the filet de sole Dubern, served by waitresses in
pleated aprons with priestly seriousness. A witch-like woman at
the next table got an appallingly noisy attack of hiccups, and
practically stood on her head in a vain attempt to stifle them. I
couldn't resist passing on our famous cure (learned in a Swiss
train) via the waitress, ending optimistically, '*Ça finira*'. Supposing it didn't! But it did, and there was much nodding and
smiling and '*Merci, Madame!*'[1]

[1]The cure consists in placing fingers in both ears and swallowing continu-
ously.

November 26th. Reached Madrid today, after a night on the cold
plateau of Burgos. Only when I came downstairs in the Hotel

Inglés did I realize in an emotional thunderclap that it was the very same hotel where Ralph and I had spent our unofficial honeymoon thirty-two years ago. The pretty blue and white staircase, the lift with its silver-painted trellis, all were startlingly familiar. When I told Ralph, who had been putting the car away, his reaction was quite different from mine. As we sat drinking our third Manzanillas in a café he fell into gloom at the difference between then and now, when he felt humiliated by age and illness and that the blaring vitality of Madrid was too much for him. 'Fell' is not the right word — he sent up a shell-burst of gloom with bits of shrapnel in it. I felt a tear or two trickling down my cheek, and didn't much mind if it was noticed by the waiters who stood around with their tragic-monkey masks and long tight-fitting aprons to the ground. Surely, I pleaded with Ralph, we could be content to watch like duennas at the ball, without removing ourselves entirely from its music and excitement. He says he'll tell me more about his thoughts on the subject, and I hope he does.

November 28th. Down the winding road from the Pass of Leon, we dipped into Churriana. In the Brenans' garden a little boy was sweeping up the leaves. Soon out came Gamel, pressed the stamp of her lipstick on our cheeks, and was followed by Gerald and Joanna Carrington. Gerald looks as if he had been through a mangle and every drop of emotion squeezed out, his eyes unfocussed. Joanna was pale, thin and composed; Gamel the most welcoming.

December 3rd — Buena Vista. Sitting over our olive-wood fire, sipping Spanish vodka, and feeling steadier and happier now that we are settled in our own domain. We have just been with Gamel to the eighteenth-century aqueduct in the *vega*, to collect specimens of the mandrake that grows there, before it finished flowering — a sinister, almost ugly plant with dirty purple flowers flush with its circular tuft of leaves. I had the time of my life with it and other specimens trying to press them on the dining-room table, where all my botanical equipment — 'flimsies', drying-papers, trowel, lenses, knives, Spanish Floras, are laid out, giving me a delightful sense of work in progress.

As well as Gerald's Maria we now have a little dark Antonia, with a passionate expression and a sweet negroid smile to look after us. She served our dinner tonight on a table by the fire, with great style and an attitude between a matador's and a Flamenco dancer's.

December 4th. Maria had told us that Gerald had a high fever, so we were surprised when he came springing in, saying he felt 'marvellous — perfectly well'. The talk was naturally all about Joanna. He had to unload what had accumulated; no need to turn the tap on, out it all came. He's not in love with her, he says, but he 'lives through her. There's nothing the three of us can talk about, but every evening Gamel goes off to write her poetry and then Joanna and I talk and talk for hours and hours. I'm a very good listener, you know. Oh, it's wonderful to have her here. Don't you think I seem rejuvenated? I was bored for years before Joanna came.'

December 7th. Gerald came for a walk with us this morning, in a different frame of mind, talking entirely about writing and works of art in general. They should always evolve as they went on, never be seen ahead and entire, above all never be the result of a flash of vision, quickly expressed. Picasso's enormous facility and versatility, and power to do that very thing, had had a fatal influence. 'An artist should always be rather stupid,' he went on, 'like Titian or Cézanne. It's very dangerous to be clever.' Of Spanish painters he said Velazquez was 'vulgar', and he didn't really 'like' El Greco, although of course he knew he was a genius. So, talking as we went, and occasionally stooping to pick or name a wild flower, we returned down the hillside.

In the evening he called on us again. 'I hope Gamel will publish her sonnets,' he said. 'Women always want success. I only want money.'

He hardly mentioned Joanna, but I think he has worn himself out with emotions about her. He's like a piece of patterned stuff that's been washed and washed until hardly any colour remains.

December 13th. The morning hours unroll happily, with sun streaming in and delicious smells. I study my flowers, press them, read, work a little at Spanish. Ralph comes down from the room where he is writing a review, calls my attention to a praying mantis in the garden and goes up again, until he finally descends to drink Montilla with me in the sun and talk about Madame de Lieven, the subject of his review. All this time the dappled light in the patio, and the knowledge that this natural beauty spreads around us, up the mountains and down to the sea, soothes and relaxes.

December 16th. Our first visitor, Sebastian, has been here two days; he is interested in everything and an eager sight-seer, so that it is a great pleasure to plan treats for him, show him the old Moorish market, the Cathedral, or the English Cemetery. He has picked up some Spanish in no time and quickly gets the hang of everything. These short days of his visit have made me admire his character more than ever — clever, rational but sensual, well-adjusted, affectionate, *good* but in no degree insipid. He has arranged for a taxi to drive him and Gerald to Granada today.

Meanwhile we took Gamel and Joanna to meet Burgo. Joanna seemed eager to see him, and very nice it was for us, too. There he was in the Hotel Bristol, Gibraltar, a little thin and pale but handsome and smiling, much impressed by the beauty of the country on one of the most ravishing days we have had, though the cold wind of fine winter days (the *terral*) was blowing.

Sebastian's last evening. I can't make out quite how much he enjoyed the Granada trip.

December 24th. Sheets of rain falling out of a grey sky. A tendency to despond, and nothing to be done except plan to go to the cinema. The Brenan party came too, and we saw a good old Gary Cooper film, which gave pleasure to all and drew loud sobs from Gerald, who was sitting next me.

Went back to the Brenans afterwards for dinner, and later to the garden room where there was a crèche made by the servants, and a village band led by our little Antonia was playing on the most extraordinary collection of instruments — a thudding 'jungle drum', bells and rattles, while the rest stood round laughing and shrieking from time to time. Then there were cries for 'Antonia! Antonia!' and our splendid girl stuffed her fat little body into a man's blue suit, snatched the gardener's hat off his head and danced and sang with passionate energy.

December 25th. Christmas lunch at the Cónsula — on the balcony, cold though it was. Their house guests were Robin and his brother-in-law Hamish Erskine, Xan and Daphne Fielding, and her son Alexander Weymouth. When we left at about five Burgo and Joanna were still there.

December 26th. Burgo got home in the small hours. They had been to a cocktail party at Torremolinos, dinner at the Cónsula, and back to Torremolinos again. Robin and Burgo had walked some of the way home through the night. The rootless existence led by the expatriates here is not attractive, and I wonder if it is a delusion that ours at Ham Spray is more solidly embedded, with taproot well down in the earth.

December 31st. The Brenans came to us for dinner and to see the New Year in. We had a very jolly evening playing paper games, at which Burgo was most amusing. Gerald's *bon mot* of the evening: 'Wives are like air. You can't breathe without them but when they are there you don't notice them.'

1958

January 1st — Buena Vista. On New Year's Eve we had walked the Brenans home and kissed goodnight in the road. Joanna kissed Ralph and Burgo, but went upstairs without kissing Gerald. This morning he came to see us to vent his resentment: 'I was in a furious rage. I took the presents I had bought for her and threw them out of the window into the street — a pair of earrings and a mantilla.'

'Didn't you go out and pick them up again?'

'Oh no, no. Some gypsy will have taken them.'

I said: 'You can't get kisses at bayonet-point.'

'No, of course not,' but he went on about gratitude, all he had done for her, pride and so on, obsessionally. The fact that she is leaving so soon has put him in a fever. 'Sunday is her last day, and just supposing the Cónsula should invite her that evening! She's fascinated by them; perhaps she would go. I'll never forgive her if she does.' He left us at our door, saying that Joanna (who had gone for a walk with Burgo) had promised to come back early. This was awkward because I knew Burgo proposed to ask her to stay to tea, and indeed there they were by the fire — Joanna's nose had begun to stream and Burgo was lending her handkerchiefs and nose-drops. They seemed rather touching together and I wouldn't for worlds have shooed her home.

January 5th. Yesterday our next guest, Robert, arrived. Today being marvellously fine we took a picnic up the mountainside to Mijas and were joined by Gerald and Joanna. There was a spectacular view of green velvet monticules stretching below us to the sea from where we sat under a group of olive trees, but Gerald sullied the beauty we were gazing at by exploding into Roman candles about the odious world of Torremolinos. 'It's a place where people come to pick up the last crumbs of sex,' was one, and another, 'Sex is distilled there — all the water of love boiled out of it.'

January 8th. We drove with Robert to the Alpujarras in search of rag rugs, eventually found a cottage where they were made and came away with eight of them. The sight of Gerald's old village Yegen, last seen in 1933, moved me deeply. Some things lie hidden in the memory, inaccessible unless they are revived; they can't be called 'forgotten' because they are capable of resuscitation by shock. Such were the dark red shining strings of pimentoes hanging against the outside walls of the houses, the slender poplars standing like ghosts against the distant view, the sound of trickling water everywhere, and the incomparable freshness of the air.

January 13th. Burgo left for home today. We shall miss him sadly. Cyril Connolly entertained us all to a great lunch party at the Gibralfaro, the Parador standing high above Malaga. Robert showed signs of anxiety that the occasion should be a success, and dressed himself in his smart London suit. It *was*, as all agreed, a great success and Cyril was brilliantly amusing as well as a very genial host. We sat at a long table on the balcony; a vase of flowers stood in front of me, and round it bulged the silhouette of the Master, haloed with tendrils of hair and backed by the sparkling sea far below in the harbour. Robert spends a lot of time at the Cónsula, and we enjoy the tidbits he brings back and the news of how the graph of Cyril's moods is doing. 'Better today.'

This evening over our fireside dinner the conversation turned to present-day pessimism, or *cafard*. Where can one look to find enthusiasm for living? I could only think of Paddy Leigh Fermor. Robert thought it existed in technical, non-intellectual circles. As for himself, he kept repeating, he was 'finished, done for' in tones of dreadful conviction. In vain we said that he made a very different impression on other people, how his energy and vitality were the envy of many. If so, what has finished him? Dare one ask him? The war; a failed marriage? His own character is what he hinted at.

January 19th. Cyril's graph not so good today. The poor Davises are getting desperate as to how he shall be entertained, and there is already talk of trips to the Canaries. Today, at a joint picnic inside a Moorish castle, Cyril wasn't grumpy at all. Dressed in a spaceman's outfit, he lay on his back on the grass, relaxed and giggling at his own jokes and even other people's. He was especially amused when Ralph described Gerald's habit of dashing up mountains to impress girls as 'competitive goatman-ship'. One of Cyril's witticisms was 'X thinks before he speaks, Gerald speaks before he thinks, and Bill thinks hard before he doesn't speak.'

I've got a request from an unknown publisher to translate Ibañez' *Sangre y Arena*. So after we got home I walked down to the Brenans to see if they had a copy I could borrow, and found a regular *tertulia* going on — Gerald and Gamel, Cyril and John Haycraft, who has a school of English at Ronda and has just written a book about it. The conversation was more of an omelette than a *soufflé*, but entertaining. I was struck by Cyril's proficiency. I took away my copy of Ibañez, and have written to say I would do it. I started my specimen pages this evening.

February 20th. Ralph and I drove to the airport to meet Raymond, and were delighted to see his brown and smiling face, but (asked how he was) he replied 'Not very well, really — rather depressed.' I hope we shall manage to cheer him up! Dinner at the Cónsula, being Cyril's last was rather orgiastic and the drinks very potent. Bill brought out some hashish. I think everyone was more or less drunk by the end of the evening.

February 22nd. Yesterday I awoke with a beating heart and compulsive craving for water. Read for an hour or so, but without properly taking in the words. I resent being made drunk against my will — it's as if someone deliberately passed me on their infectious disease. Raymond, who had a reviving afternoon sleep, was gratifyingly pleased by our olive-wood fire and our dinner (white onion soup, *cigalas* and young peas.)

Today is pleasant and sunny; we took him to the Malaga market. Gerald now pops in and out like a jack-in-the-box, and today there was an exchange between him and Ralph in which feelings began to get dangerously high. It was a question of Gerald's portrait of Ralph in *South from Granada*.

Gerald: 'Oh, it wasn't unkind at all. I merely made you out a dashing philistine who slept with actresses — just what everyone would like to be.' (The rather malicious twinkle in his eyes belied his words.) 'Anyway I sent it to you, and you passed it for publication.'

Ralph: 'Yes I did, though my solicitor thought there were grounds for libel. But what I really objected to was your picture of yourself as a selfless angelic character anxious to do everything for us, when really what you were after was seducing my wife.'[1] For some reason this seemed to revive Gerald's jealousy of Lytton.

Gerald: 'I tried to show in my book how much better Lytton's conversation was than his writing. The trouble was that he wrote to make money, or anyway for fame.' (Nothing could possibly be more untrue, and forestalling Ralph who I thought might fly off the handle, I said so.) 'Oh, there's nothing *wrong* in writing to make money. It's a very good thing to do.'

F. (now really angry): 'That's not the point, Gerald. It's a question of fact — whether Lytton actually did write for money or fame. I maintain that neither he nor any other Old Bloomsbury writer did so, and I *challenge* you to prove the contrary.'

After this the heat but not the life went out of the conversation.

[1]Carrington.

February 27th. Our days at Buena Vista are drawing to a close. We have taken Raymond to see the Malaga Cathedral and driven him up the lovely Coin valley. We ended with a dinner for the Davises and Jaime Parladé, when Maria and Antonia worked hard and successfully to make a delicious *pepitoria*. Letters have come from Janetta and Robert. Janetta writes, 'I can't tell you how I am because I simply don't know. I've been desperate, uncertain and muddled.' And Robert, 'An utterly barren and impoverished state of mind. Have never felt so useless and empty.' How sad that 0 + 0 does *not* make 1!

[After a moving farewell to Maria and Antonia we took Raymond with us in our laden car as far as Barcelona. The cold wind was inclined to give poor Ralph bouts of his angina, as sometimes did a struggle to find the way. I think he was suspicious that I was spoiling Raymond, or rather just *about to* spoil him, whereas in reality my attention was entirely focussed on *him* and his symptoms, while trying not to show it, which I knew he didn't like. In fact I had to steer an often difficult course between 'fussing' and heartlessness.]

March 12th — Ham Spray. Warmly welcomed back by Mrs Hoare and Wilde. I mentally list my resolves: To keep calm, count our blessings, look after my chief blessing carefully and lovingly but without interfering a millimetre beyond what his health requires, nor try to persuade him when he's lazy into activities he doesn't feel equal to; to remember that Burgo is a man on his own, leading his own life, even if he does sometimes enjoy the support of parental affection.

How little we thought about politics or the world when we were in Spain! Now — a new feature of life — American bombers cruise overhead *all the time*, carrying the Bomb. The people of Newbury are made deeply anxious by this activity, as we see from the local paper, and also by some alarming accident that occurred at the airfield only a week ago. Nor were they reassured by the frantic haste with which the personnel scrambled over eight-foot walls for safety, before doing anything to warn the neighbourhood. There is, it seems, quite a movement of a pacifist sort afoot. Ralph, who always rushes to the papers and wireless, has been wanting to talk about the problem ever since we got back, but I was too busy with unpacking and proofs until last night, when I settled down to read them. My feeling when I did was that I was staring into a lunatic asylum full of raving maniacs. How can people ask 'Ought we to renounce nuclear war?' *Of course* we ought to. Apart from the direct moral issue, it isn't a question of 'death rather than slavery' but of killing millions of innocent people, destroying the globe rather than slavery. Nor do I think our risk would be increased should we refuse the Bomb: those are more likely to be bombed who present a threat to others. Ralph remarked that by taking a stand against the Bomb one would find oneself in the company of cranks, emotionalists and Communists — considerations which don't affect me in the least. Later this evening he said that he really completely agreed with me. Even if the pacifist movement does gain ground, however, I don't see that it can possibly be effective. No, we shall go on building launching sites; the Bomb will go off, and whether it was by accident or design will make no difference.

March 18th. Janetta came down for a night in spite of the arctic weather and having just had flu. When I asked for news of Robert her face broke up like water into which a stone has fallen. The

cause of the 'unhappy muddle' of which she had written was that
the question of their joining forces had again come to the fore.
Though she obviously wanted to make the position clear to us she
spoke in a sort of palimpsest through which I glimpsed a very sad
position — for as one of them advanced the other retreated, and the
only clear fact that emerges is that each is terrified of the pain the
other can cause them. Also in practical terms that Janetta is going to
France with the Godleys and X, while Robert remains 'desperate'
in London.

March 20th. A night in London. Ralph lunched with Robert. When
he mentioned Janetta's departure for France next day 'Robert's
eyes flashed fire'. She had never told him; and this although —
apart from any other reason — he likes to be about for Georgie's
sake when Janetta goes away. When Ralph taxed Janetta with this
her answer was characteristic. With the most innocent expression
she said: 'But I thought he knew. I didn't *not* tell him.' The four
travellers to France were at dinner at Montpelier Square, full of
excitement and plans, which I envied them, as I also did their
youthful spirits. Kitty Godley looked touching but rather absurd,
dressed in the newest and most unbecoming fashion — a grey
tweed 'sack'. A great deal was drunk.

March 22nd — Ham Spray. Ralph and I started on our quiet working
life this morning. He retired to his library and began on a review. I
set out my paraphernalia — dictionaries, Roget's *Thesaurus* — in
the music-room and began translating *Blood and Sand*. All this is
satisfying in its way; but I wish the *cold* didn't get worse and worse,
and am horrified to have brought Ralph back into it. Next time we
should surely stay away until the end of March.

   Mary and Robin came to see us on their way out to dinner, their
first visit since Mary's very social holiday from married life in
America, wearing a new silk dress and very high heels, but her face
was still the face of level-best Mary, honest and sun-burned and
revealing. 'How do you think the New Start is going?' I asked
Ralph after they had gone, and he answered, 'Good will on both
sides.'

April 1st. After a frigid fortnight, belated spring has come to
England bringing serenity with it. Ralph is unfailingly sweet to
me; Burgo appears (at the moment anyway) to enjoy and be

interested in his life and the book he is writing for Anthony Blond; Ralph's health has been better. It rests — this happiness — precariously on dozens of tiny legs. We were able to sit out for the first time since we got back; the lawn lies in satin stripes where Wilde has mown it; Dinah sits alert and glossy by my side and the sky is blue. We had Robert and Georgie for the weekend and Burgo for one night with two friends, Francis Nichols and Michael Shone, at the start of a walking-tour.

Deep in *Blood and Sand*, I am beginning to take an obsessional and vicarious interest in bull-fighting, and spend a good deal of time reading about it.

April 12th. The Gowings to stay, great trenchermen both and their curves getting slightly out of hand. Julia expressed herself perfectly satisfied with Newcastle and what she called the 'inner life'. She is still working on the play she began in about 1940, and enjoying it I think, although it's pretty clear it will never be finished. She asked me how much I got paid for translating, and I told her about £200 for three months — not too bad. 'Ah, but for how many thousand words?' she wanted to know. 'A hundred thousand.' 'Well, of course I only write *three* words in that time,' she said, a trifle proudly I thought. After lunch both Gowings bolted upstairs like shot rabbits, and slept solidly until five, when they came down and ate a hearty tea. Ralph, Julia and I had a lovely walk through primrose-spangled woods, but she notices very little visually and not much that is said. The 'inner life' is indeed what she leads.

Coming home we were talking about the appalling difficulties of young mothers in the modern world, who wanted to remain civilized while looking after their children properly. Julia suggested that everyone should bear their children from the age of fifteen onwards. 'How could one possibly force them to?' asked Ralph. 'Oh, some "world convention" or "climate of opinion",' she replied airily, and when we both broke into hoots, she took it amiss. 'Oh well, you're so sure you're right, I shan't tell you my reasons.' There were no difficult moments during the weekend, however, and Lawrence was always appreciative. But Julia *is* a difficult guest, and reflecting in bed why this was I decided that it is because she really hates being one, and would rather have her material surroundings under her own control.

April 19th. Our monster aspen tree has been doomed to be cut in half — or pollarded rather — for reasons of safety: it is in great part hollow, and might well come down on the house in a westerly gale. So today the expert tree-fellers, whom I can only (in the light of my present obsession) think of as a *cuadrilla*, arrived to start on the job. All day the epic struggle went on until the aspen looked like a huge tuning-fork composed of two bulky but rotten limbs. Then the 'matador' — a tough man dressed all in black — climbed a series of ladders and stood dizzily on the pollarded summits, where (quite without support or ropes) he went on heroically wielding an axe to cut down all the lesser sprouting stems, each as big as a small tree, which thudded on the lawn below. When he reached the last stem on the highest stump it made me feel so ill to see him there so 'close to the bull's horns' that I retired indoors. While the matador faced danger alone, the rest of his *cuadrilla* went round chopping up the fallen wood, giving anxious glances now and then at their hero (or so I fancied him) up aloft.

The jackdaws that used to nest in the aspen are frantic with agitation, and have been flapping round in the neighbouring trees carrying twigs and moss.

April 21st. A letter from Gerald this morning refers to the conversation at Churriana last February, which had touched on sore areas of the past and embarrassed Raymond. 'Your remarks out here were unjust,' he writes. '. . . If there are moral rules in these things it was you and not Carrington or myself who broke them.' This naturally brought Ralph's hackles and prickles up until he resembled a porcupine. But when he had calmed down an interesting conversation developed. How fascinatingly human situations that one has been contemplating for years just as we have our view of the downs and the ilex tree (have the hedges grown? Has that tree got beech disease?) — how fascinatingly they emerge like negatives in developing-solution, to reveal some new picture covering the same system of facts and feelings. We all knew even before Joanna went out to Spain that Gerald would identify her with Carrington. Her own parents do it, Ralph sometimes does; I always feel it's rather hard on this charming and beautiful young girl to be saddled with the very unusual and potent personality of an aunt whom she never even knew. Now, as we talked the subject over at breakfast it came out clearly that the brief burst of hostility between Ralph and Gerald in Spain this last winter was due to the fact that Gerald was involved with _Carrington's ghost_, and that when Gerald came up to tell us how wonderfully he and Joanna were getting on, Ralph felt that the message was, 'You see, I've got Carrington after all.' As he developed this bit of the roll of film he said that he believed this was in Gerald's mind also. What an excellent plot for a novel!

Returning home after a visit this afternoon, we found that our _cuadrilla_ had finished their task, and that all that was left at the top of the huge trunk was a ring of wood round a hollow full of jackdaws' nests. 'How many were there?' Ralph asked the matador, and 'Countless', he replied. We are delighted at having the two great limbs of the tuning-fork laid low — they must have been supported by a miracle — but look at our giant aspen's pollarded head affectionately. When little shoots begin to sprout it will appear like a great Greek statue crowned with greenery.

April 30th. Tranquillity, solitude, _happiness_ alone with Ralph. Perfect weather, midsummer temperatures and a soft blue-green bloom covering all.

In the evening we listened to an argument on the Third Programme between four Oxford philosophers — or rather three and (rather absurdly) Philip Toynbee, who wasn't up to their subject, the Philosophy of Politics. It was a dazzlingly brilliant performance, arousing both admiration and envy — for surely nothing can be more enjoyable than the ability to think so clearly, and to emit streams of quick, exact and lively sentences, weaving and interweaving, with which they dealt each other tough boxer blows. Not that they got anywhere in particular though stimulating things were said all the time. Stuart Hampshire wanted to limit the scope of philosophy, confining it to the exploration of abstract and general aspects and excluding what men actually _do_ want, while poor old Philip, a sheep that had wandered into the wrong pen, bleated away in his deep rich voice about philosophy meaning love of knowledge, adding that the philosopher 'used to be thought of as a Wise Man who would teach us all how to live'.

May 17th. The Wiltshire Music Festival, to which I set off after breakfast, swept me along like a piece of paper in a gutter until I returned home at 10 p.m. Swindon Chamber Orchestra was just finishing its performance of the Purcell suite which was our competition piece, and even I could hear that ours was mousy and dim beside it. However we were awarded Grade A, and described as 'sensitive' while they got a Distinction. The most enjoyable item was our afternoon orchestral rehearsal with all the entrants, conducted by Anthony Hopkins, an engaging plump guinea-pig, who sang the themes in a soulful tenor voice and begged the cellos not to be so 'trudgy'. We had time for a whisky and a sandwich at the Bear Hotel before the actual performance in the Corn Exchange, at one end of which was a vast *cliff* of singers — Women's Institute members, colonels, and schoolchildren among whom I spotted Cressida Ridley. The proceedings were opened by the Mayor in full rig and gold chain. In the middle of the concert an old gentleman was taken short and forced his way hastily out through the huge doors behind the orchestra, creating a draught which blew much of the music off our stands. The confusion was not improved when having done what he had to, in he came again. There was an absurd moment when the conductor called for 'The one and twenties, please' (who were to sing the chorus 'When I was one and twenty') and up stood a row of ancient rosy old men with deaf-aids, and some elderly women wearing the agonized expression peculiar to part singers. 'Oh, *do* be more cheerful, ladies!' the conductor implored.

May 23rd. There has been a crisis in Algeria, including a near *coup d'état* on the part of the generals, and a declaration by de Gaulle, relayed over the wireless, that he was prepared to take over the Government. Robert is flying out there tonight as correspondent for *The Observer*. We therefore must do without his company.

June 3rd. We have been to London, disorganized as it is by a bus strike, stayed a night with Janetta, and taken Burgo and his friend Michael Shone to Strauss's *Elektra* — the music rolled round us and churned us up, an experience, if not altogether an enjoyable one. James and Alix were there; Michael compared Alix, rather brilliantly, to 'an Easter Island image'. Janetta has been so much with X that I said to Ralph it might be a good thing if she married him, as he had a talent for friendship and entering into other people's lives. Ralph was indignant, saying that I was being 'disloyal to Robert', and revealing that the last time she was here Janetta had said to him suddenly: 'I still love Robert.'

June 14th. Over to Stokke to meet Philip Toynbee and his new wife Sally. He has a large black empty stretch of unreplaced teeth in the centre of his face, his shirt is dirty and his shoes unblacked, while Sally was plump and demure in a neat grey frock, talking proudly of what Philip had done for the Anti-Bomb movement. I must say I found Philip's uncompromising slovenliness rather splendid in its way, especially in view of the fact that they were all going to dine with Daisy Fellowes, and that the Campbells were smarter and sprucer than I have ever seen them, Mary in her new brilliant pink Balmain. 'I *could* give you some blacking for your shoes,' Robin said wistfully to Philip, who replied with a silent toothless grin.

June 16th. I have finally killed off my matador, and posted him off to be typed. Robert is back, much impressed by de Gaulle's intelligence and dignity in the 'hysterical and thoroughly nasty atmosphere of Algiers'. Robert, or his Arab driver, had been shot at once, the bullet shattering the windscreen. He said: 'They have a way of rushing up and slashing your jugular artery, so I kept mine covered with a newspaper.'

Another letter from Gerald, who has a new girl-friend called Hetty, though he declares there is still room in his life for Joanna. 'Raise your glass and say "He died of happiness!"' he ended in a thoroughly embarrassing letter, the result of which was that Ralph discharged his feelings against Gerald by getting quite cross with *me*. 'Well, what *am* I to do with them?' (his feelings) he said comically. He is the reverse of William James's dog, which wagged its tail and therefore felt pleased — his voice gets angry and indignant, therefore he starts to *feel* indignant with the nearest person — in this case me, the ostensible reason being that I had asked Gamel to stay, feeling that she had been having a very thin time of it.

June 20th. Much talk with Ralph on the way to Marlow to see Alix and James. One gets so used to being inside one's own head that it's tempting to assume that other people's have similar wallpaper and furniture. Mine keeps a fairly steady pattern and I don't often move the things I bought when I first set up house, except when I rather unsuccessfully let in a little light here and there, or put in new curtains or flowers. Ralph said today that he had no such basic set-up, nor fixed 'philosophy of life': but that from time to time he got hold of what seemed an all-illuminating idea, plugged it in and flashed it round — which seems to me a brilliant analysis of his manner of thinking.

The outposts of Old Bloomsbury in the Marlow woods were as ever true to themselves. The household gods stood firm and tall — Freud, Lytton, Mozart, Fritz Busch, Stanislavsky. The Strachey family, one might add. Though admitting that Bloomsbury was now in the trough they were convinced they would rise again. Will they or not? Their figures have become very small, like those of people rapidly disappearing down a road, but whether this is perspective or their actual size I can't be sure. At lunch (off corned beef and tinned carrots) James remained quite silent while Alix proclaimed her belief that class distinctions must be brought to an end. I heartily agree, but not — as she went on to say — that public schools should be forbidden by law. She added that if the lower classes had more material blessings and free time they would become civilized in spite of themselves, yet she was too honest *not* to reveal that her housekeeper dislikes having almost nothing to do. 'She is rather bored and lonely. There's the telly of course, and now she's bought a dog.'

Delightful visit from Robert when we got home. His star is rising, his ambitions being realized, success, money and jobs just round the corner.

June 30th. At the weekend a lively argument sprang up between Janetta and me. It began in the kitchen as I was cooking *truites aux amandes* (without really knowing how) and I criticized a very rich friend for selling his house merely to make a profit. Janetta said I was being monstrously unfair, and that it was just as reasonable for a millionaire to make money as for a poor man — something I couldn't accept. His profit may be vital to the poor man, but unless the rich man wants to do something splendid or very generous with it his profit is futile. I admitted that I didn't like rich men on the whole, and thought them with some exceptions corrupted by power. 'You are being moral', said Janetta, and 'Yes, certainly, why not?' said I. At this stage we moved into the dining-room and started eating our trout and continuing the discussion with Ralph and Jonny Gathorne-Hardy. Why shouldn't a rational being think about values? I wanted to know; Janetta said she hated the idea of them and could only think of them in terms of religion. People were unique and should never be generalized about or subjected to praise and blame, but merely 'apprehended'. Interesting, though not wholly tenable if one believes generalization to be the essence of intelligent thinking. 'Can we change the subject?' she said suddenly. Jonny: 'Oh no, I want to go on talking about it.' But we didn't.

In bed that night Ralph and I pondered the question: Why do the modern 'young' dread ethical concepts — good, bad, or even true and beautiful? Ralph thought money had taken their place as something you can't do without, and the more the better. Their hopes of 'happiness' are low-pitched. Or perhaps in their eyes good, bad, et cetera seem like outworn myths believed in by their parents but not by them, just as God or the supernatural did to us.

July 5th. Warm mist encloses us, and my mind is blurred like a windscreen in a fog. Gamel arrived last week and has rested on us lightly ever since — a *good* visitor and able to keep an even keel. Yesterday evening we walked on Ham Hill among the orchids — there were Fragrant, Pyramid and Spotted, one Frog and two new patches of Musk. As we peered about and shouted to one another a big black thunder-cloud moved up from the north. Burgo and Joanna arrived in the evening and we celebrated Burgo's forthcoming twenty-third birthday with a bottle of champagne. Gamel was in whizzing form.

July 6th. All our visitors left us, including Gamel, who has I think enjoyed all her English visits, and both Ralph and I really enjoyed having her here. Ronnie Duncan[1] had liked her sonnets and made her feel she was 'an old poet of promise' she told us with her 'dove's laugh' as we call it. She spent some hours on her knees in front of a trunk from the Aldbourne cottage, as a result of which she proposed giving some of her letters from great men (such as Bertie Russell and the Powyses) to a library.

Robert told Ralph that there was 'someone new' in his life; she was 'very nice', but he wasn't in love with her. What did Ralph think of a sort of companionate marriage? Ralph has another hectic letter from Gerald saying many incompatible things about Hetty: there has been 'gaiety, gaiety', jealous scenes, she has danced wildly to jazz records, gone into a 'genuine spiritualistic trance', 'spoken with tongues', and 'got too fat'. Most of it complete *rubbish*. Then he breaks into authentic Brenanismo which I always find irresistible: 'Heigh-ho said froggy, who I dare say was the same advanced age as myself.'

Weekend at Crichel, delightful as usual, though after days of preoccupation with the crises in the Middle East and the American landings, it was strange to find them all quite uninterested, and fully occupied with their own activities. Raymond has developed such an obsession with grammar, spelling and punctuation that I caught him in the act of saying that these three ingredients alone made a good writer. It is comical to hear their fury over 'Oh really! *Folie de grandeur!*' while they remain indifferent to the fate of the world now hanging by a spider's thread.

Ralph and I sometimes feel as though we were wearing snake belts and grey flannel shorts, sitting at our desks eager for a chance to put up our hands, and dreading a quick rap on the knuckles with a ruler. Our meals were quite delicious and mostly eaten out of doors, the weather being so splendid; there was plenty of lovely music, croquet and several animated discussions, one about Free Will, and another about the monkeys and the typewriters, Raymond looking like a very alert and mischievous monkey himself.

¹Poet and dramatist.

July 23rd. — *Ham Spray.* Ralph lost his ancient but adored Parker pen, the only thing he can write with, that symbolic and valued treasure which has weathered about thirty years' constant use. We have been frantically searching for it for two days all over the garden wherever he had been pruning or fruit-picking, with loud comments to each other, while Wilde was digging the weeds under the music-room window. At last Ralph asked him if he had seen it. Wilde: 'I didn't know what you was looking for. Yes, I picked it up first thing this morning under the strawberry net.' I found myself humming a tune, and quite a bit later remembered the words: '*Mon Dieu quel homme!*' Ralph told Mary about it at lunch. She said: 'After having twice had the front gate shut in my face by Wilde I can't understand why you're so keen on that man.' Well I'm not, for one.

July 27th. Burgo and Simon Young arrived last night in full Moss Bros wedding togs, looking very charming and gay. Burgo is back again, and firmly declares that he will finish his book before he goes abroad with the Blonds; we are amazed and delighted.

We took some of our gooseberries and raspberries over to Stokke, where Robert is having a go as paterfamilias with Georgie and Rose, as Janetta has postponed her return from abroad. Later he brought them over to tea. Apparently he and Ralph were discussing the solution for Janetta's life when I was out of the room, and Ralph audaciously told him that it lay with him, Robert. 'I haven't ruled it out,' he replied. He is wonderfully good with the children. They lapped up bowls of raspberries and cream, got into the cold pool and put their big, black smelly dog in the rubber boat.

On Saturday night he brought 'my television friend', Cynthia Judah, over to dinner.

August 14th. Yesterday Ralph and I drove over to lunch with Janetta and the three little girls, who have rented a house just over the downs at Combe for a few weeks. The children played happily on two swings under the old apple-tree growing in the middle of the rough sloping lawn, while we lay in the hot sun and blustery wind talking to Janetta. Asked about her plans for the future, she said she was dreaming of leaving England, and getting away somewhere warm.

Ralph talked afterwards about her restlessness with more criticism than I feel. He thinks her desire to get away frequently from family responsibility (though the most sensitive and kind mother when with her children) is something innate and compulsive, and will probably never leave her. But I remembered her lying talking on the lawn in her check cotton blouse and with her hair tied back from her serious delicately cut profile and was touched by the image. She is as she is — someone exceptional, unique. Why try and alter her, even were it possible? Certainly she is restless at present, but I see this as the product of her native independence coupled with unhappiness.

I finished reading Ibañez' *La Maja Desnuda* yesterday, and don't think much of it. I have been busy typing out my report on his earlier books for Elek[1] and they are a very different matter. Ralph has been married to Chateaubriand, not me, for the past week. He is reluctant to put down his *Mémoires* even at mealtimes, and certainly to come for a walk.

[1] A London publisher.

[The long drawn-out separation between our dear friends Robin and Mary Campbell was now complete and had to be accepted, which being so our great desire was to remain friends with each without causing pain to the other, in the hopes that they would in the end come to be on friendly terms with each other. This of course depended entirely on them; there was little or nothing we could do about it. Happily it was the eventual outcome.

The business of 'taking sides' in personal relationships had always seemed to us an uncivilized one. 'There were no divorces in Bloomsbury,' Ralph said, and on the whole it was true — but there were re-shuffles, in one of which we had ourselves taken part; and although we never wanted any of our friends to show themselves in the least partisan when we set up together in Gordon Square in the Twenties, I do remember noticing that some of them in fact did so. I believe that the desire to 'take sides' is based on a powerful instinct as deeply rooted as human aggression, and perhaps a form of it, with all its horrible ramifications, such as jealousy, vindictiveness and even war. I have never seen that it is possible to refute Freud's theory that civilization can only be achieved by subduing the aggressive instincts. Moreover, we are at the present time and have for many years been witnessing in tangible form the proof that by amassing material objects and technical skills and fuelling them with the primitive instincts of fear and aggression modern man has got further and further away from that desirable goal.]

August 24th. Marjorie Strachey for the weekend. At seventy-six she is splendidly amusing, intelligent and active-minded. Warm-hearted too, I think, though Ralph doubts this, and says she's armour-plated like all Strachey women. She's always striking up friendships with flautists and opera-singers. On Sunday night came Robert and his friend Cynthia, both of them straight from the television world. Robert was at the top of his form and completely bowled Marjorie over. 'I've fallen madly in love with Robert,' she told us. 'I've not met anyone so fascinating for years.'

August 27th. Yesterday I got a letter from Burgo which gave me a shock in the solar plexus from which I've not yet recovered. He and the Blonds have had a horrible motor accident in Yugoslavia.

Their car, driven too fast by Anthony, skidded on a wet road and collided violently with a telegraph post. Both Anthony and Charlotte were taken to hospital, not seriously hurt, I gather; Burgo escaped with bruises. The car was a complete wreck, and the windscreen 'turned to horrible bath-salts'. I imagine it all too vividly. Burgo had to deal with the Yugoslav police, who made him stand by the wreck for an hour to warn other drivers. He then had great difficulty in finding himself a room for the night, but was at length put up in a private house, sharing a room with two workmen. Robert said comfortingly that to survive such an experience is fortifying, and I believe that this is true. They have now gone on to end their holiday, peacefully I hope, in Venice.

September 1st. Two postcards from Burgo in Venice, and a letter from Bunny who had met him there 'looking handsomer than I've ever seen him, and obviously happy, not a care in the world.'

September 9th. Hearing a while ago that poor Rosamond was shattered by the ghastly news of the death of her daughter Sally of poliomyelitis in Jakarta, we wrote and asked her to stay. She wrote back that she would like to come, if we were ready to accept the fact that 'Sally's life still went on'. We replied that we would listen with the greatest interest to anything she felt like telling us. She has just left us after two days in which we thought of nothing but her and her grief, trying to guess at what she found difficulty in saying. She was looking very splendid, but it was only necessary to talk to her for a few minutes to realize that she was shaken to the core, and we both felt profoundly moved and sorry for her. When the three of us were alone together, we embarked on the whole terrible story, and her response to it. The fact that it involved beliefs that neither of us holds made what she had to say no less tragic and interesting, and we went on talking far into the night. She described her state of mind as one of '*blinding* certainty'. She conveyed the agony she had suffered very vividly, and said more than once that she didn't want to go on living and didn't know how she could.

September 12th. Ralph decided not to come to London, so I went alone. I enjoyed looking out of the train window at the landscape hazed with autumn, and the almost miraculous way the river Kennet filled its green banks to the brim. My pleasure in the

horizontality of water is, I sometimes think, as near as I ever get
to a 'mystical' experience. In a mood to enjoy everything I saw, I
even relished the glimpse I got of engines steaming and snorting
in rows in their stalls outside Reading.

I spent most of my day with Julia, which I wanted to do. She
was in an extra censorious mood, having just returned from an
Italian holiday with Lawrence and Adrian Stokes,[1] who had
behaved so egotistically, so she said, that she was dying to write
and tell him so. Gerald was on the evening train, anxious to
inform me about the world of Hetty and 'Cool Cats'; rather
luckily the train was too noisy for conversation, and I sank into
my book.

Burgo is back from Venice and has settled briskly to work on a
translation. His description of his motor accident was horrifying,
though he managed to make a very amusing story out of it.

[1]Painter.

September 21st. The blue of the sky matches the Morning Glories
on the verandah, and Burgo's scarlet shirt (he has come down
with Simon) adds to the cheerfulness of a weekend when
everyone is in a good mood. Except Robert, who rang up in great
agitation last night to say that his father was dying. When he
arrived (with Cynthia) and we asked how he was, he replied
characteristically, 'Oh, he packed it in last night,' which was not,
needless to say, the last we heard about this event.

The weekend was in its odd way rather hilarious, except for
Robert's news. Simon and Burgo were full of jokes and chatter,
while Robert made us laugh with descriptions of his lightning
visit to Venezuela and Brazil for the telly. There was chess, bowls
and music; visits from Mary with Eduardo Paolozzi, also Janetta
and the children. Robert looked quite exhausted, and obviously
wanted to talk about his father in particular and death in general,
but there was no chance in this cheerful house-party atmosphere.
On Monday, the rest having left, Janetta reappeared with
Georgie and Rose; but as the little pitchers' ears were never far
away nothing at all personal could be said, though there was one
mysterious interchange between Ralph and Janetta.

Ralph: 'You're not thinking of doing anything frightful?'

Janetta: 'No, not at the moment — I can't really, as I didn't last
week.'

And what either of them meant I really don't know.

September 27th. A visit to Alix and James, such as we made today, gives us a glimpse of our own futures. They are just so much older and crazier than Ralph and me; like hens they have been chivvied a little closer to the execution shed, and are cackling louder and losing more feathers though they aren't yet inside. It's true there was something almost comic in their competition over their symptoms (James has been frightened by the local doctor about his blood pressure, and Alix wanted to have blood pressure, too); but the terrible plight of the old as they are herded towards death is no laughing matter at all, and there are many implications branching from the central situation, none of them pleasant. For instance, should Ralph and I ever conceivably find it too disheartening to go and see this fascinating pair of eccentrics, which I doubt, just because they have sunk a little further into the bog, what will our young friends feel about coming to see *us*?

One of the few consolations of age, I agreed with Bunny the other day, is its irresponsibility. 'This world is no longer any of my making, or much to do with me. Take it away and do what you like with it. I don't even greatly care if you drop it and break it. I'm interested in a detached way by your antics, that's all.' No, I'm afraid that won't do. Nobody wants to end up as a selfish old person insisting on having the railway carriage window up (or down, as the case may be), besides which it's physically impossible to be so disengaged.

October 8th. Mary came to dinner, freshly back from Biarritz, and bringing a wave of enjoyment into the room. Only after she had left did I begin to feel a faint sense of nausea at the thought of the people she had been describing — people both elderly and rich, who played with their toys (bridge and golf) during the hours of daylight, drank and gambled most of the night. None of them seemed to love, respect or even enjoy sex with their life companions; boredom was the great bogy and incessant jigging about the way they tried to keep it at bay. Ralph and I talked about the Sex War. He thinks we are all involved in it — we must face it, but it should be a clean fight, not a dirty one. I think one should be a pacifist in the home as well as in politics.

October 27th. Robert is with us on a working visit. Except for the extra tingle from his vitality we lead our normal life. Each of us works in a separate room and we meet for meals, walks, and talks and reading in the evening.

He took himself off at short notice on Friday just before Janetta came down. I'm not sure how deliberate that was; Janetta told us it wasn't. To us he was definite, reasonable and articulate about it. The net result was that past feelings couldn't be cancelled out, and that she could work her own problems out better without him.

November 4th. Two days completely alone with Ralph and Dinah, working at my translation, talking to Ralph, walking with Ralph through the damp yellow-green and black lanes, listening to the wireless with Ralph, spending the nights coiled up beside Ralph in our warm bed. I can even discuss with Ralph the nature of the pleasure it is living with him — perfect relaxation without dullness. Being with anyone else, even my dearest friends, imposes the faintest possible strain, gives a tiny twist to the key in the mechanical mouse's entrails. With Ralph there is absolutely *none*. We are like two mutually supporting creepers, each propping the other up and at the same time drawing sustenance and stimulation from the other's sap. But if I were to start writing down all the inestimable advantages I gain from living with Ralph I should never stop. One is being able to say *immediately* everything that comes into my mind to someone who likes to hear it. Another is the pleasure of leading two lives instead of one, and one of them male. I can't think, I can't bear to, how people manage to live without a mate. Ralph is unendingly kind and loving to me, appreciative, nicer far than I deserve. The two halves of the world's greatest pleasure are loving and being loved, and I never stop thanking my lucky stars that I have them both.

November 9th. Before dinner Burgo heaped up the fire in the music-room to such an extent that the chimney caught fire. I remembered a scene of my youth when I did the very same thing, and how guilty I felt when the episode ended in the fire brigade roaring up the drive. Not so Burgo. I noticed a sort of triumph in his manner as he made me go out of doors and look at the tall red flames pouring from the chimney into the night sky. Large lumps of molten soot fell into the grate, the house filled with an acrid smell like cabbage cooking. I felt infuriated with him, and Robert too, as they lounged on the sofa discussing whether it would be a good or bad thing if the house burned down, and leaving Ralph to take practical steps, with a calm and good humour which I confess amazed me. He knew he mustn't get agitated, and so he didn't, although this is just the sort of disaster he finds very hard to take. However, the blaze mercifully subsided peacefully.

November 15th. Days of Indian summer when we were able to breakfast on the verandah several times running. Coffee tastes extra delicious when drunk in warm if unnatural sun, and this is the season when the new plumes of the pampas grass emerge in silky beauty from their sheaths. Quite a party for the weekend — Janetta, Angelica and Desmond, with Burgo and Robert as usual. Janetta was at her prettiest and most entertaining, deluging us in Dublin Bay prawns, nuts and crème de menthe. Desmond and Angelica took to one another and we to both of them.

November 28th. Ralph made a snap decision not to come to London for the day, cancelling his doctor's appointment from a motive about which I am uncertain. I therefore got alone into my train like a fairly resigned sheep going to the slaughter of a luncheon date I didn't look forward to, with my fur jacket and *Dr Zhivago* for company. I read the latter all the way to London, with great interest and pleasure. Here for once was a new book that demanded all one's attention, that was unskippable, by which simple pragmatical test I judge it to be a good book. I finished it on the way home. I wonder how much Ralph will like it. For my part I admire it for a good many reasons; but it's a book you must take as it is, not complaining at the occasional thinness of its shimmering weblike texture, enjoying the brilliant passages of description, scenes made vivid by a poet's eye. At Harrods, with the strangest feelings, I came upon a pile of Burgo's book, published today, and bought a copy.

December 4th. Listening to a not particularly magical baritone voice singing Schubert, I suddenly — just for a moment — retrieved the taste of the glamour and excitement that life held in youth. Only music, with its hypodermic needle so quickly and subtly penetrating the unconscious, can break through the defences erected by time. We know the six-year-old is still present within us and sometimes comes to life in childish dreams and emotions; *a fortiori* the girl of twenty is enfolded within the wrappings of skin upon skin that cover that onion the human psyche.

December 8th. I feel flat and tired, I don't know why, after a most *un*-taxing weekend. Heywood and Anne are always relaxing and companionable. Burgo, though dignified, grown-up and enormously more socially equipped, seemed to be a thousand miles away behind arctic ice-floes. On Saturday we drove to Savernake forest. Burgo and Heywood strode off down the avenues, while Ralph, Anne and I meandered gently through groves of young pines carpeted by their damp and scented needles, until we reached the Grand Avenue, with its noble colonnade of beech-trunks bathed in silver-gold light. Anne was as usual spoiling for arguments — themes I remember were drink, the Royal family and money. Talk too about Janetta, and how she hates being pinned down to *plans*, a trait that is inconvenient but also part of her charm. She clearly feels they are destructive to freedom, and would like to invent everything anew for herself, nor will she ever use a current phrase, even in the ironical way that Julia and Robert sometimes do.

Everyone has now departed; there's a wintry silence, except for the crackling of logs in the grate. Paralysis of thoughts deliberately strangled at the root for fear of what they might lead to leaves my mind a blank.

[I realize that I wrote the last entry, and others that included mere hints, under the stress of sharpened misery about Ralph's health — probably due to his having had tired spells, discomfort or pain on our walks, or that change of facial expression I had learned to watch for and dread. I have always thought of myself as being more or less rational and unsuperstitious. Yet I see when I re-read these tense pages that I did *not* completely face up to the future in either of these respects. There is usually an element of uncertainty in illness, I told myself: doctors aren't always right. For instance Sawbones had tried to put us against our winter journeys to Spain, yet Ralph had visibly profited from them. At the time he was taken ill the treatment of heart patients was a great deal vaguer than it is now, when he would presumably have been given surgery; even the idea that vegetable oils produced less cholesterol than animal fats was new and unproven. 'Try it if you like,' they said, and we made it a part of his régime that he didn't resent, as he would have being forced to stop smoking.

I have suggested that I became superstitious because I remember a strong irrational feeling that if I exerted my every thought and all my energies to keeping him alive I might be able to do so, and I look back to those last years of Ralph's life as a strenuous, unabating campaign. I have no idea whether this had any effect on him — presumably not. It was merely that I was obsessed with the need to wage it. And I was unrealistic in that I do not remember ever giving my mind to the problem of how I should live without him. No, my wakeful nights were devoted to ways and means of keeping him with me. He and I never discussed the possibility of his death although there were times when I wondered if he would like to and I should have encouraged it, especially in view of our otherwise complete intimacy. I shall never be sure of the answer to that question. At the time it seemed a physical impossibility. That some loving couples do manage to talk to each other about the inevitable death of one of them I know from experience, and I greatly admire them for it.

Looking back it seems to me that I forged along my chosen path in a state of semi-numbness, and that just as one's tongue avoids a tooth with a tender hollow in it, so I tried to avoid the aching chasm in my mind.]

December 10th. Awoke feeling hardly capable of pulling myself out of the matrix of our warm bed. Ralph said afterwards that I never spoke to him once during our bathroom session. I had been unable to shake off the impression of a very good but gloomy novel which I finished last night — *The Rack* by A. E. Ellis; it is a book with no light even at the end of the tunnel, no catharsis. How much, I wonder, does the aesthetic value of a novel depend on the Aristotelian formal qualities — beginning, middle and end. And I was reminded too that Freud pointed out how the excitement of Hide and Seek, and also its shape, depended on the dreaded situation (loss of the parent) being solved in a happy way, and that 'Hide but don't find' would be no success as a game. *The Rack* fails because it gives one *no* solution happy or otherwise.

One of the worst things about my being depressed is that it sinks poor Ralph like a stone. He looks at me with the sweetest possible expression and says: 'I can't make you happy.' Whereas of course he does everything to that end. The fact is I've been unbearable company the last few days, and he has done very well to put up with me.

December 12th. Every single thing I can do to the *Maja Desnuda* is now done, and she's ready for delivery next week. Ralph thinks that's why I have been in low spirits. There was a quite good review of Burgo's book in *The Spectator*.

I spent a curious afternoon yesterday at the Prince of Wales's school at Cheam, taking part in the boys' carol concert. (This because my partner in the Newbury Orchestra, Miss Mann, is music teacher there.) I pushed through a porch full of stuffed animals in glass cases and came into a vast panelled room with red curtains and a log fire. The gnat-like voices of some little boys were arising from the grand piano in the corner, and two violins were wailing with them. I was touched by the large eyes, long lashes and glorious complexions of the boys: some had winglike ears, glowing a transparent red from the light coming in at the window. They looked about to fly away. When the rehearsal was over a longish interim followed, in which Miss Mann suggested taking us round the school, and we viewed several classrooms, and dormitories, giving off a faint smell of bed-wetting, with teddy-bears lying on most beds. We were of course shown the Prince of Wales's bed, covered like the rest with a tartan rug. Everyone crowded to look at the royal sleeping place, and from now on 'He' (in a slightly hushed voice) kept cropping up in the conversation, especially in the sewing-room, where we four visiting musicians were given tea by Miss Mann. 'I don't think Charles is going to be any good at music,' Miss Mann told us, 'he's got such great heavy hands. I tell him, "You are making an awful noise" and he gives me such an old-fashioned look.' She described the Queen as being difficult to talk to; only the Queen Mother got high praise. And all the time it was 'He' and 'You'll know Him by his leg being in plaster.' I came to the conclusion that if royalty are always to be thought of as a different species, much better educate them elsewhere. And they *are* so thought of, even when represented by a small stout boy in grey flannel, looking much like any other. Meanwhile the carol-singing began, the boys of the choir standing round the piano in their black robes and white collars, lit by a forest of candles.

Drove back through the night to describe my evening to Ralph and Janetta and read Cyril's review of Burgo's book with rather mixed feelings. I was afraid Burgo might mind some of his sharpish criticisms, but in fact I believe they were easily outweighed by his pleasure in getting such a prominent review.

December 29th. Christmas is over, and Burgo and I are both in bed with flu. He arrived in very high spirits though, bringing us a magnificent pot of caviare, and next day came Isobel, whose company is always a pleasure. She told a story of how when walking through the Park she saw a man waving wildly to her out of a car. 'I *thought* it was *Leo*nard Bing' (a friend of hers), she said, 'so I ran up and *got* in beside him. And then of course I saw it wasn't Leonard at all but a man from the Turkish Embassy.' 'What was he like?' '*Very small* and *dark.*'

After Christmas came Robert, who spent the best part of two days in the library with Ralph in earnest conversation. Serious though the subject was — for Robert is trembling on the verge of a vitally important decision — a good many bursts of laughter reached me in my bed of sickness, as well as the sound of much pacing up and down. Taken over by the eerie fungoid spread of fever and discomfort, I let my mind wander vaguely off to Robert, to Burgo, to Isobel, and then turned it off by main force to Saint-Simon and the death of the Duc de Berri. At least nothing can be done about *him* now; he has the great merit of being out of range of worry.

1959

[In the course of time some of the gilt had been wearing off the gingerbread of our winter trips to Churriana, and yet — and yet the climate was the best in Europe, and we would find Janetta there with Georgie and Rose. We decided this year on a compromise: we would spend five weeks at Buena Vista and four more in Southern Portugal as an experiment.

A few days after crossing the Pyrenees we stopped at the Parador at Benicarlo. In bed next morning Ralph told me that he had had a short attack of angina in the night, but didn't get up and swallow an emergency pill because he thought it would worry me and *I* wouldn't sleep! Such sensations were to be expected when taking exercise; it was his having it when in repose that had alarmed the doctors, and it had not occurred since the first time. I realized that I might at any moment have to make a decision, try to dominate his much stronger will, halt our advance, call a doctor and put him to bed. Of course I betrayed my preoccupation, and he insisted that he was now all right and that we should go ahead.

We reached Almería without further mishap, checked in at our hotel and went out under a pinkish lavender sky with a silver thumbnail moon, to a café which was the meeting-place for the men of Almería. Many of them had nothing but a glass of water and a newspaper in front of them. There were old men sunk in their own carnality and the weight of their ponderous stomachs, with faces a yard long, three chins, loose Hapsburg lips and gloomy eyes stewing away in dark sauce. Next to one of these sat a distinguished-looking man with silver hair, and one hand on the top of his cane, while the other held a small book of poetry, which he was reading attentively. We were in Spain all right.

'As we drove up the road to Buena Vista, "Here's Gerald," said Ralph. He was just turning off towards his house, and his companion must of course be Hetty — a stocky young woman, staring at us out of bold brown eyes, with long hair hanging loose and orange trousers. Gerald said rather uneasily: "Oh, we're not coming to call on you. You're tired — you've only just arrived." And the next moment we were being welcomed by Janetta, Georgie and Rose. Janetta had lit an olive-wood fire in our bedroom, and we felt delightfully looked after.'

We were soon encompassed by, though not really involved in, the life of the 'Coast', where gossip was the daily currency, and items of human news were picked up and tossed about like crusts of bread by pigeons, and frequent excursions were made into the 'hippy' life of Torremolinos by *voyeurs flambés* in alcohol. Gerald and Hetty, Janetta and the Davises all took part in these sorties, but they had no charm for Ralph or me. In fact there were days when I wished we had never come. But of course there was much to enjoy — for instance a refreshing visit with Janetta and Georgie to Jaime Parladé in his father's house looking out over the sea to the frowning brow of Africa. Jaime was a charming host, and we got to know him better and delight in his company. Then another day we went with the two Brenans and Janetta to dine with Mina Curtiss (née Kirstein) at her grand hotel. (We had known Mina since the Twenties, when she and her friend Henrietta Bingham arrived in London from America and took fringe Bloomsbury by storm. Mina had been the more beautiful and far the more intelligent of the two, while Henrietta had a fatal glamour for both sexes. Mina had kept in touch with her English friends and become a distinguished writer and authority on Proust. Now in middle age she was a sparkling talker and a 'character'.) The dinner she gave us was crushingly huge, the *pièce de résistance* being a battleship made of crayfish decorated with lemons, eggs and carrots all cut to look like something else, reclining on a bed of mashed potato grey with careful moulding to make it represent the sea.

Another night we went to see the famous dancer Antonio dance *The Three-Cornered Hat*. I thought as I watched him about the difference between male and female movements in the Spanish dance: the male conveys intense lust and at the same time restraint — the result being a sort of *anguish*, expressed in face and gesture. His hands appear ready to tear his partner apart, while never actually laying a finger on her. She, on the other hand, combines frenzied enticement with complete sub-mission. One talented girl left the stage leaning so far back that she was practically prostrate, with her arms twirling round her head like wild snakes.

Of course we saw a good deal of the Brenans. They too enjoyed our mountain picnics. Sometimes the movement of the car had the effect on Gerald of an analyst's couch, and loosened an uninhibited stream of memories or thoughts about age and youth, through which one could see Hetty's face. We preferred these outings to our visits to the Casa Brenan, where Gerald would put on his Cool Cat clothes, there was jazz on the gramophone and the unattractive Hetty — a well-filled bolster topped with a shiny yellow face — reigned as Queen. It was as if the dear familiar picture of Brenan life, the house decorated with Gerald's exquisite taste, his own fascinating and funny talk and Gamel's old-world eccentricities, had all been crudely bedaubed with paint. Still, after he had got the latest news about Hetty off his chest, or even said that if Gamel 'were not there' he could live happily with Hetty, he would launch out in his most harmonious and friendly style about writing, or the effect of war on young men, or every sort of subject.

Just before we left Spain we dined at the Cónsula, and Annie took me up to see Cyril, who was ill in bed. He motioned me to a chair with a royal gesture, lay with his large face on the pillow 'in music position' and began talking about Robert and Janetta. The last news he had heard was that they were going to set up house together, he said. I didn't want to be pumped and found the conversation painful. Perhaps the acutest thing he said was, 'At least Janetta has made a life for herself, even though it may be precarious and unsatisfactory, but Robert — apart from his work — has made no life at all.' Next day, February 21st, we left for Portugal.

We arrived at the small seaside town of Praia da Rocha — visited by us with Julia twenty-five years ago — and found the same yellow hotel perched above the wide sea, with its fantastic cliffs and hard sand beaches; the same horse-drawn *tartanas* for hire, jogging uphill to it, painted smartly in black and yellow with white linen curtains. We found also comfort and warmth and plenty of glassed-in verandahs. Our breakfast was brought by an elderly nanny in a starched cap, murmuring what sounded like 'Poosh-cat, poosh-cat' or 'zzzz' as she set down the tray. Both people and landscape were gentler, softer if less exciting than those of Spain, and the prune-like eyes of the Portuguese seem to express nothing but anxiety that we should be happy. We are. A splendid letter from Janetta in London, saying she has begun to hate the rat-race but both Robert and Robin tell her she mustn't, 'it's what life's about'. She's evidently seeing a lot of Robert, yet we are both now convinced of the hopelessness of our daydreams for them, and wonder why we clung to them so tenaciously. I see it as a matter of Geometry: The angle formed by Ralph and me on one side and Robert on the other = the angle formed between Ralph and me and Janetta. If two angles are both equal to the same angle they must be equal to each other. Q.E.D.

At Praia da Rocha we had found exactly what we wanted at the moment, and could carry on the sort of existence we liked, as we couldn't at Churriana with its warring stresses and strains. It hadn't been just captiousness that made us think so.

After three peaceful weeks had slid past, we set off home, by Lisbon, Coimbra and the *Chapon Fin* at Bordeaux. On March 22nd we were back at Ham Spray.]

March 23rd — Ham Spray. So here we are, having slipped imperceptibly back into our old slot. It's raining softly, but warm. Various things aren't working and require visits from 'the Men': one of these is the telephone, which gives out a gnat's voice through Atlantic rollers. Last night I said to Ralph that I thought Robert would soon tire of his wild dashes for *Panorama* (America last week, the Congo next), and that he was too critical to go on 'encapsulating' them for the public. So I was amused when this morning he burst out on the telephone: 'Really, it's absurd the way I dash about on these television journeys; it's just like taking a *pill*. The other day I looked at a map of Brazil and thought "I'd like to go there," and then I realized I'd just BEEN.' However, most of his talk was about his 'problem' which is just as acute as ever, yet the thought of a final decision makes him feel trapped and desperate.

Mary arrived to see us, spreading a glow of good humour. The gist of what she had to tell us was that Derek Jackson has been pressing her to marry him, but she was not proposing to at present. She was not in love with him, 'nor am I altogether happy about him,' she added. (Her divorce from Robin is through.)

March 26th. Easter weekend is bearing down on us, and it looks as if we shall have Burgo, Robert, and Janetta and the little girls. I can't understand why certain of life's responsibilities — those concerned with keeping our Ark afloat and with other people's troubles — put such a much greater strain on the organism than those to do with work, which positively buoy one up like cork floats. Ralph and I have been discussing the possibility of reconstructing Ham Spray to suit a recluse life for 'two elderly people'. The effort and expense would be stupendous, but it might leave us afloat, instead of being dragged under the sea.

March 30th. Our long, delicious solitude was broken on Good Friday, when the Blonds dropped Burgo with us, Robert arrived looking pale and exhausted but able to be very funny and stimulating, and soon after came Janetta with the children. None of them seem in very good shape, and ever since they began to arrive I seem to hear the steady mounting whine of a siren inside my head. Why can't human beings congregate without this fever and fret?

The ground was, as it were, well ploughed by the discovery of the happiness Ralph and I had alone in Portugal. Into it fell the seeds produced by social life and other people; and from those seeds plants have grown, which are now staring me in the face — mostly taking the form of conclusions about what I want and don't want:

I *don't want* competitive social life, or occasions when large gatherings are shouting and drinking together, but only to be with people I am fond of, old friends or stimulating new ones. I *don't want* variety and excitement for their own sake. I *do want* peace, including quite a lot of privacy, to live with my darling Ralph. I *do want* some sort of work, and opportunity to pursue my other activities like music and botany. I *do want* health, comfort, and ability to go on enjoying getting sensual pleasure from my surroundings.

A wonderfully simple charter for living! Or perhaps just 'cutting one's cloth, et cetera'? Or a Freudian flight from reality? Or acceptance of reality?

Easter weekend wasn't altogether easy, I don't know why. Burgo was helpful and friendly, telling us of his project for a new book. Janetta was kind, sweet and sympathetic, dealing with the children in a stoical, rather noble way. Delightful Rose is a little Leibniz monad, reflecting the universe *in toto* with dewdrop clarity. Georgie is temporarily fenced off and shut away. My normal manner of talking to her produced 'I don't know' and a violent shake of the head. Janetta then told me I was intimidating her, which I took greatly to heart. I think the situation between her parents has made her creep into her shell.

April 9th. As a result of indexing Freud, I awoke this morning saying to myself: 'It's a case of Mournful Prementia,' an imaginary ailment that (with its suggestion of melancholy and prediction) somewhat conveyed my mood.

After dinner at the Gowings' last night the conversation broke up two by two. Lawrence and I talked about different people's views of the universe. When I suggested that it was hard to get along with people who thought it wholly marvellous Lawrence claimed to be one of them — as an artist at any rate. When he painted a portrait, however ugly the sitter, he felt 'that every hair of their head was significant and wonderful, an integral part of the universe as a whole,' or if it was a landscape that not a leaf must be altered. As he held forth eloquently along these lines my own fundamental but buried optimism caught fire. Yet I still couldn't get beyond an ambivalent attitude — a feeling that the universe was both wonderful *and* terrible. 'The hairs may be exactly right,' I said to Lawrence, 'but what about the desperation, anxiety and loneliness inside the skull?' And he agreed. But even therein, I sometimes think, what I call 'interest' (and is perhaps the same thing as Lawrence's 'significance') is to be found. I differed from Lawrence in that what I find marvellous is consciousness itself, the sentient mind's response to its environment, rather than the shape and colour of that environment. The physical world is patently full of horror and ugliness as well as beauty and happiness, but the power of the human psyche to respond with interest to so much of both kinds is a constant marvel, like the heart's power to go on beating.

'What then,' said Ralph as we drove home, 'what then if the individual loses his power to respond?' Ah, what indeed?

April 10th. Last night, after I got into bed, the words 'Mournful Prementia' returned to my mind, and separated themselves clearly into what they obviously stand for: mournful premonitions. I felt disgusted with my optimistic theory of the day before. When I awoke this morning the telephone rang at once, and I went to it full of 'prementia' and expecting bad news. But it was only Dora Romilly asking us to dinner.

April 14th. The wind is giving half-hearted banshee wails through the bright sunlit garden. Dinah and I sit together in the little front room; we have left Ralph in the music-room because I feel my presence doing jobs when he doesn't want to do anything is fidgeting to him — for, alas, he is not feeling well. I first knew this when he got out of bed at seven this morning and took a pill, after which he lay sighing and restless in bed. I had to exercise the utmost tact to find out exactly what he was feeling. I'm certain he won't want to go to London tomorrow, nor should he; but he wants me to go without him and I *won't*. Ever since our last journey to Spain I have had an uneasy conviction that he's less well than before. It's dreadfully depressing for him but so it is for me, and he can't expect me to go on as if he were quite well when he's not. In that sense there are no frontiers where he ends and I begin.

I wish I had some mechanical thing to do instead of the new difficult Spanish translation — Unamuno — which arrived today from U.S.A. and fails to pin down my thoughts.

April 15th. Well, in the end, fortified by a talk to Janetta on the telephone and with Ralph's unwilling consent, I sent for Sawbones, and he arrived promptly, first treading fairly heavily on my feelings by telephone, which I was prepared for. He wasn't too bad. Ralph's present state must be taken as a 'warning', and he must rest absolutely for four or five days. He took all appropriate tests and left stronger sleeping-pills, which were useful.

April 16th. Two telephone calls from Janetta — *angelic*, and the best friend in the world. She's actually driving down for the night and I look forward to seeing her more than I can say. Meanwhile I'm trying not to rush blindly about like a hen with its head cut off, which is dreadfully disturbing to Ralph. He got up for a few hours today but was glad to get back to bed, doesn't want to smoke but *says* he feels better.

April 17th. I have lived through the last two days on a somehow supernormal plane, and am left rather broken but still upright, waiting for whatever comes next. I *don't* want to set down great wails of self-pity of all things, nor make lists of the symptoms which Janetta, with her unfailing sensitivity, elicited from me. Before she arrived I had suggested that Sawbones communicate with Geoff Konstam, but all through dinner and after Janetta kept up a forceful offensive for us to get him or some other specialist *at once*. She was perfectly right, and I can never be grateful enough. My difficulty is, as always, Ralph's absolute hatred of calling any doctors in. Janetta's company was enlivening to us both, but had some results not so good, in that it induced him to drink more than I now know was good for him, and eat too much of the delicious smoked salmon she brought. The night was appalling and virtually sleepless for us both. However, Geoff Konstam came as promised next day, and Janetta volunteered to stay long enough to drive him back again. So today has been the day of doctors, and had I had the energy I would have been amused at Sawbones' fantastically deferential treatment of the headmaster. Janetta and I sat talking in the music-room like husbands whose wives are having babies up aloft. After she and Geoff had left, leaving behind the news that anti-coagulants are to be tried, Ralph has become quiet, resigned and philosophical beyond belief.

April 20th. Robert and Burgo both came for the weekend. Janetta had warned us that 'Robert was in a very bad, desperate way'. But he saw Ralph several times, and had obviously not felt as shocked as Janetta at how ill he was, which was reassuring. He does in fact seem better, there is even a sign of pepperiness, on which he commented himself with a mischievous expression. In the sweetest and most touching way Burgo suggested staying on to keep me company. He has been extremely helpful and does everything I ask him.

April 22nd. Divine spring day, warm and sunny. I had my breakfast on the verandah, and have been writing letters there. I even made a start on Unamuno yesterday. Mary invited herself over and I had looked forward to a talk with her alone, and so was disappointed when Eduardo Paolozzi arrived with her. However, he had just returned from New York and when I asked about it an endless stream of highly interesting impressions poured from his mouth, with no change whatever in his round

Aberdeen Angus face. There was a lot about 'myth' and 'paradox', 'big-hearted men giving themselves a shot' or 'grabbing themselves a woman', and all-night television. I was so enthralled that I was able to retail it all to Ralph afterwards.

April 23rd. Trouble at home has blotted out public events these last days, but there is one item of news in the American paper Robert brings Ralph, which I find it hard to stomach. The controllers of rockets and satellites over there are advertising for six men to train now, and later to be sent up in rockets into the stratosphere. Something like six hundred have volunteered — all have to be in their thirties, married and with children. One man's *wife* couldn't bear him to miss the chance by being away at the time, so that she applied on his behalf! No one but me thinks anything of it, however. But I feel that much as I admire those who take fearful risks to save life or find a cure for yellow fever, to throw away their lives in this suicidal manner is just *showing off*. Mary said yesterday that she didn't want to marry Derek Jackson or anyone else.

May 3rd. Ralph is doing fine, and Geoff Konstam seems now not to want him to take anti-coagulants, which delights him. I don't know how much it is worth recording the nadir of gloomiest days, but it *is*, I believe the extraordinary power of human resilience, arguing as it does some basic kind of optimism. This evening I drove through the spring night to Marlborough for an orchestra practice, thoroughly enjoyed it, and came back purged and purified. It's as if the prevailing blackness of the craggy landscape I had been traversing, haunted by miserable worry about Ralph, threw into relief the peculiar joys that were to be had from practising a boring bit of Elgar with a heterogeneous collection of Marlborough masters and their wives.

May 6th. Again I have carried my solitary breakfast tray to the verandah. I am determined to savour this day of calm and sedation by natural beauty to the full. A warm breeze is fluttering my letters. The garden is full of swooping bird-shapes — the martins arrived yesterday; Dinah is intoxicated by them as she gazes from under my chair, and also by the quivering grasses, the general buzzing and twittering to the steady accompaniment of the cuckoo. The tulips are all out now, stiffly balanced on top of their tall stalks.

Yesterday I took my first day off since Ralph was ill, to go to Duncan's private view at the Tate. A monumentally silly conversation between two debs in the train amused me; it was interrupted by a tragedy which made the Atom bomb look small — one of them had left her wrap at Pewsey! Horrified faces: 'What on *earth* shall I do?' 'Telephone and have it put on the train.' 'Oh, but Mummy'll be *wild* — you don't know Mummy. *Goodness*, how awful!' I talked to many friends at the Tate — Morgan Forster, Freddie Ayer, Roger Senhouse, Bunny and Angelica. Raymond described a visit of Cyril and Janetta to Crichel together. 'She doesn't keep him in order, does she?' was his comment. Poor Janetta!

May 18th. I'm *delighted* with Ralph. Two days ago Sawbones came out, tested his blood-pressure and said he needn't come any more, and that Ralph might do what he liked within reason. He came down to breakfast next morning, and went with Isobel and me to have drinks at Stokke. He talks with all his old animation and doesn't get tired by people. His face has a quite different expression; it's as if he had been restored to the world, and was overjoyed to find himself in it. He is angelic to me, and anxious to get back to helping with household tasks. At Stokke we sat out in the sun talking to Freddie Ayer and Eduardo about Bertie Russell's philosophy, Madame de Staël and Duncan's pictures.

In the evening I started reading Bertie Russell's new book, as usual tougher and stiffer than one thinks it's going to be. Why try? Is any juice coming out of this mouthful, or are my teeth just going automatically up and down to no effect? Then a little squirt of something tasty goes down my throat, and it at once seems worthwhile. Faced with a fence, I often take a gallop or two round the field before my mind gets over it. And it's disheartening to find an avenue of thought blocked by 'pain of infinite regress', even though it's just what is to be expected in this mad universe.

May 24th. A soft warm wind brings the winged seeds down from the wych elms, so that walking down the avenue one seems to be shuffling through giant corn-flakes. We went to meet Gamel at the station, and took a stroll along the Kennet Canal before her train came. It was sunny and balmy, with the scent of may filling the air and some trees beginning to turn pink. Tall cow parsley and purple comfrey were flowering by the tow-path, where a huge fisherman with a face like a carp was speculatively surveying the river. The train disgorged Gamel, so weighed down by her enormous suitcase as to look very pathetic. She says Gerald is hard at work on his novel, *Mr Fisher*. Not a harsh word about Hetty, for which we give her much credit, but quite a few about Hetty's mother.

Animals are in the news. Two monkeys have been safely retrieved after being launched in rockets, and their photographs in their little space-helmets and suits were infinitely touching, their faces extremely serious and no wonder. I can't help being horrified at human beings treating them so vulgarly. 'Send up human beings,' says the RSPCA, but I wish to God they wouldn't send up anyone or anything. A hedgehog has derailed a train; and scientists fail to agree whether the strontium fall-out will produce deformed children. So the world wags along, and thank heavens we shan't be here for much more of it.

May 28th. We have Clive and Barbara Bagenal here for two nights; they seem quite a married couple, and I think it is an excellent — if unexpected — arrangement. Vanessa is said to be much relieved by it. There's no malice in Barbara: set her off on a subject like marmalade or pot-plants and she will prattle happily for hours. Clive may seem a little older, but his appetite for life is undimmed. He has brought me instructions from Vanessa that I must keep up my duties as Secretary of the Memoir Club, and that Denis Proctor is to be admitted as a member.[1] This morning our happy couple are positively spoony together, and Clive's clear voice was heard resounding through the passages: 'LITTLE Barbara, how have you slept?'

[1] Civil Servant and Chairman of the Tate Gallery.

[Barbara Hiles was a student at the Slade with Carrington, Dorothy Brett and others, one of those whom Virginia Woolf nicknamed 'the Cropheads'. In her youth she was extremely pretty, with her heart-shaped face, large blue eyes and curly dark-brown hair. Her high spirits and liveliness were much in evidence at Bloomsbury parties of the Twenties and Thirties, where she was often to be seen after most of the rest had gone home, tirelessly leaping up and down to the music like a mayfly. Among her admirers were Maynard Keynes, David Garnett and the man she married, Nicholas Bagenal, but the best known — because his devotion was lifelong though unrequited — was Saxon Sydney-Turner. I think she found his endless letters, even the boxes of chocolate and presents for the children, something of a burden, and at the time we thought her ungrateful, but when she took me to visit him in the old folks' home where he ended his days I remember being struck by her good-nature and patience with him. In middle age her marriage broke down, and she must have been over sixty when to most of their friends' astonishment she took up with Clive. 'An excellent arrangement,' as I have said, because with him her life became much more eventful, including quite a lot of foreign travel and meetings with such of his circle as Graham Sutherland, Kenneth Clark and Picasso. While in her turn she looked after him like a kind nanny. 'Barbara is too nice to mind being left out of the conversation,' he used to say, but I have forgotten who it was who remarked 'the thing is, Barbara *maids* him'.]

June 5th. I was lying with my volume of Saint-Simon on the grass bank below the verandah this afternoon, when I noticed a lot of bees hovering over it like small furry aeroplanes surveying the terrain. Very unusual bees, wearing full Elizabethan breeches (yellow with black spots). They seemed to be looking for places to bore holes, and I became so fascinated by their activities that I quite forgot the Regent and his debaucheries, and tried to help them by clearing two little bare spaces. One splendid arch-bee actually disappeared into one. I called Ralph, who said the yellow plus-fours were pollen-bags, which showed they must have nests and young in the bank. Probably I was lying on some. I moved, and sure enough the adventurous bee emerged from its hole looking exhausted, with thin brown legs where its smart bloomers had been.

June 15th. It wasn't only the ravishing weather that made this a specially good Crichel weekend. Everyone was relaxed; the talk was as good as the meals; there was croquet, walks, sitting in the sun. We were alone with Raymond on Friday night, and heard about his weekend visit to the Winston Churchills: how much he liked and admired Lady Churchill, how impossible it was to talk

to Winston, who was now quite gaga. Desmond and Eardley
arrived next day from Glyndebourne. Of the three Desmond is
the most ready to launch general ideas, springing from a liberal
and above all optimistic outlook. We talked about the Hippy
generation and their philosophy (Eardley seemed not to have
heard about them, and was indignant because they had been 'kept
from him'). He was affectionately teased by Desmond. Did we
feel differently towards the universe because of its sinister
developments of the last twenty-five years, someone asked.
Desmond was inclined to believe in progress; the rest spoke of the
universe somewhat as if it was an old friend who had shown a
new side of his character by treachery.

This is the first outing we have taken since Ralph's last bad
spell, and the great thing for me was that he never seemed in the
least uneasy, nor I about him.

June 29th — Ham Spray. It strikes me as astonishing that after
quite a long trudge through this vale of tears one should still
throw up morals with one's plough, which have a momentary
glint as of a new coin although they are anything but. For
instance: 'don't be sorry for yourself', 'keep the sense of guilt
under — or at least quiescent', and even the nursery one of 'do
your duty'. Very often it's impossible to tell what that is, though
at present mine lies plain as a pikestaff in front of me.

July 13th. Ralph came with me to London for the night, Burgo
driving up with Robert. Ralph was reading Burgo's translation in
the train, I Robert's new novel.[1]

Visiting Robert's flat, we admired his new carpet, chair, and
moving Irish gramophone records. Then came the television set,
but ah! there we were unable to follow him. He showed us
Tonight, said to be one of the best programmes. It certainly
riveted one's attention in a horrid, compulsive sort of way, yet I
was bored and rather disgusted, and longed to be able to unhook
my gaze from this little fussy square of confusion and noise on the
other side of the room. It's so old-fashioned and amateurish! 'Ah,
here's one of the great television personalities — the best-known
face in England!' said Robert, and a charmless countenance with
the manner of a Hoover-salesman dominated the screen. It's
contemptible, it has nowhere near caught up with any of the
other modes of expression; it's the LCM of the common man,

one's mind has to shrink to get inside it. It's as light-weight as a feather duster, yet vast numbers of people are daily and hourly beaten on the head with it.

Dined at the Ivy with Clive and the Colonel, Barbara, Cressida Ridley and — a pleasant surprise — Marjorie Strachey. A jolly evening.

[1]*Broadstrop in Season.*

July 23rd. Writing in the train, on the way to London and the dentist. I *hated* leaving Ralph alone. In spite of all my efforts to think ahead and arrange for his wants, I fancy he is happier when I'm there looking after him. This business of 'managing' woke me early this morning and tossing in the heat. Sometimes I feel I *can* manage quite well, when even swinging along the passage on two legs seems an amazing achievement; at others I see a pattern of success and failure more realistically. But in the basement of my mind lurks a feeling of being some awful sort of sham or fraud. Self-confidence is like the horizontal boom in the school gym. Sometimes one can walk blithely along the top — but at others it is a question of travelling along uneasily below, hand over hand, and even then only to drop off.

July 24th — Montpelier Square. London in the heat — what an unbuttoning! What a Bacchanalian rout crowds the pavements, wearing brilliant beach shirts, bare legs, sandals, crinolines, jeans. Normally many people wear their clothes rather for the unwritten things they say than because they suit them: whether it is their background (families in the Highlands, social and political values) or to declare their readiness for sex and adventure. But when it's as hot as now they strip off this print, these flags they've been waving, with one idea alone — to be cool and comfortable.

No sign of anyone at Montpelier. Then Janetta came out of her room, looking unhappy, with no voice, saying she had flu. Burgo came up from the basement shiny with sweat, about to have a bath before going to a Hinchingbrooke party, which Jonny and Janetta were also invited to. Prettily dressed in pink shantung as she was, she decided not to go after all, and soon afterwards in came Robert. Their manner to each other couldn't have been more friendly, with a distinct touch of flirtatiousness on both sides. 'Oh yes,' she said later, 'he's been perfectly all right for some time.'

Robert began walking up and down the room like a caged lion, and asking me to psycho-analyse his behaviour.

F. 'It's your animal nature trying to get out.' Then he began rolling up the bottom of his jacket. 'What am I doing now?'

F. 'Trying to get back to Eton jackets. Regression.'

Robert. 'Yes, I used to wear them. Now what?' And he rolled it even higher.

F. 'Trying to be a woman — in a bikini.'

Evening alone with Janetta, eating avocado pears and fried eggs. She told me that Robin Campbell is to marry Susan Benson, which was no surprise.

July 24th. Life begins early at Montpelier, and swells to a crescendo with the voices of the children and the Italian *au pair* girl. Janetta lay in bed looking iller than before, with her hand on the white telephone. Georgie's swimming sports and Nicky's return to school loom large. Nicky's huge trunk stood waiting to be packed, and Georgie's bathing-cap had disappeared. When I returned from my session at the dentist, the confusion was wilder than ever. Yet in spite of the mess and moments of near-collapse, the life of the house saves itself by the skin of its teeth, and perhaps gains in vitality by performing this feat. I made my way slowly up to my room on the top floor, past Janetta's bedroom, where she had retired to bed, and the nursery floor, where Robert was playing trains with Georgie and Nicky.

Then out I went to my first Memoir Club meeting as Secretary, which of course made me anxious. But dinner for fifteen went well. I sat next to Dermod and opposite Vanessa and Duncan. The reading, in Leonard's rooms, began with Julia's *Animalia*, and went on to Leonard on religious belief, both extremely typical of their writers.

August 7th — Ham Spray. After a night of *bonsoir tristesse*, slow to sleep, I wake early and lie groping among the spectres. The tent-pegs of my anxieties fasten me firmly to the old, brown, much-trampled earth. Human beings spend the first half of their lives looking forward, and trying to improve and believing in the possibility. The habit dies hard, and there's no fixed point when one can say: 'The *dégringolade* has now begun.' And long ago though I crossed this rubicon, if indeed it exists, I am still aware of stubborn stirrings within.

Have been reading Plato's *Symposium* and reflecting on the effect it and most of the rest of Greek literature must have had in fostering homosexuality in public schools, for it is subtly presented as noble and idealistic, and linked with Truth and Beauty (while heterosexuality is treated merely as a practical arrangement). And what with the knock-out personality of Socrates, how could they possibly resist?

The promise of a very hot day tormented me with thoughts of poor Burgo stewing in London — unnecessarily as it turned out, because in the middle of the morning he rang up to say he was at Stokke with the Blonds. They came over in the afternoon, bringing with them Simon Raven and a pretty girl called Jane M., and stayed until eight apparently enjoying the pool and our cool lawn. Almost our first glimpse of Simon was stark naked in the pool. He's a solid, pinkish, obviously Cambridge man. He's congenial and likes talking about the same things as we do — the shocking spread of irrationality and religion, the importance or otherwise of the Classics, sex, and harvest-bugs. He has a good sense of humour.

August 9th. Next day we had a visit from Robin and Susan, and Robin's godfather (who has the splendid name of Sir D'Arcy Godolphin Osborne), Minister to the Holy See, a tall elderly bachelor, looking out through thick glasses with the expression of a whimsical sheep, and beginning without preamble to tell us about the diarrhoea he had been suffering from for the last five days. The three menaces to civilization, he said, were Bombs, Babies and Boredom. We liked him enormously.

August 18th. This morning's bathroom conversation ranged over the wellworn area of pushpin and poetry, hot baths and houris, which has the advantage that Ralph and I don't altogether agree. I always bring up the fact that one poem leads to another and one hot bath does not — in which I'm quite aware of the holes. This had been started up when the Gowings came to dinner last night; another subject had been the dire need of a suicide technique to save one from getting caught in the trap of old age.

Witticism by Ralph: 'Wiltshire red in Rootes and Clore.'[1]

[1] Two of our local millionaires.

August 21st. A letter from Gerald, who now longs to detach himself from Hetty, and get away to Italy with Gamel — though the prospect bores him as Gamel 'is no company, just a ghost' and 'dissatisfaction is in her blood'. I doubt if this mood will last; the next letter will be full of praise of Hetty. Anyway she is the obvious alternative to what he calls '*la présence Gamellienne*'. He also had some amusing stories to tell about Ernest Hemingway and Ken Tynan, who are out there at present, getting very drunk and quarrelling about bull-fights. Was three inches from the heart too far for the final stroke? asked Hemingway. 'If you were in bed with your wife,' said Tynan, 'such a distance could make quite a difference.' Extraordinary to hear of the endless Torremolinos round going on.

Our weekend party consisted of Boris and the Hendersons, Burgo and Jane M. Boris was as ever quite magnificent, his thoughts rolling out clothed in his inimitable language and even more inimitable accent, accompanied by a stream of expressions changing from deep sadness to a great mischievous moujik's smile, revealing squat brown teeth. He and Nicko played a lot of chess, often in the garden. On one side of the table sat Boris, huge and motionless, wearing a look of deep scorn. On the other side Nicko, nervously frowning and muttering under his breath. The Hendersons' company was a great asset, and Mary one of the most tactfully helpful visitors we have ever had. But the greatest good of all was Burgo's having a girl-friend. It seems a more important event than his getting a degree, and may well be more use to him. Jane is very attractive, oncoming and friendly, with a saving grace of nervousness. She hasn't got that appalling confidence of most pretty girls.

August 26th. I am a little disconcerted at having heard nothing from America about my Unamuno translation, which is now all but finished. Otherwise we move on an even keel through this gloriously hot summer.

We have taken the excuse of having to go into Hungerford to enjoy two wonderful walks along the Kennet canal. There's a strange fascination in gazing into the clear but rotten-smelling water, with its chalky pebbles at the bottom and green mermaid's hair floating up to the surface. A margin of luscious pre-Raphaelite water-plants — fresh forget-me-nots, mint, loose-strife and bur-marigold; and in the reeds a serious, busy squadron of coots and dabchicks chugging about, while a white V on the water had as its apex a tiny moorhen hurrying to swim away from us. Water rats, a dazzling kingfisher, and once two fledglings tumbled hysterically chirping out of their nest right on to the towpath at our feet. Nothing could be more satisfying than this Turkish bath in natural beauty and solitude.

September 1st. Dined with Mary at Stokke, where Derek Jackson was staying. The evening went pretty well until Derek suddenly began boasting in his rather mad, stifled voice. He can't bear cleverness to be attributed to anyone else — it was Isaiah Berlin in this case. 'What does it all amount to? Unless a man understands *nuclear physics* he's no use at all. In the sixteenth century the engines of war were designed by the artists, Leonardo and so on. But what good was all their work in the *last war?* None at all. It's useless compared to the work *I* do.'

We thought he was badly on Mary's nerves. She murmured, 'Some people are pacifists, you know.'

Before that we had discussed the earlier and earlier age at which the young now take to sex. Ralph said that when he was at Oxford much more than half the undergraduates he knew were virgins. When I was at Newnham I only had one friend who ceased to be one while she was there, and there were a lot who didn't 'know the facts of life'. Now it's likely they will lose their virginity while still at school. But does it make much difference? Or could a kiss be just as disturbing then as the first sexual experience is now?

September 7th. We are to have a General Election next month. I asked Ralph today what reasons he would give in simple terms, to Mrs Hoare say or Georgie Kee, why one shouldn't vote Conservative? 'Because one can't trust them not to behave in a beastly way,' he said, 'either internationally as at Suez, or to the working classes. Because they really do believe themselves to be designed to rule, and superior to their fellow men.'

September 10th. Last night the wireless announced that Mary's great friend, Cathleen Mann,[1] had died, in terms suggesting suicide. Not long afterwards I had a call from Mary herself, dreadfully upset. After inadequately trying to say the right thing about the poor 'telephone doll', as we called her, I went back and told Ralph, who went on happily reading his book and was surprised when — some twenty minutes later — I wanted to go on talking about the news. 'But I had no feelings for or against the telephone doll,' he said. 'I couldn't think what Mary saw in her.'

What is the nature of the sympathetic emotion, which made me share some of Mary's sadness? I know it to be a painful faculty, which I have in excess, so that I sometimes 'share' feelings which don't even exist. It can be almost a disease, like having bad teeth. Yet I think I should worry if I didn't possess it in some degree, because I often count on it in other people. I think of it as a sort of Social Contract by which human beings support each other, and the hard walls enclosing the individual are broken down. It's intolerable to think of other people as if they were a lot of marbles rolling about and sometimes clashing. Sympathetic pain is necessary to sufferers, as one soon discovers when in trouble oneself. I thought of Janetta's feeling heart and imaginative and delicate sensibility, and how when Ralph was ill and I was desperate with worry and misery this was a comfort for which I can never be grateful enough. Who would one go to first in trouble? Janetta, Robert and Julia came quickly to mind, and I believe Burgo has the seeds of such sympathy in him. The streak of hardness in Ralph co-exists with an unusual power of understanding and analysing human emotions, as well as strong outgoing warmth.

[1] The painter, Lady Queensberry.

September 13th — Mottisfont. We had a lovely evening alone with Boris and Maud; grouse and blackberry ice for dinner. But this morning John Pope-Hennessy of the V. and A. Museum arrived — a confident, happy, vain man with a frog's face. Conversation is like Scrabble to him; you see if you can make a better word, or drop a bigger name than other people, and when doing this his voice rises to a high scream. We had to talk about what *he* wanted to talk about, which led to a lecture by him about the Romantic Exhibition during lunch, and in the evening another about the Royal family (his brother's book on Queen Mary being about to appear). Everyone except his brother (who is almost himself and therefore perfect) gets a jab from him, and a pretty sharp one, followed by a perfunctory statement of his affection — Raymond, Roy Harrod and so on.

September 16th — Ham Spray. Still not a drop of rain. Ralph and I

walked this morning up the long shallow valley beyond
Shalbourne, treading on dry biscuit-coloured grass over ash-grey
iron earth. I begin to long for the slosh and patter of rain,
especially as it no longer looks like summer, only an unearthly
paper-dry autumn. The world, seen over this arid foreground
also looks dry — the approaching Election crackles with
deadness: nobody cares about it. Nearer at hand, various couples
may or may not be getting closer: Robert and Cynthia, for
instance.

I have a Freudian index on Jokes, and a Spanish article for
U.S.A. to do by the end of the month, so am very busy. Also a
number of weekend parties loom ahead.

September 21st. I have spent the morning, clock in front of me,
doing my Spanish article, which is now in hand. Much enjoyed
the weekend with Robert, the Godleys, and Burgo. To begin at
the end, he is in some way loosened up, with curly instead of
straight lines on his face, still restless and explosive but liberated.
What he wants to be at now is a rampaging bit of sex, I believe. It
now comes often into his conversation, and he has his own style
about it — destructive, violent and funny. Robert was with us for
an afternoon before the Godleys came. We strolled across the
fields, discussing his problems, and he at once came out with the
fact that he has an appointment with a 'head-shrinker'. He talked
of his desire to 'settle down', without mentioning names, but
only 'people', 'one' and 'other people', though this anonymity
brought him to the edge and over into giggles.

September 28th. We were glad to see Anthony West and Lily after
two years' absence. However, Anthony was in a rather provoca-
tive mood. Some of the characters he attacked may have been
stand-ins for Rebecca — Madame de Staël and George Eliot, for
instance. Seeing me at work on Freud's *Jokes*, he carried it off to
the verandah, and came back with burning eyes saying: 'I was
checking up to see whether Freud had a sense of humour. He
hasn't, *has he*? These jokes aren't funny at all, *are they*?' It seemed
pointless to tell him that he was talking through his hat — the
jokes weren't Freud's, but *famous* jokes, many by Heine or
various philosophers, which had been thought funny by a lot of
people, and that Freud was taking a scientific interest in the
reason why.

On our getting up to our bedroom on Sunday night Ralph fell silent, then made the familiar gesture down his breastbone and admitted to 'discomfort'. I must not show the gloom this casts me into or he will keep such things from me.

October 6th. Returning from a weekend with the Nicholses at Lawford, Ralph sank before dinner into a state of exhaustion, with eyes half-closing, and went to bed and sleep without eating. He realistically says that Phil doesn't like him, and I am full of compunction at having let him in for the visit. I telephoned Sawbones this morning and he has been out, finds no sign of the heart being the cause, but a slight temperature. We are both relieved, but I don't feel great confidence in Sawbones' exactness.

October 17th. Janetta and I drove over to Stokke cottage, which has been rented from Mary by Robert. There we found Robert and Georgie, the house half-painted, and Cynthia upstairs interviewing an upholstress. Robert described the colour schemes: the kitchen was to be black, white and red. Janetta: 'Good heavens! Like a luxury flat of the Thirties!'

We had a whole day of talk with her alone, and she offers to drive south with us in the New Year, but she pours out for us such sweetness and sympathy that we are anxious not to trade too much on it.

November 2nd. The Toynbees are staying at Robert's cottage; they came over to us for a drink, Sally pregnant, Philip booming away in his irresistible velvety *basso profundo*. Afterwards I asked Robert about the marriage, adding that I found it hard to believe Philip capable of love. 'No, I doubt if he is,' Robert said, 'and I don't believe I am either. Though of course I recognize there is such a thing.' The relationship between Robert and Philip is like that of two businessmen, advancing and punching each other semi-comically in the chest. In an argument as to why the Labour party lost the Election they got so heated that they yelled (and boomed) at each other, both saying true and sensible things which shot past the other like missiles going wide of their target. Philip thought that if one believed one's principles were right one shouldn't scrap them just because of failure, but consider how to persuade one's adversary more forcefully; Robert that we must beat the Conservatives, and use any means to that end. Philip has a good arguer's mind, and listens to what one says as very few people do, a pleasant change from those who merely hold their breath, let their eyes glaze over and wait till one has finished.

November 6th. Winter has begun. A brilliant frosty morning, with all the dahlias and zinnias suddenly blackened and dead. Janetta arrived at lunch-time, and immediately afterwards she and I drove up on to the downs and took a walk in the already opalescent light which would soon be a fog. She talked about Cynthia entirely without malice, said that she was very kind to the children, but that she felt sorry for her as Robert was often so fierce to her.

I am insisting on a few perfectly quiet days for Ralph, but wish there could be more. A plague of visitors lies ahead, curse it! Trudge on!

November 19th. Our heaviest weekend — with the Pritchetts and the Hills — was a great success, enjoyed I believe by all including me, in spite of grey, grim weather, It ended in a long discussion about tragedy in general and *Othello* in particular. Was it one of the best tragic plots in the world or not? V.S.P. thought not, because it hinged too much on tricks and devices, and not on Fate as Aristotle thought it should. I thought that what made it so tremendous was that the violent emotions involved were common to everyone — love, jealousy, lust for power; and that whether trickery or Fate set them off didn't greatly matter.

So much for the weekend, which left Ralph and me so fresh that we took on a visit to Dora Romilly (piteously ill, poor creature), drinks at Stokke, and visits from Kitty West and Burgo.

I have just finished the nineteenth and last volume of Saint-Simon. Approaching the end of the tunnel I couldn't bear to come out, and braked hard; but now I'm through, and this vast, densely populated stretch of history lies behind me. Not until reaching the very end do I feel that in a sort of way I am conscious of it as a whole, yet I am afraid of losing or dropping that vision. Another thing I'm aware of is a warm affection for Saint-Simon himself, in spite of his vanity and snobbery. I remember his passion for truth, his curiosity, his intelligence. I shall move on to something that links with him if possible — the Letters of Madame, the Princesse des Ursins, or even the Big Miss, as

Lytton used to call her.[1] Saint-Simon is I suppose the longest book I ever read in my life.

[1]La Grande Demoiselle, cousin of Louis XIV.

November 22nd. Raymond, Joanna and Burgo arrived together. Raymond started a conversation over dinner about the difference between physical and mental afflictions. He said he sympathized with the former, but generally felt that those who had the latter were much too sorry for themselves and deserved no sympathy. I disagree with him profoundly — I see no reason to put material values before mental ones. Also the worst of mental afflictions is that they are so damnably hard to deal with. In fact I feel quite shocked at Raymond. Has he never had any? And even if he hasn't, has he no imagination?

We were drawn out on to the wet lawn carpeted with glistening leaves to watch the demise of the last of three trees beyond the badminton lawn which have had to be cut down. It still stood erect, but balanced on a narrow sliver of wood which two men were busy sawing away at. Then a wave of the hand, a distant lorry in the field beyond tightened a cable, and the tall monster toppled over with the utmost dignity and finality, dying just as one would like to die — one moment a complete, living thing and the next a prostrate corpse. The thud was stupendous, and a little old man who was watching broke into an admiring smile — admiration for the noble tree rather than for his black-browed Hercules of a son.

December 6th — Crichel. In bed at Crichel, whither we came on Friday afternoon under a luminous peacock blue sky with a crescent moon. Here we are with Eddy, elegant in a letter-box red sweater, Eardley and Raymond, and all around us this marquetry box of coloured, complicated, patterned comforts. I noticed last night how the differing styles of talk of Eardley on one side, and Raymond and Eddy on the other, show that he is an artist and they are critics. Where Eardley is responding and reflecting in a way that is entirely his own, the other two are busily amassing and assessing facts. The result is that I often find what Eardley has to say the more alive and interesting. Between several walks, meals and much lovely gramophone music we got happily to the evening, when Michael and Sonia Pitt-Rivers came to dinner. Rather to our surprise the *Crichelois* treat this marriage between a lifelong homosexual and a neurotic forty-year-old woman as if it was perfectly normal, and they would be happy ever after and why not? They certainly bounced in laughing and talking. At dinner I sat between Raymond and Michael, who is a great talker. There's hardly a subject he doesn't fall upon with the avidity of a starving man pouncing on a juicy steak, though in fact we talked mostly about trees or his travels in the far East. Lots of funny stories and excellent imitations followed one another without pause, and his memories seem to be arranged on a bookshelf in front of him, so that he finds one in a moment and takes it down. It's not so much a conversation as a very brilliant turn.

December 8th — Ham Spray. Got back with mixed feelings to our colder, much less comfortable and *soignée* house. In the very act of lolling, forgetting appearances and giving way to a certain amount of confusion (spreading the floor with newspapers and the tables with haystacks of books which are eternally being shifted in search of some important needle) there is a mixture of relief and exacerbation. Listened to *Rosenkavalier* in the evening, in preparation for seeing it next week.

December 15th. The house was unusually full of youth and masculinity last weekend (Simon Raven, Anthony Blond, Jonny, Burgo), of argument, boasting, clumping feet, and even poker chips. And Janetta for us. Burgo and Simon are going to Greece together, so there was much excited talk of plans.

The large fly in the ointment was that Ralph seemed in an undefined way dispirited and tired, and I ask myself anxiously whether we ought really to be going abroad so soon?

December 28th. Janetta and her children took over Stokke for Christmas, which was as usual a gruelling endurance test for almost everyone — except the children, who moved like ecstatic ghosts among mountains of parcels, toys, books, television sets and Balmain fur coats. Robert was a heroic figure, working manfully to live up to his standards, and backed by the devoted Cynthia. Janetta was the most worrying casualty. She looked grey with pallor and admitted to feeling 'whacked'; as she had about seventeen people to every meal it was hardly surprising, but she said that wasn't what had exhausted her, it was 'seeing people she didn't like'.

On Boxing Day Robert brought over his guests at the cottage — Woodrow Wyatt and his wife Lady Moorea. He combines socialism with snobbishness, is clever in a quick rather than in a deep way, gregarious, confident and greedy. He ate a colossal dinner, fell asleep in his chair before the music-room fire, and snored.

As for me, I am in the grip of anxiety now that our departure day approaches, especially in view of Ralph's obvious fear of being hurried or harried. I dread lest any small mishaps common to journeys might affect him and can think of no magic talisman to quell my fears except the one word COURAGE, which I have written on every page of my pocket diary.

December 29th. We had Robert to ourselves for supper last night, a perfect companion. After going over Christmas with a fine comb and deciding how everyone 'did', we got on to psycho-analysis, both in theory and practice. It was fascinating to hear about it from someone as realistic and averse to mumbo-jumbo as he is. One thing he came up with was that the infant's pleasure in suckling was fully sexual. But if so, wouldn't there be extreme differences in the psychological patterns of the breast- and bottle-fed? Robert also finds it convincing that some states of adult rage are speechless — because they refer back to the pre-speech period of infancy. I was rather struck by that. And here is a fragment of the psycho-analysis of everyday life, which has only just occurred to me: on Christmas day at Stokke I saw a pretty jewelled object lying on a table and asked what it was. Cynthia's present to Janetta, a key-ring. Something clicked at the time, but only now do I see the significance of the present of a Kee-ring.

December 31st. Last day of 1959 and last day here. Six men arrived this morning and carried off some of our furniture to prepare for re-decoration in our absence. The cushions are left on a heap on the floor, as a sign that we must *must* go.

Janetta came down to encourage us on our way, and Robert — alone now at his cottage — made a fourth at tea. We have had a cheerful, very adult postcard from Burgo in Athens. But the wind wails, and my *angst* wails with it.

1960

[A new variation had been decided on for this year's winter in the South: we would make for Alicante, an attractive town with an even better climate than Malaga, and find a comfortable hotel there with none of the burden of housekeeping and social life. If we were lucky Janetta might visit us there and we would be away for three months.

By way of Bordeaux and the *Chapon Fin* we reached the Savoy Hotel at Madrid. From the window of our comfortable bedroom I was watching the life and movement in an arcade below, when Ralph asked if I'd like to go out for a moment and I said I would. We strolled up and down admiring the coloured lights decorating the kerbside trees in readiness for tomorrow's *Los Reyes* (the Children's Christmas), when 'after five minutes, to my indescribable horror and remorse, Ralph was seized by one of his sudden bouts of exhaustion. We went back at once and he sank into an armchair. After a pause he said, "I'm all right now. I'm as right as rain." Then, *sotto voce*, "No, not right as rain. I shall never be right as rain again. That's the worst of it." Once in bed he fell asleep immediately, but I was much too anxious, and lay penetrated and saturated by grief. For it must be faced that he finds this journey much more testing than last year's.'

We were fortunate in reaching Alicante before the blizzard that a few days later brought unaccustomed cold winds and even snow, isolating a busload of people all night not far from the route we had taken. Oh, what a relief to be there, installed in our old-fashioned, very warm hotel. Ralph was soon feeling much better, and eager to walk along the esplanade with its paving of mosaics in wave pattern, set between two rows of tall palm-trees. 'The air was warm and sweet, the blue water of the harbour was full of boats, and hundreds of white doves were settling down for the night in the branches. We talked and laughed as we walked.' So it had not been all misery. 'Our fellow-guests in the hotel are mostly ancient Spanish couples,' I wrote, 'who have come South from a colder clime and are waiting for Godot. The old men glide with shuffling steps into the dining-room preceded by their wives. One such, seen from a distance is a tragic-eyed Goya, sallow-faced and with dyed black hair; looking closer one sees a fragile, bent, white-haired old woman. They are all treated gently and with respect by the staff. To Spaniards "*la vieillesse est une dignité*" (Chateaubriand, whom I've just begun to read).'

I brought no pressure to bear on Ralph to take walks or short excursions, but did my best to fall in with his desires, read his expression or tone of voice. However, 'I long for a sweet Janetta to discuss things with, and help me keep them in proportion. As I haven't got her I must swing from branch to branch through my private jungle, improvising as I go.'

So the weeks passed, and for some time the fierce cold refused to loosen its grip. Perhaps to keep his morale alive, Ralph sometimes insisted on coming out, to the Poste Restante say, when I *knew* he shouldn't, when he felt the worse for it before we got home, but stubbornly refused to take a rest in a warm café. In a rational conversation next day he admitted to having suffered from 'trouser-panic' as he called it, namely fear that I was getting too bossy. If only he could have perceived the quivering mass of uncertainty within me!

Then a telegram came from Janetta that she would join us at Almería. We were delighted, but almost scared at the thought of company, for we have been a long time alone, even if all our friends and Burgo have been splendid correspondents.

The drive to Almería went well, Ralph saying he felt 'very strong', and what joy to find Janetta there, already having moved her furniture to humanize her room. As I guessed she would, she had an invigorating effect on Ralph, and I know he felt her a support. So in a different way were the Brenans who arrived a week later, Gerald with flu, so he said. When I was alone pressing my flowers in my bedroom he came to see me. 'In the very nicest, most friendly way he asked me in detail about Ralph's health, listened attentively, and said that if at any moment we were in difficulties or needed a doctor a telegram would bring him to wherever we were. I was moved and grateful for his understanding. Gerald really isn't feeling well himself, and his friendliness in coming is a thing I shan't forget — Janetta too has been angelic.'

Janetta left with the Brenans to stay with them and with Jaime, but came back to us again for a hotter spell, of excursions and flower-hunting. Before we started on our journey home she told us she now loved the idea of leading her own life — independent except for the children.

By the monastery of Poblet and Tarragona to Paris.]

March 16th — Ham Spray. The transition from Paris to Wiltshire was almost too quick to take in, but our shock-absorbers worked so well that we have slid back with hardly a creak or squeak and already feel that we've not been away. The 'pig's bathroom'[1] looks very smart with its new marbled black, yellow and white décor. There are some pretty new curtains in the library and Mr Wells has done a lot of touching up and repainting. In fact our house doesn't look too bad at all, and a round trip of the garden showed us dogtooth violets under the beech tree and tarragon and cineraria in the greenhouse.

I am trying not to press too hard on the accelerator, but coast, as we did in Spain. It is fiendishly difficult.

[1] So-called ever since it was used to salt and 'pet' our pig in the War.

March 20th. Of all the people we saw at the weekend I feel we did well by everyone except Robert and Cynthia. Janetta was particularly and unjustifiably appreciative of — heavens knows! 'what we do for her'. We do nothing. We merely love her and are eternally grateful to her. But we also love Robert, and being with the three of them — Janetta, Robert and Cynthia — all together makes us uneasy in spite of ourselves. Robert was not at his most equable, and various mutual friends had got into his dog-house. Poor Cynthia may well be having a difficult time with him; I really felt sorry for her.

March 28th. A few minutes ago the telephone rang, and as I went to answer it I said to myself, 'It must be Burgo.' And so it was, just arrived from Paris. Asked how he was, he replied, 'Much as usual'.

I have just been listening with deep emotion to Mozart's *Requiem*. When a composer with the hand of death already on his shoulder expresses his response to his coming end in his own peculiar language, he must surely reach the summit of intense personal feeling, comparable perhaps to Shakespeare's when he writes of love and jealousy in the *Sonnets*. The *Requiem* seems to me to convey the splendour and tragedy of man's life faced with death, and bathe it in a light of *acceptability* in a way that no impurer art than music can. By thus revealing the major drama of approaching death — the whiteness to be cancelled out by dense blackness — through a mesh of logic and lucidity, the *Requiem* arouses an extraordinary sense of ecstasy that is both musical and philosophical, like the pleasure got from Beethoven's late quartets. Has it no more significance than a cold bath which sets the circulation going? I can't believe it.

March 30th. I go on thinking about the *Requiem*, trying to fit that irrational moment into my quasi-rational scheme of things, but clinging obstinately to the lifebelt of acceptance. It's no use trying to equate aesthetic emotions with logical statements about the universe or anything else, yet the very beauty of the artist's creation does seem to convince the listener or viewer that all is not lost. Maybe one reason we rate the arts so high is that they not only arouse deep pleasure, but that they also make us see the universe we are imprisoned in as *acceptable*, in many ways horrible though it is.

April 1st. Burgo came to see us, and we spent a happy evening hearing about his adventures and looking at his very good photographs of Greece. He had enjoyed Simon's company, though for such a manly-looking fellow he had turned out anxious and inefficient in practical ways. We discussed everthing except the future.

I have had a most flattering letter from Professor Tutin, to whom I sent my Spanish flowers, carefully pressed and docketed: 'The really excellent specimens arrived yesterday in the middle of a meeting of the *Flora Europea* committee. Practically all the species seem to be unrepresented in our herbarium, so you can imagine how useful a collection yours will be. Please let me know if you feel like doing any more collecting for us.' Purr, purr.

Meanwhile I have another Freudian Index, some Spanish articles for America, and a letter from an unknown Spaniard wanting me to translate a play. But far more satisfying is the fact that my life alone with Ralph has been for some while running with a smoothness and sweetness for which I'm thankful every moment of the day.

April 5th. I notice uneasily that the memory of my response to Mozart's *Requiem* is beginning to fade, and that I can't at will revive the comfort it left me with. In any case I'm mystified by the way my normal guard of literal-mindedness was lowered to let through that transcendental gleam. Last night's *St John's Passion* was glorious music, but concerned rather with the Christian myth and meekness than with man's place in the universe.

On a walk with Julia we went over something of the same ground. Her stress is on the hatefulness of the 'Cosmos', brought home to her by an article in *Encounter* about Auschwitz, whose existence I don't believe she had previously been fully aware of.

[It is plain to me now, though it was not at the time I wrote those entries, that these uncharacteristic reflections were set going by the partly conscious, but obstinately suppressed awareness that Ralph had not long to live.]

April 12th. Returning from a day in London, I met Robert arriving for dinner in the darkness of the drive. Towards the end of our pleasant evening he broke the news to us that he and Cynthia were to get married. She was going to have a child, and his only fear was that Janetta and Georgie might be upset. The terms we are on with Robert made it impossible to act an enthusiasm we didn't feel. In fact we both felt as if someone had died; but I did say truly that I was very glad to think how happy this would make Cynthia.

Janetta, who came down next day, had heard the news and took it staunchly, saying that Robert would be glad to have the child and Georgie wouldn't be upset at all. Robert is bequeathing Burgo his flat in Percy Street, a great bit of good luck for him.

April 19th. The visitors for our 'small Easter party' have just gone — Isobel, Burgo, Simon Raven and Richard Chopping, increased by extra people every day. From the social point of view it was easier having so many, as they mixed, sparkled and fizzed together, and also went off on their own. Richard was a great support, spreading his golden-hearted amiability round him.

Even so I began fraying at the edges, and Ralph said he felt 'weak' and looked it. When Annie Davis (staying at Stokke) begged us 'to come over and organize potato races for Téo's birthday party,' it was not exactly music in my ears, but Richard and I went, and found Annie struggling manfully; Téo pale with the desire always to win; Robert sulking in his tent like Achilles; rows in progress between Georgie and Téo. Janetta had taken time off to visit the Gowings, but told us that 'Easter had been ghastly'.

Robert came alone later, in a calmer mood, and able to laugh over his conversation with Cyril about marriage: 'You must just look at it as if it were a three-year contract,' he had said. He was delighted that Robert was 'joining him in the trap. There are two things that happen — either you have half your face torn away, or you just turn into a marker-buoy — *Wreck here!*'

April 20th. Janie Bussy is dead. So far we have only heard that she had been found dead in her bath at Gordon Square; that Dorothy had been moved to a nursing-home, and Pippa and Marjorie were shocked and distressed. Ralph and I felt shaken and deeply sorry. What a tragic end to her poor life!

[Jane Simone Bussy was the only child of Simon and Dorothy; she was brought up to be completely bi-lingual, in a rarefied atmosphere where only literature and painting really counted. She had the quick, acute mind of a sophisticated intellectual, but her attitude to her parents was profoundly French and emotional, as she showed by the way she devoted her life to them. After her father's death she looked after her mother until she too became senile, and then stoutly withstood all attempted persuasions of her aunts and uncles to put her in a Home. She endured the difficulties of her life stoically but not in silence — that was not her way; and she was over fifty when she died, having hardly had any life of her own.

As a girl of sixteen she and her cousin Vincent Rendel fell in love and were for a time inseparable, often to be seen travelling on the tops of buses reading poetry together. When this romance suddenly ended it was thought the family had objected, but the recent publication of Dorothy's letters to André Gide showed that this wasn't so. During the War she became violently political, took some part in the Résistance and had at least one love-affair. But though she visited us often at Ham Spray, and had rather more than mere affection for Ralph at one time, she never divulged her intimate life.

Janie had an elegant figure, beautiful hands and legs, and a face that could only be called ugly in spite of its intelligence, and relapsed into sadness when in repose. She could be suddenly tart in her remarks, yet the total impression she made was of charm, and she was a favourite at Charleston. After the war she took to painting with considerable success, producing still-lifes in bright, clear colours.

Her death was a pure accident. The gas Ralph and I smelled in the Gordon Square flat in February 1953 was an early sign of a defective geyser.]

April 24th. Poor Dora Romilly died this morning. She had been ill of cancer for some time and it must be looked on as a blessing, but what Bunny will do without her I can't imagine. In her youth she was a great beauty; she had many loving friends and no enemies.

May 23rd. Our serene progress through these last months has been shaken by the collapse of the Summit Conference, bringing the atomic cloud a little closer. We read of beastly, undiplomatic, *stupid* things said on both sides. Yet it is impossible, thank heavens, to resist the balm of some quiet days together in brilliant spring weather, with a new light on the downs that I find surprising even after these years and years of staring at them — a look of transparency, as if they and the trees were made of green glass, lit from within. Here we sit, Ralph reading some books for review, and I, hot and sweating after a morning divided between my rockery and Freud, who dazzles me as usual by the virtuosity of his mental processes and the way he finds things everywhere to start him thinking — for instance one of those little kitchen slates, cleaned by simply pulling it out, gave him a brilliant analogy for perception and memory.

The Kee wedding has taken place, and Burgo has moved into the Percy Street flat with Poppet John[1] and her husband. Robert tells us he gets on very well with them, is having his photograph taken for an article, and is working six hours a day. When Robert asked him if he was coming down here for the week-end, he replied, 'Good heavens, no!'

There has been a third death. Poor old Oliver Strachey. The
pathos was borne in on me when Julia said, 'Of course I offered to
go and sort his belongings, but Barbara said that as he had been in
his nursing-home for six years all his possessions were contained in
two small suitcases.'

[1] Daughter of Augustus.

[My first memory of meeting Oliver Strachey dates back to an
evening when he took Julia and me (aged about nine and ten) to a
play called *Baby Mine*. It was what used to be known as a 'bedroom
farce', and indeed the plot consisted in a great deal of dashing to and
fro across a landing, speculating who was inside the various
rooms, and — finally — about the parentage of the resulting baby.
Or so I remember it. I had never been to such a sophisticated
entertainment before, nor been treated so much like a young lady.
It was an evening performance and we wore our best frocks.

Oliver was the eldest surviving brother of Lytton, but unlike
him in appearance. He had the rough-hewn features characteristic
of the Stracheys, but his manner was more genial and relaxed than
Lytton's, his laugh louder and his face ruddier; a pipe was usually
sticking out of one corner of his mouth, his hands were probably in
his pockets, and his silky hair was parted down the middle to form
two parallel tunnels. As he grew older it became shining white.

Oliver was gregarious, amusing, amused, highly intelligent,
and interested in everything — music (his first love), books,
games and puzzles, women (he was something of a pouncer).
Food was an exception, and his taste embraced hardly anything
but roast meat and potatoes. 'What's THAT? A vegetable?
TOMATOES? Take them all away!' I once heard him say to a waiter.
Drink was another matter, and as he had a very bad head an
invitation to dinner entailed scooping him into a taxi in a state of
collapse at the end of the evening. Before that, however, one
would have been vastly entertained by his funny and lovable
company. He was a near genius at solving all problems and
puzzles, including the ciphers he cracked for the War Office in
both world wars. He was as fond of his friends as they were of
him, but on the whole he would be unlikely to put himself out for
them. I would call him amoral rather than selfish.

A story he told of serving as a juryman is perhaps revealing. A
seasoned burglar was being tried for 'loitering with intent'
outside a house with a jemmy down the inside of the trouser-leg.

The jury retired and chose Oliver as foreman. 'Well, I think it's a clear case,' they said to each other. 'I don't know what came over me,' Oliver told us, 'sheer devilry probably. But I suddenly thought it would be amusing to see if I could talk them round, by force of logical argument. I did, though it took some time, and we returned a verdict of Not Guilty. The judge's mouth fell open — but he wasn't nearly as surprised as the prisoner!']

[From June 1st to 9th, Ralph, Janetta and I took a short holiday in Ireland, part of whose purpose was to collect botanical records for the forthcoming *Atlas of the British Flora*. Luckily for me both my companions entered into my search with apparent enthusiasm. I read not a single book except Irish Floras and Guides, yet the time was crammed to bursting with rich sensations, mossy smells, constantly varying light, and the freshness of a satisfying draught of spring water faintly tinged with earth and growing plants. We had made no plans, but never wrangled about 'where to go'. At Kilkee we found an Irish San Sebastian, with the beaming faces of small Victorian houses ranged round its *concha*. One huge purple-faced old lady sat in the glassed-in verandah of our hotel, silently watching the world go by. There was very strong Irish whiskey, home-made brown bread, a bowl of butter, peat fires and hot bottles in our beds. Turning north next day we reached the famous and immensely tall cliffs of Moher. Janetta, suddenly panic-stricken, took one look and exclaimed, 'They're *beastly*. I hate them.' However, her V.C. blood forced her to lie down on her stomach and look over at the sheerest point.[1] At Ennistymon 'we first reached the limestone, and shrieked in unison as we came upon a great patch of the purple flowers of Bloody Cranesbill, and everywhere saxifrages and orchids. Best of all were the fantastic ash-coloured rocks of the region called the Burren, in whose crevices a mass of rare plants were growing.'

We had booked rooms at Leenane for the Whitsun weekend and from here we took a day on Achill, 'a hazy hot and still day, which suited this foreign region, where huge plantations of rhododendrons grow wild on the slopes of tall round-browed mountains rising abruptly from the plain. Their Moorish purple-pink was the dominant colour except for fuchsia red. Janetta felt a tug to the West, although it is inhabited by her ghosts, and bravely booked herself on a boat to the Aran Islands. As Ralph and I (too craven to go with her) were walking by a river a man rushed up to Ralph shouting, "Have ye got yer fishing-tackle with ye? There's three lovely throut just over there!" It was inconceivable to him that any man shouldn't own a rod.' ·

[1] Her father won the V.C. in the First World War.

June 10th — Ham Spray. Two letters from Gerald awaited Ralph here, one saying, 'Oh life! life!' and the other, 'Oh death! death!': in between the two a 'final break' with Hetty is described, caused by her having a new lover.

June 17th. We have been back here exactly a week though it seems more. Last weekend we decided to bottle our barrel of Tarragona wine. Burgo and Simon came down for a bare twenty-four hours to help, and all Sunday we had Robert, Cynthia, and Debo (the Duchess of Devonshire) helping too until about seven, giving me the restless feeling of being hostess at a weird sort of cocktail party. Were the guests getting bored and their backs beginning to ache sitting in that dusty box-room, which smelled every moment more like a bar-parlour, what with the drops soaking into the wooden floor? However, everyone emerged well from the ordeal. Burgo organized the operations very efficiently, and Robert and Simon stuck to them good-humouredly. I took the Duchess and Cynthia out for breathers into the garden and greenhouse: the former is a real charmer, very pretty, gay, quick-witted and alert to everything. I don't know much about Burgo's present life, but he seems much more grown-up and self-confident, and Simon must be given some of the credit as he's more of a friend than Burgo has had before. They have fantastically grand ideas about food and wine. I don't know the source of a (presumably apocryphal) story about Simon and his ex-wife. After he had broken with her she telegraphed: 'Wife and baby starving'. Simon is supposed to have wired back: 'Eat baby'.

June 21st. On Saturday we drove to Crichel for a weekend of continuing heatwave, all day and every day spent in the garden and all meals eaten there. A menace of thunder faded leaving a cloudless forget-me-not blue sky and a light breeze ruffling the swags of roses that covered the house. Our three hosts all looked in excellent trim, agile, thin and young for their ages. Desmond, wearing nothing but bathing pants and a thimble-shaped straw hat, slowly turned a ripe terracotta. In the evening came Kitty West and Maud Russell, both in different ways gamely fighting with their backs to the wall. Kitty is selling her house and moving to London. Maud is retreating with dignity and style before the encroaching tide of old age.

Conversation at dinner as to whether the curiosity felt about the private lives of great men was justified. Eardley firmly declared it was disgusting, even in the case of Shakespeare's Sonnets or Byron's letters. After dinner a stray remark of mine about Aaron Copland made Desmond leap spontaneously to his feet and carry some of us next door to hear his clarinet concerto not once but twice, thrusting the score into my hand. I find this elastic and excitable responsiveness of his simply charming.

On Sunday evening Cecil Beaton came to dinner and wore everyone down by staying rather too long. Dressed in a pink shirt and Palm Beach suit, his smooth pink face is rather like that of a sly moose or gnu, slit by a narrow little grin. I'm not sure how much I like him. I would guess him to be selfish and vain, malicious at times, but also affectionate in a limited way. Desmond dozed off on the sofa, Maud and I had a pleasant female talk about our sons, and Raymond and Cecil did some name-swapping.

June 22nd. To London for a mediocre performance of Verdi's *Otello*, and to visit poor little Joan Cochemé in hospital. She was lying in a small white cubicle off the T.B. Ward, with her pale face propped between pillows and her eyes closed. When she opened them and saw me she burst into tears. She has been having an appalling time, with operations on her lung under local anaesthetic. The pain was 'horrible'; I felt I was talking to someone on the rack. As I walked away down corridors as long and thickly populated as Oxford Street I was both impressed and horrified by this juggernaut of medicine on which we all depend. The sight of poor afflicted Joan lying in the middle of it, like a fly in a spider's web left a bruise on my consciousness.

June 28th — Ham Spray. Very hot and lovely weekend with Janetta and Professor Dick Sanders of Duke University, who is writing about Lytton and all the Stracheys. I wasn't sure how they would get on, but she soon saw the intensely human, emotional being that lies underneath the donnish exterior and American pursuit of culture. After lunch he said with satisfying firmness that he wanted to 'have a snooze and then go for a walk'. We found him later wandering in cornfields still sopping from a thunderstorm; so Ralph gently started him down the avenue in the direction of one of Cobbett's Rural Rides, and he was off like a shot, returning later with 'a rock' as he called it — a round black stone — as a souvenir.

We had the Kees and the Godleys to drinks on the lawn. It was quite clear which were the Professor's favourites. He took a huge fancy to Robert, and said to Ralph about Janetta, 'She's *very* attractive. Doesn't Frances ever worry about your falling for her?'

Ralph and I planned how to share Dick Sanders. I was to take him walking on the downs next day, and in the afternoon Ralph would drive him over to Alix and James. I enjoyed both the walk (it was a radiant morning) and our talk — it was largely about immortality. 'I only believe in total extinction,' he announced, 'but if I were to be offered the chance of existing for ever, in a bodily as well as spiritual form, *I should jump at it.* I love life.' This pleased me, but I confessed that personally I clung to the thought of total oblivion, whereas eternal life without ageing or maturing was an idea that filled me with dread and horror, adding that as animals in a vegetable kingdom our nature seemed to me rooted in the concept of change and decay. 'Yes,' said the Professor, 'Shakespeare really said the last word on that in *King Lear*: "ripeness is all".' So then we got on to Shakespeare, and were in complete agreement that *Othello* was the best play that he or probably anyone else ever wrote. I took him down to Combe, to peer into the little church and over the wall of the Manor, and told him the local legends about Nell Gwynne and also the gallows. He gobbles up these crumbs so eagerly that it's a pleasure to throw them to him. Indeed he's a most likeable man.

On Monday we had a letter from poor Joan, who now has a clot on her lung and is to be moved to another hospital and operated on today. I spent some time telephoning to get news of her, and then paced the lawn with Janetta, talking sadly, she of her feelings of depression, I trying to explain how I expect nothing of life and think only a week ahead. She left us, as ever sad to see her go.

July 5th. It rains and I enjoy it — it helps restore my tempo to *Andante* from *Presto*. But I must pull up my socks and write something for the next Memoir Club meeting. Burgo has paid us a short visit, with the look of release so firmly imprinted on his face that we had nothing but pleasure in his company. He will be twenty-five in three days!

July 11th. Janetta came to see us, bringing Paddy Leigh Fermor — whom we both like unreservedly. He is as ebullient and enthusiastic, as life-loving as Desmond; intoxicated with words, foreign languages and verbal jokes. We passed a hilarious afternoon, doubled up by his stories and excellent mimicry, and charmed by the way he looked lovingly at his own bleached corduroy trousers and navy-blue socks and said they reminded him of Piero della Francesca. I saw exactly what he meant.

July 25th. Looking after Marjorie Strachey has been fairly hard work, both physically bracing oneself to haul her out of her chair, and always on the run to fetch her cigarettes, matches and hot-water bottle. She responds with such touching gratitude, however, that it is well worth the effort. At breakfast this morning she began, 'Do you remember the Franklin in the *Canterbury Tales?*' 'No, Marjorie, I'm afraid I don't.' 'Well, it *snowëd* in his house of meats and drinks. *You're* like the Franklin.'

She spent most of the days sitting in a somewhat toadlike position, legs well apart, and on her face a look of almost permanent indignation. 'I *simply* CANNOT understand what they're at. Really, it's MONSTROUS. They ought to be *shot! À la lanterne!*', et cetera. Yet she contrives to get a lot of fun from life even if some of it is in the very act of disapproving.

She talked a lot about Janie's death, seeming almost to want to hold herself responsible. But no, I'm sure really that she was begging for reassurance that she was *not*. Dorothy had been getting weaker and also madder, and Marjorie and Pippa decided that they must never leave Janie alone in the house with her mother. 'And then, I can't think why — we must have been RAVING mad, we arranged that both of us should go and stay with Alix and James at Marlow for several days.' When the taxi arrived to fetch them to Marlow Pippa went up to have a last word with Janie, found the door locked and got the chauffeur to break it in.'

So that unless she believes it was suicide . . . but perhaps she does!'

Julia has been asking our advice as to how she and Lawrence can get out of taking Marjorie with them when they go out to Roquebrune to sort the Bussy pictures, books and papers. I do see that even the journey would be an impossible problem. And Julia is really rather afraid of her and can't enjoy her funny side.

'Dorothy Bussy died soon after Janie, without understanding that she was dead.

July 29th. Last night, at about half past eleven, Ralph laid the *Interpretation of Dreams* down on his knee and began to enlarge on the thoughts it aroused in him. They concerned the 'Day's residues' — those minute incidents which in Freud's view act as setters-in-motion of dreams. Ralph thought that this was because the response to some sensory stimulus had been interrupted, thus producing 'steam' which emerged in the repressed material expressed by the dream. The discussion that followed brought out in a fascinating way certain differences in our two characters and ways of thought that we must have known about for years, namely that Ralph's mind favours induction — seizes an essential particular and moves from it to a universal, in the way common to innovators; while mine is deductive and goes in the opposite direction. His is the sort of mind that makes discoveries, while mine carries out the donkey-work of criticism and analysis.

'And what about memory?' I asked him at one point. 'Oh, perfectly simple, it's just running over a tape-recorder of past stimuli,' he replied, gazing dreamily into space and obviously in a state of mind when everything was 'perfectly simple'. Of course I tried to show that it was not, but though he gave a polite appearance of listening he was really waiting until he could carry on with the thread of his own thoughts. I tried all the same to explain to him how I thought of the sensory stimuli as a swarm of bees simultaneously assaulting my five senses. He was amazed, and said he had no such feeling. How I envy his powers of concentration, his exclusion of the irrelevant, the simplicity in fact of his approach, which is something to do with the way he fell at once to sleep when we went upstairs, while I lay tossing and turning and thinking about my swarm of bees.

August 1st. Burgo and Simon Raven for Bank Holiday weekend.

We are amazed by their ideology which is a Regency, material-istic, cynical one, leaving plenty of room for pursuit of knowledge, sex and friendship, but little for love. It's a bit too highly seasoned, too suggestive of curry sauce for us, Ralph and I agreed, as we set off for our afternoon walk. Were one to plot it like a map it would overlap Robert's world a bit, and Janetta's rather less. But we aren't on their map at all; you would have to turn several pages of the atlas to come to our scale of values, and I can see how faded, priggish even, it might seem to them. But we both agree that Simon has done a lot for Burgo; he has a good head and good nature and a certain very likeable style about him.

August 5th. Staying at Kitty West's, we had a visit from Crichel. Raymond in rather melancholy mood; when asked why there had been nothing of his in last week's *Sunday Times*, he answered, 'I think they're bored of me. They want to get rid of me.' Ralph too has been expecting to be dismissed by the *New Statesman*, and was much relieved to get several consignments of books for review. Raymond described visiting Nancy Cunard in the lunatic asylum to which she was sent after setting light to a taxi and throwing her shoe at the head of the magistrate who tried her. She now appears quite sane and was allowed out for the day with Raymond and Roger Senhouse. Asked what sort of daughter he would have liked to have, Raymond replied, 'A double first'.

August 8th — Ham Spray. Joan has been with us for several days, recuperating from her operation. We took her to dinner at Kee Cottage, and a somewhat ill-matched argument arose between her and Robert about Apartheid. Joan doesn't believe she thinks the blacks are inferior, only different, and Robert — with the blazing eyes of the skilled television interviewer — was sharp enough to spot the truth though she hadn't revealed it. I was a little uneasy about my convalescent, and took Robert up for no-balling once or twice. For instance when Joan said her black cook 'was sweet and she loved him', Robert would say, 'Ah! You see? You're assuming it's *odd* for him to be sweet. Why shouldn't he be?' Or if she criticized any black person, naturally he pounced at once, so having it both ways.

September 6th. A new consignment of Spanish articles to translate has made my work-table into a battlefield. I managed, however, to get the first two off before the weekend, and there's no doubt I feel happier and droop less when I have slightly too much to do. Our weather gave us patches of brilliant blue between solid islands of cloud, and our visitors (the Godleys and Isobel) appeared to enjoy the lazy days — all they were offered — mostly spent in the garden, now luxuriant with dahlias, zinnias and groaning pear-trees. Kitty maintained that there was nothing self-indulgent about having children — it was pure altruism, an opinion which was fairly sternly contested. She went on to say that 'as they hadn't asked to be born, the least parents could do was to leave them all their money'. None was to go to spouse, friends or causes.

September 9th. Driving to the other end of Wiltshire to see Cressida Ridley, we enjoyed the beauty of the golden middle of an autumn day, and the cottage gardens blazing with late flowers and ripe red apples. We picnicked among misty downs near the romantically situated village of Imber, taken over by the army some time since. Indeed we could hear the distant booming of artillery. A little later our hackles rose at the sight of a tin-hatted sentry waiting to warn us off a piece of wild downland, and at the sound of a sergeant-major's muffled yells. Cressida's house is charming and full of signs of her taste: pretty, pale colours, dozens and dozens of well-read books, gramophone records, Mozart on the music stand. Her husband (killed in the war and never seen by us) made himself felt in 'the set of Voltaire we bought', or 'we got that at Tilshead'. We drove with her up to the downs and walked along a grass track to a piece of land that was bright purple with betony, saw-wort and the rare tuberous thistle, which we had gone to see.

September 10th — Mottisfont. Boris and Violet Bonham-Carter were here when we arrived, to be joined by Violet's son Raymond. Boris is a little muted in this house, or perhaps just by age. Some of the air has gone out of him, leaving him deflated and with dark bags under his eyes. Conversation, conversation, conversation — it goes on like a marathon: at meal-times all in the form of tête-à-têtes often without switching direction for an immense time. One snatches a breather from one's own (and a little food must be swallowed also) and sees the other pairs hard at it, looking into each other's faces with the deepest interest. What a strange go it is! Yet I am enjoying it, and so is Ralph. Yesterday after breakfast I walked out and found Boris's large shape bent meditatively over some patches of tiny cyclamens under the cedar tree. We walked off towards the river with the little woolly dog of the house bouncing beside us. Boris talked all the way about his work, obsessionally. He lives for it alone, and has no relaxation except chess problems. I was about to offer myself as a sacrifice for a game when he said it made his heart beat uncomfortably and he had given up playing. He gets up at 5.30 every morning and is at work at Barnet by eight. He goes to bed at eight.

Returning we found Noel and Giana Blakiston, a pleasant surprise. Giana saw me peering about for flowers and revealed that she too was an enthusiast, who paints her Bentham and Hooker.

Tea was like a scene in Henry James — spread under a huge tree, with cucumber sandwiches and home-made coffee cake. After it we played crazy croquet in the sideways light from the setting sun, which all at once turned into a huge red ball and disappeared, leaving us chilled. Boris's croquet style is magnificent. In his capacious trousers, cut to fit an earlier stage of corpulence, he curves his body into a vast croquet hoop, seizes his mallet low down by the head, gives his objective one searching glance, and aims — often with deadly effect.

At dinner that night he dismissed Picasso, calling him 'a clever crook' who 'cashes in by *épatant la bourgeoisie*, a couturier, a Dior always thinking up new models'. With Noel Blakiston on my other side I was discussing the importance, or otherwise, of the Classics. Thence — the transition was his I think — to belief in God. I said: 'Well, I shall ask you straight out: Do you believe in him?' He said, '*I don't know* whether I do or not.' It seemed to worry him.

On Sunday a botanical walk with Giana, looking for a local rarity. No matter that we didn't find it. The arrival of reviews of Leonard's *Autobiography* in the papers gave Violet a text to pour scorn on poor erring Bloomsbury. The gist was that they were fighting battles that had been won long ago, stating obvious conclusions that 'one' had long ago reached with no difficulty, or — in Leonard's case — being 'downright naïf'. Then came her bigger guns. '*Such* a pity that Keynes was led away, for a while, into pacifism. *So* stupid not to realize that Desmond MacCarthy was the most distinguished of the group.' Raymond and Harold Nicolson's reviews of the book she took as a form of ridicule.

Was all this leading up to her full-scale assault on pacifism to Ralph during dinner, which induced him to declare his own position openly, and particularly his horror of women who so gladly and proudly sacrificed their men? Whereupon, for the second time in our presence, she made her famous declaration: 'I would rather see both my sons DEAD AT MY FEET than under German domination!' I only heard of this interchange from Ralph later in our bedroom, but I saw from his red cheek and angry sparkling eye that feelings were high.

The Bonham-Carters left after dinner. It was like seeing a whole army disappear with flags flying, and the rest of us settled to a peaceful game of Scrabble.

September 15th — Ham Spray. Rang the Kees for news. How were they? 'Pretty bad, really,' said Robert, and went on to say he'd been having a tough time with his analyst. When I answered his question about ourselves by saying, 'Rather boringly calm at the moment,' he exclaimed, 'But that's just the trouble — *my uncalm* is so boring.'

Through Joan we hear that Craig Macfarlane has had a heart attack, and is 'resting' in a hospital at Spezia. Ralph's comment on this sad news was that he must now shelve responsibility and let other people take over. But could he? So many people lean on him, as well as his large family. I doubted it. 'He must,' Ralph said firmly. I said that neither he (Ralph) nor I had ever liked the stuff (responsibility); he was inclined to think that I do like it, but he's wrong there. I absolutely dread it, but I do sometimes force myself to take it.

Ralph has been quite exceptionally angelic to me all this summer. It is not nonsense to say I have never felt more loved. What can be the reason for it? It almost makes me anxious.

September 22nd. We were expecting Clive and Little Barbara for the weekend, both somewhat invalidish. So the very strong voice of Janetta on the telephone, just back from Spain and proposing to come down too, put courage in us both. 'I shall be quite ready to carry up trays. Shall I *bring* some trays?' She added, 'There's lots to say about Gerald and Hetty. My gosh!'

Ralph has just driven off to Marlborough in response to a summons to serve on a jury. I am green with envy.

September 28th. Janetta arrived looking fine, brown and strong in her white jersey and skirt; calm also, tolerant of Barbara and very nice to Clive and us. When Clive heard that we had asked the grieving widower, Bunny Romilly, to dinner he was quite indignant: 'NOT OLD BUNNY! Really, Fanny! Even the Crichel Boys don't ask me to meet him, and once when it was suggested Eddy said: "You don't think we'd insult any of our friends by asking them to meet *Bunny*, do you?"' Later he was heard calling from his bedroom: 'Since there's a *peer* coming to dinner I shall put on a white shirt, and perhaps Ralph could lend me a tie.' Bunny arrived a little tight from a cocktail party and couldn't get a single sentence finished, but Clive's natural good manners rose to the occasion.

Robert and Cynthia came for a drink on Sunday, and there was a splendid display of snake-charming by Robert. His technique is quite brilliant. Clive was in fits of laughter, blinking wildly and pulling his trouser-legs so far up his legs that he looked as if he was going paddling. But Robert goes one better than making people think him charming — he makes *them* be their most charming.

Some of Clive's sayings during the weekend: 'Barbara always gets everything wrong.' Of Leonard's *Autobiography*: 'I'm not a kind or affectionate man, but I do like people to be happy. Now I don't think Leonard does. I think he's cruel; he likes to see some people *un*happy.' On me: 'Fanny will never allow anyone to draw a conclusion on insufficient evidence. She's always been the same.' This said with a certain animus.

September 29th. I went with Ralph to hear the conclusion of the Marlborough case in which he is juryman. The prisoner, Barry, was accused of breaking into the Welfare Wing of Chippenham Hospital with intent to cause bodily harm to the woman he had lived with for the past thirteen years — Miss Buggins, commonly known as Mrs Barry. (Much play was made with the choice of name used by Counsels.) Miss Buggins was just in front of me; she had crisp fuzzy hair, glittering spectacles, and looked clean and rather intelligent. Over lunch at the Castle and Ball Ralph and I discussed the case in eager whispers, which is dead against the rules of this mysterio-comico-serio game. Why, if Barry intended no harm to Miss Buggins did he go back three times? I asked Ralph. 'In hopes of his weekly fuck in each case,' Ralph said, 'and to persuade her not to break with him.' And the 'grievous injury' was only 3 millimetres square as a doctor had testified. Barry having said, 'I'll strangle you' was irrelevant. Miss Buggins even admitted pushing him on to the bed and taking his shoes and tie off! With a view to sex? Surely. As in most law cases two conflicting waves of lies meet in the middle with a dull thud. Ralph was made foreman, and the verdict was Not Guilty. Poor show, really.

October 6th. Without a pause we glide from wet stormy summer to wet stormy autumn. Yesterday, an isolated day of sun and softness, I dug away all the weeds in my 'wild corner' and planted miniature daffodils, anemones and squills. Today is barely warm enough to sit on the verandah and a rumble of thunder comes from great round sulky clouds rolling over the downs.

Thoughts about the Bomb have come to the fore because of the vote for Unilateralism at the Labour Conference last week. Robert has been reporting all the political conferences. He told me on the telephone that he is now a Unilateralist, in spite of the fact that the speeches in favour were rotten, and Gaitskell's (on the other side) excellent, because he thought it showed new life and genuine feeling in the Labour Party, something also that was gaining strength. A letter from Acland in *The Times*, saying that as we were set now atomic war was inevitable and that there was literally nothing to lose by altering our present outlook, weighed with Ralph more than Robert's or my arguments. But how unreal such huge possibilities as atomic war and occupation by Russia seem as I write them down!

Henry Lamb's death was announced in *The Times* yesterday. His face looking out of the page is so vital, his gaze so piercing, that it brings the sound of his voice instantly to one's ears and makes his non-existence incredible.

October 23rd. A vivid dream that Ralph and I had decided to take suicide pills together. Ralph swallowed his and then complained with the curious logic of dreams that they hadn't worked — and why not? They had *last time*. I swallowed mine after worrying a little about Burgo and Janetta, and with a clear visual background of the green walls of our room and the garden seen through our window.

Raining steadily all day. About four o'clock, when practising my violin, I saw that it had stopped and called Ralph down from his library. We walked down the lane to the boundary with Berkshire. Opalescent clouds were parting to show cracks of blue, and though no rain was now falling everything was soused with it and gave off a damp aromatic smell. Tree-trunks a rich black, supporting a beautiful arrangement of limp orange and yellow leaves; the grasses bent over and tipped with raindrops.

A telephone call from Robert off to America for some weeks for the Telly.

November 7th. Last weekend came Bunny, Angelica and Amaryllis Garnett. My heart-cockles warmed to dear Bunny, rosy under his white thatch and overflowing with geniality. Angelica worried me, however. She radiated a feeling of desperation, and I'm ashamed that I have no idea what it's about.

But the lack of manners of Bloomsbury struck me not for the first time. When Cynthia, enormously pregnant and without Robert, came to dinner, they made no attempt to take the smallest interest in her, look at her or talk to her. Nor, my goodness, do they pass one anything — one could starve for all they care.

November 14th. At the very end of a jolly evening entertaining the Gowings, Julia brought out her 'she's made her bed and she must lie on it' attitude to Angelica. Why did she seem so desperate? I had asked. Was it hard work, cooking for seven? 'Serves her right for marrying old Bunny and having so many children,' Julia said tartly. 'Why didn't she arrange her life better? One shouldn't have children recklessly. *I* didn't. There's such a thing as family planning.' Yet in her own case, no one makes heavier weather than Julia over household chores, and the way they interfere with her peace to write in. I wonder why she is such a severe judge of her fellow men — and women — and doesn't see that conflict between strong incompatible desires is the great human predicament.

November 21st. Robert and Cynthia spent their last weekend at the cottage before the baby's arrival was due. Georgie and Rose, both touched but giggling, took me to see the baby's room — a red nest with the receptacle for the little creature itself standing lonely and expectant in the middle. I was struck to the heart by the pathos of human procreation. Robert, looking very handsome even for him, was back from America and full of his adventures. He had returned by Air India, and I liked his description of the jubilant cry of the Indian pilot on making an excellent landing: 'Oh boy! Oh boy! How is that for smooth? What you say?'

November 22nd. We spent a wonderfully pleasant relaxed evening with Mary, first drinking excellent, hot soup, and then listening to the whole of *Don Carlos* from Salzburg. What a glorious opera! The magnificent duets for male voices remain with their rich dark pattern in my mind.

November 28th. I have just driven Eddie Gathorne-Hardy, Simon and Burgo to the station. Burgo was delightfully freed from any melancholic tinge, and his mind was revolving like the efficient organ it is.

Last night before dinner I missed Ralph for a while. For the thousandth time I wondered, 'Is he all right? Could he perhaps be feeling ill?' Usually after the first panic and wild wobblings on my base, my equilibrium has been restored. This time, however, I felt it was odd that he should be in the library at this cold evening hour. I ran upstairs and found him lÿing down. No, he was *not* all right. Going through the kitchen to look at the stove he had suddenly felt a constriction in the chest, like two bars. He took a pill and then another, but remained limp and drowsy, wanting no food and unable to face the company. I am in a spurious way so armoured against these set-backs that a dreadful unearthly calm settled down on me, partly to make me able to face his dread of my 'fussing'. But along with this grey *tristesse* was the awareness of a huge crater opening, black and menacing. Paralysed in mind and hardly able to talk, I went downstairs and cooked dinner and somehow sketched a part in the conversation until the meal was over, when I was able to go up and lie beside Ralph.

This morning he swears he is better, but is in no great hurry to get up. We must 'greet the unknown' with all possible common-sense, but I am full of doubts which I cannot voice to him.

November 29th. Throughout yesterday I sank slowly into the pit, as it became gradually clear to me that 'something or other' did happen in the stove-room on Sunday night. Ralph was comatose and fighting a desperate rearguard action against admitting himself ill. He becomes furious (frighteningly so, because bad for him) if I treat him as such, and I identify myself so completely with him that the difficulty of overriding the line he has decided to take is almost insuperable. Is this another heart attack such as the second, of last spring, which was followed by three weeks in bed, or only one of the many alarming but transient 'incidents' that left no trace? During yesterday's battles my anxiety for Ralph, my agonizing dread, gradually wrenched itself away from the part of me that is identified with him, leaving a ghastly bleeding wound but at least the satisfaction of doing what I believe is right and indeed urgently necessary. I told him therefore that I had rung up the Hungerford Surgery, and arranged that Sawbones' locum should come out to see him (Sawbones himself being away). This made Ralph really indignant: 'I can never tell you about my sensations if you behave so foolishly.' I couldn't tell him that it was impossible to face another night of desperation and fear, lying with beating heart listening to his short difficult breathing. 'What would Janetta advise?' I asked myself, and I knew the answer. I rang up Geoff Konstam this morning and gave him a detailed account of Ralph's state. Oh God! He, too, is just going off on holiday. Geoff does not think it sounds serious, but he was in favour of the locum coming and has given me the name and telephone number of the heart specialist at Reading Hospital. It was a great relief to discuss things with him, and after a brief flare-up Ralph has accepted the inevitable. Words are quite useless to express my tortured state, the swords of mental pain that stab me through and through. A good nurse should keep all signs of anxiety from her patient, but how can I achieve this with Ralph, who knows me all too well, and can read everything that is written on my all-too expressive, furrowed face?

5 *p.m.* A tiny doctor with a serious face fringed with red hair came out this morning and will come again tomorrow. Absolute stillness in bed is his prescription, and it is no easy job to enforce it. He thinks there has been another slight 'infarct', and rang up Geoff to discuss the position. Meanwhile I remain in the rack, gripping as best I can on to sanity by means of practical things.

Deathly silence, the clock ticks loudly in the hall. It has been a sorrowful business for poor Ralph to accept that he *is* once more ill. I dread the evenings when my thoughts get the upper hand, and above all the nights.

November 30th. But last night was much worse than my fears. I dropped into exhausted sleep, but soon awoke and listened to Ralph's struggling breathing for four hours, while the clock snailed round its course. But why describe such agony? We are both alive this morning — that's all I can say.

Morning calls to Red-beard and Geoff, visits from Red-beard — but I have antagonized him, I see. There is something so futile about him, and I couldn't bear the snobbish reluctance he showed to get into touch with the Reading specialist who unfortunately happens to be a Lord. Yet to some extent we depend on him, and I try to choke back my horror that this little mannikin should be relevant to the health and safety of my darling Ralph. I pressed on, screaming silently from every cranny of my brain, until I got him to arrange for the lordly cardiologist to come tomorrow. Geoff seemed to take things more seriously when I described Ralph's breathing. It seems that he took two sleeping-pills while I dozed last night, one seeming insufficient, and Geoff thought this might have affected his breathing. He has recommended a new sort for tonight. I dashed in to Hungerford to get them. Not available, I have ordered them to be brought out by taxi from Newbury, and we have got them now.

Ralph does seem a little better this evening and with more appetite for his supper. He has even read more. I went downstairs while he was eating, and listened to Berlioz' *Symphonie Fantastique* on the wireless without much pleasure. I left Ralph a walking-stick to bang on the floor if he wanted me — but I never expected to hear, nor shall I ever forget that dreadful 'thump, thump, thump' . . .

December 1st. Now I am *absolutely alone and for ever.*

Index